ROUTLEDGE LIBRARY EDITIONS:
THE ANCIENT WORLD

Volume 32

# THE UNIVERSITIES OF ANCIENT GREECE

# THE UNIVERSITIES
# OF ANCIENT GREECE

JOHN W. H. WALDEN

Routledge
Taylor & Francis Group
LONDON AND NEW YORK

First published in 1912 by George Routledge & Sons, Limited

This edition first published in 2025
by Routledge
4 Park Square, Milton Park, Abingdon, Oxon OX14 4RN

and by Routledge
605 Third Avenue, New York, NY 10158

*Routledge is an imprint of the Taylor & Francis Group, an informa business*

© 1912

All rights reserved. No part of this book may be reprinted or reproduced or utilised in any form or by any electronic, mechanical, or other means, now known or hereafter invented, including photocopying and recording, or in any information storage or retrieval system, without permission in writing from the publishers.

*Trademark notice:* Product or corporate names may be trademarks or registered trademarks, and are used only for identification and explanation without intent to infringe.

*British Library Cataloguing in Publication Data*
A catalogue record for this book is available from the British Library

ISBN: 978-1-032-73414-9 (Set)
ISBN: 978-1-032-75892-3 (Volume 32) (hbk)
ISBN: 978-1-032-76039-1 (Volume 32) (pbk)
ISBN: 978-1-003-47675-7 (Volume 32) (ebk)

DOI: 10.4324/9781003476757

**Publisher's Note**
The publisher has gone to great lengths to ensure the quality of this reprint but points out that some imperfections in the original copies may be apparent.

**Disclaimer**
The publisher has made every effort to trace copyright holders and would welcome correspondence from those they have been unable to trace.

# THE UNIVERSITIES
# OF ANCIENT GREECE

BY

JOHN W. H. WALDEN, Ph.D.

FORMERLY INSTRUCTOR IN LATIN IN HARVARD UNIVERSITY

LONDON
GEORGE ROUTLEDGE & SONS, Limited
1912

Copyright, 1909, by Charles Scribner's Sons, for the
United States of America

Printed by the Scribner Press
New York, U. S. A.

*Memoriae Abunculi*

# PREFACE

THE germ of this book was first presented in the form of public lectures delivered at Harvard University in the spring of 1904. To the material then presented much other material, which it was found impossible to put in the lectures, has been added, and the whole has been thoroughly revised.

It is the feeling of the author that the Greek education of the imperial times has not received the consideration that is due to its importance. This neglect has perhaps been partly owing to the difficulty and uncertainty that have until recently attended the reading of many of the authors of this period. We now have, for Libanius's speeches—though not yet for his letters—the excellent text edition of Richard Förster, but of some other authors important for this subject there is still lacking an authoritative text.

In some measure also the neglect in question is probably to be accounted for by the general shadow under which every period of Greek antiquity not strictly to be called 'classical' has to some extent rested. Happily this shadow, which is due to the very brilliancy of the so-called 'classical' period, has been in recent years somewhat dissipated. The attitude of mind that would see in the institutions and productions of the later age only deteriorated forms of the perfect types of the earlier age, and things therefore to be disregarded, is less common now than it was formerly. It will not do to dismiss the Greek education of imperial times with the words 'barren' and 'superficial.' To those who shared in it, it was a very living thing, and it was bound up with the past life and the religion of Greece in a way which we do not find it easy fully to appreciate. To those living in the eastern part of the Empire the belief in the past of the Greek race—that brilliant past that antedated the conquests of Alexander—was what the belief in the permanency of Rome was to those living in the western part of the Empire. It was an integral and vital part of their being. The education that rested on such a basis could not be wholly barren and superficial, and any system of education that survived and performed its part in the world for eight hundred years certainly merits our closest scrutiny.

Notwithstanding the insufficiency, as measured by modern standards, of the ancient sophistical education, it is well for us in this extremely 'practical' age to hold in mind the ideal which that education proposed for itself. This ideal will be found stated on page 351. It "received its embodiment in the man who had been trained, morally, intellectually, and æsthetically, to use his powers in the interest of the state. Such a man was the orator. The orator . . . was the man of broad learning and general culture, trained to see the distinctions of right and wrong, and to act with reference to them in the service of his πόλις, or native city." A life of service in the interest of the state was here proposed—a life, however, based, not on technical knowledge or scientific attainments, but on a literary and humanistic training. Though undue stress was laid in this education on the æsthetic training, and though the intellectual training was, as judged by modern standards, defective, these facts should not be allowed to obscure the outlines of the ideal.

This book is a contribution to the study of the Greek education of imperial times. Greek education, however, was a connected whole. It is impossible fully to understand its later forms without having some understanding of those which preceded them. For this reason, a short account has been given, in the earlier chapters, of the Athenian education in pre-Alexandrian times, and of the conditions which prevailed in Grecian lands in the last three centuries B. C.

Exception may be taken to the use of the term University as applied to the congregations of professors and students described in these chapters, on the ground that no distinct charters of incorporation were granted them. At Alexandria, however, the Museum was a royal foundation and, if it did not actually receive a charter from the king of Egypt, it resembled in many other respects the modern university. The Capitolium at Constantinople, put on a new basis by Theodosius II in the fifth century, had a rigid organization and was under the immediate direction of the emperor. At other places, as at Athens and Antioch, where the educational organization was less rigid than at Constantinople, the teachers and the students formed a recognized body in the community, and the teachers were from the time of the Antonines, or even earlier, granted privileges and held subject to governmental control. But, apart from this more formal aspect of the question, the essential elements of the university, the teachers and students, the spirit of learning, the enthusiasm for intellectual ideals, were present in all these centres. There seems, therefore, to be ample justification for the use of the word University in connection with them.

The lectures which formed the nucleus of this book were designed, not only for professed students of education and of classical philology, but also for those whose interests were more general. It is hoped that the book will appeal to these three classes of readers, and that, while other investigators in this field may be assisted by the references in the notes, those whose interests are less specific may, by neglecting the notes and reading the pages of the text consecutively, gain a connected and comprehensive idea of the story of Greek education.

I desire to express my sincere thanks to Professor Herbert Weir Smyth of Harvard University for his kindness in reading a part of the proof and suggesting to me a number of improvements in the text. To my wife I am indebted for the encouragement she gave me while I was writing the lectures and for helpful suggestions.

**J. W. H. W.**

CAMBRIDGE, September 20, 1909.

# TABLE OF CONTENTS

| CHAPTER | | PAGE |
|---|---|---|
| | BIBLIOGRAPHY: SELECTED TITLES . . . | xiii |
| I. | INTRODUCTORY . . . . . . . . . | 1 |
| II. | EDUCATION AT ATHENS IN THE FIFTH AND FOURTH CENTURIES B. C. . . . . | 10 |
| III. | THE MACEDONIAN PERIOD . . . . . | 41 |
| IV. | EDUCATION AND THE STATE . . . . . | 58 |
| V. | ESTABLISHMENT OF UNIVERSITY EDUCATION IN GRECIAN LANDS . . . . . . | 68 |
| VI. | HISTORY OF UNIVERSITY EDUCATION FROM MARCUS AURELIUS TO CONSTANTINE . | 97 |
| VII. | THE DECLINE OF UNIVERSITY EDUCATION: THE CONFLICT WITH CHRISTIANITY . | 109 |
| VIII. | THE PROFESSORS: THEIR APPOINTMENT AND NUMBER . . . . . . . . . | 130 |
| IX. | THE PROFESSORS: THEIR PAY AND POSITION IN SOCIETY . . . . . . . . | 162 |
| X. | WHAT THE SOPHISTS TAUGHT AND HOW THEY TAUGHT IT . . . . . . | 195 |
| XI. | PUBLIC DISPLAYS . . . . . . . . | 218 |
| XII. | SCHOOLHOUSES, HOLIDAYS, ETC.; THE SCHOOL OF ANTIOCH . . . . . | 265 |

TABLE OF CONTENTS

| CHAPTER | | PAGE |
|---|---|---|
| XIII. | THE BOYHOOD OF A SOPHIST | 282 |
| XIV. | STUDENT DAYS | 296 |
| XV. | AFTER COLLEGE | 334 |
| XVI. | CONCLUSION | 340 |

# BIBLIOGRAPHY: SELECTED TITLES

Arnim, H. v., *Leben und Werke des Dio von Prusa.* Berlin, 1898.
Bernhardy, G., *Grundriss der griechischen Litteratur.* 5th ed. Halle, 1892.
Boissier, Gaston, *La fin du paganisme.* 3d ed. Paris, 1898.
Burgess, T. C., *Epideictic Literature.* Chicago, 1902.
Capes, W. W., *University Life in Ancient Athens.* London, 1877.
Cramer, F., *Geschichte der Erziehung und des Unterrichts im Alterthume.* Elberfeld, 1832-38.
Davidson, Thomas, *The Education of the Greek People and its Influence on Civilization.* New York, 1903.
Dill, Samuel, *Roman Society in the Last Century of the Western Empire.* 2d ed. London, 1905.
Freeman, K. J., *Schools of Hellas.* London, 1907.
Girard, Paul, *L'Éducation athénienne au Ve. et au IVe. siècle avant J.-C.* 2d ed. Paris, 1891.
Göll, Hermann, *Professoren und Studenten der römischen Kaiserzeit,* in *Kulturbilder aus Hellas und Rom.* 3d ed. Leipzig, 1880.
Grasberger, Lorenz, *Erziehung und Unterricht im klassischen Alterthum.* Würzburg, 1864-81.
Graves, F. P., *A History of Education before the Middle Ages.* New York, 1909.
Harrent, Albert, *Les écoles d'Antioche.* Paris, 1898.
Hatch, Edwin, *The Influence of Greek Ideas and Usages upon the Christian Church* (The Hibbert Lectures, 1888). 8th ed. London, 1901.
Hertzberg, G. F., *Die Geschichte Griechenlands unter der Herrschaft der Römer.* Halle, 1866-75.
Hulsebos, G. A., *De educatione et institutione apud Romanos.* Utrecht, 1875.
Krause, J. H., *Geschichte der Erziehung, des Unterrichts und der Bildung bei den Griechen, Etruskern und Römern.* Halle, 1851.

## BIBLIOGRAPHY: SELECTED TITLES

Kuhn, Emil, *Die städtische und bürgerliche Verfassung des römischen Reichs bis auf die Zeiten Justinians.* Leipzig, 1864–65.

Laurie, S. S., *Historical Survey of Pre-Christian Education.* 2d ed. London, 1900.

Lerber, Th. v., *Professoren, Studenten und Studentenleben vor 1500 Jahren.* Bern, 1867.

Mahaffy, J. P., *Old Greek Education.* London, 1881.

Monroe, Paul, *Source Book of the History of Education for the Greek and Roman Period.* New York, 1906.

—— *A Text-Book in the History of Education.* New York, 1907.

Petit de Julleville, Louis, *L'École d'Athènes au quatrième siècle après Jésus-Christ.* Paris, 1868.

—— *Histoire de la Grèce sous la domination romaine.* Paris, 1875.

Rauschen, Gerhard, *Das griechisch-römische Schulwesen zur Zeit des ausgehenden Heidentums.* Bonn, 1901.

Rohde, Erwin, *Der griechische Roman.* 2d ed. Leipzig, 1900.

Schemmel, Fritz, *Der Sophist Libanios als Schüler und Lehrer,* in *Neue Jahrbücher für das klassische Alterthum,* 20, 1907, pp. 52–69.

—— *Die Hochschule von Konstantinople im IV. Jahrhundert p. Ch. n.,* in *Neue Jahrbücher für das klassische Alterthum,* 22, 1908, pp. 147–168.

—— *Die Hochschule von Athen im IV. und V. Jahrhundert p. Ch. n.,* in *Neue Jahrbücher für das klassische Alterthum,* 22, 1908, pp. 494–513.

Sclosser, F. C., *Universitäten, Studirende und Professoren der Griechen zu Julian's und Theodosius' Zeit,* in *Archiv für Geschichte und Literatur,* 1830, 1 Bd., pp. 217–272.

Sievers, G. R., *Das Leben des Libanius.* Berlin, 1868.

Ussing, J. L., *Erziehung und Jugendunterricht bei den Griechen und Römern.* Neue Bearbeitung. Berlin, 1885.

Wilkins, A. S., *National Education in Greece in the Fourth Century before Christ.* London, 1873.

—— *Roman Education.* Cambridge, 1905.

Zumpt, H., *Ueber den Bestand der philosophischen Schulen in Athen und die Succession der Scholarchen,* in *Abhandlungen der königlichen Akademie der Wissenschaften zu Berlin,* 1844, pp. 27–119.

# THE UNIVERSITIES OF ANCIENT GREECE

## CHAPTER I

### INTRODUCTORY

THE period treated in these chapters on The Universities of Ancient Greece is the first five centuries of the Christian era, and the part of the world the eastern half of the Roman Empire — that half of it that was dominated by the Greek language and Greek civilization. Ancient Greece, as the term is commonly understood, included that small district in Europe which lay south of the Cambunian Mountains and formed the southern extremity of the Balkan Peninsula; it corresponded roughly to the modern political division of that name. More properly, however, the term is applied to all those lands in which the Greek type of civilization and Greek ideals prevailed, and in this sense it included in the fifth and fourth centuries B. C. the islands of the Ægean Sea, much of the neighboring coast-land of Europe and Asia, and many outlying districts in various directions, such as parts of Sicily and southern Italy in the west, Cyrene in the south, and numerous colonies on the shore of the Black Sea. With the advent of Macedonia into the field of Grecian politics, Greek civilization was spread still further abroad and the bounds of Greece were again widened. They now included, besides the Balkan Peninsula and the islands of the Ægean and eastern Mediterranean, Egypt and the adjacent parts of Libya, the whole of Asia Minor, with Syria, Palestine, and Arabia Petræa, Thrace, and Macedonia. It is in this broadest sense of the term that the word Greece is used in the title of the present work.

The period is one of great interest. It was the time when, throughout the Empire, the old order of things was breaking up or dissolving and the new was taking its place. In the West, Roman civilization was uniting with German arms to form the new Roman-German Empire; while, in the East, that which we call Hellenism — the later Greek civilization and culture, permeated by the ancient Greek spirit — was slowly but surely giving way before the new forces of Christianity and Byzantinism. Strictly, this is true of only the last part — approximately the last half — of the period in question; for the spirit of Byzantinism can hardly be said to have made its appearance much before the time of Diocletian, and the Christian religion was itself on the defensive as late as that emperor's reign, while the menace of the German arms was not serious in the early years of the Empire. But the seed had already been sown for the overthrow of the Hellenistic civilization before the first convert to Christianity had been made in the East, and the downfall of the Empire was foreshadowed in the corruption, profligacy, and extravagance of the Roman Court in the first century A. D. In the meantime, before the new capital had been built near the mouth of the Black Sea, and the Christian religion established as the Court religion by Constantine, and before the more serious inroads of the barbarians began along the northern border of the Empire, Greece and Rome respectively enjoyed large measures of peace and prosperity. Indeed, in the first centuries of the period before us, there was something like a genuine revival both in Roman and in Greek letters, and even in the later years the course of affairs was not always, on its face, one of steady and uninterrupted decline. Attached to both events — the breaking up of the civilization of the West and the decline and extinction of Hellenism in the East — there is a tragic interest, and it is only when we recall that on the ruins of the Roman state there was to be raised by other hands a new civilization, embodying much of the old, and that the seed of Hellenism was to be preserved through the centuries and to fructify in modern soil, that we view the events in a different light.

We have to do in these chapters, not with the wars and bloodshed, but with the educational and social life, of the times. It is, indeed, not a little singular that Greece, just at the moment when she lost her political independence, should have established another sort of rule more solid and more enduring than the other. The contrast that is here presented is striking. In the field of government Greece had never been able to establish and to maintain successfully for any length of time a federation of states. The centrifugal force among the different units of which such a federation should have been composed was too great. The Greek language and education, on the other hand, formed, in the later centuries of Hellenism, the strongest bond of union between diverse races. This it was that distinguished these races from all barbarians, and even gave them a certain superiority over their Latin-educated countrymen in the western half of the Empire. More than any other thing, it appealed to a national sentiment.[1]

In this study of ancient university life, the inquiry has been limited to those countries in which the prevailing language was Greek. Roman education in imperial times was, it is true, in the main modelled on that of the Greeks, and there were teachers of Greek learning in Gaul, as there were teachers of Latin learning at Constantinople. On the whole, however, it seems desirable to keep the two fields apart, and there is enough distinction between the two on the basis of language alone to warrant this separation.

---

[1] Lib., i. 458, 22: "Ἕλλην τις εἶ καὶ κρατεῖς Ἑλλήνων· οὕτω γὰρ ἥδιόν μοι καλεῖν τὸ τοῖς βαρβάροις ἀντίπαλον, καὶ οὐδέν μοι μέμψεται τὸ γένος Αἰνείου· ib., i. 333, 8: εἰ δὴ τοῖς λόγοις μᾶλλον ἢ τὸ γένει τὸν Ἕλληνα κλητέον. See Rohde, Gr. Rom., p. 319, and Schmid, Gr. Renais., pp. 4, 31. Greek sophistry was a protest against barbarism, and it tended to preserve the level of culture in the ancient world. Cf. H. C. Lodge, Scribner's Magazine, June, 1907, p. 658: ". . . I have often wondered how many people have stopped to consider that our language is one of the greatest bonds which hold the Union together, perhaps the strongest, as it is the most impalpable of all. . . . In the language, too, lies the best hope of assimilating and Americanizing the vast masses of immigrants who every year pour out upon our shores, for when these new-comers learn the language, they inevitably absorb, in greater or less degree, the traditions and beliefs, the aspirations and the modes of thought, the ideals and the attitude toward life, which that language alone enshrines." See p 346

The side of education that was most prominent in the centuries we are to study, and the side, therefore, that will specially engage our attention, is that known as the *sophistic*. The words *sophistry* and *sophistic* are familiar to us in English, but we must not be misled by the associations of the English words. Sophistry was, no doubt, even among the Greeks, responsible for much that was pernicious in style and in form of thought, but it was far from being the wholly bad thing that it is, probably, with us.

The phenomenon of the rise and spread of Greek sophistry had a basis of fact deep in the character of the Greek people, and its influence on the course of Greek letters we should find it hard to overestimate. The Greeks were by nature a people of speakers, and from early times the art of oratory was highly prized among them. Hardly a form — we may say, no form — of literature arose in Greece that did not owe much of its distinctive character to considerations of the spoken word. The Greeks were also, however, a people in whom the sense of fitness and proportion was highly developed. In the old days — the days to which the most perfect of the works of art and literature belong — the poet or the philosopher, the historian or the public speaker, if he had a message to convey, not only chose the appropriate form in which to convey it, but also, in making use of that form, attended to the careful adjustment of words and thought; neither of these two parts of the discourse was allowed to be out of proportion to the other; and in this careful adjustment of words and thought lay the literary perfection for which the Greeks strove. But, as time went on, men came to see more and more of the possibilities that lay in this that was called language, and to observe and wonder at the many curious things that could be done with it;[1] then they began to cultivate literary style as a thing that was to be desired for itself. Symmetry and proportion were lost sight of. Perfection was no longer sought in the careful adjustment of words and thought, but in the polish and elegance of words alone. Now it was just this cult of style for style's sake that formed the essence of sophistry. Artistic excellence, we see, was still the ideal of the Greek, but his mental vision had become perverted.

But though this was the case, the influence of sophistry on the course of Greek letters was far-reaching and important. Sophistry served, by bringing back into favor Attic words, expressions, and peculiarities of language which had fallen, or were tending to fall, into disuse, to establish, on a basis of Attic purity, the form which the Greek literary language was to retain through several centuries. The old so-called

[1] The first intimation of these possibilities was given to the Athenians by Gorgias, the famous orator and rhetorician, who came to Athens on an embassy from Leontini in Sicily in 427 B. C. "Being brought before the people," says Diodorus (xii. 53), "he spoke to the Athenians about the alliance, and the Athenians, who were naturally clever and fond of speech-making, were astounded at the strange character of his language. For he was the first to make use of exaggerated and elaborate figures, antitheses, equally balanced clauses, rhymes, and other such devices — things which nowadays [the second half of the first century B. C.] are held to smack of over-niceness and strike one as ridiculous when used to excess, but were then, owing to the novelty of the style, deemed worthy of respect."

'classic' authors, as Plato, Demosthenes, Isocrates, etc., were carefully read and studied in the schools, and collections of unfamiliar words and phrases, sometimes accompanied by explanations, were made from them. Some of these collections were designed to serve as a basis for further study, while others were meant for the use of those who wished to write in a pure Attic style. Sometimes juristic, antiquarian, or other lore was incorporated in these works, which then took on the character of encyclopædias. It is to this kind of activity that we owe such works as the *Lexicon* of Harpocration, the *Onomasticon* of Julius Pollux, and the Ἀττικισταί, or *Guides to Correct Attic*, of Phrynichus and Mœris, as well as lexica like those of Ælius Dionysius and Pausanias, which are no longer preserved, but were used by the later, Byzantine, lexicographers. Other kinds of collections were also made under the influence of the sophistic schools, such as collections of proverbs, myths, etc., and certain grammatical works stood in near relation to the study of sophistry. Compilations of the class represented by the *Deipnosophistæ* of Athenæus and the *Varia Historia* of Ælian were fostered in the same atmosphere. Certain forms of literature were of distinctly sophistic origin or development: the imaginary epistle, cultivated noticeably by Alciphron and Aristænetus; the 'description' so-called, employed by the two Philostrati in their descriptions of pictures, and by Callistratus in his descriptions of statues; and, perhaps most important of all, the novel, known to us especially through the works of Heliodorus, Longus, and Achilles Tatius. Probably no form of literature, however, was not in some measure influenced by the sophistic movement, and, indeed, the case could not well be otherwise, when nearly everybody that wrote received his training in a school of sophistry. Even the discourses of the philosophers, though more or less technical in character, tended to clothe themselves in a language of sophistical coloring and form, and some authors who were comparatively free from the mannerisms of the sophists themselves acknowledged the sophistical sway by recurring to the Attic style, which the sophists had established as a standard. The great Christian orators and writers of the fourth century, men like Gregory Nazianzene, Gregory of Nyssa, Basil the Great, John Chrysostom, were educated in the schools of sophistry, and so the sophistic standard of taste in style was carried over into the Christian literature also.

It will be seen from what has been said that the sophistic movement was one of great significance in the history of Greek letters. A movement which thus affected the course of a literature for several centuries and even exerted its influence over those who tried to deny its authority is one of the important events in the intellectual life of a nation. For a proper understanding of the later ancient Greek literature — the literature of the last five centuries of Hellenism — an understanding of Greek sophistry — its meaning and its course — is essential. These considerations alone should recommend the study of this subject to our attention; but there are other aspects under which the movement of which we are speaking may be viewed.

The sophistic training appeals to our curiosity as a method of education, and the activity of the schools of sophistry presents to us a most interesting phase of ancient Greek social life. It is to these two aspects of the movement that we purpose in these pages to direct our attention. We wish, in the first place, to obtain an idea of what the Greek higher education was like in the last five centuries of Hellenism, and we wish, in the second place, to become acquainted with the teachers and students of those days, to get as vivid an impression as possible of their activity and their personality. As a setting to this picture, we need also to know something of the course which this higher education took, and of the way in which it was affected by the different streams of Roman politics, barbarian invasion, Christianity, and what has been called the spirit of Byzantinism.

Greek education, however, was continuous. It began probably far back of the time when we begin to have historical records, and it continued, with modifications but not with interruptions, at least through the time that is included in these chapters. Some consideration, therefore, of the conditions that prevailed in the centuries preceding those in which sophistry came to the fore, as well as some account of the lower grades of education, of which the highest grade was an outgrowth, is desirable. A detailed exposition of the intellectual life of the earlier period, however, we shall not be required to give.

## CHAPTER II

### EDUCATION AT ATHENS IN THE FIFTH AND FOURTH CENTURIES B. C.

ALTHOUGH the Greeks in many parts of the world began at an early time to take a practical interest in the education of their youth, it is with regard to the educational life of the Athenians that we have the most information up to, at least, the third century B. C. In later years, when Athens became the centre of a new, Hellenistic, world, there was, among nearly all Greeks, a tendency, which grew stronger every day, to adopt the principles and methods of the Athenian education. For these reasons we may take, as the centre of our inquiry in the pre-Alexandrian period, the educational life of Athens.

The education of the Athenians in the fifth century B. C. was, as is well known, a form of training, or education in the strict sense, rather than a system of instruction. It consisted of two parts — a training for the mind and character (called μουσική), and a training for the body (called γυμναστική). Μουσική, *music* in the broad sense (as being any art presided over by a Muse), comprised reading and writing, counting, singing, and lyre or flute playing. For a long time the lyre was the only musical instrument used in the schools, but after the Persian Wars the flute came into favor; it did not, however, supersede the lyre, and in the fourth century, if not earlier, it fell into its former disfavor. The authors that were read in the schools were, of course, the poets—Homer and Hesiod perhaps first of all, and then the lyric poets. Toward the end of the fifth century the tragedians also probably came into use.[1] Large quantities of these authors were learned by heart, and some of the lyric poetry was sung to the accompaniment of the lyre. The chief aim of the Athenian education appears in the point of view from which the poets were studied: they were looked upon primarily, not as literary artists, but as moral preceptors, and were required, not so much to form the tastes as to develop the characters of the pupils. The teacher, the γραμματιστής as he was called, would be sure to find, in reading with his pupils the Homeric poems, abundant opportunity to inculcate lessons of morality based on the actions and words of the gods and heroes, while much of the lyric poetry, of course, taught its own lesson and required no interpreter. Still, although the moral side of these poems was the side chiefly dwelt upon in the instruction of the period, it is certain that the Greeks, with all their natural sensitiveness to the charm of language, did not fail to recognize an educating influence in the harmony of sweet words, as well as in that of musical sounds. The training as a whole, we should say, was directed to the harmonious development of the judgment, the taste,

---

[1] Sandys, *Hist. Clas. Schol.*, i. p. 60; Girard, *L'Éd. athén.*, pp. 149, 150. According to Lucian (*Anarch.*, 22), the laws were learned by heart in the time of Solon (*cf.* Plato, *Protag.*, 326 D).

the intelligence, the moral and the physical qualities of the youth.[1]

[1] *Cf.* Quint., *Inst. or.*, i. 8, 5. The *locus classicus* on the education of the Greek boy is Plato, *Protag.*, 325 C–326 C. The following translation is by Professor Jowett: "Education and admonition commence in the first years of childhood and last to the very end of life. Mother and nurse and father and tutor are quarrelling about the improvement of the child as soon as ever he is able to understand them: he cannot say or do anything without their setting forth to him that this is just and that is unjust; this is honourable, that is dishonourable; this is holy, that is unholy; do this and abstain from that. And if he obeys, well and good; if not, he is straightened by threats and blows, like a piece of warped wood. At a later stage they send him to teachers, and enjoin them to see to his manners even more than to his reading and music; and the teachers do as they are desired. And when the boy has learned his letters and is beginning to understand what is written, as before he understood only what was spoken, they put into his hands the works of great poets, which he reads at school; in these are contained many admonitions, and many tales, and praises, and encomia of ancient famous men, which he is required to learn by heart, in order that he may imitate or emulate them and desire to become like them. Then, again, the teachers of the lyre take similar care that their young disciple is temperate and gets into no mischief; and when they have taught him the use of the lyre, they introduce him to the poems of other excellent poets, who are the lyric poets; and these they set to music, and make their harmonies and rhythms quite familiar to the children's souls, in order that they may learn to be more gentle, and harmonious, and rhythmical, and so more fitted for speech and action; for the life of man in every part has need of harmony and rhythm. Then they send them to the master of gymnastic, in order that their bodies may better minister to the virtuous mind, and that they may not be compelled through bodily weakness to play the coward in war or on any other occasion." *Cf.* Luc., *Anarch.*, 20 *ff*. See also Monroe, *Hist. of Educ.*, p. 91: "However long it might take the boy to acquire the ability to play the lyre, mere technical skill was never the end. The task of the boy was similar to that of the work of the old bard. . . . The playing of the lyre, in the school sense, continued to be this improvising an accompaniment in harmony with the thought expressed in the passage repeated. Here was demanded both an insight and understanding in the interpreta-

Such was the type of the education of the Athenian youth through most of the fifth century B. C. In matters of detail, the education of one boy doubtless often differed from that of another. The sons of the rich, we are told,[1] went to school earlier, and left school later, than the sons of the poor, and this fact of itself implies, or suggests, in these cases a difference of attainment. Again, all teachers, we may be sure, did not teach by the same stereotyped method, and some, no doubt, were able to carry their pupils farther than others or even to give them more or less rudimentary instruction in branches not here indicated. Such teachers were Damon, Pythocleides, Agathocles, and so on — men of larger intelligence and fuller equipment than their neighbors, and so better able to carry their pupils along the lines of a more advanced instruction.

One important aspect, however, of the educational life of this period we have as yet not touched upon — that represented by the so-called sophists. As far back as the time of Thales, or even earlier, men had begun to speculate in a rational way on the phenomena of nature and to study the facts of science, and from then onward all the great speculative writers of Greece were really so many public teachers. Also, the poets and others, in so

tion of the poem and skill and creative ability in the construction and performance of its accompaniment. In both respects, there was a demand for individual ability and initiative, and hence there resulted a development of personality quite foreign to any preceding type of education. Indeed, it is to be doubted whether education as a process of developing creative power — power of expression, of initiative, and of appreciation — has ever been given a more fruitful form."

[1] Plato, *Protag.*, 326 C.

far as they showed a tendency to speculate and reason, may be regarded in the same light. Some of these men are even said to have given personal instruction, as Xenophanes to Parmenides,[1] Parmenides to Leucippus,[2] Anaxagoras to Euripides.[3] How true it is that in those days great thinkers were looked upon as teachers is shown by the fact that we so often in the history of Greek thought meet the statement that this or that distinguished man was the pupil of this or that other distinguished man. In many instances, perhaps, the former was influenced solely by the writings of the latter, and this may have been the case with at least one of the pairs just mentioned — Parmenides and Leucippus, namely. However this may be, we see that at no period of her history, at least subsequently to the time of Thales, was Greece without some measure of what is commonly called "higher learning." It was probably such learning as this that formed the staple of the instruction of the more advanced of the musical teachers of the day, such men as Damon and the others just mentioned.

But shortly after the middle of the fifth century there began to be apparent symptoms of a movement that was destined in the end to bring about an extension of knowledge in many directions. There was at that time a tendency toward the consideration of questions relating especially to moral science, practical statesmanship, and rhetoric and grammar. The representatives of this

---

[1] Diog. Laert., ix. 21.
[2] See Pauly's *Real-Encyc.*, s. v. *Leucippus*.
[3] *Vitae Eurip.*

tendency in the second half of the fifth century, as well as the successors of those who up to that time had been the inculcators of such "higher learning" as was then current, were Socrates and the sophists. These men were the signs of an intellectual stirring that was then taking place in many parts of the Greek world, and, while it is true, as stated, that the movement was at the time most noticeable in the fields of moral science, practical statesmanship, and rhetoric and grammar, it is also the case that the movement was not confined to those fields, and that in the end the impulse was felt all along the line of speculative and scientific inquiry.

The story of the fifth century sophists is well known, and it is no part of our present purpose to enter into the details of their lives and activity. They must not, of course, be confounded with the sophists of many centuries later, whose acquaintance we shall make in the subsequent chapters, nor should they even be taken as examples of what those sophists were like. As we shall see, many characteristics the two groups did have in common, but in many others they differed, and even their exact historical connection has been matter of controversy.

One of the most remarkable circumstances connected with the appearance of the fifth century sophists was the enthusiasm with which they were everywhere received by the young men of Greece. We remember [1] how the young Hippocrates, having learned late one evening that the sophist Protagoras had arrived in town, was for setting off that very night to obtain an introduc-

[1] Plato, *Protag.*, 310 A.

tion to him; but, curbing his impatience for the time being, he awoke Socrates the next morning before daylight by pounding on his door, and begged to be taken immediately to Protagoras's quarters. We recall [1] also how the youthful Theages, having heard in his country home of the wonderful doings of the sophists at Athens, was not content until he had prevailed upon his father to accompany him to the city in search of one of these men. We are induced to ask, What was the source of this great enthusiasm on the part of the young men of Greece? For we must remember that in those days there was no university, with its halo of associations and traditions, to attract the young man to a life of study: the youthful student was then something of a pioneer in the field.

One motive for seeking the society of the sophists — a motive which was perhaps not always consciously, even when actually, present — was undoubtedly the desire to obtain personal distinction in the state, either through an enlarged culture or by superior knowledge of statecraft. "I think he desires to become distinguished in the state," says Socrates, when accounting to Protagoras for Hippocrates's motive in seeking his (Protagoras's) society.[2]

Secondly, the personality of the sophists and the charm that lay in their words were powerful motives to draw many to their society. "The most of Protagoras's followers," says Socrates,[3] "seemed to be foreigners; for

[1] [Plato], *Theag.*, 121 B–122 A.
[2] Plato, *Protag.*, 316 C. Theages desired to be made clever, or wise (σοφός, *Theag.*, 121 D).
[3] Plato, *Protag.*, 315 A.

these the sophist brings with him from the various cities through which he passes, charming them, like Orpheus, with his voice, and they, charmed, follow where the voice leads."

But, after all else has been said, who will deny that to intellectual curiosity is to be ascribed a large part of this enthusiasm? The Greeks, though displaying at times a distrust and intolerance of strange doctrines — we remember the execution of Socrates and the banishment of Protagoras and others — were on the whole an intellectually curious race, wide-awake to new impressions and ready to follow out new lines of thought. The time, as has been remarked, was one of intellectual ferment, and many an eager youth must have had presented to his imagination by the professions of the sophists the prospect of wandering in new worlds of ideas, full of undefined possibilities, lying beyond the horizon of his present knowledge. Witness the impatience of the Student in the *Clouds* [1] at being interrupted in his studies by Strepsiades — for this scene, though a travesty, must have had some basis of fact. Witness also the rapt wonder and respect with which, in the *Protagoras*,[2] the followers of Hippias, gathered about their master's chair, ply the distinguished man with questions — questions about the universe and nature — and listen to his words as though they were the words of some oracle. Witness, finally, the eager interest with which on many occasions the young men of Athens leave their sports to come and engage in abstract discussions with Socrates, and the ready recep-

[1] 133 *ff.*  [2] 315 C.

tiveness they display to new ideas. Few things connected with the earlier education of the Greeks are more interesting and instructive, and few throw greater light on the intellectual life of the later centuries, than the manner in which these men — Socrates and the sophists alike — were received in Greece by the younger generation. In view of the enthusiasm, the eagerness for new ideas and new facts, the intellectual curiosity, which the young men of this age displayed, we do not find it difficult to understand how in the following centuries the philosophical and rhetorical schools of Athens were filled with students from all quarters of the world.

The influence of Socrates and the sophists on the course of Greek education was immense. Not only did the instruction that was given in the school of the γραμματιστής, or elementary teacher of letters, undergo some changes and become greatly broadened, but a number of new subjects were brought within the range of instruction. With the increase in the number of subjects that were taught, there came also a tendency to differentiate these subjects into graded groups. In the fifth century, reading and writing, counting, music in the narrower sense, and gymnastics, had answered for nearly all pupils; in the fourth century, or soon after, we find the education of the youth divided into three periods: certain studies he regularly takes in the first period, certain others in the second, and certain others in the third. If we do not press the parallelism between this system and modern systems too strongly, we may perhaps call the first period the period of elementary or primary instruction, the second the period of secondary instruction, and the third the period of college or university instruction. We are not, however, to understand that these grades were, at least at an early date, sharply defined, or that there was any hard and fast system to which all boys alike were subjected. Between the first two grades, especially, there was probably much overlapping of instruction, and the line of demarcation may here have been not always easy to find. This is the form, however, to which the Athenian education in the fourth century B. C., or in the time immediately following, approached, and, with some modifications, it was the form which probably prevailed in most Grecian cities down to the time when all pagan teaching in the world at large ceased, in the sixth century A. D.

We are also not to believe that the change here indicated took place in a day. Probably before the end of the fourth century something like a graded system — a graded system in the limited sense mentioned — had become established, but in any case the change, we are to think, was a development rather than a premeditated innovation. The end was not to be for many centuries to come, and in the meantime Greek education was to be still further broadened by the accession of new information which resulted from the scholastic movement in the period following the conquests of Alexander.[1]

[1] A graded system is distinctly mentioned in the *Axiochus* (366 D–367 A), a Platonic dialogue of uncertain date and authorship, and in an extract from Teles (of the end of the third century B. C.: see Christ, *Gr. Lit.*, p. 584), contained in Stobaeus (*Flor.*, 98, 72). Although these notices are probably both later than the fourth century, the statement contained in the text, that "before the end of the fourth century something like a graded system had become established," represents what is, on every

## 20  UNIVERSITIES OF ANCIENT GREECE

Can we, then, form any more exact idea of the changes that took place in the Athenian education in the fourth century B. C. and the centuries following? One of the subjects the study of which was specially promoted by the sophistic movement was grammar. Grammar — taken in the sense in which we use the term, for it was also used by the scholars of the Alexandrian time in a far broader sense, to include everything that pertained to the critical study and interpretation of the poets — grammar in our sense of the word was sedulously cultivated in the centuries following the early sophists, and a mass of fact and theory relative to

ground of probability, the truth. We know that the academic studies, philosophy and rhetoric, were already under way in this century, and, with the impulse given by the sophists to the study of the sciences, the latter must soon, it would seem, have taken their place between the academic studies and those of the elementary grade. See, further, on this subject, Girard, *L'Éd. athén.*, pp. 221-240. As the two passages referred to above are of interest, they are here translated. "Now when the boy," says Socrates in the *Axiochus*, "after experiencing sore trouble, has reached the age of seven, there are set over him, with their tyrannizing ways, the pedagogue, the teacher of reading and writing (γραμματιστής), and the training-master; when he has grown older (αὐξομένου δέ), the 'critic' (or 'grammarian,' κριτικός), the geometer, the tactician, and a whole swarm of masters; finally, when he has been enrolled as an ephebus, the *cosmete* with his threats of punishment, then the Lyceum and the Academy, the rule of the *gymnasiarch*, the rod, and unmeasured evils." The passage from Teles is as follows: "When he has escaped from the hands of the nurse, he is taken in charge by the pedagogue, the training-master, the teacher of reading and writing, the music-teacher, and the drawing-master. When he has advanced in age (προάγει ἡλικία), he receives, further, the arithmetician, the geometer, and the horse-trainer. . . . When he has become an ephebus, he then stands in dread of the *cosmete*, the training-master, the drill-sergeant, and the *gymnasiarch*."

words, their forms, etc., was accumulated and codified. Much of this matter must have worked its way into the instruction of the elementary teacher. In fact, we find the young pupil of the time of Dionysius of Halicarnassus, toward the end of the first century B. C., put, at the very beginning of his schooling, before he had even learned to read and write, through a systematic course of grammar, such as it would have been impossible for the boy of the time of Socrates to be taught.[1] Much else also of the multifarious knowledge accumulated by the scholars of the Alexandrian time was probably, at least as early as this, made use of by the γραμματιστής, more especially in that part of his course which had to do with the reading and expounding of the poets, and we can hardly believe that, even in respect to methods, the elementary instruction would long remain unaffected by the general spirit of scholarship.

[1] In view of present-day methods, it is interesting to see how the Greek boy, in the time of Dionysius, was taught to read. "When we learn grammar," says Dionysius (*De adm. vi dic. in Dem.*, 52, p. 1115; *cf. De comp. verb.*, 25, p. 211), "we take up first the names of the elementary sounds, called letters; then the forms and values of the letters. After we have learned these, we pass to syllables and their changes, and, these having been mastered, to the parts of speech — nouns, verbs, and connectives, together with their affections — long and short quantities, accents both acute and grave, genders, cases, numbers, modal endings, and a thousand other things of that sort. After we have compassed the knowledge of all these, then, and not till then, do we begin to write and to read — syllable by syllable at first, and slowly, as the habit is as yet new to us, but, as time goes on and continued practice gives strength and confidence to the soul, smoothly and with ease; and whatever book one puts into our hand, we then read at sight (ἅμα νοήσει), without going back over all those rules that we have learned." See Girard, *L'Éd. athén.*, pp. 130, 226.

In the fourth century B. C. — possibly not far from the middle of the century, though the exact date is naturally uncertain — a new subject was introduced into the elementary course in various Greek cities — drawing. "The subjects," says Aristotle,[1] "by which it is customary to educate children, are, we may say, four in number: letters, gymnastics, music, and, in some places, a fourth subject, drawing"; and the fact is corroborated by other evidence.[2] The introduction of drawing into the curriculum of the primary school was perhaps not directly due to the sophistic impulse; we are told by Pliny[3] that the movement started at Sicyon. In at least one place — Teos — comedy seems to have been read in the schools in the second century B. C., and it may later have been so at Athens.[4]

[1] *Polit.*, v. (viii.) 2, 3 (p. 1337 b). The reason that Aristotle gives for the teaching of drawing is that a knowledge of this subject not only prevents our being cheated in our daily commercial intercourse with men, but also enhances our appreciation of physical beauty. Compare Herbert Spencer, *An Autobiography*, vol. i. ch. xi. p. 233: "The practice of drawing or modeling is to be encouraged not merely with a view to the worth of the things produced, for, in the great majority of cases, these will be worthless; but it is to be encouraged as increasing the appreciation of both Nature and Art. There results from it a revelation of natural beauties of form and colour which to undisciplined perceptions remain invisible; and there results, also, a greatly exalted enjoyment of painting and sculpture. The pleasure which truthful rendering gives is increased by increasing the knowledge of the traits to be rendered."

[2] Stob., *Flor.*, 98, 72.

[3] *N. H.*, xxxv. 77 (*graphicen, hoc est pictura in buxo*, perhaps painting).

[4] See Girard, *L'Éd. athén.*, pp. 150, 151. In Isocrates's view, music, grammar, and all other introductory studies had simply a disciplinary value (*De antid.*, 265–267). See p. 33.

Other changes doubtless occurred in the elementary instruction of the Greeks in the period from the fourth to the first century B. C., both in respect to matter and in respect to methods. Music, for instance, was originally taught because it was considered to be a form of education for the soul, but in Aristotle's time most people studied it to give themselves and their friends pleasure. Such a change in the point of view must, we should say, have resulted in a change in the character of the instruction.¹ As early as the time of Aristophanes a new tendency in music was deplored.²

In the second period of his education the youth of these later centuries came under the direction of several instructors. First in point of importance, perhaps, was the κριτικός, the 'critic,' or, as he was later also called, the γραμματικός, the teacher or expounder of literature, especially poetic literature (not to be confounded with the γραμματιστής, or elementary teacher of letters).³ The instruction of the γραμματιστής probably did not extend very far into the region of exposition, though, where every teacher was free to teach what he could and chose

---

¹ Aristot., *Polit.*, v. (viii.) 2, 3 (p. 1337 b).

² In the famous passage in the *Clouds*, 967 ff. The simple hymns of an earlier time had given place to a more complicated music, full of strange variations.

³ [Plato], *Axiochus*, 366 E. On the words κριτικός and γραμματικός, and the duties of the 'grammarian,' see Sandys, *Hist. Clas. Schol.*, i. pp. 6–11; Girard, *L'Éd. athén.*, pp. 224–227; Quint., *Inst. or.*, i. 4 ff. Gregory Nazianzene (xliii. 23) gives the following as the 'grammarian's' duties: "to Grecize the tongue, gather information, regulate metres, and set down the laws for poems."

to, it may often have tended to encroach on the field of the γραμματικός.¹ In general, however, where the γραμματιστής left off, the γραμματικός began. The special field of the latter was the exposition and illustration of the poets, but the range of his instruction was broad and included questions from many fields — grammar, metre, history, morals, science, etc. Much attention was given to clear enunciation and good expression. The texts of the authors read were discussed and analyzed, and beauties of style and thought were pointed out and commented upon. Sometimes literary appreciations were attempted. In illustrating and expounding his authors, the teacher would take the opportunity to communicate to his pupils a mass of antiquarian and other lore, would discuss questions of etymology and the meaning of words, and would at times, doubtless, suggest emendations of the text. As time went on, the dignity and importance of the γραμματικός increased, and in the later centuries of pagan education he became in many cities a recognized factor of the university, with imperial or municipal appointment.

Other teachers whom the pupil encountered in the secondary grade were the geometer and the arithmetician.² Geometry had been in great favor as early as the fifth century, as is evident from many passages in Plato and from Aristophanes, but in the fourth century, or shortly after, it became a recognized branch of edu-

---

[1] Especially was this so in later times. Libanius, between the ages of fifteen and twenty, studied under a γραμματιστής (Lib., i. 9, 14; cf. ib., ep., 408).

[2] [Plato], *Axiochus*, 366 E; Stob., *Flor.*, 98, 72.

cation, and was taught by special teachers. The arithmetic that was taught by the arithmetician we should probably understand as something more advanced than the simple *counting* which had formed a part of the instruction of the γραμματιστής in the fifth century. Still other branches of study, as astronomy and geography, came to the fore in the fourth century and the centuries that followed,[1] though the beginnings of these studies, as of those that have already been mentioned, reached far back of that time.

One feature of the education that has here been sketched deserves special attention — the great stress that was laid in it on the cultivation of the voice. Reading meant, for the Greek boy, not reading silently, but reading aloud (ἀναγιγνώσκειν). From his earliest school-days, he was taught to utter his words clearly and distinctly, and to read with proper emphasis and expression. Most of the elementary instruction, and probably much of the more advanced, was given orally, and the boy was required to recite his lesson rather than to write it. All this is, of course, in accordance with the practice of the whole Greek people, to whom the spoken word was ever of greater importance than the written; it also accounts in part for the great vogue of the later sophists, among whom the cultivation of musical utterance and dramatic expression combined with harmonious language was developed into an art.

The age at which the boy at Athens, and probably in most other Grecian cities, was first sent to school was

[1] *Cf.* Girard, *L'Éd. athén.*, pp. 227-231.

about five or six.[1] The length of his stay depended on many considerations, not least of which, we may believe, were the means and condition of his parents. At the age of eighteen he became, at Athens, legally of age, and was then taken in hand by the state and enrolled in the college of the *ephebi*. He was also ready, at about the same age, to take up one or both of the two higher branches of learning — philosophy and rhetoric. For it was these two, philosophy and rhetoric, which, starting, at the time of the sophistic movement, from a single stream, reached forth, as it were in two arms, into the succeeding centuries, and formed the two great branches of academic study. In the earliest of these centuries they touched, on one side, the state institution of the *ephebi*. To the consideration of these three subjects, therefore, philosophy, rhetoric, and the ephebic college, we must devote a few pages before proceeding further.

Of the various schools of philosophy that were founded at Athens and elsewhere by the followers of Socrates, after the death of the latter, none survived to have an independent existence, except the four great schools, the Academic, the Peripatetic, the Stoic, and the Epicurean.[2] Almost the whole philosophical in-

---

[1] The author of the *Axiochus* sets it at seven (see p. 19, n. 1). In the second century A. D. it is stated to have been six or seven (Soranus, *Ars obs.*, 92); in the fourth century A. D., before five (Joh. Chrys., vol. iii. 109 Migne). At twelve, according to Soranus, the boy was sent to the 'grammarian' and the geometer.

[2] The Cynic teaching had for a long time great influence, and Cynics swarmed in Grecian lands as late as the second century A. D. Cynicism, however, tended to merge into Stoicism, and

struction of the eight centuries or more from the time of Plato to the closing of the Neo-Platonic school of philosophy at the beginning of the sixth century A. D. was connected with these four schools or with some one or more of them, and up to the time of Augustus, at least, Athens continued to be the head-quarters of this instruction. For it was here that the schools had been established and it was here that they had their corporate existence.

The first of the four schools to be established at Athens was the Academic. Its founder was Plato. When, in 347, Plato died, he bequeathed his house and its belongings, near the grove of the Academy, where he had been accustomed, during the last forty years of his life, to teach and converse, to his nephew Speusippus, who, at his death, bequeathed them to his pupils, or, in trust, to his successor, Xenocrates. The estate thus passed into the hands, and became the property, of the school in a corporate capacity. The members of the school formed a religious brotherhood — a $\theta$ίασος — based on a worship of the Muses. Its Head, or leader, called the *scholarch* ($\sigma\chi\delta\lambda\alpha\rho\chi\circ\varsigma$), was, in each case, either appointed by the preceding scholarch, or was chosen by the school itself, after the latter's death, and perhaps in accordance with his recommendation.[1] The purpose of

the lack of a distinct school of Cynicism in the second century A. D. is attested by the failure of Marcus Aurelius, when he at that time organized the philosophical department of the University at Athens (see p. 92), to make provision for a school of that sect.

[1] Zeller, *Phil. d. Griech.*, ii. 1, pp. 985, 986. Xenocrates was chosen by vote of the students after Speusippus's death (*Index Herculan.*, 6, 7). Occasionally a scholarch abdicated during his lifetime.

the society was twofold: scientific inquiry by the members in common and the transmission of knowledge by instruction.[1] At stated intervals banquets were held, to which guests were invited from without.

The foundation of the Peripatetic school, which was established some years later, near the Lyceum, by Theophrastus, the follower of Aristotle, was similar to that of the Academic. This, too, was a religious foundation, and the property was held in trust by a number of the members. The method of appointment to the headship of this school seems to have varied. Straton, the successor of Theophrastus, appointed in his will Lycon, and expressed the hope that the members of the school would acquiesce in this choice. Lycon left the selection of his successor to ten of his most trusted friends and pupils. In this school, too, provision was made for banquets.[2]

The Stoic school, though it had a name, had no local habitation such as the other schools had. Its members, to be sure, frequented, in the earlier part of its career, the Painted Stoa, but it acquired no private property and was not incorporated. It continued, however, to have an independent existence, and perhaps, in other respects than those mentioned (except, of course, in the matter of its tenets), it differed little from its rival schools.

---

[1] When the philosophical schools began to compete with the schools of rhetoric for the young men of all lands, they claimed to offer the only proper training for life, and so a new purpose was then added (see pp. 72; 79, n. 1).

[2] Zeller, *Phil. d. Griech.*, ii. 2, pp. 807 *ff.*, 925. For Straton and Lycon, see Diog. Laert., v. 62, 70.

The Epicurean school started on its career with the house and garden of its founder, Epicurus, but this property seems in the course of time to have been, at least in part, dissipated.[1] The members of the school, following the directions contained in Epicurus's will, met once a month to enjoy a commemorative banquet, and, besides, celebrated with an annual feast their founder's birthday. Epicurus seems to have appointed his own successor and to have contemplated that future Heads of the School would do likewise; though at a later time (121 A. D.) it appears that in case the person thus appointed proved to be an unfortunate choice, he could be set aside and another appointed in his stead by vote of the students.[2]

We see that each of these schools (with the exception, apparently, of the Stoic school) started with a certain amount of private property, and was therefore on the way toward being on an independent and self-supporting basis. From time to time, in the case of at least one of them — the Academic school — and perhaps in the case of others, bequests were made by generous patrons of learning, and thus still further means were provided for study. Before long the teachers began to take fees from their students; this had been done by the sophists in the fifth century, but Aristippus, the Cyrenaic, is said to have been the first to introduce the custom into a school, and his example was followed by Speusippus, the nephew of Plato.[3]

[1] In Cicero's time the garden was in the hands of a distinguished Roman. See Zeller, *Phil. d. Griech.*, iii. 1, p. 370, n. 1.
[2] Diog. Laert., x. 17; Dessau, *Insc. Lat. sel.*, ii. 2, 1906, No. 7784.
[3] Diog. Laert., ii. 65; iv. 2; Luc., *Vit. auct.*, 24.

With regard to the internal management of the schools, it would naturally be to the advantage of all members of any one of them to have as their Head one who could preserve harmony and command respect among the members themselves. "And I leave my garden walk," wrote Lycon, the third scholarch of the Peripatetic school, in his will,[1] "to those of my associates who have signified that they wish to use it — Bulon, Callinus, Ariston, Amphion, Lycon, Python, Aristomachus, Heracleius, Lycomedes, and my nephew Lycon. Let them elect as their Head the one whom they think most likely to remain attached to the pursuit of philosophy and most able to hold the school together. And let the rest of my associates co-operate with these, both for my sake and for the sake of the place." The other members were supposed, in a spirit of loyalty, to subordinate themselves to the Head, while they probably also gave instruction as under-teachers. Sometimes, though perhaps rarely in these earlier years, a member separated himself entirely from the school and set up a school of his own.[2]

The purpose of these details has been to show what one of the earliest forms of college in Greece was like. To these schools, or colleges, during the first three hundred years after their foundation, students of all ages came, in great numbers, from all quarters of the Greek world, and, during a part of that time, from the Western world as well; while, as we shall see later, the schools

[1] Diog. Laert., v. 70.
[2] See Zumpt, *Ueber den Bestand d. phil. Schul.*, p. 30. In general, for the history and external condition of the philosophical schools, see this article.

formed, in the second and third centuries after Christ, a part of the University of Athens. It is beyond our purpose to discuss here the tenets of the different sects, but we may observe, in passing, that the schools carried on in several directions the impulse given to study by Socrates and the sophists — noticeably in the directions of ethical, metaphysical, and scientific inquiry.

Let us now turn to the second of the three forms of college established in these early centuries on Grecian soil — the school of rhetoric. The race of sophists did not end with those distinguished members of it who lived in the second half of the fifth century, but of those who followed in the fourth century none gained such distinction, or influenced so greatly the course of Greek education, as one who, while inveighing bitterly against the sophists of his day, was himself perhaps the greatest of the sophists either of that or of the preceding age — Isocrates.

Isocrates was born in 436 B. C. and studied under some of the most famous teachers of his time — Protagoras, Prodicus, Gorgias, Theramenes — besides being influenced strongly by Socrates. After completing his education, he became a logographer, or professional writer of law speeches, and this profession he practised for a number of years, until about 390 or a little before that time. He then turned his attention to the teaching of rhetoric, and opened a school, at first, it is said, at Chios. Shortly after he removed to Athens and set up a school there. He did not die until 338, and so for about half a century his school at Athens was a gathering-point and centre of attraction for those who wished to be educated in the higher genteel learning of the day. Students flocked thither from all parts of the Greek world, and many of them were, or became in later years, famous — the statesmen Timotheus, son of Conon, and Leodamas; the orators Lycurgus, Hypercides, and Isæus; the historians Ephorus and Theopompus; and many others.

Isocrates charged for his course, which lasted from three to four years, 1,000 drachmæ ($180). Like the sophists against whom he inveighs, he professed to prepare young men for the duties of public life, but, unlike them, he attained his object rather by educating the mind and character of his pupils than by supplying them with a mass of ready-prepared material. The means to this preparation was the study of rhetoric and eloquence, or, in one word, oratory. Isocrates taught his subject, not as a cut-and-dried system, but as a *philosophy*, which was to be adapted to the aptitude and ability of the individual student. We see, in Isocrates's attitude toward his subject, again a partial explanation of the great vogue which rhetoric later had in the educational curriculum of the Greeks. Rhetoric, correctly taught, not only formed the accomplished orator or advocate, but educated the taste, the judgment, and the character. The form of eloquence to which Isocrates gave his special attention was neither the deliberative, such as was used in the public assemblies, nor the juristic, but the so-called *epideictic*, or display oratory — that form that was suited to the expounding of great political subjects of common interest.

In comparing Isocrates's school with the schools of

philosophy, we notice certain important differences. In the first place, Isocrates's school devoted less attention to form. The schools of philosophy were, generally speaking, corporations possessed of landed property and having a regular succession in the headship. The school of Isocrates was an assemblage of students drawn together by the name of one man and acknowledging, apparently, no other bond of union except a common admiration for their master and a common desire to profit by his instruction. We notice, secondly, that the teaching in the school of Isocrates was, on the one hand, less speculative, and, on the other hand, less technical and scientific than the teaching in the schools of philosophy became. It was a form of training, and it provided a broad and liberal culture. Other subjects, such as mathematics, the sciences, history, were only preparatory studies, not ends in themselves; they provided at best a technical education. We should say, then, that the rhetorical school contained more of the elements of permanency in the Greek world, for the reason that it answered more nearly to the genuinely Greek conception of education — a preparation for active life in the service of the state on the basis of the perfect development of the individual.[1] The emphasizing of

[1] Though the general tendency at this time was toward a more individualistic conception of education, there was little that was individualistic in the sophistical education of the first five centuries after Christ. Here is Isocrates's view of the educated man (*Panath.*, 30 *ff.*): "Whom, then, do I call educated, since I refuse this name to those who have learned only certain trades, or certain sciences, or have had only certain faculties developed? First, those who manage well the daily affairs of life as they arise, and whose judgment is accurate and rarely errs when aiming at

this fact at a time when the bounds of knowledge were widening in every direction, and education was undergoing a process of transformation, is one of the important services which Isocrates rendered to the cause of education. Otherwise also his influence was important: he made, namely, oratory one of the regular studies of the Grecian youth, and thus opened the way to that wonderful expansion of oratorical studies which took place in the second century after Christ. Of Isocrates's influence on the literary prose style of the Greeks, though it was most important, we are not here concerned to speak.

When Isocrates died — or even before he died, for he was ninety-eight years of age at the time of his

the expedient. Then, those who associate in dignified and honorable fashion with all with whom they come in contact, bearing easily and good-naturedly what is unpleasant or offensive in others, and softening, as much as possible, their own asperities of manner. Further, those who never become the slaves of pleasure, and who by misfortunes are not unduly cast down — bearing themselves in their presence manfully and in a manner worthy of our common nature. Fourthly, and most important of all, those who are uncorrupted by good fortune and do not lose their heads and become arrogant, but, retaining control of themselves as intelligent beings, rejoice not less in the goods they have acquired at their birth by their own nature and intelligence than in the benefits that have been cast in their way by chance. Those whose souls are in permanent and harmonious accord, not with one of these things, but with all of them, these, I say, are wise and perfect men, possessed of all the virtues. This is my opinion with regard to educated men." Elsewhere he tells us what sophistry does for a man (*De antid.*, 204): "Some (*i. e.*, of those who associate with sophists) are turned out perfect masters (*i. e.*, of the art of sophistry); some, able teachers; while those who have chosen to live a private life are rendered more cultivated in their intercourse with others than they were before, and more exact judges and counsellors of speech than the majority of men."

death — his school passed out of existence, but the influence of the man and his teaching survived and affected strongly the subsequent course of rhetorical education. Shortly after 330, Æschines is said to have transplanted the study of oratory to Rhodes. During the succeeding centuries oratory continued to be taught in the schools of Asia, and probably also to some extent in those of Athens.

The third form of college which we have to consider is the College of the *Ephebi*. The Greek word ἔφηβος signifies primarily *one who has arrived at maturity*. The legal age of maturity was, at Athens, eighteen, and the time from his eighteenth birthday (or from the beginning of the Attic official year that followed his eighteenth birthday) to his twentieth birthday (or to the beginning of the Attic official year that followed his twentieth birthday) the Athenian youth passed in an apprenticeship of arms to the state. During this whole period he was called an ἔφηβος. The whole body of young men who were at any time serving in this apprenticeship constituted the College of the *Ephebi*. When the Athenian youth was about to enter upon his nineteenth year, he presented himself, first before the citizens of his deme, and then before the βουλή, to be examined relative to his age and his parentage. It having been proven that he was really eighteen, and that he had been born of Athenian parents, his name was entered on the official register of his deme and he became a citizen forthwith. The first duty of the newly-enrolled ἔφηβος was to take the ephebic oath, which bound him not to dishonor the arms which he bore, not to desert his companion in battle, to fight for his gods and his home, to advance the interests of his country, to submit to the rule of those above him, to obey the existing laws and oppose all who attempted to break them, and to respect the religion of his ancestors. He then entered upon the course of discipline which formed the curriculum of the college and was designed to make of him one who could, in time of necessity, defend his country. The first year was a year of preliminary training; the recruit was then to be broken in. Besides receiving instruction in the ordinary athletic exercises of the gymnasium, he was taught the use of the bow, the javelin, etc., was, in some cases at least, made to engage in horse-riding and rowing, and was trained in the various military manœuvres and formations. At the end of the first year, he received from the state a buckler and lance, and was then put on patrol and guard duty along the frontier and in the various forts of Attica; at the same time he still continued his military practice. At many of the public festivals the ephebi appeared in a body and took part in the proceedings, their presence and manœuvres adding much to the pomp of the occasion.

Such, roughly, seems to have been the ephebic system as it was up to about the beginning of the third century B. C. We see that it was almost wholly military in character and that it was a state institution. The various instructors — the παιδοτρίβης, or instructor in gymnastics, the ὁπλομάχος, or instructor in the use of arms, the ἀκοντιστής, or instructor in the art of javelin-throwing, the τοξότης, or instructor in bowmanship, and others — were appointed and remunerated by the state. The σωφρονισταί, or superintendents, who were commissioned to oversee the morals and conduct of the ephebi, were state-appointed officials, and the whole college was probably under the general supervision and control of the στρατηγοί (the 'generals,' the most important of the Athenian magistrates) and the Areopagus. Had the college been nothing more than this, it would not call for our special attention here. In the course of time, however, it underwent certain changes. Toward the close of the fourth century, with the decline of the military spirit in Greece, and the advent of new conditions, apprenticeship in the college, it would seem, ceased to be obligatory on all who were entitled to carry arms, and the time of service was reduced from two years to one year. Still later, toward the end of the second century B. C. apparently, foreigners began to be admitted to the college, and from that time on they appear in great numbers on the college rolls. Not only this, but intellectual studies became a part of the curriculum of the college. We learn from the inscriptions — for it is from inscriptions that we gain the most of our information with regard to the ephebi — that the members attended the lectures of philosophers, rhetoricians, and 'grammarians,' in the gymnasia of the city, in a body and under the leadership of their Director. The Director was, in these later times, known as the κοσμητής, and his duties were to oversee the health of the students, to maintain discipline among them, to conduct them to their lectures in the gymnasia, to attend to their assignment to the various military posts, etc. Every year the outgoing ephebi presented to the gymnasium known as the *Ptolemaion*, which was probably founded through the liberality of Ptolemy Philadelphus not long after 300 B. C., a hundred books, as a contribution to the college library. At the end of the term of their apprenticeship, the ephebi appeared before the Council — the βουλή — and gave an exhibition of their proficiency in the use of arms. There seems also to have been some arrangement whereby examinations or exhibitions, either regular or occasional, were held in certain intellectual studies as well — grammar, geometry, rhetoric, and music are those mentioned. It seems possible that, in this later period, provision was also made for the preparation of students for the ephebic college. If so, the gymnasium called the *Diogeneion*, founded probably in the third century B. C., was the place where this preparation was provided, and the studies mentioned above may have been those, or a part of those, in which the candidate was required to pass a successful examination before he was admitted to the college.[1]

---

[1] For the ephebic college, see Girard, *L'Éd. athén.*, pp. 271–327, 339–342; the article *ephebi* in Daremberg and Saglio's Dictionary; Dumont, *Essai sur l'éphébie attique;* W. Dittenberger, *De ephebis atticis*. The time of the organization of the ephebic system into a military academy is uncertain and matter of controversy. The general belief has been that it dated from the early part of the fifth century B. C., but Wilamowitz-Möllendorff has called this date in question and has argued, with much plausibility, that the organization dated from about the time of Aristotle (*Arist. u. Athen*, i. pp. 191–194; followed by A. A. Bryant in *Harv. Stud. in Class. Phil.*, xviii. pp. 76–88). Two inscriptions found at Eretria and discussed by Richardson and Heermance in *Amer. Jour. of Arch.*, 11, 1896, pp. 173 ff., 188 ff.,

We see, then, how this ephebic college gradually, in the later centuries of its existence — it continued till at least the third century A. D.— became dovetailed into the higher education of the day. The military and gymnastic training of the college was originally the main feature, and the instruction in this line was provided by the state. When, in the course of time, the educational field of the Greeks became greatly enlarged, the ephebi began to attend the lectures of the philosophers, the rhetoricians, and others, but purely in a voluntary way; instruction in the intellectual branches was not provided by the state, nor was it imposed, though it seems to have been sanctioned and even favored. About the same time other changes took place which affected the character of the college. The term of service was reduced to one year, the service, apparently, ceased to be obligatory, and foreigners were admitted. The restriction on the age of entrance was also removed or allowed to fall into abeyance. The college became more and more an aristocratic body, in which the intellectual studies tended to take precedence of the military training. Many young men, after they had completed their year of ephebic service, continued

are of special interest in connection with the ephebic system. In the first (later than 146 B. C.) it is mentioned that the annual gymnasiarch furnished at his own expense a ῥήτωρ. In the second, mention is made of an ὁμηρικὸs φιλόλογοs. It is further worthy of note that the lectures were open to all who took an interest therein (1st inscr.: οἴτινες ἐσχόλαζον ἐν τῶι γυμνασίωι τοῖs τε παισίν καὶ ἐφήβοις καὶ τοῖs ἄλλοις τοῖs βουλομένοις τὴν ἀπὸ τῶν τοιούτων ὠφελίαν ἐπιδέχεσθαι. 2nd inscr.: [ὅστις ἐ] σχόλαζεν ἐν τῶ[ι] γυμνασίωι τοῖs τε ἐφήβοις καὶ [παισὶν καὶ τοῖs] ἄλλοις πᾶσι τοῖs ο]ἰκείως διακειμένοις πρὸς παιδ[είαν]).

to study with the philosophers and rhetoricians, while comparatively few of those who came to Athens to study entered the body at all. In the later centuries, the college may, for our purposes, be left out of consideration.

We have seen how, in the course of time, there was developed from the simple fifth-century education of the Greeks a system of graded education, and how, in the highest of the three grades that were evolved, there was again a threefold division. In tracing this process of development, however, we have gone far beyond the fifth and fourth centuries B. C. The process in question was gradual and occupied many centuries; it has seemed best, however, to speak of the new forms here, because the beginnings of them belonged to the fifth and fourth centuries. The ephebic system dated certainly from the fourth century, and possibly even from the fifth, while the philosophical and rhetorical schools were institutions which, in their inception, were of the fifth century.

## CHAPTER III

### THE MACEDONIAN PERIOD

In the year 334 B. C., Alexander, the son of Philip of Macedon, crossed at the head of his army into Asia and started on his march against the Great King of Persia, and in the early summer of 323 he died at Babylon. The eleven years that elapsed between these two events were most momentous in the history of Greece. They mark the opening of a new era. The political independence of Greece had been lost at the battle of Chæroneia in 338, but the conquests of Alexander opened the way to the establishment of her language and civilization throughout the East.

Although the political history of the time immediately following the death of Alexander is, at first sight, bewildering, the period, if we can disregard some of the side issues and lesser complications and keep our attention fixed on the main trend of events, is one of supreme interest. Every period is, in a way, a period of change, but at this time events were moving rapidly and the future was big with undefined possibilities. New forms, and new ideas of government, were coming to the fore, and the political map of the eastern world was undergoing transformation.

The first professed motive of action on the part of the generals of Alexander, after the death of their leader, was the desire to preserve the Empire intact for his heirs. The legitimate heirs were an imbecile youth, Philip Arrhidæus by name, half-brother of Alexander; a posthumous son; and the queen, Roxana. A regent, or protector, was immediately appointed to manage the affairs of the Empire till such time as the son should come of age. But, though the unity of the Empire was thus preserved in name, evidence was not long wanting that each of the generals was working for himself alone, and that the Empire was destined in the end either to fall apart into separate kingdoms or to become the prey of that one of the generals who should show himself the craftiest in diplomacy and the strongest in arms. It is not necessary to repeat here the story of the battles and intrigues that marked the settlement of this question, but the matter was at length decided in favor of the division of power. In Egypt was established the dynasty of the Lagidæ, or the Ptolemies, in Syria and the far-eastern lands that of the Seleucids, and in Macedonia that of the Antigonids. Many native tribes in the interior of Asia acknowledged no foreign sovereign, and most of the Greek cities in Asia Minor and on the islands enjoyed perhaps something more than a nominal independence. Greece was claimed, as an appanage, by the Macedonian kings, but they were never very successful in asserting their authority in that land. Early in the period Philetærus established the Attalid dynasty at Pergamum in Asia Minor.

This was the world in which the new Greek, or so-called Hellenistic, civilization spread, with such wonderful results in the way of literature, art, and learning, in the centuries that immediately followed the death of Alexander. Many new cities were founded by Alexander and his successors, both in the far-distant parts of the Empire, or what had once constituted the Empire, and also in the midst of the older civilization, and these cities all became centres of Hellenism.

In what, we may ask, did this Hellenism, this new-old civilization, consist? It is impossible to believe that the new cities founded by Alexander and his successors were in every case populated, even in small part, by Greeks. Some of the new cities that were planted near others that were already Greek doubtless received large contributions of population from these, and, again, many so-called new cities were nothing more than reorganizations of already-existing communities, with perhaps a change of name. In some cases, there may have been a nucleus, or a sprinkling, of Greek-Macedonian soldiery from the army of the founder, but often the main part of the population was of native origin. In what, then, if not always in population, did the Hellenism of these cities consist? Probably, first, in the architecture of many of the buildings. The new cities were, in many cases at least, built on a generous scale, with broad, straight streets crossing each other at right angles and (in the case of the main thoroughfares) flanked by colonnades and public buildings.[1] Greek architects were employed to build these and other structures, and Greek artists to embellish them. Secondly, we may

[1] The colonnades were, in some cases, of imperial date (see Förster in *Jahrbuch d. kaiserl. deutsch. arch. Inst.*, xii. [1897], pp. 121 *ff.*, and H. C. Butler in *Publ. of the Amer. Arch. Ex. to Syria in* 1899-1900, ii. pp. 50, 51).

conceive the Hellenism of these cities to have been evident in the spirit and policy of the administration. There was in most places a tendency to imitate, in governmental, educational, and other matters, the institutions and methods of procedure of Greece, or, specifically, of Athens, and the Macedonian rulers followed, so far as was compatible with monarchy, Greek precedents. Again, the language and intellectual atmosphere of the Court in the various seats of government were undoubtedly Greek.

We often wonder, in the case of some great change that has occurred in the life of a nation — such as that from republicanism to imperialism at Rome, or this in Greece that was brought about by the conquests of Alexander — what must have been the feelings and the thoughts of the people who lived at the time such change took place, and to what extent they realized it. It is not easy to escape from our own environment and to look at the events of to-day as past history, and so, unless the change in question was violent and quickly accomplished, we must guard against assuming too great consciousness on the part of the people concerned. One result of the conquests of Alexander was to raise Greece, and especially Athens, to a place apart in the imaginations of men. Her active history, so men felt, had in a way ceased; she was now to be venerated and valued for what she had done. This feeling and this spirit of reverence were particularly noticeable in the attitude of the Macedonian conquerors and of many foreign peoples toward Greece, but the Greeks themselves seem, with the loss of their political independence, to have gained, if possible, something more of veneration for their past. The Greeks, indeed, were always, even down to the days of Hadrian and far beyond, proud of their ancient glory and tenacious of old forms.

In many ways was the feeling of the Macedonian conquerors manifested. We remember how, in his far-eastern campaign, Alexander, after having, with great difficulty, crossed the Hydaspes River, exclaimed, "O ye Athenians, will ye believe what dangers I undergo to merit your praise?"[1] And this was the attitude of the Successors also. The name of Greek culture and Greek learning had been familiar to the Macedonians from their boyhood, and all their examples of human greatness were drawn from the literature and history of Greece. It is not strange, therefore, that they should wish to receive the praise of the Greeks and try to imitate by their deeds the heroes of Grecian song. Nearly all the Successors posed at one time or another as phil-Hellenes, "friends of the Greeks," and in their campaigns against one another they sought to gain prestige by proclaiming themselves "liberators of Greece." This was the battle-cry of Polysperchon when opposing Cassander in 319, of Demetrius Poliorcetes when expelling from Athens his namesake of Phalerum in 307, of Antiochus the Great when advancing on the West in 192, and of many others of these rulers again and again. This was also the cry of the Romans when they first entered the country, and we know how Flamininus, at the Isthmian games of 196, proclaimed the inde-

[1] Plut., *Alex.*, 60.

pendence of all Greece. Such proceedings were a tribute to the civilization and glory of this country and a recognition of her singular position among the peoples of the earth. Greek men of letters were honored at the courts of nearly all the Successors, and Greek philosophers were deputed by individuals and communities to serve on important missions — for the attitude of the world toward philosophers had changed since the fifth century, and they were now held in high esteem. The Macedonians, further, vied with one another in doing honor to Greek cities, and especially to Athens. Alexander, after his first victory in Asia, sent to Athens three hundred shields, and he later restored to the Athenians the statues of Harmodius and Aristogeiton, which had been carried away by Xerxes and deposited at Susa. On one occasion, after the recovery of Alexander from sickness, his mother made an offering on the acropolis at Athens. Demetrius Poliorcetes, following the example of Alexander, sent suits of armor to Athens, and Strabo says of Cassander,[1] that, while in general he showed a most tyrannical spirit, he was toward Athens, when he made that city subject to himself, considerate and indulgent. Antiochus IV — and he was only one of many — bestowed valuable gifts on the Greek cities of Asia Minor, the islands, and the European mainland — gifts such as temples, altars, colonnades, etc. Athens received from him special attention. Here he continued, on a grander scale, the construction of the great temple of Zeus, which had been begun by Peisistratus some three

[1] ix. p. 398.

hundred and fifty years before and was destined to be finished only in the time of Hadrian, three hundred years later; and he affixed to the southern wall of the acropolis, above the theatre, a gilt Gorgon's head on a gilded ægis. This same Antiochus, when he was allowed to depart from Rome, where he had been detained as a hostage, repaired to Athens, and was there made an Athenian citizen and elected to the highest Athenian magistracy, and, though a prince, he felt himself honored by the recognition. Many of the Macedonian princes in those days went to Athens to receive their education or to live for a while in the light of Greek civilization and culture. This was the case with Demetrius, younger brother of Antigonus Gonatas, and it was the case with Antiochus Grypos (Antiochus "the Hooked-nosed"). Foreign princes also, in many cases, considered it a privilege to be admitted within the pale of Hellenism, and styled themselves on their coins or otherwise *phil-Hellenes*. This was true of kings of the Jews, of kings of the Arabs, and of kings of the Parthians. The Bactrian Empire also assimilated much of the Greek culture, and the kings of Bactria boasted of being descended from Alexander. To come down to a later time: we remember how, in 53 B. C., when the news of the defeat of Crassus arrived in the Parthian capital, the Court, it is said, was witnessing a performance of the *Bacchæ* of Euripides; and how, when the frenzied Agave appeared on the stage with the head of Crassus instead of that of her murdered son, Pentheus, the audience burst into wild applause. Tigranes, King of Armenia, encouraged Greek culture at his Court, and Greek dramas were performed at Tigranocerta.[1]

We have dwelt thus long on the attitude of the Macedonian and foreign princes toward Greece, and especially toward Athens, in the centuries before Christ, in order to make intelligible the peculiar position which Athens occupied in the intellectual life of the centuries after Christ. From the time of Alexander, as has been said, Athens held a place apart in the imaginations of men. Her brilliant political history, her achievements in literature and art, the culture and learning with which her name was associated, made of this city a hallowed spot, and few were found to deny her their homage. The charm which she thus, in the time of Alexander, began to exercise over men's minds, was not broken for over eight hundred years.

But what, in the meantime, was the intellectual life of this period? It is significant of the new position which Greece occupied in the minds of men after the conquests of Alexander, that at this time the literature of the earlier days became a special object of study with men of learning. The earlier literature, like the earlier history, of Greece seemed, by these conquests, to have gained something of objectivity and perspective. But not alone in literature was the scientific spirit evident: the age was an age of learning and investigation in all departments.

The first and greatest of the new centres of learning that sprang up in Macedonian times was Alexandria, founded by Alexander in 332 B. C. Hither, early in the

[1] For the Hellenism of the East, see E. R. Bevan, *The House of Seleucus*, especially chs. xi, xii, xiii, xxxii.

third century, Ptolemy Soter, the first of the Ptolemaic kings, summoned from Greece the Peripatetic philosopher and statesman, Demetrius of Phalerum, and the two laid the foundations of the celebrated Alexandrian Library and Museum. The work was continued by Ptolemy Philadelphus, Ptolemy Soter's son. The Museum was an institution for the advancement of scientific learning; it was a sort of Round Table of erudite men. Its buildings were situated in the royal quarter of the city, adjoining the palace, and included cloisters, gardens, and a common hall for meals. Eminent literary and scientific men were invited to become members of the society, and annual stipends were allowed them by the king. Here they were to spend their lives in devotion to the Muses, and, at first at least, there was probably no provision made for teaching. The Museum resembled the philosophical schools at Athens in some respects, noticeably in being a "Temple of the Muses," a $Μουσεῖον$, headed by a president, or "priest of the Museum," who, at Alexandria, was appointed by the government. In close conjunction with the Museum was the Great Library, which in the middle of the first century B. C. is said to have contained 700,000 volumes. The librarians of this library — Zenodotus, Eratosthenes, Aristophanes of Byzantium, Aristarchus, and probably Callimachus, and Apollonius of Rhodes — are famous in the annals of classical scholarship. There was also a smaller library, which contained 42,800 volumes. In the course of time other foundations were established at Alexandria — as a Jewish college, a Christian college, and so on.

Alexandria was in Macedonian times the great centre — or, we might rather say, the one of two great centres — of scientific research. Classical learning, mathematics, astronomy, mechanics, medicine, anatomy, natural history, and whatever else of science there was — to say nothing of scholarly literature — all found a home in this city. The great rival of Alexandria was Pergamum, which, under the liberal policy of the Attalid dynasty, rose to eminence in literature, art, and science toward the close of the third century B. C. Here also was a library which, in the first century B. C., numbered 200,000 volumes, and here many distinguished literary and scientific men made their home. Another city which received a library and museum after the pattern of those at Alexandria was Antioch, founded by Seleucus shortly after 300 B. C., and enlarged and adorned by Antiochus the Great, whose reign was from 224 to 181. There was a library at Antioch as early as the end of the third century B. C., of which Euphorion of Chalcis was librarian, and much later — in the middle of the first century — a museum and library were established there by Antiochus XIII, the last of the line of Seleucid kings. Other centres of literary, philosophical, or scientific activity were: Pella, the seat of the Macedonian Court; Cos; Rhodes, where were schools of rhetoric and philosophy; Tarsus and Soli in Cilicia; and, at a later time, though founded in this period, Nicæa and Nicomedia in Bithynia.[1]

[1] In general, see Sandys, *Hist. Clas. Schol.*, i. pp. 105 *ff.*, 146 *ff.*, and the literature there cited.

And the intellectual centre of this Hellenistic world —
Athens! During the third century the material interests
of Greece suffered severely, first in consequence of the
wars of the Successors and then owing to her internal
politics in conjunction with the continued attempts of
Macedonia to gain control of the land. In 279 the
Celtic hordes from the north overran and devastated
the northern part of the country. In 221 took place the
battle of Sellasia, which closed the Cleomenic War, and
from 219 to 217 was the Social War, waged between
Philip V of Macedon and his Grecian allies on the one
hand, and the Ætolian League on the other. The condition of affairs at the close of that war is well described
by Polybius [1]: "Directly the Achæans had put an end to
the war, they . . . departed to take up once more their
regular ways and habits. Along with the Achæans the
other Peloponnesian communities also set to work to
repair the losses they had sustained; recommenced the
cultivation of the land; and re-established their national
sacrifices, games, and other religious observances peculiar to their several states. For these things had all
but sunk into oblivion in most of the states through the
persistent continuance of the late wars. . . . The Athenians, on the contrary, had by this time freed themselves from fear of Macedonia, and considered that they
had now permanently secured their independence.
They accordingly . . . took no part whatever in the
politics of the rest of Greece." This policy of abstention
from Grecian politics afforded Athens the opportunity to
devote herself more sedulously to her intellectual inter-

[1] v. 106 (trans. by Shuckburgh).

ests, and throughout this period she displayed a growing solicitude for education. The four schools of philosophy were her greatest educational asset, but rhetoric, it would seem, was also taught. The heads of the philosophical schools were in few cases Athenians; they came from all parts of the Hellenistic world. Athens was in those days gradually becoming more and more a university town, such as we see her in the centuries after Christ. Foreign potentates, as we have already seen, vied with one another in endowing her with beautiful buildings, while students of all ages and all nationalities thronged her streets and drew inspiration from her associations.

Toward the end of the third century the Romans for the first time entered into diplomatic relations with Greece and appeared with an armed force east of the Adriatic. In the year 229 the consuls Gnæus Fulvius Centumalus and Lucius Postumius Albinus crossed from Brundisium with an army and fleet, took Corcyra under their protection, and crushed the power of the Illyrian pirates. In the following year the Romans were permitted by the Corinthians to take part in the Isthmian games. In 197 the Romans defeated Philip V of Macedon at Cynocephalæ, and at the ensuing Isthmian games Flamininus proclaimed the independence of all Greece. In 168 Lucius Æmilius Paulus defeated Perseus, the son of Philip, at Pydna, and, after his victory, went on a tour through Greece, reforming the governments of the cities, bestowing gifts upon the people, and admiring the artistic treasures of the land.

We have, here recorded, three noteworthy occurrences — not the military achievements, but the events that followed these. The Romans, coming into contact with Greece, acknowledged the same charm that the Macedonians and the other nations of the East had acknowledged before them. The privilege of taking part in the Greek games was prized, for it seemed to confer on those to whom it was granted a certain standing in the civilized world; to proclaim the independence of Greece was to do homage to the Greek name; while the tour of Æmilius points to the awakening of an historical and antiquarian interest in the country.

During the second century the material condition of Greece grew constantly worse. In the year 200, Athens was obliged to witness the destruction of her gymnasia and monuments outside the walls, and the devastation of her suburbs, by the army of Philip; and the many wars which followed these events were a severe strain on the material and physical resources of all Greece. The sufferings and losses of the country culminated in this century in the siege and destruction of Corinth in 146.

Early in the first century B. C. Athens became involved in the First Mithridatic War, taking in that contest the side of Mithridates. Sulla besieged the city, and, being without sufficient material for his machines of war, he cut down the beautiful trees of the Academy and the Lyceum; and, to obtain funds wherewith to continue the contest, he broke into the sanctuaries of Greece and carried off their treasures. On the 1st of March, 86, having made a breach in the city walls, he entered the town and massacred many of its defenders. "When they had thrown down the wall," says Plutarch,[1] "and made all level betwixt the Piraic and Sacred Gate, about midnight Sulla entered the breach, with all the terrors of trumpets and cornets sounding, with the triumphant shout and cry of an army let loose to spoil and slaughter, and scouring through the streets with swords drawn. There was no numbering the slain; the amount is to this day conjectured only from the space of ground overflowed with blood. For without mentioning the execution done in other quarters of the city, the blood that was shed about the market-place spread over the whole Ceramicus within the Double-Gate, and, according to most writers, passed through the gate and overflowed the suburb. Nor did the multitudes which fell thus exceed the number of those who, out of pity and love for their country, which they believed was now finally to perish, slew themselves." Through the intercession of some Roman senators who were in the camp, and the prayer of two Grecian exiles, Sulla was at length induced to stay his hand and spare the majority of the citizens. The Peiræus was shortly after taken and almost totally destroyed by fire.

Athens seems to have recovered from this blow, and in the next years her schools of philosophy were, apparently, in as flourishing a condition as ever. More and more now did the Romans resort to Grecian lands — travellers, who were interested to see the works of art and the places associated with the famous names of history and song; students and men of culture and

[1] *Sulla*, 14 (trans. by Dryden *et al.*).

learning, who wished to live for a time in the intellectual atmosphere of the country and to converse with philosophers and orators; invalids and quasi-invalids, who, in the interests of health or of fashion, visited the cure-places of Greece. The sentiment with which men regarded Greece in those days is well brought out at the beginning of the Fifth Book of Cicero's *De Finibus* [1]: "We arranged," says Cicero, "to take our afternoon walk in the Academy, chiefly because the spot was at that time of day entirely free from the crowd. So we met in Piso's house at the appointed hour. At first — for the six stades that lie outside the Double-Gate — we whiled away the time with general conversation; but when we came to the walks of the Academy, so justly famed, we found the quiet which we had desired. Then said Piso: 'Is it due to a natural instinct or to some delusion, that when we look upon the places where, as we have been told, men worthy to be recorded in history have passed much of their time, we are more moved than when we happen to hear of the achievements or to read some writing of the men themselves? I am so moved now. For I call to mind Plato, who, tradition says, was the first to use this place habitually for debate; and his little garden, yonder, not only brings him back to my memory, but seems to place the very man before my eyes. Here stood Speusippus, here Xenocrates, here Polemo, his pupil, whose very seat we see there before us'"; and much more to the same purpose.

The two Grecian cities which most attracted the Romans were Athens and Rhodes. The list of distinguished

[1] v. 1, 1.

Romans who sojourned or studied at one or both of these places is a long one — at Athens, Quintus Metellus Numidicus, Antonius, Cicero and his brother Quintus, Brutus, Horace, and many others; at Rhodes, such men as Marcus Antonius, Julius Cæsar, Cicero, Brutus, and Cassius. The head of the Roman colony at Athens was Cicero's friend, Titus Pomponius Atticus. Athenian citizenship was eagerly sought, even in the time when it could be obtained for money,[1] and burial at Athens was considered an honor. When Servius Sulpicius begged for permission to bury his friend Marcellus within the city walls, the Areopagus refused to give its consent, and the most that could be obtained was permission to bury Marcellus in the grounds of the Academy.

> My bones and flesh the earth enfolds, a lovely child,
> My soul has upward flown into the sky;
> My name thou askest? Theogeiton, Thymuch's son,
> Of Thebes; in famous Athens do I lie,

runs an Athenian epitaph of a somewhat earlier date.[2]

We can well understand how this city, with its traditions and associations, its art treasures, its wealth of learned and cultured men, the free and democratic spirit of its people, its quiet, academic life, was destined to be, in the years to come, *the* university seat of the ancient world.

But dark days were to intervene before that time and were even now closing in. The Civil Wars began in

---

[1] Even as late as the third century A. D., Himerius sought Athenian citizenship for his son (Himer., *ec.*, vii).

[2] Kaibel, *Ep. Gr.*, 90.

49 B. C., and they lasted till 31. Many of the battles of these wars were fought out on Grecian soil, and, during the course of the wars, constant requisitions were made on the Greeks for money, troops, and supplies. At the end of the period Athens was in an exhausted condition, and her fortunes were at their lowest ebb.

We are now ready, after remarking briefly in the following chapter on the connection of the state and education in the early history of Greece, to trace, in the succeeding chapters, the regeneration of Greece, which took place in the first two or three centuries after Christ.

## CHAPTER IV

### EDUCATION AND THE STATE

WE have, in the chapters immediately before us, to trace the steps by which university education became established officially in the Greek world, and to follow its vicissitudes to the time when all pagan teaching in the world at large was brought to an end by the rescript issued by the Emperor Justinian, closing the Neo-Platonic school of philosophy at Athens, in 529 A. D. In the succeeding chapters we shall endeavor to gain a closer acquaintance with the inner life of the universities, with the teachers and students, their methods, their manners, and their work. But before we enter upon the task of tracing the outer history of the universities and observing its connection with the political and religious history of the times, it will be well to consider briefly the relation of the state to education among the Greeks in the preceding centuries.

The attitude of the state toward education at Athens in the fifth and fourth centuries B. C. was one of non-interference. Schools were private institutions, and instruction was paid for by the individual. Theorists and reasoners, like Plato and Aristotle, held that the prosperity of the state was the chief end of education, and something of the feeling which led to this attitude seems to have been an inborn characteristic of the Greek mind in general, Ionic as well as Doric, though expressing itself in the one case in less rigid form than in the other. "The legislator," says Æschines, in speaking of the legislation which went under the name of the Solonian and Draconian,¹ "thought that the child who was well brought up would, when he had become a man, make a useful citizen"; where, however, the word *well* ($καλῶς$) has a moral rather than an intellectual signification. We should have, then, the apparently anomalous condition of affairs, wherein the object of education is considered to be the perfect development of the individual, mentally, morally, and physically, for the service of the state, but yet the state fails to take cognizance of the methods by which such development is attained.

There is, however, evidence that this neglect of education by the state was not absolute at Athens. "Now," thus Plato represents the laws as saying to Socrates in the *Crito*,² "the laws which apply to the rearing and education of children — the laws under which you received your own education — do you find fault with them? Did not those of us who were set in charge of these matters order well when we enjoined it upon your father that he should educate you in music and gymnastic?" Just how much we are to understand by these words, it is difficult to say. It is possible that the "laws" in question were those simply of custom. Plato's words are supplemented by the statement of Vitruvius and others³ that at Athens the boy who had

---

¹ *Contra Timarch.*, 11.  ² 50 D.
³ Vitruv., vi. 3, translating from Alexis (*nisi eos qui liberos artibus erudissent*); Plut., *Solon*, 22 ($μὴ\ διδαξάμενον\ τέχνην$); and Galen (*Protrep.*, 8, vol. i. p. 15); *cf.* Lib., *ep.*, 137. $τέχναι$ included the liberal arts as well as trades.

not been provided with a trade or a profession by his father was relieved by law from the obligation of supporting his father when the latter grew old. These various statements possibly all refer to the same thing. The fact, however, that it is stated that, *if* the father did not provide his son with a training he could not later demand support from the latter, seems to show that there was no further penalty attached for non-compliance with the "law." However this may be, some sort of education the father was apparently required to give his son. Corroboration of the sense of Plato's words has been found [1] in the probable fact that guardians were obliged to defray the cost of their wards' education, and is also contained in the chance statement of Æschines that Athenians were under compulsion in the matter of sending their children to school.[2]

Æschines further furnishes us [3] with certain school regulations affecting the morals of pupils, which purport to go back to Solon or even to an earlier time. Thus, teachers and athletic instructors were forbidden to open their schools and palæstræ before sunrise or to keep them open after sunset; no adult person other than the teacher's son, brother, or son-in-law, was allowed, on pain of death, to enter the school-room while the pupils were within. Specific directions are also given

---

[1] Girard, *L'Éd. athén.*, p. 33.
[2] *Contra Timarch.*, 9: ἐξ ἀνάγκης. *Cf.* Isoc., *Areop.*, 37, 45.
[3] *Contra Timarch.*, 7–12. We must here distinguish between what Æschines says was the law and that which purports to be the law itself, given in the text. The former is probably true, but the latter can hardly be genuine.

as to the age at which free-born youths were to attend school, the size of the classes, etc. Furthermore, whoever undertook to defray the cost of a boy's chorus must be over forty years of age. This last provision is interesting, inasmuch as we find similar provisions as to the age of certain officers of instruction in operation in the city of Teos in Asia Minor,[1] and also recommended by Plato in the *Laws*.[2] We see, however, that the public establishment and support of schools were not involved in these regulations, and that nothing is said about courses of study, payment of teachers, and the like; it is simply a question of the right management of private institutions, and the moral education and protection of the child is the acknowledged cause of the legislation (περὶ τῆς σωφροσύνης, 7; περὶ τῆς εὐκοσμίας, 8). Some, if not all, of these laws later fell into disuse, for we find Socrates mingling freely with the young men in the palæstræ, and Theophrastus represents it as a characteristic of the Bore[3] that he drops into the athletic grounds and the schools, and, by talking with the wrestling-masters and the teachers, interrupts the progress of the lessons.

If we omit to dwell on the ephebic institution, which, as has been seen in a previous chapter, was, in the fourth century B. C., wholly military in character, but possibly later, when intellectual studies became a part of its course of training, was the cause of some official

---

[1] Dittenberger, *Syl. Inscr. Græc.*, ii. 523 a.
[2] 764 E.
[3] The character of the λάλος (*Charac.*, 7). For a later time, compare the action of Hippodromus, dropping into Megistias's school (Philos., 618); *cf.* also Lib., ii. 233, 2.

recognition being given to the philosophers and rhetoricians, we have still, in speaking of Athens, to mention a few attempts at forcible interference on the part of the government in the freedom of instruction. One of these was when, at the time of the Thirty Tyrants, a decree was passed forbidding rhetoric and philosophy to be taught at Athens.[1] Another was when, shortly after the advent of Demetrius Poliorcetes at Athens and the withdrawal of Demetrius the Phalerean, about 307 B. C., a certain Sophocles, son of Amphicleides of Sunium, secured the passage of a law to the effect that no one should open or conduct a school of philosophy in the city without the consent of the Senate and people.[2] In the first case the action was taken at the instigation of Critias, and was directed against Socrates, with whom Critias was on terms of enmity. In the second case the monarchically disposed school of the Peripatetics, which had been supported by, and had supported, the outgoing government, was the object of attack. There followed, on the second occasion, a general exodus of philosophers and students, but these all returned the next year, when Sophocles was convicted under the law against illegal procedure and his measure repealed. These proceedings, however, being due to political or private animosity, cannot in any way be said to have represented a policy, and they had not so much significance even as had the banishment of Damon, Anaxagoras, and Protagoras, the execution of Socrates, or the

[1] Xen., *Mem.*, i. 2, 31.
[2] Diog. Laert., v. 38: σχολῆς ἀφηγεῖσθαι· Poll., *Onom.*, ix. 42: διατριβὴν κατασκευάσασθαι. See also Alexis in Athen., xiii. 92, p. 610.

cumulation of honors and rewards on special philosophers and sophists by individual princes.

Of more importance, and of significance as pointing to the renewed pre-eminence of the Court of the Areopagus in local affairs relating to the habits and education of the people in the Macedonian, and especially in the Roman, period, are two occurrences, of which we have information, in the one case from Diogenes Laertius, and in the other from Plutarch. Cleanthes,[1] a poor student from Assos, who was studying at Athens under Zeno, having, in order to be able to study by day, to work all night at drawing water in gardens, was voted by the Areopagus the sum of ten minæ (about $180) for his support; "but," says Diogenes, "Zeno forbade him to accept them." Cicero (this is the other occurrence [2]) induced, on a certain occasion, the Areopagus, to request, by public decree, the Peripatetic philosopher Cratippus to stay at Athens, for the instruction of their youth and the honor of their city.

So much for Athens; of the attitude of the government toward education outside Athens, we are able to glean some information in connection with a few places. Not to dwell on the constitutions of Sparta and Crete, which were almost wholly military in character, Charondas, the legislator of Catana in Sicily, introduced, we are told, into his constitution, a piece of legislation which had been neglected by all previous legislators: he required that the sons of all citizens should be taught

[1] Diog. Laert., vii. 168, 169. Cleanthes seems also to have tended the ovens in a bakery.
[2] Plut., *Cic.*, 24.

to read and write at the public expense. The truth of this statement, which is found (with the substitution of Thurii for Catana) in Diodorus Siculus,[1] has been doubted, but, it would seem, without sufficient reason.[2]

An interesting inscription from Teos in Asia Minor, dating probably from the third century B. C., gives a curious bit of information with regard to educational affairs in that city.[3] A certain Teian, named Polythrous, son of Onesimus, had presented to his fellow-citizens the sum of 34,000 drachmæ (about $6,120) to defray the cost of instructing, in letters, all the free-born children of both sexes, and, in music and certain military exercises, all the free-born male youth. We are interested to learn from this inscription, in view of what has been said in a previous chapter with regard to graded instruction, that the instruction at Teos was divided into three apparently clearly distinguished grades.[4] But what we are specially concerned to notice here is that the instruction there provided was official in character. The teachers were to be appointed by the state, and they were to receive their pay from the state, and this system applied to all three grades. Other in-

---

[1] xii. 12

[2] *E. g.*, by Gräfenhan, *Gesch. d. klass. Phil.*, i. p. 67. See Girard, *L'Éd. athén.*, p. 20. The date of Charondas was probably the sixth century B. C. The confusion of Thurii and Catana in the account of Diodorus may be due to the fact that Thurii took much of its legislation from the Chalcidian colonies in Sicily and Italy. See, on Charondas, Niese in Pauly's *Real-Encyc.*

[3] Dittenberger, *Syl. Inscr. Græc.*, ii. 523 a.

[4] The grades in the musical and military instruction, however, seem to have been only a year apart, and it is not clear whether the grades in the literary instruction coincided with these.

scriptions from Teos tend to confirm the fact that education there was regularly public.[1]

A certain Delphian inscription, belonging apparently to the second century B. C.,[2] informs us that the people of Delphi had sent an embassy to Attalus II, King of Pergamum, "on the subject of the education of their children." Attalus had replied to the embassy by sending to the Delphians 18,000 Alexandrian drachmæ, the interest of which sum it was now determined should be used to pay the salaries of teachers.

A similar case to that last cited, showing us that there was a system of public education in Rhodes in the middle of the second century B. C., is mentioned by Polybius.[3] "They [the Rhodians]," says Polybius, "had received 280,000 medimni of corn from Eumenes [the King of Pergamum], that its value might be invested, and the interest devoted to pay the fees of the tutors and school-masters of their sons." Polybius blames the Rhodians for accepting the gift, saying that they should have guarded their dignity more jealously.

This, then, is about the extent of our information with regard to the connection of the state and education in pre-Christian times.[4] We gather therefrom that out-

---

[1] See Girard, *L'Éd. athén.*, pp. 21, 22.
[2] Haussoulier in *Bul. de correspond. hellén.*, v. pp. 157-178.
[3] xxxi. 25 (trans. by Shuckburgh).
[4] We are told by Plutarch (*Themis.*, 10) that when, at the time of the second Persian invasion, the Athenians, on the advice of Themistocles, sent their wives and children to Troezen, the people of that city passed a resolution to the effect that the fugitives should be supported by the state, and the Athenian children allowed to continue their studies in the schools of Troezen at the public expense. This statement hardly seems to point to state education at Troezen.

side Athens there was, in some places, a certain degree of state education, at least in the Macedonian period, and probably also much earlier. At Athens there existed at an early time certain laws or customs enjoining in a general way the training of the Athenian youth, and certain other laws, more definite, relative to the conditions under which instruction in the schools should be given. There does not seem, however, so far as we can make out from the evidence at hand, to have been at the same early time at Athens any state-regulated system of instruction, or any teachers appointed and salaried by the state. After the time of Alexander the tendency may have been, in many or most cities of the Greek world, for the government to interest itself more and more in the primary education of its citizens, and possibly this was the case also at Athens. In this connection, we may notice that the one point on which Polybius, doubtless comparing the Roman state of affairs with the Greek, found fault with Roman institutions on the ground of negligence, was the education of their youth; he charged the Romans with having no system of education, established by law and the same for all.[1] At Athens the Areopagus and the chief civil functionary, the στρατηγὸς ἐπὶ τὰ ὅπλα, as well as others of the στρατηγοί, apparently asserted, in the Macedonian and early Roman periods, a certain amount of authority even over the higher education by virtue of their connection with the state institution of the *ephebi*. The establishment, however, of the higher education of the day on an official basis,

---

[1] Cic., *De repub.*, iv. 3.

though, as we see, all things were tending toward it, was left to the personal initiative of the Roman emperors of the second century A. D.[1]

[1] For the connection of the state and education among the Greeks, see, in general, Girard, *L'Éd. athén.*, pp. 1-61, and Grasberger, *Erzieh. u. Unterr. im klass. Alterth.*, iii. pp. 554-594.

## CHAPTER V

### ESTABLISHMENT OF UNIVERSITY EDUCATION IN GRECIAN LANDS.

DURING the years that elapsed from the establishment of the Empire under Augustus to the last quarter of the first century of our era we have comparatively little direct information with regard to the intellectual condition of Greece.[1] The country was at that time but slowly recovering from the distress and exhaustion occasioned by the Civil Wars, and was likewise for part of the period suffering from the neglect of the reigning emperors. Diminution of population, impoverishment of the people and land, paralysis of trade and commerce were some of the misfortunes which the Civil Wars, often fought out on Grecian soil, brought in their immediate train. Already, as we have seen, at the time of the First Mithridatic War, when Sulla invested Athens and the Peiræus, and, for want of material for his machines of war, cut down the beautiful

[1] From the time of Tiberius to the time of Vespasian there was a singular dearth of Greek writers, and the literature of the preceding period was an expatriated literature. Diodorus Siculus, Dionysius of Halicarnassus, and Strabo all lived and wrote outside Greece. In the last quarter of the century we have, as important sources of information on Greece, Plutarch and Dio Chrysostom. See, in general, on the condition of the country in this century, Mommsen, *The Provinces of the Roman Empire* (trans.), i. ch. vii.; Hertzberg, *Gesch. Griech.*, i. ch. v.; ii. chs. i. and ii.; Mahaffy, *The Greek World under Roman Sway (The Silver Age of the Greek World)*, ch. xii.

trees of the Academy and the Lyceum, and then, entering the city, caused the streets of Athens to flow with blood, the people had suffered terribly, but from that blow they seem to have recovered quickly, and in the following years Athens was the seat of a large colony of Roman youths and men, eager to make acquaintance at first hand with the culture and education of Greece. The Civil Wars, however, once more laid waste the land and impoverished the people, and this time the recovery was less quick than before. "Empty Athens" (*vacuas . . . Athenas*), says Horace,[1] contrasting the rural quiet of the city by the Ilissus with the noise and bustle of Rome. The picture drawn by Strabo and Dio Chrysostom, of the devastated condition of Greece in the first century of our era; of once thriving cities lying in ruins or reduced to villages; of depopulated towns, where in the gymnasia the statues of the gods stand half hidden by the crops, and flocks of sheep graze in the market-places and about the council-halls; of large tracts of land lying untilled for want of hands, is indeed a mournful one. Asia Minor and the islands of the Ægean suffered less in these wars than the mainland of Greece, and in their descriptions of this part of the world Dio and Strabo painted in colors correspondingly brighter.

Still, we know that during these years the educational institutions of Greece were gradually crystallizing into the form which we find they have taken when the veil is at last lifted toward the end of the first century A. D. We know that, even in those days, intellectual

[1] *Ep.*, ii. 2, 81.

life did not stagnate. There were Greek philosophers and other men of letters in the cities of Europe and Asia, and they were important personages in the communities in which they moved. Greece was still to many Romans the land of pious pilgrimage, and Greek men of learning were welcomed in the capital of the West. Probably, however, Grecian lands were at this time no longer holding their own in the struggle for intellectual supremacy, and Athens perhaps was even falling behind other Grecian cities. Strabo could say in the reign of Tiberius that Marseilles, with her sophists and philosophers, was drawing the noblest Roman youths thither and away from Athens,[1] and that Tarsus even surpassed Athens as a university centre. "Such an enthusiasm," he says, speaking of Tarsus,[2] "for philosophy and all the other parts of a liberal education, has been developed in the people of this city, that they have surpassed Athens and Alexandria and all other places one might mention as seats of learning and philosophical study. . . . They have schools for all branches of literary culture." He notes, however, that at Tarsus, which differed in this respect from most other seats of learning, the students were nearly all natives, and that very few strangers came to reside there.

In the last half of the first century, however, we already meet premonitory symptoms that Greece is awakening from her long slumber. Oratory, which, after the fall of Greek liberty, retired into private life and became a thing of the schools, begins, under the changed

[1] iv. p. 181.
[2] xiv. p. 673 (trans. by E. R. Bevan).

conditions which now prevail, to come once more into closer relation to life, and the teachers of oratory, the sophists, gain a new distinction.

As this is the first time, in the course of our survey, that we have had occasion to speak of these later sophists, it will be well if we stop here for a moment to render some account of these men and to trace, as accurately as may be, their history and lineage. We are familiar with the so-called sophists of the fifth and fourth centuries B. C.— those men who travelled from place to place, instructing the Greek youth in the higher learning of the day and training them for active service in the state and for the duties and successes of private life. These men, though differing to some extent in what they taught and including in their range of studies a great variety of subjects, probably without exception laid special stress on rhetoric and the art of public speaking. The art of managing words skilfully and effectively was almost a necessity in the public and private life of the Athenians of that day, it appealed to the delicate artistic sense of the Greeks, and it was justified to those who were the teachers of wisdom by its importance in the transmission of knowledge itself. Isocrates, in the fourth century, was the first to give to the epideictic eloquence an artistic treatment, and in his hands this department of oratory gained a new meaning and a new force; he raised the study of rhetoric and oratory to an independent position in the educational curriculum of the Greek youth. With the loss of Greek independence, the field for an inspired national oratory — an cratory such as that of Demosthenes and Hypereides —

was cut off, and the art of public speaking retreated, as has been said, into the schools. Here it led a forced and artificial existence, and was dissected and worked over like a body from which the spirit has flown. It still appeared, on occasion, in public, in the presence of selected audiences, before the magistrates, in assemblies, in the courts, and on embassies, but the orators at such times were generally professional rhetoricians and teachers of eloquence, who were interested first of all in the display of their own art. When Alexander conquered the East and opened the way to the extension of the Greek civilization and language in that quarter of the world, an enlargement of the field for the practice of oratory no doubt gradually took place in the free communities of the East, and men there were who received their education, in whole or in part, at the rhetoricians' hands and employed it in the service of the commonwealths. Oratory had, however, at that time, to contend with the rival claims of philosophy, and it was never, in the last three centuries before Christ, received so enthusiastically and unreservedly by the majority of the population as was the case at a later time; it remained distinctively a school oratory, quite different from the inspired oratory of an earlier period, and the general tendency seems to have been for it to separate itself more and more from the life of the people,[1] although it never renounced the claim to be

[1] This is clear from many passages in the *De rhetorica* of the Epicurean philosopher Philodemus (who, however, we must bear in mind, wrote from a partisan point of view); *e. g.*, i. p. 41, 8 (ed. Sudh.): μεθοδικόν τε γὰρ οὐδὲν οἱ σοφισταὶ παραδιδόασιν ἐν ταῖς μελέταις πρὸς μάθησιν τῆς ἐν τοῖς ἀληθινοῖς ἀγῶσιν δυνάμεως. *Cf.*

the chief preparation for life. A certain popular oratory, it would seem, still lingered about the courts,[1] and it is a question to what extent the numerous *rhetors* referred to by Strabo in his *Geography*[2] as being active in the cities of Asia Minor, were educated in the schools of sophistry.[3] Although Asia Minor and some islands of the Ægean, such as Rhodes and Lesbos, seem

*Epicurea* (Usener), p. 113, 18. That the tendency in the schools at this time was to run to scholasticism, or at least to formalism, is clear from the text-books that were written on the various branches of rhetoric; e. g., Philod., ii. p. 110, 9: τεχνολογίαι σοφιστικαί· i. p. 195, 22: τέχναι (of gesticulation and the management of the voice); i. p. 138, 17: παραδόσεις (θεωρημάτων πολιτικῶν). A good picture of the sophist as he was in the first century B. C. is gained from the scattered notices in the pages of Philodemus. The sophist of this period dealt with the three kinds of speeches, the judicial, the deliberative, and the epideictic (i. p. 212, 21, 25), and claimed that his art was the mother of all other arts and sciences (i. p. 223, 13). Advocates and popular speakers sent their sons to him to be educated (i. p. 38, 5). He had set rules for the treatment of the parts of the speech, such as the introduction, the narrative, etc., which, however, not all men followed (i. p. 201, 12). He gave precepts for the cultivation of style and the improvement of the memory (i. p. 79, 23). He had rules for the management of the voice and the body (i. p. 193, 16). He treated of metaphors (i. p. 170, 24), of enthymemes (i. p. 78, 16), of allegories (i. p. 181, 25), and of hyperbata (i. p. 160, 15). He held 'displays' (ἐπιδείξεις), and gave examples of judicial, deliberative, and ambassadorial speeches (i. p. 134, 2); and he also dealt with themes called θετικά (i. p. 206, 22). The sophist of this period no longer, apparently, professed to instruct young men in all and every branch of practical learning; he was distinctively the teacher of (rhetorical) oratory. See Brandstätter, *Leipz. Stud.*, 15, p. 226.

[1] See p. 87, n. 3.
[2] *E. g.*, xiii. pp. 614, 617, 627.
[3] Dionysius of Halicarnassus (*De comp. verb.*, 25, p. 206; *cf. De or. ant.*, 1) says that some orators of his time (presumably the so-called Asiatic, or Asianic, orators) lacked a general education as well as systematic rhetorical training.

to have been the special fields in which these schools throve, there was a school at Athens in the first century B. C.,[1] and we are probably justified in believing that rhetoric was taught at Athens from the time of Isocrates down.

But although the general tendency of oratorical instruction in the centuries before Christ was such as we have described, another tendency there was of diametrically opposite character at work during the same period — a tendency which was destined to lead in later times to important results. We are told that toward the end of the fourth century or the beginning of the third century B. C. the study of oratory underwent a change. Before that time those who were known as sophists had been accustomed to deal with subjects that allowed of a more or less eulogistic treatment, or to discuss such half-philosophical questions as, What is the nature of virtue? What is the nature of the gods and the universe? but now supposititious cases drawn from the experience of life, especially cases resembling those which occurred in the law courts and the assemblies, began to be used.[2] The sophistical oratory was primarily epideictic, and the introduction into the schools

[1] See Blass, *Griech. Bered.*, p. 95.

[2] According to Quintilian, it was about the time of Demetrius of Phalerum that fictitious cases in imitation of pleadings in the forum and in public councils were introduced into the practice of the sophistical schools (*Inst. or.*, ii. 4, 41, 42; *cf.* ii. 10). Philostratus (481) and Photius (*Bibl.*, cod. 61) assign the new tendency to Æschines. Philodemus (i. 122, 25–136, 20) says that the imitation court and assembly speeches as practised in the schools formed no real and natural part of the sophist's profession. So, also, the rhetorician, Menander (Speng., *Rh. Gr.*, iii. p. 331; see p. 224, n. 4).

## UNIVERSITY EDUCATION ESTABLISHED 75

of a subject-matter that did not properly belong to them was a movement, apparently, in the way of popularizing such oratory — it was, we should say, a recognition of the claims of daily life. The epideictic, or display, oratory may thus be conceived to have gained a wider significance; the new matter was given an epideictic, or sophistical, treatment; 'displays' of judicial and deliberative themes, as of the properly epideictic speeches, were held. It was under such conditions as these that on the one hand the sophistical training could at that time claim to be a preparation for active life and that many could send their sons to the schools of sophistry in this belief, while on the other hand some could deny to this training all right to be considered preparatory to life.[1] For the time the sophistical tendency seems to have prevailed, but in later centuries — in the centuries after Christ — as we shall see, a saner taste came in, and then the judicial and deliberative oratory formed an essential part of the sophistical training.

The name *Sophist*, as applied to a professional teacher, either of learning in general or specifically of oratory, never went out of existence from the time it was so first used,[2] and the sophists of the second and follow-

---

[1] We must remember, however, that some part of this difference of opinion is to be accounted for by the rivalry that existed between philosophy and rhetoric, each claiming to furnish the only proper training for the future citizen.

[2] Brandstätter, *Leipz. Stud.*, 15, pp. 258, 259; Rohde, *Gr. Rom.*, p. 315, n. 2. The word *Sophist* was originally used of any man who had superior wisdom or ability in a single line, and it naturally came to be applied in the fifth century B. C. to those men who claimed to have a more or less general acquaintance with many subjects. This change of application was a step in the direction of making the term technical. The first man, so far as

ing centuries A. D., though in their profession and many of their characteristics different from the sophists of the fifth and fourth centuries B. C., were historically the direct lineal descendants of these men.[1] The later sophists, however, were not, like the earlier sophists, teachers of all learning with a leaning toward oratory, but they were teachers and expounders of the art of public speaking exclusively.

Toward the end of the first century of our era the school oratory of which we have spoken began once more to come into closer relation to life. One sign of this tendency was its leaning toward the judicial and deliberative oratory.[2] The oratory of the imperial age first pre-

can be determined, to use the word in its purely technical sense of an epideictic orator and teacher of (epideictic) oratory Brandstätter (pp. 228, 258) makes out to have been Epicurus.

[1] The exact historical connection of the imperial sophistry has been matter of controversy. The view of Rohde (*Gr. Rom.*, p. 312, n. 1, and in *Rhein. Mus.*, 41, pp. 170-190) is that it was a direct outgrowth of the so-called earlier *Asiatic* oratory. This view is supported by Brandstätter, *Leipz. Stud.*, 15, pp. 260 *ff*. The Asiatic oratory, however, must have become in the hands of the sophists distinctly modified by the Atticistic tendency inaugurated, or strongly promoted, in the Augustan age by Dionysius of Halicarnassus and Cæcilius (*Rhein. Mus.*, 41, p. 172). The sophists of the time of Philodemus are said to have used solecisms and barbarisms (Philod., i. p. 154, 4; *cf.* p. 159, 20), while Polemo purged oratory of the Asiatic word-jugglery (Procop., *ep.*, 116, but see Schmid, *Gr. Renais.*, p. 43, n. 76; see also the following note). Another view is that of Kaibel (*Hermes*, 20, pp. 497-513), who connects the later sophistry with the teaching of the fifth and fourth centuries B. C. and with the Atticistic tendency of Dionysius and Cæcilius. Wilamowitz-Möllendorff (*Hermes*, 35, pp. 1-52) emphasizes the historical connection of the earlier and the later sophists.

[2] See Philos., 511, 518, 595, 600, 626, 628. The general interest taken by the sophists of the second and third centuries A. D. in municipal politics is suggestive of the fact that the

sents itself to our view, not at Athens, but in Asia Minor; Nicetes, its first great light, was a native of Smyrna, and almost all the other important sophists of the second century came from the Greek cities of Asia.[1] Now it was precisely in these cities that the Romans, when they came into contact with the Greeks, met the most active and vigorous municipal life. It was the policy of the Romans not to interfere in the internal politics of the conquered states further than was necessary to uphold the imperial dignity and to preserve order in the cities. Thus, in the Greek communities of Asia Minor, the old forms of democratic polity were for the most part still in existence in the first century of the Christian era; assemblies and courts met as of yore, and magistrates, elected by the people, governed under the old names.

oratory which they taught was coming nearer to the life of the people. Many of these men held important positions in the cities; thus, Lollianus was στρατηγὸς ἐπὶ τῶν ὅπλων at Athens (Philos., 526), as were also Theodotus (*ib.*, 566) and Apollonius (*ib.*, 600); Apollonius was also archon eponymus. Note also the public activity of Polemo at Smyrna (*ib.*, 531, 532). These examples might be many times multiplied (see p. 164). Secondly, sophistry, we are told, underwent a wonderful expansion at the hands of Nicetes (*ib.*, 511). This statement seems to point to the beginning of a new era for the subject. Also, the false rhetoric of the earlier oratory was giving way to a saner style (see the preceding note, and the following passages: Philos., 588, 589, 598, 613, 616; Hippodromus wished to find somebody educated in the Asiatic style of oratory: *ib.*, 618, 619; for a sample of the inflated style of the sophists of an age not long preceding that of Lucian, see Lucian's *Lexiphanes; cf. ib., Rhet. præc.*, 17). It did not always happen, however, that the sophist was at home in the court or assembly room (Philos., 614; Lib., *ep.*, 1038; Eumen., *Pro rest. scol.*, 2; *cf.* Seneca, *Contr.*, iii. *præf.*, 16–18).

[1] Philos., 511, and under the various biographies. *Cf.* Sopater, *Proleg. in Aristeid.*, iii. p. 737, and Himer., *or.*, xi. 2. Ephesus was a literary centre in the time of Domitian (Philos., 339).

The country was prosperous and at peace, and enjoyed a large measure of happiness. Notwithstanding the levelling tendency of the Roman government in imperial times, and the increasing necessity (caused by the inability of the municipal authorities to cope with the question of taxation, the burden of which was growing heavier and heavier every year) for interference on the part of the central government in the internal affairs of the cities, much of the old feeling of political independence and national patriotism must still have existed in these communities at that time. Under these circumstances, it was found, in a greater degree than before, that the widest field for public activity was opened to those who possessed an oratorical training.[1] It needed,

---

[1] That the sophistical training was a preparation for active political and professional life is clear from many passages. Senators, advocates, and judges, especially, came from the sophist's school (Lib., i. 334, 5 ff.; ii. 279, 4; 284, 3; 286, 13; 295, 5; iii. 229, 2; ep., 973, 1107); officials of the imperial government (ib., i. 202, 8; 334, 10; iii. 435, 12; ep., 80, 140, 780, 781, 1143); even emperors (ib., iii. 283, 10); and Christians, as well as pagans (Choric., p. 109). The ability to speak was the high-road to official positions (Lib., ep., 248: καὶ σύ τοι τὸ ἄρχειν ἔχεις ἀπὸ τοῦ δύνασθαι λέγειν). Julian tried to fill the imperial positions in the provinces with educated men (Himer., or., v. 10). The sophist beheld young men issuing from his school into the walks of life (Lib., iii. 199, 5: ἐπὶ βίων ὁδούς). The speaker trained in the sophist's school spoke in the assemblies on war and peace (ib., iii. 198, 17). The sophistical education is called the most *useful* of all accomplishments (ib., i. 334, 4). The two requirements for a senator were financial means and the ability to speak on the subjects of the day (ib., iii. 447, 17). The calling of the sophist was to turn out public speakers (ib., i. 617, 17; ep., 780). Influential positions were obtained through rhetoric (ib., ep., 823; cf. 1454). Perhaps the clearest description of the sophist's profession is in Themistius, 339 b, c: εἰ μὲν πρὸς ἀργύριον βλέπεις . . . ζητεῖν ἐκείνους τοὺς λόγους οἳ χρήματά σοι βλαστήσουσιν. ἔστι δὲ

# UNIVERSITY EDUCATION ESTABLISHED 79

however, the favor and encouragement of the ruling power to give to the study of oratory that impulse that should bring it once more into prominence. These, in the last half of the first century A. D., were not long lacking. The emperors, as the century wore on, began to respond to the charm which Greece never for long failed to exert over those who came within the circle of her influence.[1]

πολὺ τὸ σπέρμα τοῦτο καὶ ἐν δικαστηρίοις καὶ ἐν ἐκκλησίαις, καὶ μάλιστα εὐθαλεῖ περὶ τὴν ἀγορὰν καὶ τὸ βῆμα. μηνύσαιμι δ' ἄν σοι καὶ ἐγὼ τοὺς ἐνθάδε ἀφθόνον αὐτὸ κεκτημένους· οἷς εἰ προσίοις τε καὶ θεραπεύοις, ταχύ σου μεγάλην τὴν γλῶτταν καὶ περιττὴν ἀποδείξουσι. . . . οὕτως ἡμῖν οἱ σοφισταὶ δεξιοί εἰσιν. Philostratus in his *Lives* rarely mentions pupils other than sophists, but Chrestus turned out, besides other distinguished men, several famous political orators (591). Oratory, according to Libanius, was an ornament in all walks of life (*ep.*, 140: πανταχοῦ δὲ οἷον σαυτῷ καὶ τὸ λέγειν προσήκειν. οὐδεὶς γὰρ βίος ὑπὸ ῥητορικῆς αἰσχύνεται). Rhetoric was the savior and support of municipal life (Procop., *ep.*, 80: τὴν Ἑλλάδα ῥητορικήν, ἐφ' ἧς ἑστήκασιν αἱ πόλεις). Compare Lib., i. 102, 11: ὧν (public speakers) οἰχομένων ἐζημίωνται μὲν βουλαὶ καὶ διοικήσεις πόλεων, ἐζημίωνται δὲ δίκαι, λόγων τῷ δικαίῳ συμμάχων ἐστερημέναι, ἐζημίωνται δὲ θρόνοι, ὧν τοὺς μὲν Ἑρμῆς, τοὺς δὲ ἐφορᾷ θέμις. See p. 119.

[1] Even in the previous century Julius Cæsar had shown his interest in education by granting the franchise to all physicians and teachers of liberal arts who were living or should live at Rome (Suet., *Jul.*, 42), while Augustus, in banishing foreigners from Rome, made an exception in favor of these two classes (*ib.*, *Aug.*, 42). The history of Greek sophistry for the centuries lying between the time of Isocrates and the end of the first century A. D. is hard to make out owing to the lack of material. H. v. Arnim, *Leben u. Werke d. Dio von Prusa*, ch. i. (followed by Wilamowitz-Möllendorff, *Hermes*, 35, pp. 1–52), gives the presumable course of the struggle for supremacy between the rhetorical and the philosophical education during this period somewhat as follows: At first the contest was about evenly balanced, but when Aristotle gave to rhetoric the protection of his favor, this subject gained a temporary advantage. With the conquests of Alexander in the East, there was opened a broader field for the practice of the rhetor, and victory lay for a time with the oratorical training. In the third century the individual sciences were emancipated

The Emperor Claudius (41–54) was from the first well disposed toward Greece and showed in various ways his interest in the country and its people. He restored to their original homes many Grecian works of art which had been carried out of the land in the reigns of his predecessors,[1] and under him Greek freedmen rose to a new importance in the Roman Court and state. His fondness for the Greek language and literature is well known. He also established a foundation at Alexandria, bearing his own name.[2]

Nero (54–68) refined upon the Hellenism of Claudius and carried it a step further. He never, it is true, out of regard for the avenging Eumenides — he himself, like Orestes, being a matricide — visited Athens, but he imitated, from pure egotism no doubt, the example of Flamininus at Corinth, and proclaimed, at the Isthmian games of 67, the freedom of all the Greeks. It is not necessary to repeat here the history of the extravagant manner in which this emperor testified to his admiration for all things Greek, and sought to exalt his own

---

from philosophy and came to the fore. Toward the end of the third century rhetoric began to make a system for itself, and philosophy fell to the rear. The second half of the second century was filled with the contest over the question, whether rhetoric was a $\tau\acute{\epsilon}\chi\nu\eta$ or not, and over the $\tau\acute{\epsilon}\lambda$os and the $\breve{\epsilon}\rho\gamma o\nu$ of rhetoric. Next, the contest was carried to Rome and made much of there. Cicero tried to restore to philosophy something of her ancient rights, but he secured no permanent results; philosophy became with the Romans an $\grave{\epsilon}\gamma\kappa\acute{\nu}\kappa\lambda\iota o\nu$ $\pi\alpha\acute{\iota}\delta\epsilon\nu\mu\alpha$. Among the Greeks it still retained some remnant of its former glory. Bury (*Roman Empire*, p. 573) aptly compares the controversy waged under the Empire between the merits of philosophy and rhetoric to the controversy raised in modern times as to the respective educational values of classical literature and science.

[1] Paus., ix. 27, 3; Dio Cass., lx. 6.   [2] Suet., *Claud.*, 42.

skill and understanding by an appeal to the Greek standard. Though his conduct was based on vanity and egotism, it was, by its very extravagance, a tribute to the superiority of the Grecian intellect and to the influence which that superiority exerted over other nations — an undignified and uncouth tribute, no doubt, but still a tribute. There was in it a sort of recognition of the fact that Greece did, by her own right, possess a certain claim to the world's homage.

The empty honor of "freedom for all the Greeks," bestowed by Nero, was withdrawn by Vespasian (69–79), who also, after the loose management of his predecessors, drew the financial reins of his government tighter. Though his rule was for these reasons probably felt as a hardship by the Greeks, it was in another way of genuine benefit to them, for he, first of the emperors, gave marked official recognition to Greek studies. He endowed at Rome chairs of Greek and Roman eloquence, with annual salaries of 100,000 sesterces ($5,000), and rewarded with large sums distinguished poets and artists.[1] The first to receive appointment to the Latin chair was Quintilian.[2] Vespasian also relieved from certain public duties 'grammarians,' rhetors, physicians, and philosophers.[3]

[1] Suet., *Vesp.*, 18.
[2] Though it would seem that the first payment was made in the reign of Domitian, for Jerome says (in *Euseb. Chron.*), under the year 90 A. D.: *Quintilianus ex Hispania Calagurritanus primus Romæ publicam scholam et salarium e fisco accepit et claruit.*
[3] From the words of Charisius in the *Digests* (l. 4, 18, 30), it would appear that the measure went even back of the time of Vespasian: *magistris, qui civilium munerum vacationem habent, item grammaticis et oratoribus et medicis et philosophis, ne hospitem*

The reign of Domitian (81–96) was again unfavorable to all studies, both Greek and Roman. Though Domitian was so far Hellenic in his tastes that he organized at Rome contests on the pattern of the Olympic games and presided at the same in Greek dress, he on the other hand drove from the city and from Italy all philosophers and teachers of wisdom.[1] Athens had at this time, it would appear, re-established her pre-eminence in the educational world, for Philostratus, who, to be sure, wrote long after and may have interpreted this period somewhat in the light of his own, speaks of the young men who in the reign of Domitian flocked to the schools of Athens from all quarters of the earth.[2]

With Nerva and Trajan freedom of thought was again restored to the Greek and to the Roman world. We have not much information with regard to the personal connection of these two emperors with Greece, but their reigns must have been felt, there as elsewhere, as a relief after the long and unpropitious reign of Domitian. Nerva (96–98), in the short period during which he was emperor, found time to recall from exile the Greek rhetor Dio Chrysostom, and this famous man retained

*reciperent, a principibus fuisse immunitatem indultam et divus Vespasianus et divus Hadrianus rescripserunt.* Although immunity from the burden of quartering public officials is alone mentioned here as being the gift of Vespasian, immunity from other burdens was probably granted by him (Plin., *Ep. ad Trai.*, lviii. (lxvi.): *cum citarem iudices, domine, conventum inchoaturus, Flavius Archippus vacationem petere cœpit ut philosophus;* see also Tac., *Dial. de or.*, 9).

[1] Suet., *Domit.*, 10; Tac., *Agric.*, 2. See, further, Hertzberg, *Gesch. Griech.*, ii. p. 142, n. 42. Titus confirmed all Vespasian's rescripts (Suet., *Tit.*, 8). [2] 359.

## UNIVERSITY EDUCATION ESTABLISHED 83

the favor and friendship of the following emperor, Trajan (98-117). Trajan, further, so we are told by Philostratus,[1] bestowed upon the distinguished sophist Polemo the privilege of travelling by land and sea free of charge, a privilege which was extended by Hadrian to the sophist's children. More and more, we see, the emperors were taking an intelligent interest in this land to the east, and the time was not far distant when its schools were to be given an official standing.

Thus it was that Hadrian (117-138), he who was so fully imbued with the spirit of Hellenism that, as we are told by a late historian,[2] he completely adopted the studies, the manner of life, the language, and the whole culture of the Athenians, and who, even after he had become emperor, lived on terms of perfect intimacy and friendship with Greek philosophers and sophists, determined to restore to Greece her proper place among the peoples; and with him begins a new era for the country, a new inspiration of national life. Hadrian aimed to unite, under Athens as a head, the scattered fragments of the Greek race. For this purpose he instituted at Athens the Pan-Hellenic synod, or assembly, and a new national assembly, called the *Pan-Hellenia*, to both of which all Greek communities, wherever established, were permitted to send representatives. As a place of congress and centre of the new nationality, he built the temple of Zeus Pan-Hellenios. This was but one, and not the most important, of the many buildings with which he adorned Athens. The temple of the Olympian Zeus, begun by Peisistratus, continued by

[1] 532.     [2] Aurelius Victor, *Epit.*, 14.

Antiochus Epiphanes, and now completed by Hadrian, a pantheon patterned after that at Rome, a gymnasium, a stoa and library, and many other buildings, arose within a few years. A whole new quarter of the city was laid out and built to the south-east of the Acropolis, near the Ilissus, and separated from the old city by an arch commemorating the event. In many other parts of Greece also Hadrian caused fine buildings to be erected, but it was upon Athens that he bestowed his special favor.

His activity, however, was not confined to the erection of fine buildings. In many ways he showed his interest in Greek studies, and he bestowed many favors on Grecian philosophers and other men of learning. He confirmed the decrees of previous emperors, granting immunity to teachers and others, and granted still further privileges at first hand.[1] The impulse which he gave to the cause of learning must have been immense, and well might the Athenians begin to number their years anew from the date of the first arrival of Hadrian at Athens.[2]

One act of Hadrian — an act relative to the succession to the headship in one of the philosophical schools at Athens — shows how far these schools had already become objects of oversight and control to the imperial government at Rome. Plotina, the mother of the emperor, was a member of the Epicurean school. It was a regulation bearing upon this school (and probably upon the other schools as well) that none but

---

[1] *Dig.*, l. 4, 18, 30; Philos., 532.
[2] Dittenberger, in *Hermes*, 7, 213.

Roman citizens should be appointed to the headship, while it was also a law of the realm that wills (except for bequests in trust) should be written in Latin. These restrictions were felt by the members of the school to be onerous. Accordingly Plotina wrote to the emperor, begging that the incumbent of the headship, Popillius Theotimus, be permitted to write in Greek that part of his will which referred to school matters, and that he further be allowed to select his successor from among citizens and non-citizens alike. It was pointed out that the restriction that was set upon the selection of a Head made it difficult to find the right man for the place, while the privilege possessed by the members of the school of passing upon the selection made by the testator and, on occasion, of substituting another man in his stead had been the source of nothing but good to the school. The request was granted by Hadrian, who made the privilege to apply not only to Theotimus, but to future Heads of the school as well.[1]

One of the most important acts of Hadrian was the establishment at Rome of the *Athenæum*, which was designed as a rallying-place and theatre of display for Greek and Roman sophists and poets, and afterward became the centre of the University of Rome. The name, of course, speaks of the beloved Athens. He also

[1] For the inscription, containing Plotina's letter to the emperor in Latin, the emperor's reply to Plotina in Latin, and Plotina's proclamation of the result of her petition, to the members of the school, in Greek, see Dessau, *Insc. Lat. scl.*, ii. 2, 1906, No. 7784. Hadrian is referred to in Plotina's proclamation in the following terms: τῶι ὡς ἀληθῶς εὐεργέτηι καὶ πάσης π[α]ιδείας κοσμητῆι ὄντι. See also Diels, *Archiv. f. Gesch. d. Philos.*, 4, pp. 486–491.

confirmed the privileges of the Museum at Alexandria, and honored several sophists and other men of learning by making them members of this institution. Thus, the sophists, Polemo of Smyrna and Dionysius of Miletus, as well as Pancrates, a poet, were so distinguished.[1]

The movement which was thus started by Hadrian was continued by the two succeeding emperors and by the wealthy sophist, Herodes Atticus. Herodes, though a private individual, rivalled, with his almost fabulous wealth, even the emperors themselves in his zeal for building and his lavish expenditure of money. The beautiful Odeum, on the south-western slope of the Acropolis, built in memory of his wife Regilla, and the Panathenaic stadium, near the Ilissus, remodelled and constructed entirely of Pentelic marble, testified to his generous love for Athens. One of the foremost sophists of his day, he was also an admirer and patron of sophists, and he lived on terms of friendly intimacy with three emperors. He died late in the reign of Marcus Aurelius.

Antoninus Pius (138–161), though he seems, after becoming emperor, never to have visited Athens, was an earnest friend of learning, and showed his interest in the philosophers and rhetoricians in a very material and important way. He gave, we are told, honors and salaries to rhetoricians and philosophers throughout the provinces.[2] The honors, apparently, consisted for the most part of exemption from certain taxes and immunity from certain public duties. These duties, or a

---

[1] Philos., 532, 533, 524; Athen., xv. 21, p. 677.
[2] Jul. Capit., *Anton. Pius*, 11.

part of them, are mentioned in the *Digests*:[1] ædileships, priestships, jury service, the superintendency of palæstræ and the paying of training-masters, army service, etc. Physicians and 'grammarians' were also exempted from these duties. It is interesting to note that physicians were, from the earliest times, recognized as public benefactors, and were so treated by Greek legislators. Diodorus Siculus tells us that in very early times they received salaries from the state.[2]

With regard to the salaries ordained by Antoninus Pius, it seems probable that these were to be paid by the cities themselves, and that, only when the cities were unable to pay them, were they paid from the Fiscus, or imperial chest. As we are told that Antoninus made these regulations to apply to *all* the provinces, we should be led to expect that at Athens a beginning was now made of establishing academic chairs with salaries attached, and such, in fact, seems to have been the case. A chair of rhetoric was, it would appear, established, and the first man to occupy it, according to Philostratus, was Lollianus of Ephesus.[3] Either now or in the reign of

[1] xxvii. 1, 6. The honors nearly all, however, went back to a time earlier than Hadrian; Antoninus simply confirmed edicts issued by Hadrian and preceding emperors. It was the usual practice of emperors, on coming into power, to confirm the acts of their predecessors, as each emperor's acts were considered to be personal to himself and to expire with his recession from power.   [2] xii. 13.

[3] Philos., 526. That the salaries were to be paid by the municipalities, and that, only in case the municipalities could not pay them, were they paid by the emperor, is the view of Zumpt (*Ueber den Bestand d. phil. Schul.*, p. 45). This view, though probable, is not certain. The *political* chair held by Apollonius of Athens (Philos., 600: τοῦ πολιτικοῦ θρόνου) Zumpt (p. 49) understands to be a municipal chair at Athens, while the chair

the following emperor a chair of 'grammar' was also probably established at Athens, while some provision

later established by Marcus Aurelius, the so-called *chair of the sophists*, or *sophistical chair* (Philos., 588: τοῦ τῶν σοφιστῶν θρόνου· 618: τὸν 'Αθήνησι τῶν σοφιστῶν θρόνον· Sopater in *Proleg. ad Aristeid.*, iii. p. 739: τὸν θρόνον τὸν σοφιστικόν· Phot., *Bibl.*, cod. 80, p. 60: τὸν σοφιστικὸν θρόνον), he takes to be an imperial endowment. That the latter was the case would seem to be certain (Philos., 566: ἐπὶ ταῖς ἐκ βασιλέως μυρίαις· *cf.* 591). Brandstätter (*Leipz. Stud.*, 15, pp. 194, 244), from a comparison of the words πολιτικός and σοφιστικός as they are used by Greek writers, concludes that they here have reference to the character of the eloquence taught, and that the political chair was a chair of judicial eloquence (see also Liebenam, *Städteverwaltung*, p. 79, n. 2). The following considerations seems to support Zumpt's view rather than Brandstatter's: 1. We nowhere else find mention made of an endowed chair of judicial oratory, while there were chairs of sophistry municipally endowed in various parts of the Empire at this, and at a later, time (see p. 134; *Dig.*, l. 9, 4, 2). 2. The chair here called πολιτικός is called by Philostratus in 526, and perhaps elsewhere (see p. 94, n. 1), ὁ 'Αθήνησι θρόνος. 3. There is a difficulty in distinguishing between the activities of the incumbents of the *political* chair and those of the incumbents of the sophist's chair. Thus, Theodotus was appointed to the sophistical chair, though he is called ἀγωνιστὴς τῶν πολιτικῶν λόγων καὶ ῥητορικῆς ὄφελος (Philos., 567). The holders of the *political* chair are classed as sophists, and they seem to have differed in no respect from those who are known to have held the sophistical chair. Thus, Apollonius the Athenian wrote in a metrical style quite out of keeping with what we are told should be the style of a teacher of political eloquence (*ib.*, 601, 602), and Lollianus, besides having a sophistical style, held 'displays' and spoke extempore (*ib.*, 527). Apollonius of Naucratis, though a rival of Heracleides, who apparently held the sophistical chair, practised political speeches (*ib.*, 599). 4. There is a recognized use of πολιτικός in the sense of *publicus, civilis, municipalis*, as applied to public services, or liturgies; *e. g., Dig.*, xxvii. 1, 15, 12; see *ib.*, l. 4, 14 and 18; also Kuhn, *Verf. d. röm. Reichs*, i. p. 40. On the other hand, there were undoubtedly in various cities teachers of a base oratory, forensic or judicial (Philos., 274, 331, 566, 570, 614; [Luc.], *Amores*, 9; Lib., iii. 449, 17; Isoc., *De antid.*, 30, 37-41), and it is possible that some of these held endowed chairs. If the 'political chair' at Athens was one of the latter, it may

## UNIVERSITY EDUCATION ESTABLISHED 89

seems to have been made at this time for the granting of salaries to philosophers.[1]

With regard to the number of sophists, 'grammarians,' and physicians, whom it was permitted to honor in the aforesaid ways, Antoninus gave very specific directions. Small cities might have privileged five physicians, three sophists, and three 'grammarians'; larger cities, that is, those in which there were courts established, seven physicians, four sophists, and four 'grammarians'; capital cities, ten physicians, five

have been endowed by the city or it may have been endowed by the emperor. At the beginning of the second half of the third century there were still two chairs of rhetoric at Athens (Eunap., p. 11). Tatian (Or. ad Græc., 19) says: οἱ γὰρ παρ' ὑμῖν φιλόσοφοι τοσοῦτον ἀποδέουσι τῆς ἀσκήσεως ὥστε παρὰ τοῦ Ῥωμαίων βασιλέως ἐτησίους χρυσοῦς ἑξακοσίους λαμβάνειν τινὰς εἰς οὐδὲν χρήσιμον ἢ ὅπως μηδὲ τὸ γένειον δωρεὰν καθειμένον αὐτῶν ἔχουσιν. The date of this speech has been set as early as 152 A. D. (Christ, Gr. Lit., p. 891) and as late as 173 A. D. (see Aimé Puech, Recherches sur le discours aux Grecs de Tatien, pp. 10, 96). At this time, therefore, salaries had already been assigned to certain philosophers. The amount of the salary, six hundred gold pieces (= 60,000 sesterces = $3,000), was greater than the amount of the salary given to philosophers at Athens. Sophists at Rome received a higher salary than sophists at Athens (see p. 81), but the reference here can hardly be to philosophers at Rome. It is possible that the philosophers at Athens are meant, and that the discrepancy between Philostratus's 10,000 drachmæ and Tatian's 600 aurei is to be explained as a case of inexactness of statement or as due to a change in currency values. An amusing inscription to Lollianus has been found at Athens (Kaibel, Ep. Gr., No. 877).

[1] For the 'grammarian,' see Eunap., p. 7: Λογγῖνος (in the third century) . . . κρίνειν γε τοὺς παλαιοὺς ἐπετέτακτο, καθάπερ πρὸ ἐκείνου πολλοί τινες ἕτεροι, καὶ ὁ ἐκ Καρίας Διονύσιος· Suidas, s. v. Παμπρέπιος· παρὰ τῆς πόλεως γραμματικὸς αἱρεθείς (in the fifth century). Cf. Phot., Bibl., cod. 242, p. 346 b: οἱ δὲ Ἀθηναῖοι γραμματικὸν αὐτὸν ἐποιήσαντο καὶ ἐπὶ νέοις διδάσκαλον ἔστησαν. For the philosophers, see Jul. Capit., Anton. Pius, 11, and the passage in Tatian cited in the preceding note.

sophists, and five 'grammarians.' This number might not, on any pretext whatever, be exceeded, but, in the case of certain duties, it might, on occasion, be diminished. Immunity was to be granted only after formal vote of the local council and enrolment of the beneficiary in the official list of beneficiaries. No limit was set to the number of philosophers who might be honored, as they were in any case not numerous.[1]

These do not exhaust the regulations set forth by Antoninus Pius relative to the appointments to what may be called the "Fellowships of Arts and Sciences."[2] We can see from these, however, that the appointments were made the subject of a formal and elaborate system; they were no longer meant to be given arbitrarily and at caprice to individual professors by individual emperors, though, as will be evident later, famous sophists

[1] *Dig.*, xxvii. ii., 6. It is suggested by Mommsen, *The Provinces of the Roman Empire* (trans.), i. p. 393, that the edict of Antoninus Pius, limiting the number of persons who might be privileged, was called for by the burdensomeness of the existing arrangement, whereby unrestricted exemption was possible; this measure, therefore, would imply previous imperial grants.

[2] Thus, Antoninus stated that it was expected that philosophers who had the means would voluntarily render to their country services involving the expenditure of money. At a later time, Septimius Severus and Caracalla established the law that a teacher or physician who was born in one city and was teaching or practising in another might not claim immunity in the city of his birth; but under Antoninus provision was made for honoring thus men of exceptional skill who were teaching or practising in cities in which the legal number of appointments had already been made. Teachers of sophistry, and probably other teachers also (*cf. Dig.*, l. 5, 9), whether salaried or not, if established at Rome, were so privileged; the theory in this case being that he who was teaching at Rome was teaching in the common fatherland of all. Teachers of law, while privileged at Rome, were not privileged in the provinces. See *Dig.*, xxvii. 1, 6, 7, 9-12; 1. 5, 9.

were often specially honored, and sometimes dishonored as well.

The university thus established at Athens, through the agency of Antoninus Pius, was developed by Marcus Aurelius (161–180). Marcus Aurelius, from his youth a friend and companion of Greek philosophers and sophists, a student of Herodes Atticus, with whom he, even after he had become emperor, continued on terms of intimacy and whose lectures he continued to attend, was a firm friend of Greek learning, but he found, owing to the exigencies of his reign, little time to devote to peaceful pursuits. He did, however, in the intervals of his campaigns, carry on the work begun by his predecessor in the Greek schools. Early in the second half of his reign, apparently, he established at Athens, by the side of the already-existing chair of rhetoric, which was possibly salaried by the city, a second chair, with much higher salary attached. The salary of this chair was to be paid from the imperial chest. The first sophist to be appointed to the new chair was Theodotus, and he held the position two years, till his death. Then, whether immediately after or not is uncertain, but presumably so, Adrian of Tyre, a pupil of Herodes Atticus and one of the most famous sophists of the time, was called by the emperor to fill the position. When Marcus made this appointment, he had neither heard Adrian declaim, nor had he even seen him, but he called the man solely on the basis of his great reputation. So it was that, when Marcus, in 176, passed through Athens on his way to Rome from the East, he determined to listen to a sample of Adrian's eloquence, and he set the sophist a theme to discuss. Adrian was so successful in his treatment of the theme that Marcus, well pleased with his oratory, bestowed upon him many gifts and honors.[1] After this, the emperor completed the work which he had begun, and endowed several chairs (probably two in each school) in the four schools of philosophy — the Academic, the Peripatetic, the Stoic, and the Epicurean.[2]

[1] All that is certain with regard to the date at which this chair was established is that it was not later than 174. We know that Marcus was at Smyrna in the spring of 176 (Clinton, *Fasti Romani*, ad an. 176), and that he later in the same year repaired to Athens, where he was initiated into the Eleusinian Mysteries (Jul. Capit., *Marc. Ant. Phil.*, 27). At that time Adrian already held the chair of sophistry at Athens (Philos., 588). Zumpt (*Ueber den Bestand d. phil. Schul.*, p. 51) conjectures, as the date, 168, when the emperor was at Sirmium, and Hertzberg (*Gesch. Griech.*, ii. p. 411) puts it in the second half of Marcus's reign. All that Philostratus says on the matter is ἐκράτει μὲν ἤδη τοῦ τῶν σοφιστῶν θρόνου (588). If this suggests that the appointment of Adrian was recent at the time of Marcus's visit to Athens, the establishment of the chair was also probably of recent date, for, as stated in the text, Theodotus, the immediate predecessor, as it would seem, of Adrian, was the first to occupy the chair, and he held it two years until his death (*ib.*, 566, 567). Adrian was in Rome between the years 164 and 168 and attended a clinic of Galen there (Galen, xiv. p. 627). This was before the sophist was established at Athens (οὔπω σοφιστεύων). Sopater (*Proleg. ad Aristeid.*, iii. p. 739) says that Herodes Atticus held the chair of sophistry at Athens, but this seems not to have been the case.

[2] The number of philosophical chairs established by Marcus Aurelius is nowhere definitely stated. The two passages bearing on the subject are these: Philos., 566: τοὺς μὲν Πλατωνείους καὶ τοὺς ἀπὸ τῆς Στοᾶς καὶ τοὺς ἀπὸ τοῦ Περιπάτου καὶ αὐτοῦ Ἐπικούρου προσέταξεν ὁ Μάρκος τῷ Ἡρώδῃ κρῖναι, and Luc., *Eunuch.*, 3: συντέτακται μέν . . . ἐκ βασιλέως μισθοφορά τις οὐ φαύλη κατὰ γένη τοῖς φιλοσόφοις, Στωϊκοῖς λέγω καὶ Πλατωνικοῖς καὶ Ἐπικουρείοις, ἔτι δὲ καὶ τοῖς ἐκ τοῦ Περιπάτου, τὰ ἴσα τούτοις ἅπασιν. ἔδει δὲ ἀποθανόντος αὐτῶν τινος ἄλλον ἀντικαθίστασθαι. . . . καὶ τὰ ἆθλα . . . μύριαι κατὰ τὸν ἐνιαυτόν. . . . οἶδα ταῦτα. καί τινά φασιν αὐτῶν ἔναγχος ἀποθανεῖν, τῶν Περιπατητικῶν οἶμαι τὸν ἕτερον. These passages would seem to

## UNIVERSITY EDUCATION ESTABLISHED 93

"Marcus," says Dio Cassius, "after he had come to Athens and been initiated, gave to the Athenians honors, and to the whole world teachers at Athens, with annual salaries, in every branch of literary study," and Zonaras adds that the salaries were to be paid from the imperial coffers.[1] The appointments to the philosophical chairs were to be made, after examination of the candidates, by the venerable sophist, Herodes Atticus, while, in the case of the chair of sophistry, the appointment was made now, and for some time to come, by the emperor himself.

It is evident from all the passages bearing on the subject that Marcus aimed to make of Athens a real university centre, and that the measures he took in furtherance of his aim were thorough-going and extensive. It is possible, as has been said above, that certain salaries had already been assigned to philosophers at Athens by Antoninus Pius, but, if this was so, Marcus, we may believe, increased their number and value, while he changed the method of appointment to the philosophical chairs, and not improbably made other changes in the management of the schools. These changes were apparently in the direction of a loss of independence on the part of the schools and greater

---

point to two chairs in each school, but Zumpt (*Ueber den Bestand d. phil. Schul.*, p. 50) understands that there was but one chair established in each school by Marcus, while the second was that supported by the school itself. But it is not improbable that the succession in nearly all the schools had at this time run out (see p. 102, n. 1). See, further, Sandys, *Hist. Clas. Schol.*, i. p. 309, and Grasberger, *Erzieh. u. Unterr. im klass. Alterth.*, iii. p. 445.

[1] Dio. Cass., lxxi. 31; Zon., xii. 3.

oversight and control of the schools on the part of the emperor. The holder of the chair of sophistry, if not actually put over the University as a whole, at least ranked in dignity above the other professors.[1] At this time, the philosophical and the rhetorical department were kept more or less apart, but in the fourth century, after the decline of philosophy at Athens, the chair of sophistry was undoubtedly of commanding importance, and then the incumbent of this chair was probably also the Head of the University.[2]

Such is the history of the establishment of the University of Athens. The period of nearly three quarters of a century (117–180), embracing the reigns of Hadrian and the first two Antonines, was a period of happiness

---

[1] The following expressions point to this conclusion: Philos., 566: προύστη δὲ καὶ τῆς Ἀθηναίων νεότητος πρῶτός ἐπὶ ταῖς ἐκ βασιλέως μυρίαις· ib., p. 567: ἐπέκρινε τοῖς νέοις· ib., 588: ἐπέταξεν αὐτὸν τοῖς νέοις. Elsewhere the chair is called "the chair of the sophists" (ib., 588: τοῦ τῶν σοφιστῶν θρόνου), "the chair of the sophists at Athens" (ib., 618: τὸν Ἀθήνησι τῶν σοφιστῶν θρόνον), or simply "the chair at Athens" (ib., 587, twice: τοῦ Ἀθήνησι θρόνου). In the following places the context makes it certain that the same chair is referred to: ib., 566, 567, 591, 593, 621, 622, 623. In ib., 526, though the same expression, τοῦ Ἀθήνησι θρόνου, is used, the reference must be to the *political* chair, for Theodotus was the first to hold the more exalted chair (ib., 566). The following references are less certain than those given above, but the sophistical chair is probably meant: ib., 594, 599, 613, 627. ἐπὶ τῆς καθέδρας occurs in an inscription (Dittenberger, *Syl. Inscr. Græc.*, i. No. 382; date, 244–249 A. D.). Of a later time, in Athens, τοῦ θρόνου (Eunap., p. 95), and τοῦ παιδευτικοῦ θρόνου (ib., p. 95; but see p. 220, n. 4). See also p. 87, n. 3, and p. 142, n. 3. Sophists not infrequently resigned the chair at Athens in order to accept the chair at Rome (called ὁ κατὰ τὴν Ῥώμην θρόνος or ὁ ἄνω θρόνος· Philos., 580, 589, 594, 596, 627). The sophist was sometimes said to 'have his seat' in the place where he taught (e. g., Lib., i. 126, 6: παρὰ Βιθυνοῖς ἐκαθήμην).

[2] Compare the School of Antioch (pp. 270 *ff.*).

## UNIVERSITY EDUCATION ESTABLISHED 95

and well-being for all Grecian lands. Sophists and other men of learning thronged in the cities of Greece and Asia Minor, and crowds of eager students, young and old, flocked to their lectures. Education had never before been at so high a premium. "All Ionia," says Philostratus, "is like a college of learned men, but Smyrna holds the first place, like the bridge upon the cithara."[1] At other cities also there were famous schools, some of which became even more famous in succeeding centuries, as at Berytus, Tarsus, Antioch, Ephesus, etc. Most famous of all, perhaps, though not so much in the line of sophistry as of scientific learning and philosophy, was Alexandria, with its museum and libraries. This was the age of the distinguished sophists, Polemo of Laodicea in Caria, Lollianus of Ephesus, Adrian of Tyre, Theodotus the Athenian, Scopelian of Clazomenæ, Philager the Cilician, Hermogenes of Tarsus, the oft-mentioned Herodes Atticus, and many more. Of many of these men we have no literary remains, and, in fact, the reputation of most of them was based on the spoken, rather than on the written, word. Of Herodes and Polemo we have one short speech each, and of Hermogenes several works of some value on the theory of rhetoric. Aristeides of Adriani in Mysia, who was compared by the ancients themselves to Demosthenes, has left us a considerable body of writings, as has the more important Dio of Prusa, called the "Golden-mouthed," of an earlier age. The biographer of these men is Philostratus, himself a sophist, who lived in the first half of the third century, and wrote his work,

[1] 516. *Cf.* Aristeid., i. p. 376.

*The Lives of the Sophists,* in the reign of Alexander Severus. Nor must we omit to mention the most original of all the sophists of this period, one in whose pages we see the manners of the age depicted from their most amusing side — Lucian.

It does not come within the province of these chapters to deal with every field of literary and scientific activity, and some mention has already been made in a previous chapter [1] of those branches of learning that stood in close relation to the study of sophistry. There was much activity in all lines of scientific and philological research in this century and the centuries that followed, but there were few names in any line to be compared with the great names of the Alexandrian period. Rhetoric, the technical side of sophistry, was of course cultivated, while, in the field of grammar, more scientific methods came to the fore, and the foundations of Greek syntax were laid. The study of geography, which had received a fresh impulse at the time of the conquests of Alexander, was continued with vigor in the early imperial times; but mathematics and astronomy, though not wholly neglected in the first centuries of the Christian era — witness the name of Ptolemy — were at this time suffering a temporary relapse, after their great activity in the Alexandrian period. Medicine was well represented. Of philosophy we shall have occasion to speak in connection with the next century.

[1] Ch. I.

## CHAPTER VI

### HISTORY OF UNIVERSITY EDUCATION FROM MARCUS AURELIUS TO CONSTANTINE

NEVER again, after the death of Marcus Aurelius, did Greece enjoy the benefits of imperial favor as she had done during the preceding sixty or seventy years. After that time, those who sat on the throne were often men of little cultivation, with no taste for literature or learning, and, if there was occasionally one who had the inclination to patronize letters, the time and opportunity were for the most part lacking. Dark clouds also soon began to gather round the state. Civil wars and military revolutions, intrigues of rival claimants and foreign campaigns, served to occupy the attention of the reigning monarchs and to sap the strength of the Empire. Occasionally, also, was heard the distant thunder of the barbarian hordes along the northern frontier, giving warning of the storm that was soon to break. Plagues and earthquakes, and an increasing uncertainty as to how the financial needs of the government were, from year to year, to be met, added to the confusion of the times.

Still, this was not, up to the middle of the third century at least, the worst period which Greece had experienced. The Severi if not enthusiastic patrons of literature and education, were not for the most part inimical to them, and, under more favorable circumstances, they might, in some cases, have proved of genuine benefit. The appointments to the imperial chair of sophistry, as is evident from Philostratus,[1] continued to be made by the emperors, and the emperors confirmed and expanded, on occasion, the edicts of Antoninus Pius and Marcus Aurelius relative to the privileges of sophists, philosophers, and others. Commodus (180–193), the last of the Antonines, was not insensible to the charms of oratory, and he raised to honorable position two famous sophists, Adrian of Tyre and Polydeuces of Naucratis.[2] Septimius Severus (193–211), it is true, deprived Heracleides the Lycian of the immunities attaching to his position as Professor of Sophistry at Athens, because the latter failed in a speech made in the imperial presence,[3] but otherwise he seems to have been not ill-disposed toward Greece and to have stood in close personal relation to the Greek cities. Athens alone, unfortunately, incurred, for a trifling reason, his resentment, and was deprived of certain privileges, probably either political or territorial. The refined Julia Domna, wife of Septimius Severus and mother of Caracalla, was herself a student and a friend and patron of students. She procured, in the reign of her son, the professorship at Athens for the sophist, Philiscus of Eordæa in Macedonia,[4] and she was a friend of Philostratus, who wrote his *Life of Apollonius of*

[1] *E. g.*, 591, 593, 622.
[2] Philos., 590, 593; *cf. Dig.*, xxvii. 1, 6, 8. For Pertinax, see Jul. Capit., *Pert.*, 11.   [3] Philos., 601, 614.
[4] Philos., 622; *cf.* Dio Cass., lxxv. 15; lxxvii. 18.

*Tyana* at her request. Little that is favorable can be said of Caracalla (211-217) from our point of view, if from any. Not only did he deprive Philiscus of the immunities attaching to his position, but he in a fit of anger threatened to do the same for all sophists, though he seems not to have meant the threat seriously, for he never carried it into execution.[1] His treatment of the Peripatetic philosophers was still more harsh. Accusing Aristotle of having been accessory to the death of Alexander the Great, for whom the emperor had a fanciful admiration, he threatened to burn the books, wherever found, of all the philosopher's followers, and he actually deprived the Peripatetics of their salaries and other emoluments at Alexandria.[2] Alexander Severus (222-235) received a Greek education, and, like Septimius Severus, was one of the better emperors of this period. He established salaries and built lecture-rooms at Rome for rhetors, 'grammarians,' physicians, astrologers, architects, and others, and instituted a system whereby free-born children of poor parents should have the cost of their education defrayed by the state. He also granted certain favors of a financial character to legal orators in the provinces.[3]

We should say, then, that, although the University of Athens did not, in this period, that is, during the half-century immediately following the death of Marcus Aurelius, enjoy the particular favor of the emperors, it was still, having been firmly established by the An-

---

[1] Philos., 623. Compare his conduct toward the sophists Philostratus and Heliodorus (*ib.*, 623, 626).
[2] Dio Cass., lxxvii. 7.  [3] Lamprid., *Alex. Sev.*, 44.

tonines on a basis of its own, in a hardly less flourishing condition than in the previous period. The list of famous sophists whose names appear in the pages of Philostratus is a long one, and includes Antipater of Hierapolis, Polydeuces (otherwise Pollux) of Naucratis, Hippodromus of Larissa, Heracleides the Lycian, Apollonius and Proclus of Naucratis, Apollonius the Athenian, and Philiscus of Eordæa.

One tendency of this period we have specially to notice. We saw [1] that Antoninus Pius, in defining the number of teachers and others whom it was permitted in the different classes of cities to honor officially with immunity from public burdens, put no restriction on the number of philosophers, holding that the philosophers altogether were not many, and that the number of such who would be likely to apply for immunity would not be large. From the pages of Lucian we should hardly infer that there was in his time any lack of self-styled philosophers in Greece and the lands inhabited by Greeks — and, indeed, we are told that, in consequence of the favor shown by Marcus Aurelius to men of learning, a large crop of philosophical weeds immediately sprang up [2] — but it was undoubtedly the case that in

[1] P. 90.
[2] Dio Cass., lxxi. 35, 2; Herodian, i. 2. There seem, however, to have been more philosophers outside Attica than at Athens (Luc., *Drap.*, 24, 25); Attica was too poor to attract many— Philippopolis, in Thrace, near the rich gold and silver mines of that country, offered greater attractions. *Cf.* Bury, *Roman Empire*, p. 574: "The towns of Greece swarmed with them [spurious philosophers]. Everywhere, Lucian tells us, one meets in the streets their long beards, their rolls of books, their threadbare cloaks, and their big sticks. Poor cobblers and carpenters leave their shops to rove about the country as begging Cynics.

those days philosophy was no longer the power in the intellectual world that it had once been, and that it was gradually declining from year to year in importance and interest. Rhetoric and eloquence, which had for long contended on almost equal terms with philosophy, were now forging to the head. Still, the race of philosophers was far from being extinct even in the second quarter of the third century. "There were many philosophers when I was a boy," says the rhetorician Longinus,[1] referring to that period, "but now," he continues, speaking of a later time, "it is impossible to describe how utterly this subject is neglected." Many circumstances conduced to the decline of philosophy: the changed condition and taste of the times, the inner barrenness of the subject as then taught and studied, and the rise and spread of Christianity. The philosophers of that period did little more than repeat in new words and phrases, or expound and comment on, the old doctrines. Much time was also spent in useless argumentation and quibbling.[2] The Peripatetic school long maintained itself by the stress which it laid on positive science and logic, but, as time went on, it gradually tended to merge into the Academic school.[3]

. . . In the second century the country was infested with begging philosophers, carrying scrip and staff like the begging monks of the Middle Ages. . . .

"But, although unpopular and mercilessly jibed at, the philosophers exercised great influence; and the very existence of a multitude of spurious philosophers proves the repute which the true philosophers enjoyed."

[1] Porphyr., *Vit. Plotin.*, 20.

[2] Porphyr., *Vit. Plotin.*, 20; Luc., *Hermot.*, 79, 81, 82.

[3] On the tendency of the philosophies at this time to look to a common end, see Themis., 236 b; Jul., *or.*, vi. 184 C–186 A.

In the Epicurean and Stoic teachings the ethical element was always strong, and this now failed to satisfy the needs of the age. Much that was permanent in the Greek ethical teaching had been taken up by Christianity, while the spiritually or philosophically inclined who were out of sympathy with the new religion arrayed themselves from this time on more and more in the ranks of Neo-Platonism. This doctrine, which formed the last expression of Greek philosophic and religious thought, played a more important part in the two centuries that followed, and we shall therefore speak more at length of it later. The endowments of the various schools still existed in the first half of the third century — and, indeed, regular διάδοχοι, or 'successors,' are mentioned, in the case of at least one school, the Academic, as late as, or even later than, the reign of Gallienus (260–268), and, in the case of other schools, in the reign of Caracalla — but the study of philosophy was gradually becoming entirely secondary to the study of rhetoric and eloquence.[1]

[1] Eubulus was διάδοχος of the Academic school at Athens between the time when Porphyry went to Rome to study (262) and the time when Plotinus died (270): Porphyr., *Vit. Plotin.*, 15. Eubulus and Theodotus were διάδοχοι in the youth of Longinus (230–240): *ib.*, 20. Athenæus and Musonius, the Stoics, and Ammonius and Ptolemy, the Peripatetics, are mentioned (*ib.*, 20) in the same connection as Eubulus and Theodotus, and, though not called διάδοχοι, they doubtless were so. Alexander of Aphrodisias held an official appointment as teacher of the Peripatetic philosophy in the time of Septimius Severus and Caracalla (Alex. Aphr., *De fato*, 1). Seneca, writing in the first century A. D. (*N. Q.*, vii. 32, 2), says: *tot familiæ philosophorum sine successore deficiunt: Academici et veteres et minores nullum antistitem reliquerunt.* Diogenes Laertius in the third century A. D. (x. 9) says that the succession in about all the schools but the Epicurean had

Soon after the middle of the century, the storm which had been gathering about the state broke. The financial embarrassment of the government, which had been increasing from year to year, was now at its height. Reckless extravagance on the part of the emperors, poor management of the public funds, the increased cost of supporting the army, which, since the attitude of the barbarians had become more threatening, had been greatly enlarged — these, with other, subsidiary, causes, had brought the state almost to the verge of bankruptcy. Owing to the exportation of large quan-

run out, but he is probably quoting from an earlier writer. Diels (*Archiv. f. Gesch. d. Philos.*, 4, pp. 490, 491) refers Diogenes's statement to the jubilation occasioned by the rescript of Hadrian relative to the Epicurean school, made in 121 A. D. (see p. 84, above; also Zeller, *Phil. d. Griech.*, iii. 1, p. 378). The Seneca passage certainly, and probably the Diogenes passage also, dates from a time before the reorganization of the schools under Marcus Aurelius, and most of the schools may well have been languishing at that time. The renewal of life given by Marcus's reorganization is testified to by Galen (xix. p. 50): νυνὶ δὲ ἀφ' οὗ καὶ διαδοχαὶ αἱρέσεών εἰσιν, οὐκ ὀλίγοι κατὰ τήνδε τὴν πρόφασιν ἀναγορεύουσιν ἑαυτοὺς ἀπὸ τῆς αἱρέσεως, ὅθεν ἀνατρέφονται. From this passage, combined with the passage from Porphyry given above, in which *two* διάδοχοι in the Academic school are mentioned, it would appear that the word διάδοχος at this time referred to the regular state appointed and salaried philosophers of the different sects, rather than to 'heads' of the schools in the old pre-Christian sense. It is probable that, when Marcus Aurelius established the philosophical department of the University of Athens, the name διάδοχος was transferred from the 'heads,' or 'successors,' appointed by the schools to the new state-appointed 'heads,' or, if the succession had run out, that the word was again brought into use with this change of meaning. The schools of philosophy, each with two salaried professors, would thus be parallel to the school of sophistry. Only the Academic teaching maintained itself with any vigor up to the advent of Neo-Platonism. *Cf.* Eunap., p. 6.

tities of gold and silver to the provinces, and the conversion of other large quantities into objects of art, the precious metals had become in later years more and more rare.[1] To add to the confusion and distress, the depreciation of the currency, which had been begun by Nero, and had been recklessly continued by succeeding emperors, notably by Caracalla and Elagabalus, had reached the point where the silver coinage was equal to only a fraction of its nominal value, and even gold was quite uncertain in its standard.

With the year 235, when the reign and life of Alexander Severus came to an end, began a long list of lesser emperors. Most of these were mere military commanders, raised to the throne by acclamation of their soldiers, and few of them reigned longer than two or three years. None was able to cope successfully with the difficulties of the time.

In the year 250 the Goths, descending from the river Dniester, crossed the lower Danube and overran the province of Mœsia. This inroad was the first of a constant succession of similar inroads, made by the tribes of the north and lasting through twenty years. In or about 267, a band of the Heruli, who lived to the northwest of the Black Sea, embarking on ships, sailed through the Hellespont, and, ravaging the cities of Asia Minor and the islands of the Ægean, advanced as far as

---

[1] Seeck (*Untergang der antiken Welt*, ii. p. 201) mentions, as a further cause of diminution in the supply of the precious metals, the custom, which had become common in those days, when barbarian inroads, civil wars, and imperial greed rendered the possession of any treasure uncertain, of burying large sums of gold and silver.

the coast of the mainland of Greece. Then they went through the country, plundering and burning, and entered Athens itself. But Dexippus, a distinguished schoolman and historian, and worthy successor of his famous countrymen of old, collecting a determined band of patriots, two thousand strong, lay in wait for the Goths not far from the city, and, swooping down upon them, drove them in flight from the land.

This period was the darkest that Greece had experienced for many years, and it probably marks the point of least prosperity for the University of Athens. Imperial favor had long been wanting to the University, and at this time the imperial salaries, both those of the philosophcal schools and those of the chairs of rhetoric and 'grammar,' seem to have been withdrawn. The former, with the possible exception of those of the Academic school,[1] were perhaps never restored, but the latter, when better times returned, were either renewed or provided for under a different arrangement. The regulations relative to honors and immunities also now fell into abeyance, and the whole system was in a condition of disarrangement. Fewer students, we can hardly doubt, came in those days to Greece, and the number of teachers waned.

But Athens was not the only university town that suffered at the hands of the barbarians at this time. Throughout Thrace, Macedonia, Asia Minor, and the islands of the Ægean, cities were sacked and burned, the countryside was laid waste, temples and shrines were pillaged, women and children were put to the

[1] See the quotation from Procopius, p. 126, n. 2.

sword. Few towns in that section of the world escaped uninjured. Philippopolis, Byzantium, Trapezus, Nicæa, Nicomedia, were either plundered or burned. Even Antioch in Syria suffered from invasions of the Persians. Such conditions as these in fully one-half of the Greek world at this time were not conducive to the pursuit of academical studies.

The period of depression, however, was not of long duration. With the accession of the Emperor Claudius, in 268, a new spirit entered the conduct of public affairs, and this spirit was sustained under the immediately succeeding emperors — Aurelian, Tacitus, Probus, and Carus. In 284 Diocletian came to the throne, and he immediately set about instituting a series of reforms, which, while they changed the character of the government, restored to it something of its former strength and credit. The work of reorganization thus begun by Diocletian was continued and brought to a completion by Constantine the Great, at the beginning of the next century. Under this ruler the Empire entered upon another long period of prosperity and efficiency. Among the matters which engaged the attention of Constantine was the condition of university teaching throughout the Empire. In a series of edicts[1] he confirmed the benefits which had been conferred by the earlier emperors on teachers and physicians, but in the stormy period which had recently passed had been allowed to lapse, and added to these still others. The salaries and privileges of the sophists, 'grammarians,' and physicians were under some system restored, and

[1] See the edicts in *Cod. Th.*, xiii. 3, and *Cod. Jus.*, x. 53.

the privileges were extended to their wives, children, and goods. It was forbidden for any one to injure a sophist, 'grammarian,' or physician, or to bring him into court. No special mention is made of philosophers. It is probable that there were comparatively few philosophers at Athens, or indeed elsewhere in Greek lands, at this time, and the salaries of the different schools, if we except those of the Academic school, seem, as has been said, not to have been restored. The original endowment of the Academic school still remained.

There now began for Athens and for all Greek lands the second and last great period of academical activity — a period when the Greek university received its most complete development and when many of the distinctive features of Greek university life existed in their most pronounced form. The period is marked by such giants of sophistry as Julian (not Julian the Emperor, but Julian the Sophist), Proæresius, who lived and taught in the full exercise of his powers till his ninety-second year, Himerius, Themistius (who, though he called himself a philosopher, had many of the characteristics of a sophist), and Libanius, one of the most famous men of his time, the friend of Christians and pagans, and a successful sophist in Constantinople, Nicomedia, and Antioch, and by others hardly less distinguished — Epiphanius, Diophantus, Tuscianus, Hephæstion, etc. Of some of these we have considerable literary remains, and the lives of most of them are told in the pages of Eunapius, who is the historian of the sophistry of this century, as Philostratus is of that of the second and third centuries. The works of Libanius, apart from their great historical value, abound in interesting details of the life of teachers and students in this period, and other sources give us much additional information.

In several ways, however, the new régime instituted by Constantine was destined to be of disadvantage to Athens. Constantinople, the new capital built by Constantine on the foundations of the old Greek city of Byzantium, was designed to rival Rome in its grandeur and importance. Here was the Court of the emperors of the East, and "hither," says Libanius,[1] "men prominent for their learning thronged from all quarters of the Empire to make their home." Here also was established, possibly at a somewhat later date, a new university under especial imperial favor. All these facts could not but in the end tend to throw into the shade many a smaller and less favored Greek community. The immediate effect on Athens, however, was not great, and for many years she continued in the enjoyment of her newly won prosperity. What, however, contained the germs of more serious consequences, and contributed in largest measure to the fall of the University of Athens, was the establishment at this time of Christianity as the Court religion.

[1] i. 23, 9.

## CHAPTER VII

### THE DECLINE OF UNIVERSITY EDUCATION: THE CONFLICT WITH CHRISTIANITY

IN order to understand the antagonism that existed, or was generally supposed to exist, in the last centuries of paganism, between the new religion and the old education, we need to understand that the old education and culture and the ancient form of devotion and ceremonial were, in most men's minds, inseparable. The links between the two were so many and so strong that the fall of the one meant, in the minds of pagans and Christians alike, the fall of the other. All the literary material which formed the basis of study in the schools was drawn from the ancient life and history of Greece, and all the associations of literature and art were connected with the ancient religion. "There has come back from exile, Emperor" — these are the first words of the formal greeting which Libanius extended to the Emperor Julian when the latter, soon after his accession to the throne, came to take up his head-quarters at Antioch [1] — "there has come back from exile, in company with the practice of holy rites, honor for the study of letters; not alone because letters are, perhaps, not the least part of such practice, but also because you were aroused by no less a thing than letters to reverence

[1] i. 405, 1.

for the gods." And again [1]: "These two things, letters and the practice of holy rites, seem to me to be closely allied and akin to each other."

And yet that the new religion and the old culture were not incompatible is evident, if we needed such evidence, from the fact that many faithful Christians studied at Athens side by side with pagans, under the same pagan teachers. Prominent among these were the two famous churchmen, Basil the Great and Gregory Nazianzene.

[1] iii. 437, 1. This attitude is well brought out in the following letter (42) of Julian, in which he gives his reasons for issuing the edict mentioned below in the text: "Right education I consider to be not the gracefulness that resides in words and on the tongue, but a healthy disposition of an intelligent mind, and true opinions about the good and the bad, the noble and the base. Whoever, therefore, believes one thing and teaches his pupils another, would seem to fall as far short of being educated as he does of being a good man. Now if the variance between the belief and the teaching is in small matters, the result must, it is true, be considered bad, but it is still in a way endurable. But if in the greatest matters a man believes one thing and teaches the opposite of what he believes, how does he differ at all from the huckster — not the good huckster, but the rascally one, who teaches most what he thinks most valueless, cheating and enticing by his praises those to whom he wishes to sell his probably worthless wares? All, therefore, who profess to teach, be the thing they teach what it may, should be of good character, and should not hold opinions at variance with those of the world at large, and especially is this true, I think, of those who instruct young men in letters — making of themselves interpreters of the ancient writings — whether they be rhetors or 'grammarians,' and still more if they be sophists. For these intend, in addition to what else they do, to teach, not language alone, but morals as well, and they say that what they teach is the philosophy of citizenship. . . . Did not Homer and Hesiod and Demosthenes and Herodotus and Thucydides and Isocrates and Lysias look upon the gods as the guides to all instruction? . . . It is unreasonable, it seems to me, for those who interpret the works of these men to dishonor the gods who were honored by them. But I do not, because their conduct is unreasonable, say that they

Both these men held that there was no real antagonism between pagan learning and Christian belief, and Basil, in a special discourse, endeavored to show that the pagan literature was full of examples, precepts, facts of history, and anecdotes, of a character to elevate the mind, furnish it with good and beautiful ideas, and prepare it for Christian teaching.[1] A single sophist, of the sophists that we know of this period, but he one of the greatest of all, Proæresius, is reputed to have been a Christian,[2] but there were others, for an edict of Julian

must change their faith and so keep on with their teaching. I give them the option of not teaching what they do not consider of worth, or, if they wish to teach, of first convincing their pupils in a practical way that neither Homer nor Hesiod nor any one of those whom they interpret and whom they have accused of having been impious and ignorant and in error with regard to the gods was in fact such. . . . Up to the present time there have been many reasons why they should not frequent the temples, and the general fear that has threatened has made it pardonable if one has concealed his inmost belief with regard to the gods. But now that we have received from the gods freedom, it seems to me strange that men should teach what they do not look upon as right. If, then, they believe in the wisdom of those men whom they interpret and of whom they profess to be, as it were, the prophets, let them first imitate their piety toward the gods. If, on the other hand, they feel that those men were in error in regard to the highest truth, let them go into the churches of the Galileans and interpret Matthew and Luke. . . . No young man who wishes to attend a teacher has been deprived of the opportunity to do so. For it would be illogical to bar boys, who do not yet know whither to turn, from the best road, and then drive them by fear and against their will into the course that their fathers took. And yet these, like delirious persons, should be cured even against their will; though we should have consideration for all in the case of such a sickness. For, I believe, we should instruct, and not punish, those who are not in their right mind."

[1] *Cf.* Sandys, *Hist. Clas. Schol.*, i. p. 349; also Monroe, *Hist. of Educ.*, pp. 238–240.

[2] Eunap., p. 92. His Christianity has, however, been doubted (Bernhardy, *Griech. Lit.*, p. 693).

made it illegal for Christians to teach the pagan culture.[1]

Libanius, when he saw the old religious rites no longer observed, or observed only in secret, the temples closed and public sacrifices forbidden, festivals and processions fallen into disuse and oracles unvisited, was in sore distress, and, in the anguish of his heart, he exclaimed bitterly against the Christian religion. In the pages of this author we have an interesting picture of the conflict between Christianity and paganism from the pagan point of view. The religion of the gods, it should be remembered, had existed for centuries by right of prior occupation; it was a part of the old established order of things; and Christianity had, until recently, as being the new-comer, been obliged to sustain the burden of proof. And so Christ seemed to Libanius that one who "in an evil hour burst in upon us like a drunken reveller."[2]

The condition of affairs here indicated reached a climax under the Emperor Constantius (337–361).

Constantius [says Libanius[3]], taking from his father a spark of evil, enlarged the thing into a mighty flame. Constantine, to be sure, stripped the gods of their wealth, but Constantius destroyed their temples, and, wiping out every

---

[1] Eunap., p. 92; Amm. Marc., xxii. 10, 7; xxv. 4, 20. A Christian sophist is mentioned in Lib., i. 526, 9. Of course there were Christian sophists at a later time in the school of Gaza.

[2] i. 408, 15.

[3] Lib., iii. 436, 18. The policy of Constantius in restraint of liberal studies was perhaps less felt at Athens, in Egypt, and in Palestine than in certain other places, such as Constantinople, Nicomedia, and Antioch (Lib., iii. 439, 4). Still, Athens did not escape (Himer., *or.*, iv. 3, 8, 9; xiii. 2; xiv. 6, 33; xxi. 1, 2).

sacred law, put himself in the hands of those of whom we need not be reminded; and he extended the dishonor from religion to letters. . . . Philosophers and sophists and others whose lives were dedicated to Homer and the Muses he never on any occasion invited to the palace; he never saw one of them; he never praised one of them; he never spoke to them, or heard them speak; those whom he admired and kept about himself and made his advisers and teachers were barbarous men, certain pernicious eunuchs. He renounced his imperial duties in their favor, and though the acts went under his name, and the show of dress was his, the real power was theirs. They persecuted the study of letters in every way, humbling those who had any share in it and exhorting one another to see that no man of wisdom secretly worked his way into the friendship of the emperor. They introduced the pale-faced throng (*i. e.*, Christians), the haters of the gods, the worshippers of tombs, whose proudest achievement it is to disparage Helios and Zeus and the fellow-rulers of Zeus. They brought back into line the secretaries, who were no better than their own slaves either in head or in heart. . . . The change was swift. The butcher's son, the fuller's son, the gutter-snipe, he who had thought it luxury to be free from want, suddenly appeared in grand style on a horse of grand appearance, with brow raised aloft, and attended by a throng of followers — the possessor of a large house, much land, flatterers, banquets, and gold! If a rhetor did happen, by their gift, to hold some office, he had obtained it as the price of flattery. It would have been better for such a one, had he been wise enough to see it, to become even more abject than he was, than to be raised up through their means. The abominable and drunken eunuchs carried their outrage and insolence so far that they actually placed the secretaries in the seats of the provincial viceroys. And the excellent Constantius rejoiced at all this, as though he had been fortunate enough to find the one means that would preserve the state!

Education being in disgrace at the Court, students no longer turned to the study of letters, and the professors' classes fell off in numbers.

Well might Libanius, under the circumstances, look upon the accession of Julian, who, he says,[1] "in a prince's station, loved wisdom more than any philosopher," as the dawn of a new life, for letters as well as for religion, and greet it with the wild and jubilant exultation of one beside himself for joy: "Then did I laugh," he says,[2] "and leap, and make and deliver speeches in my joy. Altars took again their wonted blood, smoke rolled heavenward the savor of the sacrifice, gods were honored with festivals — festivals which few, old men they, remember ever to have seen — divination recovered its license, and rhetoric its respect; Roman men took heart, and barbarians were defeated or threatened with defeat."

But the joy of those who, like Libanius, looked forward to a complete restoration of the old order of things under the new emperor, was short-lived. On the 26th of June, 363, less than three years after he had been proclaimed emperor by his soldiers, Julian was killed by a Persian arrow while conducting a campaign in the East. Libanius's grief at this event was not less than his joy at the accession of Julian. "At first," he says,[3] "I looked to the sword, feeling that any death, however harsh, would be less painful than life." And then this unavailing lament to the gods:[4] "Oh! ye gods and divinities, why did ye not fulfil the hopes we had placed

[1] i. 81, 6.   [2] i. 81, 9.   [3] i. 91, 13.
[4] i. 616, 13; *cf.* 507 *ff.*

## DECLINE OF UNIVERSITY EDUCATION 115

in you? . . . Did he not raise up your altars? Did he not build for you temples? Did he not reverence magnificently gods and heroes, the air, heaven, earth, and sea, the springs and rivers? Did he not make war upon those who had made war upon you? Was he not more temperate than Hippolytus, more just than Radamanthus, more sagacious than Themistocles, braver than Brasidas? . . . And we fondly hoped that all the Persian land would become a part of the Roman domain, and would obey our laws, . . . and that Greek sophists in Susa would mould the Persian youth into orators."

Only a short time before his death, Julian had sent envoys to Delphi to restore the oracle in that place, and these had returned with the prophetic response,

εἴπατε τῷ βασιλῆι, χάμαι πέσε δαίδαλος αὐλά.
οὐκέτι Φοῖβος ἔχει καλύβαν, οὐ μάντιδα δάφνην,
οὐ παγὰν λαλεοῦσαν· ἀπέσβετο καὶ λάλον ὕδωρ,

which has been recently translated,[1]

"Tell ye the king: to the ground hath fallen the glorious dwelling;
Now no longer hath Phœbus a cell, or a laurel prophetic;
Hushed is the voiceful spring, and quenched the oracular fountain."

After the death of Julian, the study of rhetoric began rapidly to decline.[2] At this time the most important Greek university centres were Athens, Constantinople, Nicomedia, Antioch, Berytus, and Alexandria, but prob-

[1] By Sandys, *Hist. Clas. Schol.*, i. p. 347. The original is in Cedrenus, *Hist. comp.*, i. 304, p. 532. [2] Lib., iii. 440, 15 *ff*.

ably no city of any size was without its active university life. Of the places named, Athens, Antioch, and, in a lesser degree, Nicomedia, were famous for their sophistry, Constantinople and Berytus were celebrated for their schools of law, while philosophy found a home at Constantinople and Alexandria. At Alexandria there was also much activity in the line of medicine. The regulation of the universities continued from time to time to engage the attention of the different emperors, but Constantinople, under the special favor of the Court, grew and increased at the expense of the other centres.[1]

[1] Sophists swarmed on land and sea (Themis., 341 d). Themistius received his oratorical training in a remote city of the East, near the Phasis river (*ib.*, 332 d). There were cleverer sophists at Constantinople than elsewhere, says Themistius (339 d; *cf.* 346 c). There was a chair of sophistry at Thessalonica in the time of Himerius (Himer., *or.*, v. 9). Many places are mentioned by Libanius as being seats of sophistry (*e. g.*, Ancyra, *ep.*, 358, 1079, 1181; Cyzicus, *ep.*, 441; Tarsus, *ep.*, 343; Chalcis in Syria, iii. 158, 1 *ff.*; Tyre, *ep.*, 930, etc.; Pamphylia, *ep.*, 781, etc.; Galatia, *ep.*, 839; Palestine, *ep.*, 875, etc.; Cappadocia, *ep.*, 1211). Syria was a hot-bed of sophistry (*ib.*, *ep.*, 1033). See also Schemmel, *Neue Jahrb.*, 22, p. 150. Philosophical studies seem to have increased somewhat in the second half of the century, perhaps at the expense of sophistry. Jovian endeavored to bring the subject back into favor (Themis., 63 c; Eunap., p. 58). This Constantius had also claimed to do (Themis., 20 d). Alexandria is lauded as a seat of philosophical studies (Lib., ii. 397, 5); Constantinople also (Themis., 20 d; Himer., *or.*, vii. 13). According to Themistius, there were large schools of philosophy in Greece and Ionia, as well as at Constantinople, in the time of Theodosius (294 b). But, on the other hand, philosophy did not now court the market-place and the light of day, as it had done in the time of Socrates (*ib.*, 341 d), while Themistius says that it was in bad repute (246 c), and also that it had thinned out and died away (341 d). For medicine, see Kuhn, *Verf. d. röm. Reichs*, i. pp. 88 *ff.*; Bozzoni, *I Medici ed il Diritto Romano;* Pohl, *De græc. med. pub.* See also pp. 142 *ff.*

## DECLINE OF UNIVERSITY EDUCATION 117

In the last half of the century, the persecution of the old faith became more and more severe. A series of edicts was put forth, forbidding the practice of all pagan rites, ordering the closing of the temples, and finally confiscating the property of the gods. No place was left for the old faith to rest in. Bands of black-robed votaries went through the land seizing and appropriating to their own use and that of their orders the wealth of the pagan temples.

But now this black-robed throng [says Libanius[1]], who, though they try to conceal the fact by an artificial pallor, eat more gluttonously than elephants and by their frequent draughts tire out the patience of the congregation, which accompanies each potation with a chant — these black-robed votaries, Emperor, though the law forbids such practices, hurry to the temples, carrying beams and stones and iron bars; while some, not having these, are ready even with their hands and feet. Then, without the slightest compunction or restraint, they rip off roofs, tear down walls, drag down images, and overthrow altars; and the priests must either say nothing or lose their lives. . . . So they go through the land like mountain torrents, laying waste the country under pretext of attacking the temples. . . . They say that they are warring against the temples, but their warfare is really a means of private gain, both for those who attack the temples and for those who plunder the possessions of the poor inhabitants, carrying off their beasts and the contents of their storehouses. . . . Some even go farther than this, and appropriate the land, saying that So-and-So's land is consecrated ground; and many a landholder has been deprived of his estate under a false charge. Those who do these acts live in luxury and grow fat on the profit of other men's misfortunes — they

[1] ii. 164, 4; cf. Eunap., pp. 44 f.

who reverence their god, as they say, by starving their bodies! If those who have been robbed of their goods go to the city "pastor"—for so they call some worthless fellow — and complain, telling him of the injustice they have suffered, the "pastor" praises the wrong-doers, and drives the suppliants from his presence, giving them to understand that they are fortunate not to have suffered even worse. And yet, Emperor, these are of your Empire no less than the others, and are as much more valuable than the others as those who work are more valuable than those who do not; for these are the workers and the others are the drones. If these drones hear of an estate that contains anything that can be plundered, straightway that estate is engaged in unholy practices and is committing an unpardonable sin; a campaign must be instituted against it, and the inspectors immediately appear. "Campaign" is the name they give to this robbery, if robbery be not too weak a word to use — for robbers try to escape observation and deny their deeds; and, if you call them robbers, you insult them; but these men are proud of their actions and strive to outdo one another, giving instruction in the art to those who are unacquainted with it and proclaiming themselves deserving of honor.

And then, with less bitterness:[1]

It is necessary, in matters of belief, to use persuasion, not force. For if one, being unable to accomplish one's purpose by the former, makes use of the latter, nothing is gained, though something seems to be. It is even said to be contrary to the Christian commandment to use force; while persuasion is therein recommended. Why, then, do you display such spite against the pagan temples? . . . Clearly, in so doing, you transgress your own laws.

[1] ii. 178, 2; *cf.* i. 562, 21. The same idea is expressed by Themistius (68 a, b, 155 d, 156 c), and by Julian (424 B.) Libanius pleads for the preservation of the pagan temples as works of art (ii. 189, 11 *ff.*).

More and more also, as the century wore on, it became evident that, in competition with other studies, Greek letters and oratory were failing to hold their own. Under the blighting policy of the imperial Court at Constantinople, municipal freedom, which in earlier times had been the mainstay of a healthy national life, was greatly retrenched, and there was no longer room for the exercise of those professions for which sophistry had formed the preparation. Owing to the increased burdensomeness of taxation, which fell in the first instance on the members of the municipal councils, these bodies constantly tended to decrease in size. Lack of public spirit took the place of former civic pride.[1] Again and again Libanius complains that students are going to Berytus and Rome to study law and Latin, and that, while sophistry has ceased to lead to anything profitable, the acquisition of culture for its own sake is a thing no longer desired or thought worth the striving for. There is for us almost a tragic interest in beholding this aged sophist, whose thoughts and interests all lay in the past of his race, and whose early days had coincided with the palmiest days of sophistry, compelled to look upon the decay of his religion and the degradation of his favorite

[1] Nowhere is the connection of the local councils and rhetoric more definitely set forth than in the oration in which Libanius urges the Emperor Theodosius to restore the former size and influence of the councils. "This (*i. e.*, rhetoric)," he says (ii. 587, 15), "has fallen into decay and been ruined along with the councils, just as, when the councils throve, rhetoric was in honor and had many lovers. . . . With the understanding, then, that, in aiding the councils, you will also aid the books which are now cast aside, . . . bring it about that both recover their vigor — council-houses and schools." See p. 78, n. 1.

studies. "Another misfortune," he says in one place,[1] "a misfortune which shook the art to its foundation, was involved in the stampede from the Greek tongue and the migration to Italy of those who sought to converse in the Latin language. The Latin language, it was said, had become of more value than the Greek: with the one were power and riches, with the other was nothing but the language itself. I was not moved by the advice of those who urged me to give up teaching. Though I well knew to what a pass matters had come, I did not think it right to desert my post. I should not have deserted my mother had she fallen into misfortune, and Greek letters claimed my respect no less than my mother." And again[2]: "More than ever now has Greek given place to Latin, so that I even fear that Greek will be banished altogether, through the agency of the law. Law and proclamation, however, have not brought about this thing, but the honor and power that become the portion of those who learn the Latin language. But the gods, who have given Greek letters, will attend to their victory, and will see that they regain the influence which once was theirs." Latin was still, at this time, the language of the Court at Constantinople, and law had become the stepping-stone to many civil offices. "Letters formerly drew young men from every quarter," says Libanius again,[3] "but now they are valued not at

[1] i. 133, 14.     [2] i. 142, 21.
[3] i. 185, 17. Formerly the orator did not need to study law further than he studied it in his sophistical course; for the rest he hired the services of one versed in the legal books (*cf.* Mitteis, *Reichsrecht u. Volksrecht*, pp. 189 *ff.*). The case was different as early as 364 (Lib., *ep.*, 1116, 1123, 1160), but even then the prospective law student often took a course in sophistry (Lib., *ep.*,

## DECLINE OF UNIVERSITY EDUCATION 121

all. They are, it would seem, like rocks, whereon it is a madman that would cast his seed. . . . The harvest is reaped from other soil, from the Latin tongue, O Mistress Athene, and from the law. In former days, the expert in law stood in court, with his roll in hand, looking at the speaker and waiting for the order to read; now even secretaries fill the very highest offices." Naturally, Libanius had no very great affection for the study of the law; "the law," he says in one place,[1] "a study for those who are slow of intellect." Another branch which had many votaries in these later years was short-hand-writing.[2]

Libanius was himself the last of the great sophists, and when he was asked on his death-bed to whom he would wish to bequeath his school, he replied, it is said, to John (meaning John Chrysostom, the great Christian orator), if the Christians had not won him.[3] Libanius died in 394 or 395, at the age of eighty or eighty-one, and shortly after his death the tide of barbarian invasion rolled once more toward the shores of Greece. All through the last half of the fourth century the muttering thunder of the barbarian arms had been heard in the northern provinces of the Empire still more threateningly than in the previous century, and now Alaric, at the head of his West Gothic hordes, swept down, through the pass of Thermopylæ, and overran the country. Athens alone, of the cities of Greece, such is the tradition, was

---

117, 1124; Procop., *ep.*, 41, 117, 151, 153; *cf.* Lib., i. 214, 2; iii. 441, 23 *ff.*; Theodoret, *ep.*, 10). So students went from Libanius's school to a school of medicine (Lib., *ep.*, 1178). We thus have the inception of the graduate professional school (see p. 197).

[1] i. 214, 2.  [2] Lib., iii. 440, 7.
[3] Sozom., *H. E.*, viii. 2; Cedrenus, i. p. 574.

providentially saved. The aged Priscus, philosopher in the University of Athens, died at this time, from grief (it is intimated) at the sad lot of his fatherland; and many other distinguished men either succumbed to the same fate or died a voluntary death; while not a few fell at the hands of the Goths.[1] At about the same time, in 395, namely, Theodosius the Great died, and the Empire was divided between his two sons, Arcadius taking the East and Honorius the West.

At the beginning of the next century we seem already in the midst of a new life. There were still sophists and other teachers of language at Athens, but their importance was not what it had once been. The old glitter had gone from the study of sophistry. Many works of art had been removed by orders of the emperors, to decorate the new city by the Bosporus, and Athens, apparently, was in danger of becoming a quiet rural village.[2] Let us hear the judgment of Synesius, the Neo-Platonist, and (later) Christian bishop, of Cyrene, on the Athens of this period: "I shall not only gain relief from my present trouble by this voyage," he writes to his brother before going to Athens,[3] "but I shall also free myself from the necessity of prostrating myself in the future, out of respect for their learning, before those who

---

[1] Eunap., p. 67.

[2] Its decline in the fourth century is indicated by Eunapius, who says that Libanius chose Constantinople rather than Athens wherein to settle, because he did not wish to bury himself in a small city and decline with the city's decline (p. 97). Of Emesa, formerly the most thriving town of Phœnicia and a famous seat of learning, Libanius says, in the year 388, that it has been reduced to a few houses, which are themselves on the way to decay (*ep.*, 766). [3] *Ep.*, 54.

come from that city. These people differ in no way from us other mortals, at least as far as their understanding of Aristotle and Plato goes. But they walk among us like demi-gods among demi-asses (*i. e.*, mules), because they have seen the Academy and the Lyceum, and the fresco-painted Hall, wherein Zeno taught — which is no longer fresco-painted, for the Governor has stripped the place of its paintings." After he has seen Athens, he writes again to his brother thus[1]: "Cursed be the ship-captain that brought me to this spot. There is nothing in the Athens of to-day of any note, except the famous names of places. Just as, when a beast has been sacrificed, only the skin remains as a reminder of the living thing that was within, so here, now that philosophy has taken its departure from this spot, there is nothing left to do but to roam about and gaze in wonder at the Academy, and the Lyceum, and, forsooth! the Painted Stoa, which gave its name to the philosophy of Chrysippus, but is now no longer painted, since the Governor has carried off the pictures in which the Thasian Polygnotus stored his art. In our days it is Egypt which nourishes the seeds which she has received from Hypatia. Athens, once the home of wise men, is now famous only for her beehive-keepers. So it is with the pair of learned Plutarch-scholars, who fill their halls with students, not by the reputation of their lectures, but by the wine-jars of Hymettus."

We recognize in these outbursts the jealousy of an adherent of the rival school of Alexandria,[2] but we also

[1] *Ep.*, 136.
[2] See Zumpt., *Ueber den Bestand d. phil. Schul.*, p. 79.

see that Athens, "holy Athens," as Synesius himself calls it,[1] was still, even in those days, the sacred hearth of learning, whose place no other city could usurp.

An important seat of sophistry toward the end of the fifth century was Gaza, in Palestine, where taught the two sophists Procopius and Choricius, but other cities in the neighborhood enjoyed their sophistical schools, as Tyre, Cæsarea, and even Alexandria. Alexandria had suffered in the third century (272), when the Emperor Aurelian laid waste much of the royal quarter of the city, and again late in the fourth century (391), when, under Theodosius, the temple of Serapis, where was stored the smaller of the two libraries which the city originally possessed, was destroyed; but men of learning never ceased to flock thither, and in the fifth century she was prominent, not only by reason of her philosophical school, but also through her studies in mathematics and astronomy. Antioch and Nicomedia had seen their best days in the fourth century, but at Antioch at least there was still in the fifth century a school of sophistry. Cæsarea in Cappadocia was in the fifth century the seat of 'grammatical' and rhetorical studies, while at Ancyra, in Galatia, there were schools of rhetoric and philosophy. Berytus was famous for its school of law; and, lastly, the University of Constantinople, put on a new basis in 425 by Theodosius II, offered courses in rhetoric and 'grammar' (in two languages, Greek and Latin), in law, and in philosophy.[2]

[1] *Ep.*, 54.
[2] For Gaza, see Croiset, *Hist. lit. grec.*, v. 984, and the works of Procopius and Choricius. For Antioch, Tyre, and Cæsarea in Palestine, see Chor., p. 6. For Ancyra, see Mommsen, *The*

## DECLINE OF UNIVERSITY EDUCATION 125

At this time, when the study of rhetoric was falling into disfavor and was becoming more and more a matter of technical detail, Neo-Platonism at Athens reached its stage of greatest prosperity. This doctrine, which pretended to be simply a development of the ideas contained in the writings of Plato, but really contained elements from the doctrines of many schools, had started at Alexandria toward the beginning of the third century. The immediate predecessor of the real line of Neo-Platonists was Ammonius Saccas, and under his pupil, Plotinus, and Plotinus's pupil, Porphyry, the Neo-Platonic philosophy was established, in the last half of the third century, at Rome. At the beginning of the fourth century it was transferred by Iamblichus to Syria, where it assumed more and more the character of a religion, tinged with Eastern mysticism. The pupils of Iamblichus were numerous, and they spread the doctrine into many parts of the Greek world. It gained a footing at Athens about the middle of the fourth century, and rose to great favor in the next century, under Plutarch, Syrianus, and Proclus. In the meantime, another line of professors was expounding the doctrine in the Alexandrian school, prominent among whom were Theon and his daughter, the beautiful and accomplished Hypatia, she who was afterward killed by an infuriated mob of Alexandrian Christians.

Neo-Platonism at this time represented all the philosophy of the age, and it was a religion as well as a philosophy. Those who were opposed to Christianity and

*Provinces of the Roman Empire* (trans.), i. p. 342, and Lib., *ep.*, 358, 1079, 1181. See also pp. 142 *ff*.

were attached to the old culture and education and the old traditions arrayed themselves in general on the side of this faith. The Neo-Platonic school at Athens passed for the lineal descendant and legitimate successor of the old Academy of Plato, and enjoyed the endowment of the Academy.[1] But, as time went on, it became more and more apparent that the continuation of this last stronghold of the pagan faith in an otherwise Christianized world was a thing that the Christian emperors could not long endure. Edict after edict was put forth, directed against the old religion, and making it harder and harder for the faithful few who remained to continue in its practice. The death-blow finally came in a rescript of Justinian of the year 529, forbidding the teaching of all philosophy and the expounding of the law at Athens; the study of jurisprudence in the East was hereafter to be confined to Constantinople and Berytus. All grants of public funds made by previous emperors in the interests of learning were withdrawn, and the endowment of the philosophical school at Athens was confiscated.[2]

[1] For the endowment and income of the Academy in the fifth century A. D., see the quotation from Damascius's Life of Isidor in Suidas, s. v. *Plato*. The same is given in slightly different form in Photius, *Bibl.*, cod. 242, p. 346 a.

[2] The closing of the schools at Athens is mentioned by Malalas and Procopius. The story has given rise to some discussion, and I cannot do better than quote here Professor Bury's note to Gibbon's *History*, vol. iv, ch. xl, p. 266: "The suppression of the schools by Justinian has been unsuccessfully called in question by Paparrigopulos and Gregorovius. . . . The authority of Malalas is good for the reign of Justinian. . . . His words are: (Justinian) θεσπίσας πρόσταξιν ἔπεμψεν ἐν ᾿Αθήναις κελεύσας μηδένα διδάσκειν φιλοσοφίαν μήτε νόμιμα ἐξηγεῖσθαι κ.τ.λ. (p. 449, ed. Bonn). Justinian had already taken stringent measures against pagans. . . . It is not difficult to guess what happened. The edicts against

Seven philosophers, the last remnant of the Athenian University, refusing to conform to the new order of things, left Greece a few years later and took up their residence in a foreign land, Persia, but, finding their surroundings there uncongenial, they secured from the Roman Emperor, through the intercession of the Persian King, permission to return to their native country and to remain in undisturbed possession of their ancient faith. Let us hear the words of the historian Agathias on this last event connected with the University of Athens [1]:

Damascius the Syrian, Simplicius the Cilician, Eulamius the Phrygian, Priscian the Lydian, Hermeias and Diogenes of Phœnicia, and Isidor of Gaza, the flower . . . of the philosophers of our age, being dissatisfied with the new

paganism, strictly interpreted, involved the cessation of Neoplatonic propagandism at Athens. The schools went on as before, and in a month or two the proconsul of Achaia would communicate with the Emperor on the subject and ask his pleasure. The πρόσταξις mentioned by Malalas was the rescript to the proconsul. At the same time the closing of the schools was ensured by withdrawing the revenue, as we may infer from Procopius, Anecd. c. 26, ἀλλὰ καὶ τοὺς ἰατρούς τε καὶ διδασκάλους τῶν ἐλευθερίων τῶν ἀναγκαίων στερεῖσθαι πεποίηκε. τάς τε γὰρ σιτήσεις ἃς οἱ πρότερον βεβασιλευκότες ἐκ τοῦ δημοσίου χορηγεῖσθαι τούτοις δὴ τοῖς ἐπιτηδεύμασιν ἔταξαν, ταύτας δὴ οὗτος ἀφείλετο πάσας. It should be observed that the teaching of law was expressly forbidden. The study of jurisprudence was to be limited to the schools of Constantinople and Berytus. The statement of Malalas that Justinian sent his Code, A. D. 529, to Athens and Berytus, is remarkable, and has been used, by Gregorovius to throw doubt on the other statement of Malalas, by Hertzberg to support it. We may grant Gregorovius that there was no solemn formal abolition of the schools, but there is no reason to question that they were directly and suddenly suppressed through a rescript to the proconsul. . . ." For the course of study pursued in the Neo-Platonic school, see Schemmel, *Neue Jahrb.*, 22, pp. 505–513. Grammar and rhetoric, Schemmel holds, were in some measure still taught at Athens (p. 513).

[1] ii. 30.

faith which had spread through the world, thought that the kingdom of Persia would be a far better place to live in. For they believed, with the majority of their countrymen, that the ruling power in Persia was most just and such as Plato would have had, a union of philosophy and kingly rule, while the people, they thought, were in the highest degree temperate and orderly. . . . Taking these popular reports to be true and encouraged by them, and being, further, owing to their refusal to conform to the established order at home, prevented from living in safety in Greece, they straightway wandered forth, and settled in a strange and foreign land, there to live for the rest of their days. At first, finding those in power overbearing and beyond measure arrogant, they abominated them and called them all manner of names. And after that they saw that house-breakers and thieves existed in great numbers, some of whom were caught, while others escaped; and every kind of injustice was done. . . . For all these reasons the philosophers were distressed, and grieved that they had left their homes. Then, when they conversed with the king, and found to their disappointment that, while he made some pretence to a liking for philosophy, he knew nothing at all of the deeper learning, and was firmly wedded to other beliefs than their own, . . . they straightway departed, and, though Chosroes admired them and would have had them remain, they continued, thinking it better to step foot once more in Roman dominions and then, if need be, die, than to remain in Persia and be the recipients of all manner of gifts. . . . This good, however, they gained from their sojourn: . . . they were able from that day forth to live according to their pleasure. For, the Romans and the Persians being at the time on the point of concluding a treaty, Chosroes made it one of the terms of the treaty, that the philosophers should be allowed to return to their homes and live for the rest of their days in peace, without being obliged to profess a faith which they did not believe or change their ancestral religion.

The seven philosophers, on their return, settled in Alexandria, but the spirit of Hellenism was dead in the world at large, and the University of Athens did not again in ancient times open its doors.

## CHAPTER VIII

### THE PROFESSORS: THEIR APPOINTMENT AND NUMBER

THIS Athens — the Athens of Hadrian and Antoninus Pius and Marcus Aurelius, the Athens of Herodes Atticus and the other great sophists and philosophers who made the fame and established the traditions of the University in the second century A. D.— what was it like? what was its appearance and what its life? Brilliant, indeed, in outer aspect must it have been, for, besides the great number of works of art which had been preserved from earlier times, there were now the many magnificent buildings erected, or in process of erection, through the generosity of Hadrian and the other emperors and Herodes Atticus. All Greece was a museum of beautiful works, and Athens, according to the orator, the "eye of Greece."[1]

With the establishment of the Roman supremacy throughout the Mediterranean lands, the importance of Greece, politically and commercially, had decreased. Landed property had tended to fall more and more into the hands of large proprietors, and the rural population

---

[1] τοῦ τῆς Ἑλλάδος ὀφθαλμοῦ, Lib., i. 531, 9. *Cf. ib., ep.*, 866: τὸν ἀστέρα δὲ τὸν Ἑλλάδος τὴν Ἀθηναίων πόλιν· Cic., *Pro leg. Man.*, 5 (of Corinth): *totius Græciæ lumen;* Hegesias in Photius, *Bibl.*, cod. 250, p. 446 b.

had, as a consequence, flocked to the towns. Many foreigners also came to make their home at Athens. Still, the city, notwithstanding this increased population, was never, even in a slight degree, another Rome. It was distinctly a university town, and its teachers and students were among its most important assets. "Empty Athens" (*vacuas . . . Athenas*), as we have noted, Horace had said in a previous century, contrasting the rural quiet of this city with the noise and bustle of Rome, and probably the epithet well characterized that partial silence, so charming a feature of some European cities of to-day, which forms the atmosphere of a town, once bustling and politically important, but now, in the ripeness of its age, resting in the memories of its past and its consciousness of present wisdom and dignity. Let us hear Lucian, following the description given by the philosopher Nigrinus, discourse on the Athens of his day and the ways of her people:[1]

Nigrinus began by praising Greece and the men at Athens, saying that these are bred from their youth to be friends of philosophy and poverty, and that they look upon no man with favor, either native or foreigner, who tries to introduce among them ways of luxury and wantonness. If any one comes among them who is thus disposed, they try quietly to change his ways, and, working upon him by degrees, mould him to a purer manner of life. He cited the case of a man — one of the very wealthy — who, coming to Athens with a large retinue of followers, made a disgusting display of fine clothes and gold, and thought to fill the whole town with envy and amazement. Everybody looked upon the poor wretch as one in misfortune, and they took

[1] *Nigr.*, 12–14.

him in hand to train him — not harshly, or directly dissuading him, for the city was free and he could live as he pleased. But when he appeared in the gymnasia or the baths and made himself obnoxious by jostling with his attendants, or crowding into a corner, those whom he met, some one would say in an undertone, pretending not to be observed and as though not directing his speech at him, "He's afraid of being slain while taking his bath. Strange! for there's peace in the bath-house. He has no need of an army here." And he, hearing what was the truth, would take the lesson to heart. His Dolly Varden dress and his long purple robes they caused him to drop, by ridiculing, with much wit, their gay colors. "Spring's come," they would say, or "Where'd that peacock come from?" or "Perhaps they are his mother's," or something of that sort. They ridiculed other things about him in the same way — the number of his rings, his carefully arranged hair, the extravagance of his life — so that little by little he was trained to a more sober way of living. . . . Such praise Nigrinus gave to the people, and he also spoke in admiration of the free and democratic spirit which reigned among them, and of the quiet and restful life that was found at Athens. He showed to me how thoroughly this life is in accord with the teachings of philosophy, and how it is able to guard a pure and upright spirit in the breast, being, for the man of serious principles, who has been brought up to despise riches and lives in accordance with nature, the very best life.

We breathe in these words the air of intellectual freedom and academic peace, and that such were characteristics of the Athens of those days, is clear not alone from this passage. Proclus of Naucratis, we are told, left his home and went to live at Athens, "because he enjoyed the quiet that was there."[1] Aulus Gellius is

[1] Philos., 603.

fond, on occasion, of dwelling on the remembrances of his happy student days at Athens. Sometimes, he tells us,[1] in the long, hot days of summer, when the schools were closed and the sophist ceased to drone, Herodes Atticus would invite a party of friends, mostly students, to his suburban villa, Cephisia, and there, amid pleasant shades and murmuring streams and walks that were cool and refreshing, entertain them with a banquet and social or learned discourse. Again, it is the philosopher Taurus, who sits at his door conversing with his students after lecture,[2] or goes to visit them when he hears that they are sick,[3] or invites them to a modest repast at his house.[4]

What a feature of the times seem these banquets, where learned discourse mingled with good cheer! A famous one, and doubtless the prototype of many, was that described by Plutarch in the Ninth Symposiac. The occasion was the festival of the Muses at Athens. Ammonius, the distinguished philosopher, who, as supreme magistrate of the city, had general supervision of the schools, held an examination of those students who were studying 'grammar,' geometry, rhetoric, and music, in the gymnasium called the *Diogeneion*. Then he invited the most famous professors of the city to a banquet. Here met many of the old student friends of Plutarch, and here the wit outrivalled the viands.

In this Athens, brilliant in outward appearance, but quiet and rural in its atmosphere, we have to imagine, as the most important feature, that which gave life and

[1] i. 2.   [2] ii. 2.   [3] xii. 5.
[4] vii. 13; xvii. 8, 20; *cf.* iii. 19.

color to the rest, the University. The disputes between members of the different schools of philosophy, the jealous bickerings of sophists and philosophers, the rivalry and competition that ensued, when it became known that a vacancy had occurred in one of the much-coveted chairs, the grand displays of eloquence, to which the whole town flocked, the appearance in public of some famous sophist, clad in a gay and jewelled robe, or driving, like Adrian,[1] to his lectures in a chariot with silver trappings, and returning, the centre of a throng of young men gathered from all quarters of the Greek world, and, finally, the various companies of students, betraying by their faces and their dress their different nationalities — all these features gave a most distinctive character to the town.

We saw, in an earlier chapter,[2] that when Marcus Aurelius, by granting to the professors of philosophy and sophistry at Athens fixed salaries, gave to the University an official standing, he assigned to the honored sophist, Herodes Atticus, the duty of making the appointments to the philosophical chairs, while he reserved to himself the privilege of filling the chair of sophistry.[3] This arrangement, so far as concerns the sophistical chair, continued up to the time when the whole mechan-

[1] Philos., 587.  
[2] P. 93.  
[3] That is, the imperial chair. The appointment to the municipal chair (if municipal chair it was) would probably be made by the βουλή. *Cf.* the case of Nicostratus at Rhodes (*C. I. G.*, xii. 1, No. 83), and the case of Soterus at Ephesus (Kaibel, *Ep. Gr.*, No. 877 a). 'Grammarians' were also appointed by the council, and both 'grammarians' and sophists could be deposed if they did not perform their duties satisfactorily (*Cod. Jus.*, x. 53, 2, edict of Gordian).

ism of the University was thrown into disorder by the confusion occasioned by the inroads of the barbarians and the internal distress of the Empire, in the third quarter of the third century.[1]

With the philosophical chairs, however, the case was different. Herodes Atticus died about 179, hardly more than three years, if so long as that, after he had been put in charge of the philosophical department of the University. After his death, the duty of examining the candidates and making the appointments in this department was assigned to a 'board of electors,' the constitution of which is not quite certain. The members of this board are called by Lucian "the best, the oldest, and the wisest of those in the city," but whether they were members of the philosophical schools, or simply representative citizens, or whether they formed a permanent board or were chosen for the occasion, is not made clear.[2] The rivalry of the different candidates, on the day when an examination, preliminary to the filling of a vacancy, was to be held, was doubtless intense, and we may trust Lucian to make the most of

[1] See Philos., 591, 593, 622, 623.
[2] *Eunuch.*, 2: οἱ ἄριστοι καὶ πρεσβύτατοι καὶ σοφώτατοι τῶν ἐν τῇ πόλει· 3: ψήφῳ τῶν ἀρίστων. They seem to be the same body as the *probatissimi* in *Cod. Th.*, xiii. 3, 7 (*Cod. Jus.*, x. 53, 8): *exceptis his, qui a probatissimis approbati ab hac debent colluvione secerni.* Zumpt (*Ueber den Bestand d. phil. Schul.*, p. 52) conjectures that they were members of the βουλή, or Areopagus, but in *Cod. Th.*, xiii. 3, 5 (*Cod. Jus.*, x. 53, 7): *iubeo, quisquis docere vult, . . . iudicio ordinis probatus decretum curialium mereatur, optimorum conspirante consensu*, they are distinct from the local council. *Cf.* Diogenes's indictment of Lucian in Luc., *Pisc.*, 26: ὁ δὲ τοὺς ἀρίστους συγκαλῶν, . . . μεγάλῃ τῇ φωνῇ διαγορεύει κακῶς Πλάτωνα κ.τ.λ.; also Lib., i. 66, 1; Luc., *De domo*, 3; *ib.*, *Dial. mort.*, 9, 2 and 4.

the humor of such an occasion. He describes to us in one of his pieces[1] an amusing scene of this sort. A vacancy has occurred in the Peripatetic school, one of the two professors having died, and several candidates present themselves in competition for the coveted place. The judges are, as has been said, "the best, the oldest, and the wisest of those in the city, men before whom one would be ashamed even to say anything out of order, much more to act in the disgraceful way in which these men acted." Two of the candidates are superior to the rest and make the decision in the end doubtful. Both are thoroughly familiar with the tenets of the school, both are orthodox Aristotelians in their belief, and both prove themselves proficient in the art of discussing. Finally, when each has shown himself in these respects the equal of the other, they turn to personalities, and carry things so far that the judges, unable to decide between them, refer the matter in the end to the emperor at Rome.

We see from this piece what the qualifications required of a candidate for a chair of philosophy at this time were — familiarity with the tenets of his sect, orthodoxy in his philosophical belief, and, apparently, some facility in the use of language.[2] The 'board of

---

[1] The *Eunuchus*.

[2] *Eunuch.*, 4: τὰ μὲν οὖν τῶν λόγων (the tenets of the sect) προηγώνιστο αὐτοῖς καὶ τὴν ἐμπειρίαν ἑκάτερος τῶν δογμάτων ἐπεδέδεικτο καὶ ὅτι τοῦ 'Αριστοτέλους καὶ τῶν ἐκείνῳ δοκούντων εἴχετο. Some facility in the use of language seems to be implied in 9: τοῦ δὲ οὐ σωματικὴν λέγοντος εἶναι τὴν κρίσιν, ἀλλ' ἀλκὴν ψυχῆς καὶ τῆς γνώμης ἐξέτασιν δεῖν γίγνεσθαι καὶ τῆς τῶν δογμάτων ἐπιστήμης, and in 13: εὐξαίμην ἂν οὐ τὴν γνώμην οὐδὲ τὴν γλῶτταν (ἑτοίμην) . . . ἐς φιλοσοφίαν ἔχειν. Not all philosophers, however, could speak with

electors' may, however, have been competent to make the appointment on any basis on which it chose, and the moral fitness of the candidate no doubt often came into serious consideration. Pamphilus and Lucinus, indeed, the two interlocutors of this dialogue — voicing therein, we may believe, the sentiment of Lucian — agree that, if they were judges, they should consider the character of the candidate first of all. We are reminded of the edict of Valentinian and Valens [1] of the year 369, wherein it is provided that all who have adopted the garb of philosophers, without being entitled thereto, shall, if found in a foreign city, be transported back to their homes; "excepting only," continues the edict, "such as have been approved by the *best* and deserve to be separated by them and set aside from this worthless throng; for it is base, if a man who professes to endure the blows of fortune cannot endure the burdens of his citizenship." In other edicts also fitness of the candidate from a moral point of view was made a prerequisite to appointment or to the receiving of a license to teach. Thus, an edict of Julian,[2] dated 362, requires that all professors and

fluency (Luc., *Jup. trag.*, 27; Themis., 261 c, 342 b), but more and more, as time went on, even the philosophers came under the sophistic influence, and eloquence came to be an accomplishment of the philosopher (*cf.* Themis., 328 *ff.*). Themistius may be taken as an example — Libanius (*ep.*, 703) says that he taught eloquence as well as philosophy — and compare Lib., i. 385, 3, and Eunap., p. 112. If philosophers are included in the edicts *Cod. Th.*, xiii. 3, 5 (*Cod. Jus.*, x. 53, 7) and 3, 6, eloquence is specifically named as a qualification required of the teacher of philosophy. See p. 138, n. 1.

[1] *Cod. Th.*, xiii. 3, 7 (*Cod. Jus.*, x. 53, 8).

[2] *Cod. Th.*, xiii. 3, 5 (*Cod. Jus.*, x, 53, 7). A similar requirement is contained in an edict of Valentinian and Valens of the year 364 (*Cod. Th.*, xiii. 3, 6), and in another of Theodosius of the year 425 (*Cod. Th.*, vi. 21, 1 [*Cod. Jus.*, xii. 15, 1]).

other teachers of liberal studies shall excel, first in moral character, and then in eloquence. It is to be noted that these edicts applied apparently, not alone to philosophers, but to teachers of all liberal studies, including teachers of the law.[1]

We also see from this piece of Lucian that, in case the 'board' was unable to decide between the candidates, the matter was referred to the emperor. It would seem from a passage in Alexander of Aphrodisias,[2] who was Head of the Peripatetic school in the time of Septimius Severus, that the announcement of the appointment was in any case made by the emperor. So, at a later time, in the case of the sophists, the call was sometimes made by the emperor, after the selection had been made by the council.[3]

After the reorganization of the Empire under Diocletian and Constantine at the beginning of the fourth century, the philosophical schools fell into the back-

[1] Philosophers are not specifically mentioned in *Cod. Th.*, xiii. 3, 5 and 6, and vi. 21, 1, but they would seem to be included under the expressions *magistros studiorum doctoresque* (xiii. 3, 5), *si qui erudiendis adolescentibus vita pariter et facundia idoneus erit* (xiii. 3, 6), and *quicunque alii ad id doctrinae genus, quod unusquisque profitetur* (vi. 21, 1). See, however, *Dig.*, l. 13, 1. *Cf.* Eumen., *Pro rest. scol.*, 14. In inscriptions, morals and eloquence are often mentioned together; *e. g.*, Ἐφημ. ἀρχ., 1883, p. 20: ἀρετῆς ἕνεκα καὶ λόγων· *C. I. G.*, 4679: ἐπὶ ἀνδραγαθίᾳ καὶ λόγοις· *C. I. A.*, iii. 769: διά τε τὴν ἐν τῷ ἐπιτηδεύματι ὑπεροχὴν καὶ τὴν περὶ τὰ ἤθη σεμνότητα (see Wilhelm, *Jahresb. d. österr. arch. Inst.*, 2, 1899, p. 275).

[2] *De fato*, 1: οὗ (Aristotle) τῆς φιλοσοφίας προΐσταμαι ὑπὸ τῆς ὑμετέρας μαρτυρίας διδάσκαλος αὐτῆς κεκηρυγμένος· though this may have been a case of appeal, in which Alexander was actually appointed by the emperor. Or does Alexander mean simply that he was appointed by authority delegated by the emperor?

[3] See p. 140.

## THE PROFESSORS: THEIR APPOINTMENT

ground,[1] and the method of appointment to the chairs of sophistry was changed. The emperor, though he was, of course, at all times the court of last appeal, no longer regularly and on every occasion exercised the right of selection. Though the method of appointment, in this later period, may not have been, for all places and for all times, the same, in general the municipal councils, acting under the authority, expressed or implied, of the local magistrates, seem to have been competent to determine the personnel of the various universities. Thus, in Greece, the proconsul, who had his seat at Corinth, acted as a sort of curator to the University at Athens.[2] He could appoint and he could depose, and when, as was often the case, the students got into a fight with one another or with the townsmen, or in any other way broke the peace, he summoned them to appear before his tribunal, to answer for their conduct.[3] But, though the control of the University of Athens was at times thus interfered with by action of the proconsul, the independence of the council was in general re-

---

[1] Appointments in the Neo-Platonic school at Athens in the fifth century were made by members of the school or by the outgoing Head (Hertzberg, *Gesch. Griech.*, iii. p. 532).

[2] *Cf.* Himer., *or.*, xiv. 37. See also Hertzberg, *Gesch. Griech.*, iii. p. 85.

[3] A celebrated case of this sort was the hand-to-hand contest that took place between the students of Apsines and those of Julian (Eunap., p. 69). On another occasion the students became so unruly and caused such disturbance in the town that the proconsul, holding the professors to account for the conduct of their students, deposed three of the sophists and appointed three others in their stead, among whom was Libanius (Lib., i. 19, 11; 176, 13). The proconsul could also forbid a professor to hold public displays (Himer., *or.*, xiii. 2, 3).

spected.¹ It is probable that a similar state of affairs existed at most of the other university centres. Sometimes the call to a professorship came from the community itself, and was expressed in the form of a decree passed by the local council and signed, or otherwise approved, by the emperor or the emperor's representative in the province.² At other times, upon a simple request of the community, the emperor or the emperor's representative issued an edict, calling upon a professor to accept a certain chair.³ Naturally the emperor would be more apt to interfere in educational matters at Constantinople than in smaller cities in which there was no Court. At Antioch and some other places the local council, acting by itself, seems to have been, under ordinary circumstances, competent to dispose of the fortunes of its teachers,⁴ but there is no doubt

¹ The proconsul on one occasion urged the council to extend a call to Libanius (Lib., i. 58 and 59; 73, 12; cf. 176, 22, and iii. 457, 5). This is stated to have been the first time that a sophist was called to Athens from without to teach; sometimes students stayed on at Athens year after year, waiting for an opening that never came (ib., i. 21, 6). Libanius refused to accept the call, though he recognized the honor done him (ib., i. 59 and 60). Libanius was also called to Egypt by the council and the prefect (ib., ep., 1050; i. 176, 22). Cf. ib., iii. 204, 5: ψηφίσματι καὶ γνώμῃ.

² Cod. Th., xiii. 3, 5 (if it is to be applied to the official appointments); cf. Cod. Jus., x. 53, 7. Libanius was called to Nicomedia by a formal vote, passed, by special permission of the governor of Bithynia, after petition made by the citizens (Lib., i. 36, 13). See preceding note.

³ Lib., i. 27, 3; cf. 54, 1. Even in the second century an embassy was sometimes sent to the emperor to beg for the appointment of this or that professor (Philos., 591). Proæresius recovered his chair at Athens through the intervention of the emperor (Eunap., p. 80).

⁴ At Antioch (Lib., ii. 213, 12; ep., 209, 453, 825). At Cæsarea (ib., ii. 220, 20). At Apamea (ib., ep., 1449). At Cyzicus (ib.,

that in these cases also the emperor or the emperor's representative would at any time have felt himself at liberty to interfere.¹ In fact, it is evident from many passages in Libanius that intrigue and politics played at times no unimportant part in determining the sophist's lot. Sometimes, notably on occasion of the appointment of the Head of the rhetorical school at Athens, a rhetorical contest was instituted among the various candidates.²

Oftentimes a single speech was sufficient to establish the reputation of a sophist and insure his appointment to an excellent position.³ Popularity had its dangers, however. If a professor received a call, voiced by the emperor, it was generally wise for him to accept.⁴ Release from service or change of position was also, if the professor was popular and his services were desired, often difficult to obtain. Libanius tells us that, after he had set up a school at Constantinople and the stu-

---

ep., 441). And see ib., ii. 80, where the power (in ordinary cases) of the local council is emphasized: βαρυτάτη δέ οἱ καὶ ἡ βουλὴ δέσποινα ἐπίκειται γράμμασιν ὀλίγοις αἴρειν τε αὐτὸν καὶ καθαιρεῖν ἔχουσα στρέφειν τε ὅπῃ βούλοιτο τὰς ἐκείνου τύχας ἐκβάλλειν τε, εἰ τοῦτο ἀρέσκοι, καὶ πλῆθος ἀντιτέχνων ἐγκαθιστάναι ἄλλα τε μικρὰ δοκοῦντα εἶναι μεγάλην φέροντα τὴν λύπην. But it is stated in what follows that the sophist may be able to evade the action of the council if he can obtain the favor of the emperor or of a magistrate. Eumenius was appointed professor at Autun, in Gaul, near the end of the third century by the emperor (Eumen., Pro rest. scol., 14).

[1] See preceding note, and Lib., ii. 601, 8. Just after Libanius's removal to Antioch there came an edict from the emperor calling him back to Constantinople (ib., ep., 407, 1242).

[2] Eunap., p. 79. See, for this passage, p. 142, n. 3, and p. 153. An examination on the two subjects, moral character and eloquence, seems to be implied in Cod. Th., xiii. 3, 5 (Cod. Jus., x. 53, 7) and 3, 6. Cf. Augustin., Confess., v. 13.

[3] E. g., Lib., i. 27, 5.   [4] Lib., i. 20, 4; 54, 1; 126, 9; 177, 9.

dents had begun to flock to his lectures, the emperor, fearing that he might wish to transfer his residence to Antioch, his home, issued a decree enjoining his stay in the capital.[1] At a later time, when Libanius actually undertook to leave Constantinople and to remove to Antioch, he found it necessary to engage in an endless amount of wire-pulling. First, he interested several physicians in his case. These were to depose that the climate of Constantinople was bad for his head — he had been troubled from his youth with vertigo and headache — while that of Antioch was beneficial. Next, the mayor of the city was to agree to accept this deposition without question. Finally, an influential man at Court was worked upon, by an appeal to his feeling of self-importance, to support the physicians' statement and to add his own prayers thereto for Libanius's release. The manœuvre was partly successful: Libanius received a temporary leave of absence, which was, however, afterward made permanent.[2]

The number of official sophists at Athens in the fourth century is uncertain. There seem to have been at least three, and there may possibly have been more. Of these, one held a position superior to the positions of the others, and was known as the Head of the school.[3]

[1] i. 29, 11.
[2] i. 66, 8; *ep.*, 394a, 395. Even for a temporary leave of absence of four months during the summer, he had to sue for the emperor's consent (*ib.*, i. 61, 14).
[3] An important passage for determining the number of official sophists at Athens is Eunap., pp. 79 *ff.*: ὡς δέ, ἀπελθόντος Ἰουλιανοῦ κ. τ. λ. (translated, p. 154, below). The passage has been differently understood. Zumpt (*Ueber den Bestand d. phil. Schul.*, p. 56) and Hertzberg (*Gesch. Griech.*, iii. p. 328) under-

At Constantinople, provision was made at the beginning of the next century for three Latin and five Greek chairs of sophistry. There was also at least one official 'grammarian' at Athens, while at Constantinople there were, at the beginning of the fifth century, ten Latin

stood it to mean that there was a preliminary examination of all the candidates, at which six were chosen to compete in a further contest for the chair, while according to the view of Bernhardy, K. O. Müller (see Zumpt, p. 56, n. 2), and Schlosser (*Univ., Stud. u. Prof. d. Griech.* in *Archiv für Gesch. u. Lit.*, i. p. 219), there was no nomination and no contest to be followed by an appointment, but simply an appointment and a struggle for ascendancy afterward. Eunapius's language, though not wholly free from ambiguity, seems tolerably clear. It is evident that there arose at Athens after Julian's death a question about the *succession* to the emoluments of some *position* connected with *sophistry* (τὰς Ἀθήνας εἶχεν ἔρως τῆς διαδοχῆς τῶν ἐπὶ τοῖς λόγοις πλεονεκτημάτων); it is also evident that a large number of candidates presented themselves, each resting his claim to the right of appointment on the statement that he held the supremacy in the sophistical field (παραγγέλλουσι μὲν ἐπὶ τῷ κράτει τῆς σοφιστικῆς πολλοί κ.τ.λ.). The matter to be decided, then, before the succession to the emoluments could be conferred, was which of all the claimants was the strongest. Six passed muster and were chosen to compete (χειροτονοῦνται δὲ δοκιμασθέντες ἁπάσαις κρίσεσι) — four as being likely candidates, two simply to fill up the number; "for there had to be at Athens, according to the Roman law (or custom), a number of speakers and a number of auditors" (ἔδει γὰρ πολλοὺς εἶναι, κατὰ τὸν νόμον τὸν Ῥωμαϊκόν, Ἀθήνησι τοὺς μὲν λέγοντας, τοὺς δὲ ἀκούοντας). The last words may offer some difficulty, but they seem to mean that the Roman law or custom required that the appointment should be made only from a large number of candidates (as to-day it is the custom at auctions not to make a sale on a single bid) and only after a thorough trial of strength. The struggle that followed was long-drawn-out, and probably extended over many months, if not longer; the whole eastern part of the Empire (not simply Athens) was divided in its sympathies, and sent its students to this or that sophist in accordance with these sympathies. The rivalry was intense. Proæresius at one time was even driven from the city. A new proconsul, coming to Greece, summoned the rival sophists to appear in a contest in his presence. Finally, the

and ten Greek 'grammarians,' besides one philosopher and two lawyers. At Antioch, there were, at one time in the second half of the fourth century, at least three Greek sophists holding regular appointments, Libanius, Zenobius, and Acacius, and later we find Libanius at

superiority of Proæresius was acknowledged by all; as Eunapius says, "after that, no one dared oppose Proæresius, but all, as if struck by a bolt from Heaven, acknowledged his superiority," and "the rule of Proæresius resembled that of a tyrant, and he was famed far and wide for his eloquence" (p. 84: ἅπαντες συνεχώρησαν αὐτῷ εἶναι κρείττονι· p. 85: τυραννὶς ἐδόκει τις εἶναι· cf. p. 68: καὶ ἐτυράννει γε τῶν 'Αθηνῶν· p. 78: πρὸς τὸν Οὐλπιανὸν κρατοῦντα τῆς 'Αντιοχείας ἐπὶ λόγοις· p. 80: τὴν ἐπὶ λόγοις βασιλείαν εἶχον αὐτοί· p. 90: τὸν βασιλεύοντα τῶν λόγων· Lib., i. 24, 15; ii. 313, 1; Philos., 559). Eunapius does not say in so many words that Proæresius now received "the emoluments of the succession," but this result would follow as a matter of course. Our understanding of the Eunapius passage has a bearing on the question of the number of official sophists at Athens. Zumpt and Hertzberg supposed that there was but one official sophist here mentioned; Bernhardy, Müller, and Schlosser, that there were six. A comparison of affairs at Antioch in this century (see pp. 270 ff.) and at Athens in the two preceding centuries (see p. 94) makes it probable that there were at Athens at this time a number of sophists holding regular appointments, but that one of these had a position above the others and was the Head of the school. A statement in Photius lends further reason to this view, for he speaks of Himerius as being "at the head of the rhetorical school at Athens" (*Bibl.*, cod. 165, p. 109a: τὸν ἐν 'Αθήνησι κατὰ ῥητορείαν προὔστη διδασκαλείου). Furthermore, Eunapius says that the son of Sopolis was said to have held "the chair" at Athens (p. 95: ἐπιβεβηκέναι τοῦ θρόνου τὸν παῖδα φάσκουσιν), and that Parnasius "held the educational chair" (p. 95: ἐν τούτοις ἦν τοῖς χρόνοις καὶ Παρνάσιος ἐπὶ τοῦ παιδευτικοῦ θρόνου), while Photius tells us that Leontius was raised to "the sophistical chair" (*Bibl.*, cod. 80, p. 60b: εἰς τὸν σοφιστικὸν θρόνον). In all these cases (except, possibly, in the passage referring to Parnasius: see p. 220, n. 4), we may believe, the chief position, or the chair at the head of the school, is meant. It is to be said, however, that the term 'chair' was sometimes used rather loosely. Thus, Himerius speaks of Isocrates as having held "the chair" at Athens at a time when official chairs were quite unknown (*or.*, xxxii. 2:

## THE PROFESSORS: THEIR APPOINTMENT 145

the head of a school consisting of four sophists, or rhetors, besides himself. There may have been other official sophists at Antioch, and there certainly was an official 'grammarian.' As the fourth century wore on and law and Latin usurped, in the popular favor, the

Ἰσοκράτης τὸν μὲν θρόνον εἶχεν Ἀθηναίων). It is probably in this loose sense that Herodes Atticus is said to have held the chair at Athens (see p. 92, n. 1). We have several intimations that there were a number of official sophists at Athens in the fourth century. When Libanius was a student there, the proconsul on one occasion deposed three sophists and appointed three others in their stead (Lib., i. 19, 16). Not long after, Libanius was called to Athens, but whether, if he had accepted the call, he would have made a fourth, is uncertain (ib., i. 59, 3). Elsewhere 'chairs' of sophistry are spoken of as existing at Athens (ib., i. 333, 13). Possibly the Head of the school alone was chosen by contest, while the other members were appointed by the council and proconsul. When in 356-7 (see Seeck, Briefe d. Lib., p. 62), apparently some years after the contest here in question (for the date of the sophist Julian's death, see Hertzberg, Gesch. Griech., iii. p. 323, n. 69, and p. 329, n. 84), Anatolius came to Athens, he instituted another contest among the sophists (Eunap., pp. 85 ff.). Himerius was then one of the number (ib., p. 87). Each of the sophists discussed from a different point of view the theme propounded, and Anatolius afterward remarked that, had there been more than thirteen ("more than a dozen," we should say; cf. the "thirteen-cubits man" in Theoc., xv. 17; see, however, Wyttenbach's note) sophists, the result would have been the same (ib., p. 89). This remark, which suggests a number less than thirteen, would seem to have reference to the *official* sophists, for of official and unofficial sophists together there must have been a great many more than thirteen (when Julian died, those who applied for his position were "so many," says Eunapius, p. 79, "that I should have difficulty in telling their names"). Whether all the six sophists nominated at the time of Julian's death were official sophists, is not clear, but perhaps the two of least importance were not. Harrent, who combats the idea that there was in any city a school with an official head, holds, with Bernhardy, Müller, and Schlosser, that there were six sophists elected after Julian's death (Les écoles d'Antioche, pp. 44, 227). Schemmel (Neue Jahrb., 20, p. 56; 22, p. 495) considers that there were three official sophists at Athens and three at Antioch.

place of Greek, chairs of these subjects were established in other cities than Constantinople. Thus Antioch received, apparently, a Latin sophist and a lawyer.[1] The great seat of law, however, in the East, was Berytus, where were established several chairs of this subject.[2] Nicæa, Nicomedia, Cæsarea in Palestine, and many other smaller places in Asia and elsewhere supported at least one Greek sophist each.[3] Indeed, the Greek sophist then was an indispensable and inevitable feature of every Greek community; he was the centre of the intellectual life of the community, and held to that life much the same relation that the academy or the college holds to the life of the American community to-day.[4]

There were in all the large university centres many professors and tutors outside the official list, who depended for their income solely on the fees of their students, but these were, at least in the fourth century, more or less under the supervision and control of the imperial government. Thus, in the case referred to

[1] For Constantinople, see *Cod. Th.*, xiv. 9, 3 (*Cod. Jus.*, xi. 19, 1); for the 'grammarian' at Athens, Eunap., p. 7, and Suidas, s. v. Παμπρέπιος. As early as the first half of the fourth century there were at least two official sophists at Constantinople (Lib., i. 27, 3; 29, 5). For the case of Antioch, see pp. 295 *ff.*, and Lib., i. 153, 7; iii. 261, 262; *ep.*, 209, 1240. Libanius found it necessary, as time went on and Latin became indispensable to the advocate, to provide instruction in that subject in his school under a special teacher (*ep.*, 448, 453); and perhaps also in law.

[2] In Justinian's time probably four, and four at Constantinople (*Dig.*, *præf. omnem*). Cæsarea, Athens, and Alexandria also had schools of law.

[3] Nicæa (Lib., i. 36, 10); Nicomedia (*ib.*, i. 36, 14); Cæsarea (Choric, p. 6). *Cf.* also Lib., *ep.*, 1449; Himer., *or.*, v. 9; and see pp. 116, 124.

[4] The sophist's profession is called the ' mind of the city" (νοῦν πόλεως, Lib., i. 332, 14).

above, in which Libanius was forbidden by an edict of the emperor to remove from Constantinople to Antioch, he was at the time a private instructor receiving no salary from the government. Again, in the edict issued by the Emperor Julian in 362, to which reference has already been made, it was ordained that a professor or tutor who wished to set up a school of his own must first receive formal permission from the local council, which permission was to be given by the advice and with the consent of the *best*. The decree embodying this permission was then to be sent to the emperor for his signature; "in order," thus concludes the edict, "that the teacher may approach his task of instructing the young of the community with the added honor of my approval." These restrictions were, at least in part, removed two years later, when Valentinian announced that any one who possessed the requisite moral and intellectual qualifications might, without further ado, set up a school.[1] These semi-official, or licensed, teachers corresponded in a way to the *Privat-Docenten* of the German universities of the present day. Under the edict of Julian, it is hard to see wherein, except in the matter of salary, the licensed teachers differed greatly from those with regular appointment.

In the first half of the fifth century, Theodosius II, with whom at this time Valentinian III was associated

[1] *Cod. Th.*, xiii. 3, 6. It would seem, however, that under both edicts some sort of an examination was necessary to determine the possession of the qualifications required. It is generally recognized that the first of the two edicts was designed to exclude Christians from the privilege of teaching at the universities (*cf.* Jul., *ep.*, 42).

## 148   UNIVERSITIES OF ANCIENT GREECE

as emperor of the West, gave to the University at Constantinople a more rigid organization and limited still further in certain ways the right of private instruction. The regulations of Theodosius and Valentinian are contained in three sections of the Theodosian Code,[1] and are repeated in part in two sections of the Justinian Code.[2] As an interesting specimen of ancient university legislation, the sections of the Theodosian Code are here translated in full. They are all dated in the year 425. The first[3] deals with the right of private instruction, the number of official chairs, and the assignment of rooms for lectures; it is addressed to the city prefect.

All who [thus runs the edict], wrongfully calling themselves *Professors*, have been accustomed to meet their students, gathered from any quarter, in the public halls and lecture-rooms, and to go with them from place to place, are hereby forbidden to teach in public. If this practice, which is now condemned and forbidden, be, after the present proclamation of Our Divine Will, again attempted in the future, let him, who shall have disobeyed Our injunction, not only receive the mark of disgrace which he deserves, but also understand that he is to be expelled from the city, in which he is unlawfully living. Those, on the other hand, who have been accustomed to go from house to house and to teach privately the same subjects in different houses, shall, if they have chosen to devote themselves to private pupils, taught in private houses, in no way be affected by this ban. If, however, there be any of this number who are seen to hold an appointment at the University, be it understood that they are strictly forbidden to engage in any teaching within private walls whatever, and

---

[1] vi. 21, 1; xiv. 9, 3; xv. 1, 53.
[2] xi. 19, 1; xii. 15, 1.                           [3] xiv. 9, 3.

## THE PROFESSORS: THEIR APPOINTMENT 149

if it shall be discovered that they are acting contrary to this Our Divine Commandment, they shall enjoy none of the privileges which are granted deservedly to those who are appointed to teach exclusively in the University.—Let there teach, as regular Professors, in this University of Ours: — of those who are recommended by their knowledge of Roman eloquence, three orators and ten 'grammarians'; of those who are known for their power in Greek eloquence, five sophists and again ten 'grammarians.' And since it is Our wish that the youth who are ambitious of glory should not be instructed in these arts alone, we add for the first time to the Professors already mentioned teachers of profounder knowledge and education: let there, namely, be appointed, in addition to the others, one who shall examine into the secrets of philosophy and two who shall expound the principles of law and justice.—Special rooms shall be assigned and appointed by Your Eminence to each of the Professors, so that neither the students nor the teachers shall annoy one another, and that the confusion occasioned by the mingling of tongues and voices may not disturb the ears, or distract the attention, of those engaged in study.

The second edict [1] deals with the disposition of rooms in the porticos of the Capitol, some of which rooms were assigned to the professors and their classes.

Rooms which are seen to be adjacent to the north portico and are shown to be of a size and splendor to render them, owing to the admiration caused by their spaciousness and beauty, fit to accommodate public business, are to be assigned by the city prefect to the aforementioned instructors, to be used as class-rooms. Those on the east and west sides, which have no approach and no public exit from a main street, making them open passageways, are

[1] xv. 1, 53.

to be fitted up, as heretofore, as restaurants. Rooms, however, which are considered too small or too mean, must be enlarged, by adding space from the adjacent rooms on either side, so that neither the occupants nor the users shall be cramped. If any person whose room is taken can show that he has obtained it by imperial favor, or in any other way as a gift or by lawful purchase, Your Eminence shall see that he be reimbursed for the same from the public treasury.

The third edict [1] provides for a system of honoring with title professors who have taught with success twenty years.

The Greek 'grammarians,' Helladius and Syrianus; the Latin 'grammarian,' Theophilus; the sophists, Martinus and Maximus; the lawyer, Leontius: — these men it has been decided to honor with the title of Count of the First Order, now bestowed by Our Imperial Majesties; and they are to rank in dignity with those who are ex-Vicars. Furthermore, every other, who shall have been recommended in his particular profession, provided he shall have led a moral and praiseworthy life, and provided he shall have given evidence of skill in teaching, eloquence in speaking, subtlety in interpretation, and ability in reasoning, and have been found worthy, in the judgment of the most honored assemblage of our city, of holding the position of Professor in the aforementioned University, shall, when he has for twenty years continued in uninterrupted and sedulous performance of his duty of teaching, enjoy the like dignities with these men.

One essential difference we see between the ancient university and the modern: in the ancient university there was no governing or examining board — no board

[1] vi. 21, 1.

which arranged and co-ordinated the studies or conducted examinations and gave degrees. The point at which the different streams of education met was either the local council, which, as we have seen, usually made appointments, or the emperor, who, either in his own person or through his representative, retained general oversight and control of the teachers and students. No attempt, however, was made by either of these, the council or the emperor, to regulate the kind or the amount of instruction. There is a possible, but very uncertain, intimation that at Athens, toward the beginning of the fifth century, something in the nature of a degree was given by a voluntary union of the instructors themselves.[1] The intimation, however, is so *very* uncertain that we cannot with safety build much upon it. There are also some indications of co-operative action among the various members of the teaching corps at Antioch in the fourth century, and almost certainly there was one sophist at Antioch in this century, Libanius, who possessed a certain degree of authority, delegated to him by the council, over the teachers and schools of the city as a whole.[2] These phenomena, however, were but the beginnings of what, had conditions been more favorable, might in the end have led to some more compact union of interests among the teachers. The strictest control from above over the teaching force of any city seems to have been exerted at Constantinople, where, as we have seen, the emperor in the fifth century limited considerably the right of private instruction. Taken as a whole, however, and in their essential nat-

[1] See p. 303, n. 1.　　　　[2] See pp. 270 *ff*.

ure, the ancient Greek universities offer us the phenomenon of a voluntary congregation of professors and students, all filled with a like zeal for learning, and each professor having his faithful band of enthusiastic followers, bound to him by ties of sentiment and loyalty.[1]

There was, among the sophists of the fourth century — the case was not so bad in the preceding centuries — little, if any, of that spirit of brotherhood and generous freemasonry that usually exists in a community of scholars at the present day. Instead, there were jealousy, spite, and often unrelenting hatred. Each sophist felt himself in an attitude of antagonism toward his brother sophists and saw in them his natural enemies. The rivalry was intense and often bitter, partaking more of the character of personal animosity than of professional emulation, and descending in many cases to acts of persecution, and even violence.[2] So it was that,

[1] The nearest approach to a single word for the idea of University was the name of a building; *e. g.*, the Athenæum at Rome, the *auditorium* (*Cod. Th.*, vi. 21, 1), the *Capitolium*, or the *auditorium Capitoli* (*ib.*, xiv. 9, 3) at Constantinople, the Museum at Alexandria and possibly at Antioch (Lib., i. 71, 10).

[2] A notable statement of the spirit of envy which prevailed among teachers in the fourth century is contained in the words of Synesius, *Dion*, 13: "Now the life of the teacher is this: . . . As soon as he has secured a following of youthful admirers, he will speak no word of praise for anything that any man says, for he is in danger of being looked down upon and of having to behold his troop flock to another school. . . . It is part of the teacher's lot to be made up of envy, the greatest and the most worldly of the passions. He will pray that no man other than himself may shine with wisdom in the city, and, if some man do, he will detract from that man's good name and try to make himself the sole object of regard." Similarly Themistius, 254 b, c: "Workers in metal and carpenters, and, if you please, poets and other such artists (*i. e.*, sophists), have a right, if one says anything, to rebel and show themselves jealous, for the emoluments of their arts

when an election or appointment to a chair was to take place, cabals and intrigues were the order of the day. In order to illustrate the condition of affairs here referred to, we may be allowed to give, at this point, translating from Eunapius, an account of what occurred at Athens at the time of the death of the sophist Julian and the appointment of his successor, Proæresius. Julian, the first in point of time of the great sophists of the fourth century, was famous far and wide for his wonderful gifts as a teacher and interpreter of the art of sophistry, and drew large crowds of students from many quarters of the Empire. His favorite and most gifted pupil was Proæresius, who himself afterward came, in the words of his biographer, to exercise an educational control at Athens that resembled a *tyranny*.[1] When Julian died, about 337, he bequeathed to Proæresius his house, which Eunapius describes as being small and simply furnished, but as breathing the atmosphere of a shrine of the Muses,[2] and would, no doubt, have had his pupil succeed him as Head of the school at Athens. The power of appointment to the headship, however, lay at this time in the hands of a special body, probably the local council, and the appointment was to be made only after a rhetorical contest. Six candidates were nominated to take part in the contest, and a long and bitter struggle for supremacy ensued.[3]

are either money or money and glory, and the one who is worsted cannot have an equal share of these with those who are victorious." "Rivalry begets envy even in wise men," says Philostratus (490), and "Man is naturally an envious thing" (*ib.*, 515).

[1] Eunap., p. 85.     [2] P. 68.
[3] P. 79. For a discussion of this passage, see p. 142, n. 3. The text of Eunapius is uncertain in some places.

But when [says Eunapius], after the death of Julian, the city was all agog to learn who would be his successor as Head of the school, a large number of aspirants presented themselves, each claiming to be supreme in the field of sophistry — so many were there that I should have difficulty in telling their names. But these successfully passed the test and were nominated by unanimous vote: Proæresius, Hephæstion, Epiphanius, and Diophantus — and two others: Sopolis, who was pulled in by the hair, simply to fill up the ranks, and one Parnasius, who was of no special note. For there had to be at Athens, according to the Roman law (or custom), a number of speakers and a number of auditors.

Now, although all these were nominated, the two of least importance had only the name of being so, and their power ended with the platform and the desk. But in the case of the others, who were more powerful, the sympathies of the city became straightway divided, and not of the city only, but of the whole Roman Empire, and the division took place, not on the question of eloquence, but on the question of nationality in the matter of eloquence. For the East was clearly reserved, like a huge fee, for Epiphanius, Arabia fell to the lot of Diophantus, Hephæstion, out of respect for Proæresius, withdrew from Athens and went into retirement, while to Proæresius were sent the students from the whole of Pontus and the neighboring regions — for the people there admired the man as a treasure that was their own — and not from Pontus only, but from all Bithynia as well, the Hellespont, and the parts above Lydia, stretching through what is now called Asia, to Caria and Lycia, and ending at Pamphylia and the Taurus. All Egypt fell to his lot, as a portion of his oratorical realm, and the parts which, stretching above Egypt toward Libya, are bounded on one side by a *terra incognita*, and on the other by lands which are habitable. This that I have said was true in general, for, strictly speaking, there were some differences in these nations in the case of a few youths, and then again there were changes,

# THE PROFESSORS: THEIR APPOINTMENT

as when one, finding himself at first deceived, went over to another sophist.

Now, Proæresius was so pre-eminently superior to his rivals that he soon gathered about him an extraordinarily large body of student followers. But the followers of the others, all banding together, proved so strong that, after bribing the proconsul, they drove Proæresius from the city, and so held the power, in the world of letters, in their own hands. Proæresius, who, in addition to his flight, was beset by dire poverty, being, like Peisistratus, driven into exile, later returned. . . . Good fortune attended him, for there was a new proconsul in charge of affairs in Greece, who, according to the report, was very indignant at what had happened.

But no sooner had Proæresius, through a reversal of fortune and by permission of the emperor, re-entered Athens, than his enemies, coiling and twisting themselves anew, raised their heads to strike another blow. . . . In the meantime, Proæresius having, like another Odysseus, returned after long absence, found but few of his former pupils . . . of the same mind as of yore, and these looked upon him in astonishment, distrusting what had occurred. Encouraged at finding even these, he told them to wait till the new proconsul arrived. The proconsul arrived sooner than was expected. Entering Athens, he straightway called the sophists to a conference, thereby causing in their ranks general consternation. However, they came, though reluctantly and with many a hem and haw. Themes were set, and the sophists, being unable to escape, spoke, each striving to do his best. The applause was given as pre-arranged, by bands of summoned claqueurs, and so all separated, dismay reigning supreme in the ranks of Proæresius's friends.

The proconsul, however, summoned them all again, as if to reward them, and then, giving orders that they should be detained, suddenly called in Proæresius. The sophists had come, quite ignorant of what was about to happen.

Then the proconsul, raising his voice, said, "I intend to set for you all to-day a single theme, and to hear you discuss it at once. Proæresius shall speak too — after you, or in whatever turn you may wish."

It was evident that the sophists were trying to escape, . . . but the proconsul, raising his voice a second time, said, "Proæresius, do you speak." Then Proæresius, gracefully saying a few words of introduction from his chair, and touching on the merits of extempore speech, arose, with confidence, when he came to the main part of his task, and, as the proconsul was about to propound a theme, raised his eyes and looked about the room. Seeing the enemy's faction in great force, and his own small and retiring, he naturally for a moment lost heart. But, as his spirit began to boil within him and he grew hot for the fray, he cast his eyes over the crowd, and seeing, in the far end of the room, two men, wrapped in their cloaks, whom he recognized as past-masters of the art of sophistry and the chief offenders against himself, he raised his voice and shouted, "Aha! behold my two gallant friends! command these, Proconsul, to propound the theme. Then perhaps they will learn that they have treated me wrongfully."

The two, when they heard these words, disappeared in the crowd and tried to escape observation. But the proconsul, sending his officers through the room, caused the men to be taken and brought to the front, and then urged them to propound the theme, as it is called. After putting their heads together and deliberating for a while, they finally gave a subject, the hardest and the most unsatisfactory subject they could find, one, besides, which was on a private matter and did not readily lend itself to rhetorical treatment. Proæresius, looking at the men with fire in his eyes, said to the proconsul, "Whatever I ask before the contest that is fair, I beg that you will grant." The proconsul telling him that nothing that was fair should be refused, "Then," said Proæresius, "I request that the short-hand-writers be allowed to enter, and, as they every day take notes of what is said in the courts of law, so now that they be permitted to record what is said by me."

When the most skilful of the writers had been allowed to enter, they took their stand on either side, ready to begin their writing, but none knew what was about to happen. Then Proæresius said again, "One other thing I ask, which is not so easy to grant." The proconsul bidding him speak, "It is," he said, "that no one shall applaud me." When, much to the alarm of all, this request too had been granted, Proæresius began to speak — fluently, and with a sonorous ring at the end of every period. The audience, which had been enjoined to keep silence, was unable to contain itself for wonder, and a deep murmur went through the room. As the speaker advanced in his subject, and was carried beyond all bounds of what would be considered for any human being possible, he entered upon the second part of his speech, and filled out the statement of the case; but, leaping about the platform and acting as if inspired, he left that part, as though it needed no defence, and turned quickly to the other side of the argument. The short-hand-writers could hardly keep pace with him, and the audience, moved to break their silence, were speaking in all parts of the room. Then Proæresius, turning to the writers, said, "Observe now, carefully, whether I remember all that I have so far said," and, word for word, without making a single slip, he went over the whole case a second time. Then not even the proconsul regarded longer his own injunction, nor did the audience care for his threats, but, caressing the breast of the sophist, as if he were the statue of some god breathing inspiration, all who were present prostrated themselves before his hands and feet, and some called him a god, and some the image of Hermes the Eloquent. His rivals lay, racked with envy, but even so some of them did not fail to praise him. The proconsul, with his body-guard and officers, escorted him from the lecture-room. After that no one dared oppose Proæresius, but all, as if struck by a bolt from heaven, acknowledged his superiority.

Some time later, his rivals, again gaining strength, arose, like the heads of Hydra, and returned to their former methods. By offering rich banquets and dainty maids, they won over to their side some of those who were of most influence. In acting thus, they were only following the example of kings, who, when they have been defeated in regular battle, finding themselves reduced to the last extremity, have recourse to their light-armed troops, their slingers, and their auxiliary forces, on which they place little dependence; not that they really value these, but they are compelled to use them owing to their need. So the sophists, resorting to the help to which they were obliged to resort, devised such plots as these — which were disgraceful enough, but are without reproach if a man is basely in love with himself. At any rate, their stratagem met with success, and they obtained a considerable following. But the rule of Proæresius resembled that of a tyrant, and he was famed far and wide for his eloquence. For either all those who had intelligence joined themselves to him, or else those who came to him straightway, because of their choice, gained intelligence.

This passage presents a vivid and comprehensive picture of the sophistical activity in the fourth century, and there are many features in it to which we shall recur at a later time; but what we are specially interested to note here is the bitter and unrelenting character of the rivalry that existed among the different sophists — a rivalry that, as we shall also see, was often reflected in the conduct of their students. As regards the teachers, indeed, if we are to believe Libanius, even fathers and mothers of families were not exempt from persecution at the hands of disgruntled sophists to whom they failed to send their sons for instruction. "You say," says

Libanius, addressing one of his students,[1] "that your father has been injured by the sophist whom you deemed unworthy to be your teacher. How many other fathers have been injured for the same reason, when the teachers, saying that they have been insulted, have waxed wroth and sought to wreak their vengeance on those at hand, since they could not catch those who had gone away? Have not mothers, in cases where the father is dead, been dragged into the market-place, though unused to such treatment, and handed over to the violent hands of the police? And when a boy has had neither father nor mother, these miscreants have gone against his house-slaves and his lands and those who have had the care of his lands, and, by throttling the men and choking them, have compelled them to cry out against their masters, who have left for other parts."

We should remember, however, that such proceedings as those described form but one side of what is, after all, a two-sided picture. There were, in the preceding centuries, often much good-will and generous recognition of others' merits among the various sophists, and it could have been, at any period, only the smallest sophists that acted in the barbarous spirit described by Libanius.[2]

In the year 393, when Libanius was seventy-nine years of age, he was urged, after an illness which had confined him some time to his house and his bed, to appear once more in his class-room. The friend from whom this request came expected that there would be

[1] iii. 192, 1.
[2] For the other side of the picture, see p. 255.

a general concourse of rejoicing teachers to Libanius's room to welcome the sophist back to his old haunts; but Libanius knew better. Only two appeared, "and these," he says,[1] "will probably be punished by the others for having come." Such, in the fourth century, was the jealousy displayed toward the greatest sophist of his time by his own fellow-workers and countrymen.[2]

[1] *Ep.*, 995.
[2] The experience of Libanius when he first tried to get a footing as a teacher at Constantinople well illustrates the methods that were employed in this sophistic warfare. When Libanius arrived at Constantinople, after his second visit to Athens, there were two sophists established there. He was at first discouraged, but soon proceeded to make his name known to the city; he announced a declamation. Then took place a battle of displays between Libanius on the one side and the two sophists on the other. The aim of each side was to outdo the other and attract the favor of the city to itself. Libanius seems in the end to have prevailed, for he soon secured a class of over eighty. Students even came to him from outside the city. An edict was put forth by the emperor enjoining his stay in Constantinople. But his opponents, though defeated, were not silenced; they immediately entered upon a campaign of vilification. At this juncture, one Bemarchius came on the scene. This sophist had formerly been established at Constantinople and was high in favor with the emperor, Constantius. Though an adherent of the old religion, he had recently made a triumphal march through Asia and as far as Egypt with a speech in which he lauded Christ and described at length a certain church built by Constantius. Returning at this time, he expected to find things at Constantinople as he had left them, but none of his former pupils returned to him. He then attended a display of Libanius, and came away disheartened. A month later he held a display himself, in which he thought easily to show his superiority to Libanius. In this attempt he was unsuccessful, but soon gave another display, in which he presented the speech with which he had recently met with such favor. This proved to be so obscurely written that no one, according to Libanius, could understand it. Bemarchius's next move was to forestall any further attempt of Libanius to give a display, by inducing the Governor to withdraw his patronage from him and to refuse to attend his lectures.

Seeing, however, that he was unequal to Libanius in the field of oratory, Bemarchius next accused Libanius of employing the services of an astrologer, and proceeded to form a large personal faction, with the view of eventually bringing about Libanius's ruin. Just at this time there occurred a political revolution at Constantinople, of which Bemarchius and his followers determined to take advantage, in order to seize and imprison their opponents. Probably Libanius owed his freedom from imprisonment at this time to the fact that the revolution was soon quashed. With the restoration of order, a new governor came to Constantinople. He was a bitter enemy of Libanius, and he advised the latter to leave the city if he valued his life. Libanius left, intending to go to Nicomedia, but an edict from Constantinople warned him off from that city. He therefore went to Nicaea, but later succeeded in settling at Nicomedia. Here also he met with persecution, due to the jealousy of the local sophist. He stayed at Nicomedia, however, five years, at the end of which time he was recalled to Constantinople (Lib., i. 27 *ff*.).

## CHAPTER IX

## THE PROFESSORS: THEIR PAY AND POSITION IN SOCIETY

BRILLIANT indeed must have been the condition of the successful sophist in the flourishing period of sophistry. The old feeling of latent hatred and distrust which marked the attitude of many well-meaning people of the fifth century B. C. toward those who professed a higher learning had all disappeared in the centuries after Christ. No member of the community was then more admired or more honored or more loved than the teacher of sophistry.[1] His approach to a city was hailed with delight, and the people ran to welcome him from

[1] *Cf.* Luc., *Rhet. præc.*, 1, for the dignity of the sophist's name and profession: τὸ σεμνότατον τοῦτο καὶ πάντιμον ὄνομα, σοφιστής· also Eunap., p. 99: τῶν . . . βασιλέων καὶ τῶν ἀξιωμάτων τὸ μέγιστον αὐτῷ (Libanius) προσθέντων, . . . οὐκ ἐδέξατο, φήσας τὸν σοφιστὴν εἶναι μείζονα, and Philos., 624: οὐδὲ ἐπήρθη ὑπὸ τοῦ ὀνόματος οὕτω μεγάλου ὄντος. Glory, wealth, and recognized position in society were the portion of the successful sophist (Luc., *Rhet. præc.*, 2, 6). A literary education was considered the only road to wealth by one whose family had become impoverished (Lib., *ep.*, 349). *Cf. ib., ep.*, 655: εἰς μὲν χρημάτων λόγον ἔσχατος, εἰς δὲ λόγων ἐπιθυμίαν πρῶτος· οἶδε γὰρ ὀρθῶς, ὅτι τοῖς ἐκείνων ἀποροῦσι τούσδε κτητέον, οἳ κἀκεῖνα δύνανται φέρειν. Chrysostom speaks of the man who obtained high office, a rich wife, and wealth by his eloquence (*Adv. oppug. vit. mon.*, iii. 5, Migne, i. 357), as a typical case. Scopelian was overjoyed when Herodes called him his teacher (Philos., 521: καὶ τῶν τοῦ Πακτωλοῦ πηγῶν ἥδιον). A governor of a province thought himself disgraced if he was not eulogized by the sophist (Lib., ii. 374). *Cf.* Dio Chrys., xviii. 473 R.

## THE PROFESSORS: THEIR PAY

all quarters; if he condescended to remain among them, he was considered to have conferred upon them a great honor. By his presence the city was benefited in many ways. When Polemo took up his residence at Smyrna, crowds of picked youths flocked thither from all parts of the Greek world to hear him lecture, and the place gained a new importance. The people, who had for long been at strife with one another, became reconciled and learned new ways of governing and of regulating justice. By his address and great persuasive powers, Polemo secured for them many advantages from the emperor, and when he drove forth, accompanied by a large retinue and seated in a Phrygian or Celtic carriage drawn by horses with silver-studded harness, he brought great glory to the city; "for," says Philostratus,[1] "a city is set off by a family in thriving circumstances, just as it is by a fine market-place or a grand display of houses." The sophist was, as a rule, the most able and important man in the community, and his influence was exerted on the side of good. Sometimes he was a generous benefactor of the city, giving of his means to erect costly buildings or to relieve the needs of the poor.[2] At

[1] 531, 532. The people of Clazomenæ urged Nicetes to settle among them because they thought the prestige of the city would be greatly enhanced by his presence (*ib.*, 516). See, further, *ib.*, 511, 605, 606, 613; Lib., i. 332, 13. A man would glorify his country by acquiring eloquence (Lib., *ep.*, 23). The sophist Julian drew young men from all quarters of the world (Eunap., p. 68). When Scopelian went on an embassy to Italy, the youth of the land followed him back to Ionia (Philos., 520).

[2] *E. g.*, Philos., 568, 605. Themistius helped the needy (Lib., *ep.*, 379). *Cf.* the case of Eumenius, who offered to devote his whole salary, for as long a time as the need therefor should exist, to the restoration of the university-building at Autun (Eumen., *Pro rest. scol.*, 11).

other times, as in the case of Polemo, he guided, by his wise counsel, the politics of the state, and was often, either by the state or by the emperor, raised to positions of official trust.[1] He, of all men, was chosen to go on important embassies, and then his eloquence and the favor enjoyed by his class stood him in good stead. Cities and individuals vied with one another in honoring him while he lived, and, after his death, they raised to his memory statues and other memorials.[2]

An important privilege attaching to the educational profession in those days was the immunity from taxation and other public burdens (*ateleia*, ἀτέλεια, as it was called)[3] enjoyed, in some measure at least, by nearly

[1] The imperial secretaryship was often filled by a distinguished sophist; *e. g.*, by Adrian (Philos., 590), and by Antipater (*ib.*, 607). For other positions, see *ib.*, 596, 600, 601, 607. Libanius speaks of a sophist τὴν πόλιν ἀπὸ νευμάτων ἄγοντι (ii. 581, 9). See p. 76, n. 2.

[2] Lollianus (Philos., 527), Polemo (*ib.*, 543), Aristeides (*ib.*, 582), and Proæresius (Eunap., p. 90) were honored by statues. Busts of Varus were set up in a temple or sacred precinct (Philos., 576). Philostratus (543) says that it was evident that Polemo was not buried at Smyrna, for the reason that, if he had been, no shrine would have been considered too sacred to hold his remains. Dionysius was appointed governor of a large province, and was made a Roman knight and a " Fellow " of the Alexandrian Museum (*ib.*, 524). Themistius was made a member of the Senate of Constantinople (Themis., 313 c), received a silver chariot with heralds (*ib.*, 353 d), and was honored in many other ways (*ib.*, 146 b, 214 a, b). See also Philos., 611. A title was offered Libanius, which he refused to accept (Lib., i. 174, 2; Eunap., p. 100). He was intimate with the highest officials, who strove to do him honor. A magistrate had Libanius's picture painted and put in a public place (*ib.*, ii. 413, 414). Libanius pleads that officials should close their doors to sophists, as some sophists use their influence at Court to advance their own interests and increase the size of their classes (*ib.*, ii. 600, 1 *ff.*; iii. 80, 9; 91, 6; 103, 5). See Liebenam, *Städteverwaltung*, p. 78.

[3] Also ἀλειτουργησία, *vacatio, immunitas, excusatio*.

## THE PROFESSORS: THEIR PAY

all teachers from the time of Vespasian or even earlier.[1] This was a privilege that was then much sought after and highly prized. The duties of public life, which in the beginning had been more or less voluntary, had, as time went on, become both more numerous and more burdensome, and they were now obligatory on all men of means; in most instances they involved large expenditures of money and much sacrifice of time. Not only this, but taxation was pressing more and more heavily on all classes of society alike. To escape from this twofold burden was in itself no small remuneration. Some mention has already been made in a previous chapter[2] of the immunities enjoyed by professors, and it is not necessary to repeat here all that was there said. According to an edict of Commodus,[3] which was based on edicts of earlier emperors, philosophers, sophists, 'grammarians,' and physicians were excused from acting as guardians, trustees, superintendents of palæstræ, ædiles, priests, commissaries of grain and of oil, and judges, were not liable to have officers of the government quartered on them, and were not obliged to serve against their will on embassies and in the army; in fact, no service, national or other, was required of them except by their own consent. From time to time these privileges were confirmed and amplified by subsequent emperors, and were even extended to the families and possessions of the beneficiaries; "to the end," says an edict of Constantine,[4] " that those engaged in teaching

[1] See p. 81, n. 3.
[2] Ch. V.   [3] *Dig.*, xxvii. 1, 6, 8; *cf.* 6, 1.
[4] See *Cod. Th.*, xiii. 3, 3. The sections in the *Codices*, etc., bearing on the immunity of teachers are the following: *Cod. Th.*,

may with more ease instruct many in the arts and sciences."

There seems originally, as the edict of Commodus shows, to have been no distinction made, in the matter of immunities, between philosophers and other teachers,[1] but the comments of the third century jurists,[2] as well as the rescript of Diocletian and Maximian quoted below, make it evident that a change had taken place in this regard in their time. Even in an edict of Antoninus Pius it was stated that philosophers were expected, in case they were very rich, to serve the state in ways which called for the expenditure of money; "if," continues the edict,[3] "they raise any question about their wealth, they will by that very fact be seen to be no philosophers." "Your profession and your request are at variance with each other," wrote Diocletian and Maximian to the philosopher Polymnestus, who had claimed immunity from certain duties involving the expenditure of money;[4] "for while you profess to be a philosopher, you are convicted of the blindness of avarice, and you alone try to avoid the burdens which are attached to your patrimony. You may learn from the example of all others that your request is vain."

xiii. 3, 1; 3, 3; 3, 10; 3, 16; 3, 17; 3, 18; *Cod. Jus.*, x. 42, 6; 47, 1; 48, 12, 1; 53, 6 and 11; xii. 40, 8; *Dig.*, xxvii. 1, 6; l. 4, 18, 30; 5, 2, 8; 5, 8, 4; 5, 9; 5, 10; *Inst.*, i. 25, 15; *Frag. Vat.*, 149, 150. Students were also sometimes granted immunity (*Cod. Jus.*, x. 50, 1 and 2).

[1] See also *Dig.*, l. 4, 18, 30; *Frag. Vat.*, 149. Favorinus claimed immunity from the priestship on the ground that he was a philosopher (Philos., 490), and Flavius Archippus immunity from jury service on the same ground (Plin., *Ep. ad Trai.*, lviii. [lxvi.]).

[2] *Dig.*, xxvii. 1, 6; l. 5, 8, 4.

[3] *Dig.*, xxvii. 1, 6, 7.     [4] *Cod. Jus.*, x. 42, 6.

## THE PROFESSORS: THEIR PAY

In this matter, as in the matter of their pay, to be considered later, the philosophers were, by their very profession, placed at a disadvantage. In the third century they enjoyed immunity from the burdens of guardianship and from the so-called *munera sordida corporalia* (physical services considered degrading, such as the baking of bread, the burning of lime, etc.) only.[1] Except in one edict, of the year 369,[2] there is no further mention of philosophers in the *Codices* or the *Digests* until we come to the edict of Honorius and Theodosius of the year 414, in which immunity is granted to certain philosophers at Constantinople;[3] though it is possible that philosophers are included under such expressions as *magistri studiorum, professores literarum*, which occur in some of the edicts.[4] This omission of practically all reference to philosophers in the edicts and rescripts of the fourth century may be due to the comparatively small number of philosophers that then existed and to their decreasing importance.

The basis on which immunity was granted to teachers was that, in exercising their profession, they were already serving the state; a double service could not be required of them.[5] The same principle was accountable for the granting of immunity to practising physicians.[6] It is noteworthy that, when Diocletian and Maximian

---

[1] *Dig.*, l. 5, 8, 4. See also Kuhn, *Verf. d. röm. Reichs*, i. p. 119.
[2] *Cod. Th.*, xiii. 3, 7 (*Cod. Jus.*, x. 53, 8).
[3] *Cod. Th.*, xiii. 3, 16 (*Cod. Jus.*, x. 53, 11).
[4] See p. 138, n. 1.
[5] *Cf.* Lib., ii. 211, 22: οὓς εἴ τις φαίη λειτουργεῖν, ἴσως οὐκ ἂν ἁμάρτοι. See also Kuhn, *Verf. d. röm. Reichs*, i. p. 120, n. 908.
[6] Lib., *ep.*, 635.

forbade the municipal councils to grant immunity, they made an exception in favor of teachers of liberal studies and physicians. It was a corollary of this principle that a sophist, 'grammarian,' or physician, who was born in one place and was teaching or practising in another, could not, except in certain specified cases, enjoy immunity in the place of his birth.[1] The case of the sophist Philiscus will illustrate what has here been said.[2] Philiscus, whose mother was a native of the district of Eordæa, in Macedonia, was engaged in teaching at Athens in the reign of Caracalla. The Eordæans, with whom it was a custom to claim for services all who were citizens of their land by either parent, called upon the sophist on one occasion to perform some local service in the interest of the community. Philiscus objected, and the case was carried for settlement to Rome and to the emperor. Meanwhile, Philiscus, designing to outmanœuvre the Eordæans, hastened to Rome, attached himself to the following of the literary Julia, mother of the emperor, and through her secured his appointment to the chair of sophistry at Athens, before his antagonists arrived on the scene. When the case of the Eordæans came up, Caracalla was furious to find that he had been outwitted. He called on the sophist to plead his own cause in court, and then, when the latter appeared, would hardly hear him to an end. The words, the manner, the dress of Philiscus, all gave him offence, and he interrupted the speaker from time to time with sarcastic remarks and questions. Finally, the case having been decided in favor of the Eordæans, Philiscus ventured

[1] *Dig.*, xxvii. 1. 6, 9 *ff.*; l. 5, 9.  [2] Philos., 622, 623.

to remind the Emperor that his (Philiscus's) position of sophist at Athens afforded him protection in the present instance. Thereupon the emperor burst forth with great indignation: "Neither you nor any other teacher shall go free of burdens. I will not have the cities deprived of their due services for the sake of a few paltry declamations." So Philiscus held the chair of sophistry at Athens for seven years, without the immunities that were usually attached thereto. In this case, in so far as Caracalla deprived Philiscus of his immunity at Eordæa, he seems to have acted in accordance with the law as set down in a previous edict,[1] but in depriving the sophist of his Athenian immunity, he exercised the imperial prerogative of arbitrary action. Notwithstanding this fact, he afterward granted to Philostratus, the Lemnian, immunity for a single speech.[2]

It not infrequently happened that a professor voluntarily accepted an office or performed a service for his city out of a feeling of patriotism, but such action on his part was not to be held to prejudice his case or to serve as a precedent for future requisitions on the part of the community.[3] In the latter half of the fourth century, however, when, owing to the increased taxation and the growth of a large body of privileged functionaries attached to the imperial service, it became yearly more difficult for the communities to meet the requirements of the government, a city did sometimes try to impose burdens upon those to whom it had granted immunity.

[1] *Dig.*, xxvii. 1, 6, 9.    [2] Philos., 623.
[3] This is distinctly stated in an inscription in Dittenberger, *Syl. Inscr. Græc.*, No. 414, and in *Cod. Jus.*, x. 44, 2.

Such a case was that of Eusebius, a former pupil of Libanius. Eusebius had been appointed sophist at Antioch by vote of the municipal council. The council had also passed several decrees — four in all — begging the emperor to confer upon Eusebius some distinction — seemingly a title or the honor of a special edict which should have the effect of confirming their own votes conferring upon the sophist immunity from civic duties. This the emperor had done. Later, Eusebius was induced to serve on an embassy to the Court at Constantinople, with the understanding that this service should not stand as a precedent for future loss of privileges. Certain of his fellow-citizens, however, while themselves on an embassy to Constantinople, made the effort to have his immunity withdrawn. The attempt was unsuccessful, but Eusebius won his case only after proceeding twice to Constantinople and pleading at the Court in person.[1] Though the enjoyment of immunity by the teacher is spoken of as being a matter of law,[2] and though it so appears in the edicts, it is evident from this account that appointment to a chair and immunity from service were not so inseparably united that it was not thought desirable at times to have a special decree, or an edict, or even a title, specifically conferring the latter.[3]

[1] Lib., *ep.*, 789, 797 a–798, 820–827, 836–839; i. 154, 12; ii. 224, 14; iii. 160, 9 *ff.*; see also Seeck, *Briefe d. Lib.*, pp. 143, 144. The attempt was also made to deprive Libanius of his immunity (Lib., i. 154, 7), and, apparently, one Gerontius at Apamea (*ib.*, *ep.*, 1163–1165, 1297, 1428, 1431, 1449).
[2] Lib., i. 154, 8; *ep.*, 825.
[3] In general, on the subject of immunities, see Kuhn, *Verf. d. röm. Reichs*, i. pp. 83–122, and Liebenam, *Städteverwaltung*, pp. 417 *ff.*

The financial remuneration of the Greek professor came in several ways. If he enjoyed a regular appointment at some one of the university centres, he received a fixed salary, which, in the second and third centuries, was paid either by the city or by the emperor, according as the chair which he filled was a municipal or an imperial donation.[1] If it was the latter, the professor was said to be "eating the emperor's bread."[2] The amount of the salary is in some cases known. That of the 'political' chair of rhetoric at Athens, founded by Antoninus Pius, was, in the second century, one talent ($1,080),[3] while that of the imperial chair, established by Marcus Aurelius, as well as that of each of the several chairs of philosophy, was 10,000 drachmæ ($1,800).[4] Philosophers in some city are said to have received as high as 600 aurei ($3,000).[5] In the troubled period which followed the death of Alexander Severus the salaries of the different professors were apparently allowed to lapse. Those of the philosophical schools, with the possible exception of the Academic school,[6] seem never to have been restored, but, after the reorganization of the Empire under Diocletian and Constantine, at the beginning of the fourth century, the

[1] Philos., 566, 591; Luc., *Eunuch.*, 3, 8; *Dig.*, l. 9, 4, 2. Caracalla deprived the Peripatetics at Alexandria of their salaries (Dio Cass., lxxvii. 7.)

[2] Lib., i. 29, 4: τῶν βασιλέως ἐσθίειν· ep., 488: τῆς ἐκ βασιλέως τροφῆς. *Cf.* Fielding, *Tom Jones*, bk. xii. ch. 7: "'Why, certainly,'" replied the exciseman, "'I should be a very ill man, if I did not honor the king, whose bread I eat.'"

[3] Philos., 600.

[4] Philos., 566, 591; Luc., *Eunuch.*, 3, 8.

[5] See p. 87, n. 3.

[6] See Procop., *Anecd.*, c. 26, quoted p. 126, n. 2; and also p. 105.

salaries of the sophists and 'grammarians' were once more made available.[1]

To what extent these salaries were now paid by the emperor, independently of the communities, it is difficult to say, for the evidence on this point is conflicting. The emperor is certainly mentioned in several passages as being the source of a sophist's salary, as, for example, that of Libanius at Constantinople and that of Eudæmon at Elusa.[2] On the other hand, the local council is no less distinctly declared to be in certain places the paymaster. When, nearly at the close of the third century, Constantius Chlorus reorganized the University at Autun, in Gaul, he fixed the salary of the new Head of the school, Eumenius, at 600,000 nummi, but he also directed that this amount be paid from the city funds.[3] The edict of the emperors, Valens, Gratian, and Valentinian, directing that salaries be paid to professors in the various cities of Gaul, prescribes that these be taken from the *fiscus*.[4] The words *fiscus* and *ærarium*, however, were often used at this time indiscriminately,[5] and it is probable that the city treasuries are here meant, for the edict contains the further statement that the cities have not the liberty of donating salaries to their professors at their own pleasure. Again, the city of Chalcis, in Syria, is said to have

[1] *Cod. Th.*, xiii. 3, 1 (*Cod. Jus.*, x. 53, 6).
[2] Lib., *ep.*, 488, 132; *cf.* i. 29, 5.
[3] Eumen., *Pro. rest. scol.*, 14 (*ex rei publicæ viribus*). The nummus in this case Mommsen (*Hermes*, 25, p. 27) considers to be the Diocletian denarius (see p. 184, below), so that Eumenius's salary would be between $2,500 and $3,000.
[4] *Cod. Th.*, xiii. 3, 11.
[5] Hirschfeld, *Die kais. Ver. bis auf Dioc.*, p. 17, n. 2.

## THE PROFESSORS: THEIR PAY 173

voted its sophist, Domninus, a salary,[1] and the sophist Priscio was drawn from Antioch to Cæsarea by an offer on the part of the Cæsareans of greater emoluments, which probably means salary.[2] Gerontius was raised to the chair of sophistry at Apamea by his countrymen, and was granted by them a considerable income.[3] The argument of the Twenty-ninth Oration of Libanius,[4] in which a plea is made for the better remuneration of the rhetors of Antioch, seems to rest on the assumption that the salaries of these rhetors were derived from the city funds. Finally, the Emperor Probus (276–282) is said to have established salaries at Antioch ἐκ τοῦ δημοσίου.[5]

In view of this discrepancy, we should be inclined to conclude that some salaries were paid by the city and some by the emperor, and this was probably the case. One, indeed, would naturally assume that the duty of payment was a concomitant of the privilege of appointment. As we shall presently see, a single sophist's salary was sometimes made up of contributions from different sources. The very same salary which Libanius in two places says he received from the emperor at Constantinople, he in another passage says he received

---

[1] Lib., iii. 158, 1.    [2] Lib., ii. 220, 21; cf. i. 76, 7.
[3] Though this seems to be distinguished from the *salary* (Lib., ep., 1431, 1449).
[4] ii. 204–223 (the Thirty-first in Förster). See, especially, pp. 211, 213, 214.
[5] Malalas, xii. p. 302. The word δημόσιον, however, was sometimes used of city funds (Liebenam, *Städteverwaltung*, p. 298, n. 1), sometimes of state funds (Hirschfeld, *Die kais. Ver. bis auf Dioc.*, p. 13, n. 3; p. 30, n. 2); here and in the Themistius passage cited below (p. 174, n. 1) it probably refers to state funds. *Cf.* Procop., *Anecd.*, c. 26, quoted p. 126, n. 2, and Eunap., p. 90.

from the city; and he also says that this salary was taken away from him by order of the emperor.[1] Probably Libanius's salary at Constantinople, while an imperial grant, was partly paid from city funds.

We should also remember, however, that confusion was likely to occur, owing to the close interest which the imperial government took, in the fourth century, in the financial affairs of the municipalities. As the financial requirements of the government increased, the emperor became increasingly jealous of the management of the city funds, and felt more and more inclined to hedge them around with restrictive regulations. Thus, municipalities were forbidden, unauthorized, to expend public moneys for the erection of buildings; new taxes might not be imposed by the cities without the emperor's consent; and the raising of loans was absolutely forbidden to the communities.[2] And so, even as early as the third century, local councils were forbidden to assign salaries to any but professors of the liberal arts and physicians,[3] while in the fourth century, by an edict of Constantine of the year 349, no salaries at all were to be voted by the municipal councils without the special direction of the emperor;[4] and, as we have already seen, Valens, Gratian, and Valentinian, in their edict to the governor of Gaul in 376, warned the municipalities against donating salaries to professors on their own responsibility.[5] Furthermore, it appears

[1] *Ep.*, 1254: ἥν τε ἐκαρπούμην ἐκ τῆς πόλεως τροφήν, and γνώμῃ βασιλέως. *Cf.* Themis., 291d-292 c.
[2] Seeck, *Untergang der antiken Welt*, ii. pp. 168, 169.
[3] *Dig.*, l. 9, 4, 2.    [4] *Cod. Th.*, xii. 2, 1 (*Cod. Jus.*, x. 37).
[5] *Cod. Th.*, xiii. 3, 11.

that even in cases in which the salary was granted by the municipality, the sophist had sometimes to plead with the imperial magistrates before he could obtain his money.[1] Under these conditions, when the emperor's hand was so strongly felt in all local financial matters, it is not surprising if even municipal grants were at times felt to be due to the emperor's favor; they were made, at least with his implied, if not with his actual, consent, and sometimes by his direction, and they were subject to his control.

Some idea of the actual conditions under which sophists at this time got and retained their official salaries may be gained from the stray notices which Libanius gives of his experience at the time of his removal from Constantinople to Antioch. Libanius removed to Antioch from Constantinople in the spring of 354. While at Constantinople, he had been in receipt of an official salary, which he at one time says came from the emperor, and at another time from the city,[2] and when he removed to Antioch this salary seems not to have been stopped at once. Why this was the case we are not told, but we may surmise that it was because Libanius had not yet received full discharge from his duties at Constantinople; he for some time stood in constant dread of being recalled to that city.[3] Not long after his removal, however, apparently in the next year, one whose

---

[1] *E. g.*, Lib., ii. 212, 12 *ff*.      [2] See pp. 172, 173.

[3] When his salary was finally withdrawn, he was, he says, quite resigned to the loss, as it was better that he should sever all connection with the city (*ep.*, 488). Acacius was in the enjoyment of a salary at Antioch; when he went to Palestine, an effort was made to take this salary away, which effort Libanius opposed (*ib.*, *ep.*, 292).

name is not given secured, first the cessation of further payments to Libanius, and then, by imperial edict, the transference of the salary to another sophist, presumably one who was at the time teaching at Constantinople; and he even went so far as to write to the Prætorian Prefect of the East, within whose jurisdiction Antioch was, with the object of demanding back from Libanius that part of the salary that had already been paid since Libanius's removal. The prefect at this time was Strategius; being a man who exercised justice in his office, and was withal an admirer of Libanius, he refused to listen to the request.[1] Through his efforts, the attempt to extort past payments from Libanius was stopped, and apparently even a postponement of the withdrawal of the salary was effected. Libanius sent a special messenger, one Agrœcius, to Constantinople to secure the arrears that were due him, and he wrote to Themistius, the famous philosopher of Constantinople, and to Photius, probably the proconsul of the province in which Constantinople was situated, to assist the messenger in his mission.[2] Just when the salary was finally withdrawn for good we do not know, but apparently in the spring of 357; there remained some arrears which were never paid.[3] We are also ignorant of the exact time when Libanius first received a salary at Antioch, but it was earlier than the winter of 358–359, for we find him then reminding Polychronius, the proconsul of Phœnicia, of the fact that he had been instrumental in lowering, or even totally withdrawing,

[1] Lib., *ep.*, 1254, 1247.   [2] Lib., *ep.*, 1261, 1262.
[3] Lib., *ep.*, 488.

that salary;[1] and it would seem from certain other indications that it was possibly as early even as 354, in which case Libanius was receiving a salary from Constantinople and another from Antioch at the same time.[2] The man who instigated the movement to take away Libanius's salary at Antioch was Helpidius, at that time Prætorian Prefect of the East. This salary was restored in 362 by Salustius or Salutius, successor of Helpidius. Half of it was then to come from Antioch and half from Phœnicia; the obtaining of the latter half, it was hoped, would be expedited by Julian, the proconsul of Phœnicia.[3] Gaianus, the successor of Julian, was later reminded by Libanius that he had the power of increasing or diminishing the amount of the salary.[4]

Several interesting pieces of information are derived from this account. It is evident, in the first place, that the imperial magistrates were very influential in determining the size of the teacher's salary; and, secondly, it is evident that the teacher's salary sometimes came from different sources. Libanius's position, though part of his salary was derived from the city of Antioch, may be considered as an imperial donation—imperial, for instance, as distinguished from the positions of the rhetors at Antioch, to be considered later.[5] Probably there were other such imperial chairs at Antioch (as the chair held by Acacius), and also at Constantinople and some smaller cities. The salary in each of these cases may have been derived from several sources.

---

[1] Lib., *ep.*, 27.

[2] See p. 267, n. 1. For the dating of the letters of Libanius, see Seeck, *Briefe d. Lib.*

[3] Lib., *ep.*, 652.    [4] Lib., *ep.*, 710.    [5] Ch. XII.

In consequence of the frequent and often serious fluctuations in prices to which the Roman market was in those days subject, the salaries of professors were, in the fourth century, in common with most other salaries, generally paid in kind or at rates varying as the price of some staple commodity, such as wheat or oil. Thus, in the edict of Valens, Gratian, and Valentinian, of the year 376, relative to professors in Gaul, it was directed that the Latin or Greek sophist should be paid a salary of twenty-four annonæ, the 'grammarian' a salary of twelve annonæ; in the specially flourishing city of Trèves the sophist was to receive thirty annonæ, the Latin 'grammarian' twenty, the Greek 'grammarian' (if one worthy could be found) twelve. The annona was the allowance of a common soldier, and it apparently sufficed, though in slender measure, for a man and his family;[1] it comprised such articles as bread, pork, mutton, salt, wine, and oil. Themistius, who held an appointment at the University of Constantinople, was entitled to a salary of two hundred medimni (*i. e.*, about three hundred bushels) of wheat, and the same number of jars of oil, probably monthly, though of this we are not told.[2] Themistius speaks most disparagingly of the philosopher who weighs his salt fish, wrangles with the paymaster about the weight of his goods, and tries to convert his wine and provisions into money.[3]

[1] See Seeck, *Untergang der antiken Welt*, ii. p. 540. The salary was called τροφή (Lib., *ep.*, 132), τροφαί (*ib.*, *ep.*, 27), πυροί (*ib.*, i. 76, 7), σῖτος (*ib.*, *ep.*, 710), τιμή (*ib.*, *ep.*, 652), τιμαί (*ib.*, *ep.*, 710); more technically, σύνταξις (*ib.*, ii. 212, 22), σίτησις (Malalas, xii. p. 302). [2] Themis., 292 a.

[3] Themis., 292 c. Besides salt fish, ὄψα are here mentioned; barley, in Lib., *ep.*, 27, 710. Sometimes part payment was still made in money (*ib.*, *ep.*, 710; ii. 211, 5).

The conversion of surplus goods into money, however, must have been no unusual proceeding, and it probably caused the sophist no little trouble and anxiety.[1] Sometimes the professor's income was increased in still other ways — by valuable gifts, as in the case of Libanius at Constantinople, or by the assignment of a piece of land for use during the professor's lifetime, as happened more than once at Antioch.[2]

Those sophists who had no official appointment subsisted upon the fees of their students.[3] Whether fees were also a form of income for the officially appointed sophists is not for all periods and for all places certain. There is evidence that they were, if the sophist chose to make them so, at Athens in the second century, and at Antioch in the fourth century,[4] and probably the same is true of every place up to the end of the fourth century. In the fifth century, however, under the stricter regulations of Theodosius, the case may have been otherwise, at least at Constantinople.

The size of the fee was — except under the circumstances immediately to be noted — determined by the sophist himself, and depended in great measure on the

[1] Libanius speaks of a sophist, Eudæmon, who was concerned to turn his 'allowance' into money (*ep.*, 132).
[2] Lib., i. 57, 9; ii. 208, 10; 211, 9; 213, 2. Libanius at Constantinople seems to have enjoyed the income from a piece of land.
[3] Called $\mu\iota\sigma\theta\delta s$ (Themis., 288 d); $\dot{a}\mu o\iota\beta a\iota$ (Lib., i. 197, 16).
[4] The sophists of Antioch took fees while in the enjoyment of a salary (Lib., ii. 215, 1). Themistius at Constantinople prided himself on not taking fees from his students (Themis., 288 c, 289 a, 291 c, 294 a). But he also waived his salary, so we can hardly draw an argument from his case. For Athens, see Philos., 526. See also Lib., *ep.*, 1449.

breadth of the sophist's reputation and the depth of the student's, or the student's father's, purse. If the sophist was famous and drew large audiences, he could, if he was so disposed, demand and obtain almost any price for his lectures. Not always, however, did the professor have a fixed price for his course, to be imposed on all students alike; sometimes an agreement as to the size of the fee was made with the student or the student's parent or guardian before work in the course began;[1] and at other times the professor left it to the student himself to give whatever he could and would. Rich students were inclined to be generous toward favorite sophists, and often gave them voluntarily large sums of money, as a mark of admiration and respect. When the sophist Scopelian came to Athens, early in the second century, Herodes Atticus was a boy, studying under the tutorship of his father. Scopelian was famous in the line of extempore speaking, and the young Herodes, after hearing him declaim, imitated so well his style and manner that the father, pleased with the boy's attainment, rewarded both him and the sophist. To the former he gave five hundred talents, to the latter fifteen ($540,000 and $16,200, respectively). Out of his present Herodes gave to his teacher another fifteen talents, and the father, asserting that all other sophists — those of an earlier age — had done nothing but

---

[1] Lib., ii. 342, 13; Themis., 288 d. Lucian tells of a case in which it was agreed that payments should be made on the last day of the month (*Hermot.*, 80). Elsewhere the first of January is mentioned as the regular pay-day (Lib., i. 259, 20; ii. 427, 3, 11). Sometimes presents of money, fruit, wine, oil, etc., were sent to the sophist by the student's father (*ib.*, iii. 135, 10).

corrupt his son's tongue, destroyed their busts, which had been arranged along the corridors of his house.[1]

The well-known generosity of Herodes was doubtless often taken advantage of. On one occasion he sent to the distinguished sophist Polemo, whom he had shortly before heard declaim, the sum of 150,000 drachmæ ($27,000). Polemo refused to accept the gift, and Herodes thought himself held in scorn, until a friendly interceder suggested that possibly the offended sophist might accept 250,000 drachmæ ($45,000). Herodes added the extra 100,000 drachmæ, and had the pleasure of beholding his gift accepted.[2]

These sums seem in this connection fabulous, but it must be remembered that they were given for single recitals, not for courses of lectures, and they cannot be considered typical except of what the most famous sophists would occasionally receive from princes and wealthy patrons of the art.[3] We must also bear in mind that this was practically the only way in which a prince or wealthy patron could testify materially to his admiration for the art of letters and his gratitude toward his alma mater. To bestow valuable gifts and privileges on individual teachers was, in fact, to donate to the university itself. The corporate alma mater (if we except the philosophical schools, to which, as we have elsewhere seen, funds were also sometimes given) existed not at this period. The fees which Damianus gave, however, were considerably more moderate than those of Herodes,

---

[1] Philos., 521.  [2] Philos., 538.
[3] Such another wealthy patron was Theagenes, chief magistrate of Athens, in the fifth century: ἀναλοῦτο δὲ αὐτῷ πολλὰ τῶν χρημάτων εἴς τε διδασκάλους καὶ ἰατροὺς κ. τ. λ. (Suidas, s. v. Θεαγένης).

182    UNIVERSITIES OF ANCIENT GREECE

but still generous.[1] Damianus later became a sophist himself, and, while studying as a young man in Asia, he gave to each of the great sophists whose lectures he attended, Aristeides of Adriani, and Adrian of Tyre, 10,000 drachmæ ($1,800). Damianus, however, was accounted wealthy, and, though the prices which he paid to his two teachers were apparently for courses of lectures, not for single recitals, they were still in the nature of gifts, and were considered exceptional. The fee which Proclus set for his course, on the other hand, was probably somewhat below the usual price demanded.[2] He required, once for all, from each of his students, the sum of one hundred drachmæ ($18), and then allowed him to attend lectures as long as he would. Proclus also provided a library for the special use of his students, so that they might supplement his lectures by private reading.

We do not find that, as a rule, the sophists, even the greatest of them, were exorbitant in their charges for regular instruction, while they were certainly often most generous and considerate toward their poorer pupils. Thus, Scopelian, who was so richly rewarded by Atticus for improving his son's style, graded his fees according to the circumstances of his pupils.[3] The wealthy Damianus, while teaching at Ephesus, took no fees at all from students who came from abroad, provided he

---

[1] Philos., 605.
[2] Philos., 604. In 361, Libanius says that probably a man could obtain more for his teaching in Antioch than elsewhere — probably elsewhere in Asia is meant (*ep.*, 277). For the price of a sophist at Rome, see Juv., vii. 186; of a 'grammarian,' *ib.*, 215 *ff*.
[3] Philos., 519.

saw that they could not afford to pay,[1] while Themistius, the sophist-philosopher of Constantinople, prided himself on not making money out of his pupils, and was even ready on occasion to lend a helping hand to those who stood in need.[2] Lollianus, who was sophist and at the same time the chief magistrate at Athens, collected on one occasion a contribution from his students to relieve a threatened famine, and then made up the amount so collected by remitting the fees for his lectures.[3] From these and other [4] cases we may see that the sophist was not, as a rule, inclined to press hard on his poorer students, and that the way to a higher education in those days was probably rarely closed to a boy by reason of the cost of tuition alone. It is evident from many passages in the sophists themselves that the studying youth was then, as it is now, made up of both rich and poor alike.[5] This democratic mingling of all classes in the sophist's school-room must, we should say,

[1] Philos., 606. Isocrates, at an earlier time, took fees from foreigners, and those well-to-do foreigners, only (Isoc., *De antid.*, 39, 164).

[2] Themis., 288–291; Lib., *ep.*, 379. [3] Philos., 526, 527.

[4] See, for example, the case of Libanius (p. 187), who in his later years took no fees from his students. He says that it was pay enough if the students displayed a disposition to learn (*ep.*, 1583). Similarly, Themistius thought it pay enough if his students turned out modest in their bearing, restrained in their passions, well-mannered, lacking in awkwardness, and not without common sense, etc. (Themis., 289 a). *Cf.* also *Lib.*, iii. 346, 7; Philos., 600. The philosopher in Luc., *Hermot.*, 9, must have loaned money to his student. See also p. 331, n. 5. The sophist probably felt under moral obligation to give instruction free to his poorer students, when he himself was not in need of the fees (*cf.* p. 190, n. 3).

[5] See, for example, Themis., 288 c; Lib., i. 198, 6. Note also the case of Proæresius and Hephæstion (p. 329).

have been an influence of counteractive tendency in a society that was growing more and more aristocratic every day.

Teaching in the palmy days of sophistry seems to have been for many a not unprofitable profession. The evidence that this was so is plentiful.[1] We must, however, guard against believing that the road of sophistry was paved with gold for all. Competition was great, and the success of the most distinguished sophists probably serves to conceal the fact that there were many others whose condition was hardly more than tolerable. The profession of the philosopher, unless, like Themistius, he held an official appointment, was probably less remunerative at this time than that of the sophist, for the sophist was the incarnation of the university, and the halo that hung about his head drew students toward his class-room and away from that of the philosopher.[2]

Toward the beginning of the fourth century, owing to the high prices that at that time prevailed, Diocletian undertook to establish a maximum scale of prices for commodities and services. In this scale, the highest fee that a sophist was allowed to charge a student was two hundred and fifty denarii a month. The denarius, originally a silver coin of about the value of the drachma (eighteen cents), was, under the system of Diocletian, a

[1] Only a few references can be given. Lollianus made a good living out of his teaching (Philos., 527). Many at one time got rich by teaching at Antioch (Lib., ii. 215, 6; 421, 7). *Cf.*, further, Luc., *Apol.*, 15; Philos., 615; and see p. 162, n. 1. But the situation was different in the reign of Constantius and toward the end of the fourth century (see pp. 112, 119 *ff.*, 191).

[2] Timocles, the Stoic, however, took μισθοὺς οὐκ ὀλίγους (Luc., *Jup. trag.*, 27).

small copper coin worth between two-fifths and one-half of a cent. The sophist was, therefore, at that time allowed to charge his pupil a little over one dollar a month. This restriction on prices, however, did not long remain in force.[1]

Of course, the sophist's income depended in large measure on the number of his students. From a few intimations we are enabled to gain some idea of what the size of the classes was; as a rule, they appear, in the case of the more famous sophists, to have been large. Chrestus of Byzantium is said to have had a hundred paying pupils at one time.[2] Libanius, at the beginning of his career, was promised forty pupils if he would set up a school in Constantinople, and, when he actually did so, he gathered more than eighty.[3] Afterward,

---

[1] Until 1890 the value of the Diocletian denarius was uncertain and was variously estimated. In that year Mommsen, through a valuable discovery recently made, was enabled to determine its value as slightly over one and four-fifths pfennigs, German money, that is, a little over two-fifths of a cent (*Hermes*, 25, pp. 17–35). For the Diocletian tariff, see *Der Maximaltarif des Diocletian*, Mommsen and Blümner. Other rates given in this tariff for those connected with the teacher's profession are: for the teacher of gymnastics (*ceromatitœ*), 50 denarii; for the hired pedagogue (*pœdagogo*), 50 denarii; for the teacher of letters, or teacher of lowest grade (*magistro institutori litterarum*), 50 denarii; for the teacher of arithmetic (*calculatori*), 75 denarii; for the teacher of short-hand-writing (*notario*), 75 denarii; for the teacher of the copyist's art (*librario sive antiquario*), 50 denarii; for the 'grammarian' (*grammatico*), 200 denarii; for the geometer (*geometrœ*), 200 denarii; for the teacher of architecture (*architecto magistro*), 100 denarii. In each case the rate was for a single student for a month. Blümner (p. 116) understands that it applied, not to those who taught in private houses, but to those who set up schools in the city.

[2] Philos., 591. Another sophist, three hundred pupils (Schemmel, *Neue Jahrb.*, 22, p. 494). [3] Lib., i. 24, 15; 29, 7.

removing to Antioch, he had in that city, at first fifteen, then over thirty, later fifty, and at last so many that, as he says, he could not get to the end of them before sundown.[1] With his fifteen pupils Libanius was in despair, considering that he was living in idleness.[2] At the time of the great riot at Antioch, his class dwindled, first to twelve, and then to seven; "but still," he says,[3] "for so small a number I continued to go down to the school, and I did so just as readily as before." For a number less than ten he declined on most occasions to make up a class.[4] Philosophers and the less popular sophists doubtless had to content themselves with fewer pupils.[5]

Sometimes, under the stress of competition, sophists did not hesitate to resort to unbecoming measures to enlarge their classes. We have already seen how the rivals of Proæresius tried, by rich banquets and other more questionable inducements, to increase their following and draw students away from Proæresius. Occasionally a sophist offered money to those who would join his class. Libanius tells of a case of this kind,[6] and

[1] Lib., i. 70, 13; 71, 10; 73, 4; *ep.*, 407. Förster (ed. Lib., i. p. 133), following Cobet, reads in Lib., i. 71, 10, πλειόνων ἢ δὶς τοσούτων νέων, thus eliminating the number thirty.

[2] Lib., i. 70, 13.     [3] ii. 272, 6.     [4] Lib., ii. 273, 6.

[5] Themis., 30 c. *Cf.* the jest on Aristeides (Aristeid., iii. p. 741).

[6] i. 45, 11. Men (or was it the sophist Acacius?) were bribed by dinners to oppose Libanius (Lib., *ep.*, 418, 443). On one occasion Libanius played the following trick on his rival Acacius: He sent one of his students to the sophist with instructions to pretend that he wished to leave Libanius's school and join the forces of Acacius. The student was warmly welcomed by Acacius, who allowed himself to be escorted home by the new recruit. When the sophist's door was reached, the student bounded off

Themistius was accused of buying students at prices ranging from a mina to a talent each (from $18 to $1,080), a charge which he, however, indignantly denies.[1] Adrian won the favor of his pupils in more legitimate ways: by joining in their sports and drinking-bouts, instituting hunting expeditions, and celebrating the national festivals in their company.[2]

One of those sophists who were inclined to be lenient in the matter of fees was Libanius. In the latter part of his career he allowed his students to do as they pleased with regard to giving payment for their instruction, the understanding being that those who were financially able to pay should do so, according to their means. Few, however, of the well-to-do students were found to act as their consciences should have directed, and, as a practical scheme, this honor system fell to the ground. Sorrowfully, Libanius acknowledges[3] that it is to the advantage neither of the professor nor of the student that instruction should be given free. "For," says he,[4] "what one can get free, one makes no exertion to obtain, and what has cost nothing, one does not

and joined the forces of Libanius, who were waiting in the neighborhood, and who greeted the sophist with a shout of laughter (Lib., *ep.*, 634).

[1] 289 b, 290 c, 291 d, 294 a. *Cf. ib.*, 293 d; Aristeid., ii. p. 532; Lib., *ep.*, 407. Sometimes pedagogues would sell their wards to the highest bidder (Lib., *ep.*, 407). Libanius tried to put an end to this practice. He thought it also unbecoming to canvass for pupils (*ib., ep.*, 87).

[2] Philos., 587.      [3] i. 199, 3.

[4] iii. 441, 12. *Cf.* Philos., 494. Also J. R. Lowell, *Harv. Anniv.* (*Works*, vi. p. 170): "Our ancestors believed in education, but not in making it wholly eleemosynary. And they were wise in this, for men do not value what they can get for nothing. . . ."

value;" while for him who is engaged in instructing youth, thought about material needs clogs the springs of the tongue.[1] We cannot help feeling that, in Libanius's case at least, the fear of frightening away students and the difficulty of collecting fees had much to do with the sophist's attitude in the matter of charging for instruction. The competition for students was, as we have seen, keen, and rival sophists were always looking with malicious glee for signs of discontent in the enemy's camp. "But what can I do?" says Libanius,[2] "expel the students and diminish the size of my class? In what way could I give greater satisfaction to Priam and the followers of Priam, who are always on the tiptoe of expectancy to behold the size of my class diminished and the number of my students fewer? I have in my time seen a general who, although the men under his command were worthless, did still determine to put up with the indignity, for fear that his army would fall an easy prey to the enemy." It is also clearly evident that the poor sophist was often sorely harassed by his inability to collect his fees. "For this is certainly enough," says Libanius in another place,[3] "to stir a man to indignation and make him cease from declaiming: that a boy, after receiving money from his father to bring to his sophist, should squander this on wine and dice and the pleasures of the body."

Occasionally the distracted sophist or philosopher had recourse to the law for the recovery of his debts.

[1] ii. 212, 8.     [2] i. 206, 15.
[3] i. 197, 17. See, further, on Libanius and his fees, i. 213, 11; ii. 217, 6 *ff.;* 267, 14; 311, 16.

Lucian tells us, in an amusing scene,[1] of a philosopher who, seizing by the scruff of the neck a pupil who was dilatory in the matter of repaying a loan, was for dragging him off to court, and would have done so, "and would," says Lucian, "have chewed his nose from his face, had the boy's friends not intervened." Herein the philosopher stood, in most cases, by his very profession, at a disadvantage, and Lucian is never tired of pointing the contrast between principle and practice in the philosopher who showed anxiety about his debts. The feeling that gave rise to these gibes was the same as that which in time caused the philosophers to be deprived of certain of the immunities originally granted to them by law — immunities which the other professors continued to enjoy as long as their kind existed — and it is an interesting fact that the attitude of the Roman jurists toward the philosopher's profession was exactly that of the satirist Lucian. The philosopher was for once taken at his word. The famous jurist Ulpian gave it as his legal opinion that philosophers should not be given judgment by provincial magistrates in cases brought for the collection of fees, for the reason that philosophers, by their very profession, should scorn mercenary rewards;[2] and we recollect that Antoninus Pius stated in an edict that if philosophers, when called upon to serve

[1] *Hermot.*, 9. *Cf. ib., Symp.*, 32; Juv., vii. 228; Augustin., *Confess.*, v. 12. Agathocles, the Stoic, went to law with his pupil about his fee (Luc., *Icaromen.*, 16). See also Lib., i. 213, 11; ii. 423, 11; iii. 446, 12. In Isocrates's time philosophers sometimes required the fees to be put in the hands of a third person before the instruction began (Isoc., *Contra soph.*, 5). So, in Lucian, the sophist demanded a retainer (Luc., *Rhet. præc.*, 9).
[2] *Dig.*, 1. 13, 1.

the state, made a discussion as to the amount of their wealth, they were shown to be no philosophers;[1] while an edict of Valentinian, already referred to, sarcastically observed, in directing that all unworthy philosophers found in a foreign city should be shipped back to their homes, that it was disgraceful if one who professed to support the burdens laid upon him by fortune could not support those put upon him by the state.[2] One would have thought that the jurists and emperors would have spared the Peripatetic philosophers at least, for it was one of the tenets of this sect that money was a 'good' and was not a thing to be despised. For the rest, this feeling that it was a derogation to the philosopher's dignity and inconsistent with the philosopher's profession that the philosopher should be particular with regard to the proceeds of his teaching was probably as old as the history of philosophy itself in Greece. It accounts in a measure for the attitude of Socrates and Plato toward the sophists of their time, as men who took pay for their instruction, and it appears again in the conduct of such men as Diogenes of Sinope. In the time of which we are treating, it influenced Themistius to waive the salary to which he was entitled,[3] and it explains why Apollonius of Tyana should have made it a reproach to philosophers in general that they accepted any salary at all.[4] It is noteworthy as showing that there existed in the world at large a strong tendency to

---

[1] P. 166.     [2] *Cod. Th.*, xiii. 3, 7.
[3] Themis., 260 b, 292, 293; *cf.* 25 c. It was a sign of the greatest penuriousness, he says, for a teacher to take money for his teaching when he did not need it (289 c).
[4] Philos., 386, 398; *cf.* Luc., *Nigr.*, 25.

regard the philosopher's profession as something more than a profession — as a thing not to be laid aside with the issuance from the school-room or the lecture-hall; it suggests the reverse of the picture drawn by Lucian.

As the fourth century wore on, the condition of those engaged in the teaching of liberal studies grew worse and worse. Latin, law, and short-hand-writing usurped in the popular favor the place of oratory and Greek, not because the former were in themselves more highly prized, but because they were favored by the Court and opened the way to influential and paying positions in the state.[1] Many old families, too, that could have been depended on to adhere to the old régime, had in the course of time become impoverished, and new families, with little taste for intellectual pursuits, had come to the fore. The classes of the sophist were diminished, while he found it ever harder and harder to collect his fees. "Few men nowadays," says Libanius, writing in the reign of Constantius,[2] "grow rich by teaching. Workmen and shopkeepers, sitting at their doors, count up the students of the sophist, and reckon that he reaps a goodly harvest. But far different is the case. The fact that many grew rich by this profession in former days makes it seem that many must do so now. But times have changed. The study of sophistry is dishonored by those in power, and wealth and consideration flow from other sources."

It also becomes year by year increasingly more difficult for the poor sophist to collect his regular salary.

[1] Lib., i. 133, 134, 143.
[2] ii. 214, 23 (paraphrased). *Cf.* 600, 14.

"Sometimes he gets only a part, sometimes none at all, sometimes it comes by driblets. And then, the bother that he is put to, to get it even so! He must go to the governor, or to the governor's attendants, or to the city treasurer, and demean himself by fawning upon his inferiors and begging for what is his own, and these are actions which, I am very sure, the man of self-respect, such as the teacher should be, would almost rather starve than do. And then, the meanness of this salary! Some call it enough, but I am ashamed to mention how small it is."[1] A hard lot altogether is the sophist's in these dark years of the reign of Constantius.

Such was the condition of affairs at Antioch; it could not have been much different at Athens. After Libanius settled at Antioch and when the darkness and discouragement of the reign of Constantius were nearly at their worst, one of the distinguished sophists of Antioch, Zenobius, died, and four other sophists (or rhetors) were appointed by the city to receive his salary, the single salary being divided among the four. Zenobius, during his last years, had been in possession of a valuable estate, which had been presented to him by the city and from which he derived an income that served to supplement, very respectably, his none too generous salary. Libanius, taking Zenobius's case as a precedent, came, in the interest of the four sophists, before the local council, and begged that a like dispensation might be made in their favor. The five formed a sort of school — the rhetorical department, or, more probably, one section of the rhetorical department, of the Univer-

[1] Lib., ii. 212, 12 (paraphrased).

## THE PROFESSORS: THEIR PAY 193

sity of Antioch — with Libanius at its head; he spoke, therefore, as one who had a personal interest in the welfare of all. Let us, from his description, obtain one last glimpse of the sophist's lot at this period:

Some of these sophists [he says[1]] do not even have homes of their own, but, like cobblers, they live in rented houses. Those who have bought houses are still in debt for the purchase money, and are therefore in worse plight than those who have not. One of them has three servants, another two, and a third not even two, and the servants are all insolent and ill-behaved, because they are so few in number. . . . This sophist blesses his stars that he has only one child, that, having several children, thinks himself in great misfortune, a third has to be careful that he gets no children, while the fourth acts the sensible part and avoids matrimony altogether. It used to be the case that those who were engaged in this profession went to the silversmith's and left orders for goods, and then, standing by, conversed with those who did the work, sometimes finding fault with the workmanship, and sometimes pointing out something better; sometimes praising those who were quick, and sometimes urging on the slow. But these have the most of their conversation — and let no one distrust my word — with the bakers, not asking for the bread that has been promised them or demanding back their money, but making excuses for what they themselves owe. Always saying that they will pay, they are always compelled to take more, and so, beset by two opposing evils, they have to avoid and seek the same persons; for they avoid by reason of their debts, and they seek by reason of their needs. . . . Then, when the debts have grown to great size and there is nothing wherewith to pay them, they take their wives' ear-rings or bracelets, removing them from their wives' persons, and, carrying them to the baker's, leave them in his hands,

[1] ii. 208, 27.

cursing, as they do so, the profession of letters. They have no time to consider how they shall replace what they have taken, for they must think what there is in the house that they can go to next. Again, when they have finished their lectures, they do not, as they should, straightway leave the scene of their labors and go home to rest, but they linger and hang about the lecture-hall, for to go home, they know, would only be to feel their trouble the more keenly. Then they sit down together and talk over in sorrow their hard lot, and one, thinking his position the worst, hears of even bitterer things from his neighbor. I, who am at the head of this school and at the same time a native of Antioch, hide my head in shame when I see such things.

Whether Libanius was successful in his petition to the council of Antioch, we do not know, but he may well have been so, for, although the petition was made between the years 355 and 361, during the reign of the unenlightened Constantius, Libanius was a sophist of great repute and influence in his native city, and whatever request he made was likely to receive favorable consideration.[1]

[1] Lib., ii. 221, 23.

## CHAPTER X

### WHAT THE SOPHISTS TAUGHT AND HOW THEY TAUGHT IT

WHEN, about the middle of the fourth century, Professor Himerius, of the University of Athens, welcomed to the college cloisters the proconsul Hermogenes, who was on a visit to the city and the University, he took occasion, in a speech delivered at the time,[1] to describe his friend's life and education. Brought up in the Court of the emperor at Constantinople, Hermogenes had imbibed from his boyhood the principles and beliefs of the old faith, before the old faith was proscribed, and had received the education which was proper for a youth of his condition. On reaching the age of manhood, he left the Court, and devoted himself for a number of years to the life of a student. First, he studied dialectic, and learned how to reason and how to demonstrate, and how to distinguish the true argument from the false and the specious. Then he turned to the art of rhetoric and learned how to add to bare words the charm of harmonious discourse. After that he delved into the mysteries of philosophy, and mastered the subject in its three branches: morals, physics, and theology. In this subject he did not stop with one system or one

[1] *Or.*, xiv. 18–30.

set of beliefs, but went, from beginning to end, through all that had been said and thought by the various schools in the different periods of their existence. Neo-Platonism, the doctrines of Plato and Aristotle, the dogmas of the Stoics and the Epicureans — with all he became familiar. From philosophy he went to astronomy and geography, and, in order to familiarize himself with the face of nature, he travelled in nearly all parts of the known globe. Finally, political science and the art of governing men engaged his attention, and here he made use of the Latin as well as the Greek tongue.

The great Christian orator and writer, Gregory Nazianzene, tells us, in his account of his friend Basil the Great's life,[1] how Basil, when a student at Athens, studied and excelled in all branches of academic learning. "Who," says Gregory, "was to be compared with him in rhetoric, . . . though he had not the rhetorician's cast of mind? Who excelled him in philology and in the understanding and practice of the Greek tongue? Who gathered more narratives, understood better the forms of metre, or laid down the laws of poetry more exactly? Who went deeper into the mysteries of philosophy, both that high philosophy which holds its face upward toward the sky, and that which is speculative and is more concerned with the daily actions of life, as well as that third kind which deals with demonstrations, oppositions, and arguments, and is called *Dialectic?* . . . Of astronomy, and geometry, and the properties of numbers, he obtained such an insight that even with

[1] *Or.*, xliii. 23.

the best he could hold his own. . . . And with medicine, . . . both theoretical and practical, he made himself thoroughly familiar."

From these two accounts we gain some idea of what the education of a man of broad and general culture was in the fourth century of our era. It may seem surprising, on first consideration, in view of the prominent part which the schools of sophistry played in the education of the day, that so little, comparatively, is made in these accounts of the study of rhetoric and eloquence. We must remember, however, in the first place, that the two men whose education is here described are presented to us in the aspect of exceptional cases. It is not to be supposed that all, or even a large part, of the young men who sought an education in those days studied every one of the subjects that these men studied, or studied it in the same way. Some, indeed, of these branches, as arithmetic, geometry, and others, were taught, in an elementary way, in what we should call the grammar, or the high, school. As probably studied by Basil and Hermogenes, they were more in the line of the specialists, the number of whom is always small and little in evidence compared to that of the great body of studying youth. Mathematics, then, in its various branches, astronomy, geography, law, and medicine, were, in so far as some of these were not studied in their elements in the grammar, or the high, school, either graduate or professional studies, while the two great departments of academic instruction, those which we may consider as constituting the college proper, were the departments of sophistry and philosophy. So, Libanius tells us[1] that the Emperor Julian, while he was yet a young man and before he had become emperor, set his mind upon the possession of two jewels, more beautiful than royalty itself — philosophy and rhetoric (φιλοσοφίᾳ καὶ λόγοις). Both of these he acquired and mingled in his soul —"the higher power," says Libanius,[2] "through the knowledge of things heavenly, and fluency of speech through association with sophists." And the ecclesiastical historian Socrates, in speaking of the Christian orator John Chrysostom, tells us who was his teacher in philosophy and who in rhetoric.[3]

But, secondly, we have to observe, in connection with the education of Basil and Hermogenes, that the philosophy of the fourth century, in so far as it was *taught*, was probably all, or nearly all, either of the Neo-Platonic type or of a type represented by, but greatly

[1] i. 375, 14.      [2] i. 376, 1. *Cf.* 409, 3.
[3] vi. 3. Lucian seems to say in a passage that is defective (*Parasit.*, 26) that rhetoric and philosophy are generally recognized to be pre-eminent among the arts, and Philostratus (274) represents Apollonius of Tyana as referring to the philosophers and the sophists as the dispensers of all wisdom: εἰ μὲν γὰρ παῖδά σε ἑώρων ἔτι, ξυνεβούλευον ἂν φοιτᾶν ἐπὶ φιλοσόφων τε καὶ σοφιστῶν θύρας καὶ σοφίᾳ πάσῃ τὴν οἰκίαν τὴν σεαυτοῦ φράττειν. Themistius says (303 a) that there are two chambers in the soul, one of which is inhabited by rhetoric, the other by philosophy. *Cf.*, further, Lib., i. 400, 6. The ἐγκύκλιος παιδεία (ἐγκύκλια παιδεύματα, ἐγκύκλια μαθήματα), 'the common round of subjects,' which every boy was supposed to study, seems not always to have included the seven liberal arts, grammar, logic, rhetoric, geometry, arithmetic, astronomy, and music. Maximus of Tyre, to be sure (*Diss.*, 37), includes, under the term, philosophy, rhetoric, and even poetics (*cf.* Vitruv., i. 1, 12), but Seneca (*ep.*, 88) makes no mention of philosophy and rhetoric, while Theon (*Progym.*, i. p. 146 [Speng., *Rh., Gr.*, ii. p. 59]), and Quintilian (*Inst. or.*, i. 10, 1) restrict the name to the elementary subjects, excluding philosophy and rhetoric. *Cf.* Strabo, i. p. 13.

inferior to, the philosophy of Themistius, an eclectic philanthropism, based on the doctrines of Plato and Aristotle, and combined with expositions of those authors' works. When Libanius, as just noted, speaks of the education of the Emperor Julian, he characterizes the philosophy which Julian learned as "the higher power, gained through the knowledge of things heavenly"— that is, as essentially a religion — and, in general, philosophy meant to Libanius the new doctrine of Neo-Platonism, which had already taken firm hold upon the East, but was only just becoming established at Athens.[1] Themistius held an appointment at the University of Constantinople, and, though we are not acquainted with the constitution of this University in the fourth century, we know that in the fifth century there was on its faculty, which included eight sophists, twenty 'grammarians,' and two lawyers, but one philosopher.[2] The chair of philosophy was not a chair of any special sect, but it is probable that the incumbent thereof busied himself, like Themistius, especially with the interpretation of the works of Plato and Aristotle. The Academic school, and possibly the Peripatetic, still subsisted at Athens in the fourth century, but that representatives of the Epicurean and Stoic sects were then teaching at Athens or elsewhere, in regular course, is hard to believe, though there may have been men here and there who professed for a price to expound the literature of these schools.[3] So, when it is said that Her-

[1] See, for example, i. 516, 15.
[2] *Cod. Th.*, xiv. 9, 3 (*Cod. Jus.*, xi. 19, 1).
[3] See Themis., 287 a. Themistius often speaks of Plato and Aristotle, but rarely refers to philosophers of the Epicurean and

mogenes made himself familiar with the systems and beliefs of the four schools of philosophy, we are perhaps to understand that he gained no small part of his information through private reading rather than through regular instruction.

The usual tendency of the fourth century student — of the student who was neither, like Basil and Hermogenes, filled with the desire to acquire, in the field of knowledge, all that there was to acquire, nor, like the scholars of Alexandria and elsewhere, inclined to the way of the specialist — was, it is to be feared, to overrate the comparative value of sophistry and to consider all other subjects as subsidiary to this; and, indeed, perhaps his attitude was but the reflection of that of most sophists and of the world at large. Eager to enter as soon as possible upon this study, which appealed in so popular a way to the æsthetic tastes of the Greek-educated peoples, and led to remunerative and influential positions in the state, the young student was all too apt to neglect those branches which should have preceded sophistry. "The old rhetoricians," says the rhetorician Theon,[1] "and especially those among them who were famous, used to consider that the student

---

Stoic sects. Julian says that in his time most of the writings of Epicurus and Pyrrho had perished (*Frag. ep.*, 301 C). See pp. 100 ff.

[1] *Progym.*, 1, p. 145 (Speng., *Rh. Gr.*, ii. p. 59). Compare with this Lucian's humorous account of the way to become a sophist (*Rhet. præc.*, 14). It makes no difference, says Lucian, whether the preliminary studies are taken or not; one may even skip reading and writing. For the value put upon a sophistical education by many fathers, see Lib., iii. 199, 23. They prize it more than all wealth, or even than life itself.

should not approach the study of rhetoric until he had gained some knowledge of philosophy and had filled his mind with philosophy's inspiring beliefs. Nowadays most young men, far from taking up philosophy before they come to the study of eloquence, do not even touch the ordinary elementary branches, and, worst of all, they attempt to handle forensic and deliberative themes before they have gone through the necessary preliminary training." This probably represents the attitude of many people toward education in the second, third, and fourth centuries: sophistry, the end and aim of all instruction, and every other subject secondary to this.

Theon, in the passage just quoted, says that it had once been considered by rhetoricians the proper thing for students to study philosophy before they studied rhetoric. The practice in this respect probably varied. Libanius heard the philosophers Priscus and Maximus while he was studying rhetoric at Athens,[1] while some students, especially such as were inclined to specialize in philosophy, doubtless took up the subject, or continued it, after the completion of their rhetorical course. This was the case, as we have seen, with Hermogenes, who, however, studied one branch of philosophy, dialectic, before he reached the rhetorician's course.

However, even such students as did not go through the regular course of elementary subjects probably in few cases failed to study under a 'grammarian.' The duties of this teacher have been sketched in Chapter II. He it was who grounded the young pupil in the language and literature of ancient Greece — the poetic literature

[1] Lib., *ep.*, 685, 866.

chiefly, though at times perhaps he expounded certain prose writers, as, for instance, the historians — and his course was introductory to that of the teacher of rhetoric. The term 'grammar,' however, as has already been explained, was much broader than the term as used in English, and the 'grammarian's' instruction extended over many fields. Of the two courses, the course of the 'grammarian' and that of the rhetorician, or sophist, the former was, in a general way, a course of instruction, while the latter was more distinctively a course of training; in the former the pupil was taught to read and write correctly, and was made acquainted with the language, literature, and life of the Greek race; in the latter he was trained to individual effort in the use of language and argument. These definitions are of course not to be considered as wholly exclusive of each other: some training in initiative probably accompanied the instruction given by the 'grammarian' in reading, writing, and literature, and sometimes the 'grammarian' anticipated composition subjects usually taught by the rhetorician; while, on the other hand, the rhetorician's course doubtless contained much that was wholly didactic in character. In general, however, the distinction here drawn held.[1]

This sophistry, then, that was made so much of in the education of those days — what, we have to ask, was its nature and how was it taught? Sophistry we may roughly define as the art of public speaking—in one word,

---

[1] For the duties of the 'grammarian' in the Roman education, see Quintilian, *Inst. or.*, Bk. I. Sometimes a boy attended a rhetorician while he was still studying under a 'grammarian.'

oratory. In so far as training in oratory depended on a body of fixed principles and precepts, it involved also a study of formal rhetoric, and thus the sophist, when he undertook to give a course in sophistry, had a twofold task to perform. He had, in the first place, to introduce his pupils to the theoretical and technical side of his subject, to acquaint them with the various divisions of rhetoric, together with the name and meaning of each, and he had, secondly, to train them in the art of speaking readily and fluently. It was this second aspect of the subject which was given the greater emphasis in the flourishing periods of sophistry, in the second, third, and fourth centuries, but in the fifth century, when sophistry was in its decline, the art tended to become more and more a matter of bare technical detail. Some sophists, indeed, in the earlier period, depended more, for the formation of their own style and delivery, on natural ability and intuition than on the precepts of their art. This was the case, we are told,[1] with Polydeuces, and Libanius, who in his student days attended more to his books than to his professor's lectures, showed in his declamations ignorance of technical details which, says Eunapius,[2] were familiar to every school-boy.

Early in the course, we are told,[3] the instructor

[1] Philos., 592.
[2] P. 98. Detractors of Libanius asserted that his success had been due to luck and that he had no rhetorical art (Lib., *ep.*, 123; *cf. ep.*, 140). *Cf.* Quint., *Inst. or.*, ii. 11.
[3] Theon, *Progym.*, 2, p. 158 (Speng., *Rh. Gr.*, ii. p. 65). Theon has here given us the best ancient description of the course pursued in the Greek schools of sophistry. The methods of the Roman schools were in general those of the Greek schools; therefore, Quintilian's account of the former may help us in forming

should, in order to impress upon his students the meanings of terms, select from the ancient authors good examples of the various kinds of discourse, such as the fictitious story, the narrative of fact, the eulogy, the description, the so-called commonplace, etc., and assign these to be memorized. Later he may himself compose other examples — examples of 'construction' and 'refutation' — and set these also before his students. Much time, meanwhile, is to be spent in studying the ancient authors, Demosthenes, Plato, Homer, Aristotle, etc., and, as these are read, either by the student or by the instructor, opportunity is found for the discussion of the writer's treatment of subject, his point of view, his arrangement of material, his language and style, and so on, wherein these are good and wherein they may be improved. At last, when the students are themselves ready to put pen to paper, they begin by imitating the models which they have had set before them, and gradually, as they advance under instruction, gain greater and greater freedom and self-dependence. Now the instructor takes occasion to explain to his students the proper arrangement of topics and of proofs, and he also tells them when to introduce digressions and when to expand, and discourses on the appropriate methods of treatment for the different kinds of cases. Remarks are also made on vocabulary and style, and the students are instructed to avoid rhythmical prose, such as that of Hegesias and others, and to strive first of all for dignity

our estimate of the latter. It is well, however, not to assume too great correspondence of detail. Theon's account has here been supplemented by a few notices drawn from other sources.

and clearness. Themes are set for the students to expand, first those of the purely declamatory type, afterward those of the deliberative and judicial types. Training in elocution follows, and the students are required to declaim, sometimes speeches and arguments from the authors they have studied, at other times their own compositions.

The instruction here sketched varied, of course, in its details, and the really able teacher, we may be sure, adapted his methods to the aptitude and ability of the individual student. Like Isocrates several centuries before, he tried to develop the judgment of his pupils, and depended more, for their improvement, on practice and example and wise guidance than on the use of fixed rules. The necessity of following some such method as this was recognized by the educators of those days quite fully. "We are not all born with equal aptitude for all things," says Theon;[1] ". . . We should, therefore, try to develop our naturally strong points and to make amends for our weak points, so that we may be able to handle, not large subjects only, like Æschines, or small subjects only, like Lysias, but all sorts of subjects equally well, like Demosthenes." The practice of one of the foremost teachers of the day — Libanius — was quite in accord with this precept. "No one of those who conversed with Libanius," says his biographer, Eunapius,[2] "or were honored with his intimacy, went away untouched. He could recognize a man's character in a moment, and see whether the good or the bad pre-

---
[1] *Progym.*, 2, p. 171 (Speng., *Rh. Gr.*, ii. 72).
[2] P. 97. *Cf.* Lib., *ep.*, 358, 1203; Quint., *Inst. or.*, ii. 8, 1–5.

dominated in his make-up, and he had equal tact when it came to conforming to that man's ways." Of course, this character applied to Libanius the teacher as well as to Libanius the man of the world.

In another respect also we have evidence that a wise discretion was a part of the ancient educator's outfit. "When the written work of the pupil is to be corrected," says Theon,[1] "the teacher should not begin by correcting all at once every error, large and small, that is on the paper. If he does, the pupil is in danger of becoming discouraged at the outset, and of thinking that there is no prospect of his making any advancement. The teacher should first correct a few of the more prominent errors, and from these go on at a later time to the more minute. When the teacher corrects an error, he should at the same time show wherein it consists and in what way an improvement in the pupil's work may be made." It is refreshing, in the face of the obloquy which has sometimes been heaped, in ancient as in modern times, on the art of Greek sophistry, to meet such thoroughly sensible remarks as these in one of the best of the ancient writers on the subject. They show us that, as we might have supposed, there were two sides to the matter, and that, in spite of Synesius's gibe, to the effect that the sophist sits like a jar filled to the brim with wisdom,[2] he was expected to dispense his wisdom in a judicious and rational way.

In order to obtain an idea of the thoroughness of the sophistical training, we may take one of the various

[1] *Progym.*, 2, p. 171 (Speng., *Rh. Gr.*, ii. p. 72) paraphrased.
[2] *Dion*, 13.

forms of discourse used in the sophist's school-room and see how the subject was there treated. Let this be the "fable" (μῦθος). This is described by Theon [1] as "a false narrative presenting the semblance of truth" (λόγος ψευδὴς εἰκονίζων ἀλήθειαν). In the first place, the student was taught the appropriate style for a fable. This differed from the style of any other kind of discourse and was distinguished by the characteristics of simplicity, naturalness, lack of artificiality, and clearness. The student would recognize the appropriateness of these characteristics, because he had already memorized examples of the fable, taken from the best authors. Secondly, the form of the story came under consideration. The student was taught to tell the story, at one time in direct narrative, as a piece of his own knowledge or experience, at another time in indirect narrative, as if on another's authority. In the Greek language, of course, this difference of form involved a difference of case, mood, person, etc. Sometimes, to compass an air of unaffectedness, the two forms were combined in one fable. After the student had thus learned to construct the fable in the correct style and form, he was taught to make proper application thereof. Thus, given a certain fable, as, for instance, that of the camel which, wishing for horns, lost even his ears, he must find an occurrence in history which, in its main features, resembled this, such as the case of Crœsus, who lost even the kingdom which he had, while striving for one that was larger; and, *vice versa*, if he was given

---

[1] *Progym.*, 3, p. 172 (Speng., *Rh. Gr.*, ii. p. 72).

a fact of history, he was to find a fable that would apply thereto. Again, he was required to draw a moral from a given fable, or, if the moral was given, to construct a fable from which it might be drawn. Further, he was taught how to expand and how to contract fables. To expand, he might, for instance, lengthen his descriptions or insert more narrative matter, and to contract, he might follow the opposite course. Finally, his work was examined, as a whole and in detail, with reference to various qualities, such as clearness, plausibility, dignity, consistency, order, and relevancy of parts.

The fable, it should be remembered, was only one of a variety of forms of discourse which received similar treatment to this. Some of these have been already mentioned — the narrative of fact, the fictitious narrative, the eulogy, the description, the commonplace, etc. One of the most striking facts in connection with this instruction is the emphasis that was laid in it on the study of literary style. It may be doubted whether there has ever been another period of the world's history when the youthful student has been taught with such systematic thoroughness to distinguish between the different qualities that should characterize the different forms of discourse. That the style of the fable should differ from the style of the narrative of fact, and that the eulogy and the description should be constructed in different moulds, with different words, different constructions, and a different literary atmosphere, are truths which we all recognize and which instinct teaches the artist to apply, but they represent a stage of literary nicety to which, it is to be feared, our instruction does not in the main strive to attain.[1]

Two of the most important exercises to which the ancient student was subjected were the 'refutation' and the 'construction' so-called (ἀνασκευή and κατασκευή). "In these exercises," says the rhetorician Aphthonius,[2] "is contained the whole force of the sophist's art." The 'refutation' was the argument attacking, the 'construction' the argument supporting, a given statement or story. The two arguments followed certain fixed lines, and were conducted on the basis of clearness, possibility, dignity, consistency, and advantage. We have the briefs for the plaintiff and the defendant in a case in which the Daphne-Apollo legend is at stake.[3] The 'refutation' must begin, we are told, with a depreciation of those who are the authors of the story, in this case the poets. Following the depreciation comes a statement of the story itself, and then the argument. The story is incredible, (1) because it is obscure. For what union of the Earth and a river can we conceive of? An overflowing of the Earth by the river's waters? Then are all rivers men. Can man beget a river, as a river, man? Wedlock is of bodies that have sensation, but the Earth has no sensation. Furthermore, how could Daphne be the daughter of the Earth and a river? We must suppose either that Daphne was a stream or

[1] Quintilian (*Inst. or.*, i. 9; ii. 1) says that the Latin 'grammarian' frequently anticipated a part of the work of the rhetorician and taught in a simple way some of the exercises referred to above. Apparently this practice was less frequent among the Greeks.

[2] *Progym.*, 5, p. 72 (Speng., *Rh. Gr.*, ii. p. 28); 6, p. 77 (*ib.*, p. 30).

[3] Aph., 5 and 6, pp. 72-80 (Speng., *Rh. Gr.*, ii. pp. 27-32).

that the river was a mortal. (2) Because it is impossible. Granted that Daphne was born of the Earth and a river, how could she have been brought up? Either in the water, in which case she would have been drowned, or under the earth, in which case she would not have been seen by Apollo. (3) Because it lacks dignity. It is beneath the dignity of a god to fall a victim to love. (4) Because it is inconsistent. Gods are superior to mortals; how, then, could Apollo have been outwitted by a woman among mortals? Also, why should the Earth have defended her daughter from Apollo? If wedlock is an evil, how was the Earth herself born? If it is a good, she unjustly deprived Daphne of what would have been to the latter's advantage. Either, therefore, the Earth was never born, or, being born, she was evil. (5) Because it is objectless. For why did the Earth act so contradictorily? She pained Apollo by saving him, but she also deluded him by leading him on. Again, she united the laurel-branch, a symbol of pleasure, which is fleeting, with virtue, which is the opposite of pleasure, and with prophecy, which is perennial. The case for the defence, following the same lines as the case for the prosecution, begins with a laudation of the originators of the story, and then proceeds to the argument, supporting the story on the basis of its clearness, possibility, dignity, consistency, and advantage.

The sophist Choricius, in eulogizing the class-room methods of his teacher Procopius, says:[1] "Not a word that was not Attic escaped his notice, not a thought that

[1] P. 5.

wandered from the point, not a construction that was inharmonious, not a syllable that jarred on the ear. It would have been easier for one, striking a wrong note on the cithara, to escape the notice of Arion of Methymna, or of the Lesbian Terpander, than for one who spoke a word out of tune to have done so unobserved by him." These words contain in brief a statement of the chief aim of the sophistic training: to teach appropriateness and orderliness of thought (*inventio* and *dispositio*), and purity and elegance of language (*elocutio*), under the latter being included choice of words and style. Again and again, in the descriptions of the sophist's trade, are these two features — thought and expression — combined.[1] One of the chief means employed to this end was the study of the ancients. Demosthenes, Plato, Thucydides, Isocrates, Lysias, Æschines, Homer, Hesiod, Aristotle, and even Aristophanes and the tragedians, were read and reread, learned by heart, discussed, and analyzed, in the schools.[2] So important

---

[1] *E. g.*, Syn., *Dion*, 4: περιττὸς ἀνὴρ εἰπεῖν τε καὶ γνῶναι· Choric., p. 14: δεινὸς τὰ δέοντα γνῶναι καὶ λαμπρὸς ἑρμηνεῦσαι· also Luc., *Rhet. præc.*, 1; Philos., 498, 511, 527, 544. *Cf.* Thuc., ii. 60, 5. It was, we remember (p. 5), in the careful adjustment of these two, the thought and the form, that the literary excellence of the earlier Greeks consisted. A third feature, subsidiary to the other two, but also an integral part of the art, was the delivery (*pronuntiatio*), which included the management of the voice, gestures, etc.

[2] See Jul., *ep.*, 42, p. 423 A; Lib., i. 179, 15; 202, 2; iii. 438, 10, 24; 439, 15; *ep.*, 828; Themis., 289 c; Luc., *Rhet. præc.*, 17; Philos., 518. Sometimes complaints were made that the pupils lingered too long over a single book (Lib., ii. 273, 1; *cf.* Themis., 289 a; Lib., *ep.*, 812). For the ἅμιλλαι (Lib., *ep.*, 246, 286, 407), engaged in by both students and teachers, see Sievers, *Leben des Lib.*, p. 24, n. 78, and Schemmel, *Neue Jahrb.*, 20, p. 61. The

a part in the sophistic training did study of these authors play, that the sophist was sometimes described as the

ἅμιλλα seems to have been an argument based on a passage or passages of an author, in which the speaker took a stand opposed to that of the author (see Luc., *Parasit.*, 58). Sometimes the students studied more modern authors, as Aristeides. Libanius recommends his own letters (*ep.*, 954), and says that his own speeches were studied in the schools (i. 103, 15). On one occasion Libanius received a letter from a friend during school hours, and he read the letter to the class instead of going on with the lesson (*ep.*, 128). At another time, receiving a letter, he conversed with his pupils about the sender (*ep.*, 607). Epistle-writing was one of the subjects taught in the schools. We obtain here and there in the authors a few glimpses of the class-room and of class-room methods. Once, when the students were not present, one of the boys came to Libanius and recited his own composition, about which some discussion had arisen. At first they both stood, Libanius near the door, and the boy apparently on the platform, in the rear of the room. After the boy had read about two hundred lines, they both became seated, each at his own desk (*ib.*, i. 238, 4). Libanius's students gave 'displays,' and after a 'display' of this sort school was dismissed for the rest of the day (*ib.*, ii. 267, 7, 16; 268, 11; 280, 15; *cf.* Themis., 312 b). This was done as a mark of honor to the boy who declaimed, and was customary (*ib.*, ii. 267, 16: τά τε οὖν ἄλλα τιμᾶν αὐτὸν παρῄνει τῷ μηδὲν προστεθῆναι τοῖς δεδειγμένοις λόγοις, καὶ νόμος ἦν ἀρχαῖος τοῦτο οὕτως ἔχειν ἐθέλων· *ib.*, 268, 3: τοῦτο δὲ ἦν, μηδὲν ἕτερον τοῖς ὑπὸ τοῦ νέου ῥηθεῖσιν ἐπεισενεγκεῖν). In general, for one orator to speak *after another*, ἐπ' ἄλλῳ, μετ' ἄλλον, seems to have involved some disrespect toward the latter. Hippodromus, being requested to give a display after one of his pupils, refused, saying, οὐκ ἐπαποδύσομαι τοῖς ἐμαυτοῦ σπλάγχνοις (Philos., 617). A similar honor was paid by Herodes to Polemo: ἔδωκε τῷ Πολέμωνι ὁ Ἡρώδης καὶ τὸ μὴ παρελθεῖν ἐπ' αὐτῷ ἐς λόγων ἐπίδειξιν, μηδ' ἐπαγωνίσασθαί οἱ (*ib.*, 538). Libanius objected to a poet reciting after him a poem on the same subject on which he had himself just delivered a speech: μὴ μετ' ἐμέ τις ἐπὶ τοῖς ἴσοις ἕξει τὸν σὸν ἀδελφόν (Lib., ii. 372, 19; *cf.* 23). The words *after Libanius*, attached to the announcement, were especially objectionable: προσθέντα τούτῳ τὸ μετ' ἐμέ (*ib.*, ii. 373, 3). *Cf.*, further, *ib.*, ii. 376, 14: ἐπῆγεν ἔπη τοῖς εἰρημένοις λόγοις, and 377, 15: τό τινα εἶναι τὸν ἐπ' ἐμοὶ λέξοντα· also *ib.*, ii. 281, 2: ὡς ἐπὶ μηδενὶ πεπραγμένῳ, and Luc., *Charid.*, 13. Students took notes of their lectures

## WHAT THE SOPHISTS TAUGHT

one who led young men to a knowledge of the ancients;[1] and constant conning of the classic authors was said to be essential for the good speaker.[2] To assist the teacher and the student in their cultivation of Attic style, handbooks of Attic words and constructions, such as those referred to in the first chapter of this book, were prepared.

The sophistical education aimed at preparing young men for the professions and pursuits of active life, both public and private. The judge, the advocate, the senator, the ruler of provinces, the city magistrate, all received their training, before the time when Christianity and the altered favor of the imperial Court drove

(Luc., *Hermot.*, 2; Lib., ii. 293, 16; *cf.* Quint., *Inst. or.*, i. *praefat.*, 7; ii. 11, 7). Sometimes they went through the streets studying their lessons or thinking up questions to ask their teacher (Luc., *Hermot.*, 1). Occasionally they interrupted the teacher with objections (*ib.*, 13; *cf.* Plut., *De rect. rat. aud.*, 4, 10, 18). Sometimes the work of other teachers was taken up for criticism, and the philosophers at times discussed the tenets of other sects and showed their weak points (Luc., *Hermot.*, 32). The philosopher Taurus used to give his students an opportunity to ask questions at the close of his lecture (Gell., i. 26). When the professor lectured, or read, to his students, he was said ἐπαναγνῶναι (Epictet., i. 10, 8). In *ep.*, 812, Libanius gives the account of his work in class for four months. Herodes, in addition to his regular lectures, held a *privatissime* (τὸ Κλεψύδριον), to which his ten most promising students were invited. At these lectures a water-clock was set for the length of time required to recite a hundred lines, and these Herodes recited at a stretch, first requesting his students not to interrupt by applause. The members of this seminar were called by outsiders *Thirsters*, διψῶντες (Philos., 585, 586, 594).

[1] Lib., ii. 207, 11: ἡγούμενοι τοῖς νέοις ἐπὶ τὴν γνῶσιν τῶν ἀρχαίων· Choric., p. 4: δύο γὰρ ὄντων οἷς ἀρετὴ βασανίζεται σοφιστοῦ, τοῦ τε καταπλήττειν τὰ θέατρα συνέσει λόγων καὶ κάλλει, τοῦ τε τοὺς νέους μυσταγωγεῖν τοῖς τῶν ἀρχαίων ὀργίοις. *Cf.* Jul., *ep.*, 42; Lib., *ep.*, 367.

[2] Lib., ii. 289, 19; 291, 25; 292, 2; 294, 23; 295, 6.

sophistry into exile, in the sophist's class-room.¹ Such being the case, we should expect to find in this training a wise adaptation of methods to the requirements of life, and in this expectation we are not deceived.

A central point in the Greek sophistical education was the training of the memory. The Greek student of eloquence was required to learn by heart large quantities of the ancient authors, as well as many of his own, and his professor's, compositions. Discourse on common topics, such topics as would frequently arise in the course of the student's professional career, was also prepared and given to be memorized. By this process not only was the memory of the student, or, at least, the skill with which the student used his memory, improved, but his mind was filled with a ready store of material and illustration. We remember the famous *tour de force* of Proæresius—how on one occasion, after delivering an extempore oration on a subject just propounded to him, he turned to the short-hand-writers at his side, and, telling them to observe carefully what they had taken down, astounded all his hearers by repeating, word for word, without making a single slip, the whole speech from beginning to end.² This feat, which was not unique, fairly put the audience into raptures of delight. Eunapius says of himself that when he arrived at Athens, at the age of sixteen, he had the ancients at his tongue's end,³ and a similar statement

¹ See p. 78, n. 1.
² See p. 157. *Cf.* Pliny, *ep.*, ii. 3, 3 (of Isæus); Quint., *Inst. or.*, x. 6, 4; xi. 2; Cic., *De or.*, ii. 74 and 86; Sen., *Contr.*, i. *praefat.*, 2, 3, 17–19.
³ P. 75.

is made with regard to the philosopher Priscus.[1] The importance attached by the sophists themselves to the cultivation of the memory is suggested by the anecdote that is told of Polemo.[2] Polemo once, seeing a robber of many misdeeds writhing on the rack and hearing the officer who was in charge of the culprit remark that he knew not what punishment was good enough for the man, said, "Order him to commit to memory the writings of the ancients." "For Polemo," says Philostratus, "although his own mind was stored with matter, considered that the hardest thing of all in the sophistic training was learning by heart." The students of Dionysius of Miletus were famed in their day for their good memory, and some people even went so far as to say that Dionysius made use in his teaching of mnemonic arts derived from the Chaldæans.[3] But this allegation Philostratus denies, accounting for the good memory of Dionysius's students on the simple ground of practice and constant repetition. "There *are* no arts of memory," says Philostratus, "nor could there be, for memory gives us arts, but it is itself unteachable; nor is it to be acquired by any art; it is a gift of nature and a part of the imperishable soul."

In active life the advocate must at all times be prepared to defend either side of a case, and, whichever side he defends, to look at his own as his adversary's, and his adversary's as his own. This was the exact method employed in the preparation furnished by the

---
[1] Eunap., p. 65. [2] Philos., 541.
[3] Philos., 523. *Cf. ib.*, 618; Syn., *Dion*, 11. On cultivating the memory in children, see Plut., *De lib. educ.*, 13.

sophistic schools. Fictitious cases, drawn, when not wholly general in character, from the ancient history and mythology, were constructed, and the students were required to defend first one side and then the other. Sometimes these cases were those of actual or probable occurrence, but often they were purely imaginary, and at times most ingeniously intricate in construction. Thus, there is a law to the effect that, when a tyrant is slain, his children shall be slain with him. There is another law which grants to tyrannicides whatever they may ask. A woman who is married to a tyrant kills her husband and then asks for the possession of her children. The student is to plead the cause of the woman.[1] The Potidæans, being besieged by the Athenians, have been driven by hunger to taste one another's flesh. The Athenians are accused by the Corinthians of impiety. The student is to argue the case for the Corinthians.[2] There is a law at Lacedæmon that no one under thirty shall speak in the public assembly. After the battle of Leuctra, the Thebans send ambassadors to the Lacedæmonians, threatening war if the Lacedæmonians do not grant independence to Messene. Some advise compliance with the Theban demand, but Archidamus, a young man, speaks in favor of war. His counsel prevails, and the enemy are defeated. Then Archidamus is indicted on a charge of illegal action. The student is to support the cause of Archidamus.[3] Judicial themes were considered the most difficult kind of themes, and were therefore given to the student last of all. He was

[1] Lib., iv. 798.   [2] Lib., iv. 348.   [3] Lib., iv. 420.

## WHAT THE SOPHISTS TAUGHT 217

first trained in declamatory and deliberative themes.[1] In many cases, it will be noticed, the student was required to put himself into the position of another person and to imagine what that other person's thoughts and emotions would be in a given set of circumstances. Sometimes actual impersonation was demanded. Cimon, son of Miltiades, pleads before the Athenian people to be allowed to take his father's place in prison;[2] Patroclus tries, by tears and reproval, to reconcile Achilles to the Grecian host;[3] Timon, in love with Alcibiades, brings an accusation against himself in the Athenian senate.[4] These are situations for which the student is required to find expression in words and in action. The last case, the treatment of which involves a reconciliation of conflicting emotions, is one of a large class of cases. Libanius, from whose collection it is taken, says with regard to it, in his introductory remarks: "This is a difficult theme, for the student has to represent two antagonistic characters, the misanthrope and the lover. Care must be taken not to introduce thoughts that are inappropriate to either character. The misanthrope, however, must in the end prevail over the lover."

Much was also made in the sophistic training of extempore speaking, but the display of this accomplishment we can better observe in the grand show declamations of the sophists themselves; and to these we now turn.

---

[1] Theon, *Progym.*, 1, 151 (Speng., *Rh. Gr.*, ii. 61); Tac., *Dial. de or.*, 35. See Volkmann, *Rhetorik*, p. 293.
[2] Lib., iv. 335.    [3] Lib., iv. 80.    [4] Lib., iv. 181.

## CHAPTER XI

### PUBLIC DISPLAYS

IN the preceding chapter we have touched upon one side of the sophist's profession — the purely pedagogic, or class-room, side. The more picturesque side was brought into view when the sophist himself came forward as the interpreter of his own art.[1] This took place on various occasions. Libanius made it a practice, at one period of his life while teaching at Antioch, to give a public display of his art at regular intervals, during the winter and spring months, those being the months when college was in session and the town was full of students.[2] During the long vacation, in summer and early autumn, sophists had an opportunity of travelling about from place to place, and then often friendly contests were instituted.[3] Sometimes the governor of a province or other magistrate, while passing through a town, would

---

[1] The two most important duties of the sophist were to hold public displays and to introduce boys to the ancients, that is, to teach (see the quotation from Choricius, p. 213, n. 1).

[2] Lib., i. 196, 7; 199, 10. *Cf. ep.*, 1292. He gave displays in summer also (*ib., ep.*, 394 a). At Antioch, when a display was given, there seems to have been a general holiday among the sophists, so that all students could attend (*ib.*, ii. 279, 11). It may have been under some such regulation as this that Libanius heard three sophists at Athens (*ib.*, i. 14, 5; see p. 304).

[3] See pp. 256 *ff. Cf.* Eunap., p. 17; Lib., i. 176; *ep.*, 394 a. Sometimes the contest was not so friendly (Eunap., pp. 81, 86).

PUBLIC DISPLAYS 219

call upon a distinguished sophist to give a sample of his eloquence, or he would travel a long distance to see and hear one who was famous. Even emperors, on occasion, visited the sophist's hall or gave a hearing at the Court.[1]

Generally the displays were open to the public, but at times, as when they were given by special request, for the benefit of a prince or high official, they were held before limited audiences. Libanius, in the latter part of his career, finding that the people complained of the number of his speeches, excluded the public on these occasions, though he had earlier admitted them.[2] Sometimes invitations were sent out several days before the declamation was to be held, or servants were despatched through the town to 'round up' the students and bring them to the lecture.[3] The students, it is clear,

[1] This was done by Hadrian and others of the early emperors, and also by some of those of the fourth century. The Emperor Julian, when he visited Antioch for the purpose of taking up the war in the East, inquired first of all for the sophist Libanius, and, when he saw Libanius, his first words were, "When shall I hear you speak?" (Lib., i. 81, 22). On one occasion a provincial governor, whose official residence was at Antioch, sent to Libanius, requesting a sample of his art, but Libanius refused to speak unless the governor would leave the palace and come to his (Libanius's) lecture-room (ib., i. 77, 4). A similar story is told of Polemo, who once, by repeated refusals to speak, actually compelled a certain magistrate, high in power, to come to his door with a gift of ten talents ($10,800) and a prayer for recognition (Philos., 535).

[2] Lib., i. 180, 1. Maximus held δημοσίας ἐπιδείξεις (Eunap., p. 61; cf. Himer., or., xvii). ἐν ὁμίλῳ κοινῷ (Lib., ep., 25). Cf. ib., ep., 244, 964. A speech delivered before an audience of four (ib., ep., 31); with closed doors (ib., ep., 286); the audience limited to fifteen by request (ib., i. 50, 12).

[3] Invitations sent out three days beforehand (Themis., 313 d); the day beforehand (ib., 243 a). Servants sent to 'round up' the students (Lib., i. 199, 11; cf. Philos., 589). The sophist some-

were, in Libanius's later years, not always ready to come, but in the 'good old days' of sophistry they needed no urging, if the sophist was distinguished, but flocked to the lecture-hall in throngs.[1]

Generally, at least at Antioch, no fee was charged for admission to these lectures.[2] Occasionally a sophist made it, in the case of a wealthy patron, a condition of speaking, that the patron should reward him with a substantial gift,[3] while in other cases the patron was quite ready to testify unasked to his regard for the sophist. At Athens an admission fee may sometimes have been charged.[4]

---

times went personally to invite his friends (Syn., *Dion*, 11). Audiences were collected by flattery (Lib., i. 62, 16). See also *ib.*, *ep.*,173, 546, 1292. Jealousy was sometimes caused if a person was overlooked when the invitations were sent out (*ib.*, i. 205, 18; iii. 446, 9). It was considered an honor to receive an invitation (*ib.*, *ep.*, 173). Libanius sought to stifle jealousy by multiplying his displays (*ib.*, *ep.*, 394 a). He says in one place that he is constantly requested, even during the summer, to give displays, and that he has invited the whole city to a display (*ep.*, 1292; *cf.* 1296). The word used for 'sending an invitation,' 'inviting,' is καλέω (*ib.*, i. 199, 11); for 'collecting an audience,' ἀγείρω (Themis., 282 d). Aristeides says (ii. p. 575) that it is a degradation of the sophist's profession to go about drumming up an audience.

[1] Lib., i. 199, 7. People were also backward about coming to Aristeides's displays at Smyrna (Aristeid., ii. pp. 573, 579). Aristeides, however, was not an extempore speaker, and he was not much in favor with the people (Philos., 581, 582).

[2] Lib., i. 200, 18.

[3] See the case of Polemo (Philos., 535).

[4] The question turns on our understanding of the following passages of Philostratus: 519: τὰς δὲ μελέτας μισθοῦ μὲν ἐποιεῖτο, ὁ δὲ μισθὸς ἦν ἄλλος ἄλλου καὶ ὡς ἕκαστος οἴκου εἶχεν· 527: μισθοὺς δὲ γενναίους ἐπράττετο τὰς συνουσίας οὐ μελετηρὰς μόνον, ἀλλὰ καὶ διδασκαλικὰς παρέχων· 604: τὰ δὲ τῆς μελέτης πάτρια τῷ ἀνδρὶ τούτῳ διέκειτο ὧδε· ἑκατὸν δραχμὰς ἅπαξ καταβαλόντι ἐξῆν ἀκροᾶσθαι τὸν ἀεὶ χρόνον. ἦν δὲ αὐτῷ καὶ θήκη βιβλίων ἐπὶ τῆς οἰκίας, ὧν μετῆν τοῖς

In these public, or semi-public, displays the student had the opportunity of seeing illustrated the principles which he had been taught in the class-room. The displays were, in fact, primarily designed to supplement the class-room instruction, and they formed a regular part of the sophist's course. In them the sophists

ξυλλεγομένοις ἐς τὸ πλήρωμα τῆς ἀκροάσεως. Were the public admitted to these μελέται, which were primarily for the students, or not, and, if they were, did they, as well as the students, have to pay? μελέτη generally suggests a *public* display. On the whole, however, it seems probable that the displays here referred to were not public, but that there were others given more especially for the benefit of the public, for which no charges were made (see, *e. g.*, *ib.*, 571, 572, 579, 617). The inference from the wording of the second passage may be that the less advanced and more mechanical part of the course — that part which consisted strictly of teaching — as distinguished from the more advanced and elocutionary part — the displays — was at this time not usually given by the sophist himself, but by an assistant. This view is supported by the statement of Quintilian (*Inst. or.*, ii. 1, 1 *ff.*) that rhetoricians had come to think it their business simply to declaim and to teach the art and practice of declaiming, leaving the more elementary parts of their subject to the 'grammarians.' (That a distinction was sometimes made between practising the sophist's profession and teaching, is clear from *Dig.*, xxvii. 1, 6, 9: ἐὰν γὰρ Κομανεὺς ὢν ἐν Νεοκαισαρείᾳ σοφεστεύῃ ἢ θεραπεύῃ ἢ διδάσκῃ . . .). Indeed, it is not improbable that the sophists of the second and third centuries gave much of their instruction through examples—that is, in the form of displays (*cf.* Brandstätter, *Hermes*, 15, pp. 239, 240. Therefore, possibly the παιδευτικὸς θρόνος of Eunapius, p. 95, refers, not to the chief sophistical chair at Athens, but to a subordinate chair; see p. 142, n. 3). If this view is correct, it will account for the use of the word μελέτη in the other passages. Compare also the verb in Philos., 528, 529; and see the case of Libanius's school at Antioch (p. 271, n. 1). The usual words for the association of teacher and student are συνουσία (*ib.*, 604), and ὁμιλία (Porphyr., *Vit. Plotin.*, 5), while ἀκρόασις, which, with ἐπίδειξις (see below), is commonly used of public displays (*e. g.* Philos., 586, 589; Lib., i. 199. 11), is also used of the sophist's course in general (*e. g.*, Philos., 615: γῄδιον . . . ἐωνημένον ἐκ τῶν

brought into play all the arts and devices of the sophistic trade.[1] It is important that we gain an idea of what these displays were like, for on these occasions the sophist appeared in his moments of greatest triumph.

ἀκροάσεων· 606: ἠφίει τούτοις τὸν μισθὸν τῆς ἀκροάσεως). So, the noun ἀκροατής and the verb ἀκροάομαι (ib., 579, 583; p. 343, below). μελέτη is used with reference to the kind of speech and is often contrasted with διάλεξις (e. g., ib., 592, 593). The two were distinct in style and treatment. The πλάσματα of Lib., i. 275, 8, were probably μελέται (cf. ib., ep., 407). Menander (see below) speaks of the μελέτην ἀγώνων, and ἀγών is also used (Philos., 514), as well as λόγων ἀγών (Lib., ep., 367), ὁ κατὰ μελέτην ἀγών (ib., ep., 574), and ὁ ὑπὲρ μελέτης ἀγών (Philos., 601). σπουδή is used of teaching (ib., 587). μελέτη, of course, referred primarily to a prepared speech or exercise, and it is sometimes contrasted with extempore speech (ib., 628), but it is also sometimes used to include extempore speech (ib., 570: τὰς μὲν οὖν μελέτας αὐτοσχεδίους ἐποιεῖτο· 514: τὰς δὲ μελέτας οὐκ αὐτοσχεδίους ἐποιεῖτο· cf. also 619; 604: ἡ μελέτη δὲ κ. τ. λ.; the verb in 626), and it was the common word used for the deliberative or the controversial speech, extempore or prepared, delivered on the occasion of a display (Volkmann, Rhetorik, p. 361, therefore, is to be corrected). ἐπίδειξις is commonly used of a public display (Lib., i. 199, 8). Students also gave ἐπιδείξεις either in public or before the whole school (p. 211, n. 2; see also Themis., 304 a). The rhetorician Menander (Speng., Rh. Gr., iii. p. 331) would seem to restrict the word to the γένος ἐπιδεικτικόν (ἃς γὰρ ἐπιδείξεις λόγων πολιτικῶν οἱ σοφισταὶ καλούμενοι ποιοῦνται, μελέτην ἀγώνων εἶναί φαμεν, οὐκ ἐπίδειξιν). So the word is used in Choric., p. 125. Originally, of course, it had this meaning, but when the γένη δικανικόν and συμβουλευτικόν became a part of the sophist's stock in trade and took on a 'display' character (see p. 74, n. 2), it was made to include these also. So Philos., 626: ἀνάθες μοι καιρὸν ἐς ἐπίδειξιν μελέτης (also ib., 619), and then without μελέτης (ib., 537: ἐς τὰς ἐπιδείξεις). ἐπίδειξις λόγων is also found (ib., 539). ἐπίδειξις was sometimes used of the διάλεξις (Himer., or., vi. 1). In Philos., 579, it is used of both the διάλεξις and the μελέτη.

[1] Choric., p. 5: ἐποίει δὲ τοῦτο πολλάκις εἰς ἔρωτα λόγων ἐγείρων τοὺς νέους· Lib., ii. 280, 2: ὁ λέγων ἃ χρὴ μιμεῖσθαι· ib., ii. 280, 10: οὐκοῦν καὶ ὅστις ἐθέλει ποιῆσαι ῥήτορας, παρεχέτω τοῖς τοῦτο δυνησομένοις ἑαυτὸν παράδειγμα καὶ τὸν μὲν οὐ βουλόμενον λέγειν ὁ νέος ἀποδιδρασκέτω, τὸν δὲ καὶ ποιοῦντα καὶ δεικνύοντα λόγους διωκέτω.

Generally the sophist, especially if he came from foreign parts and was a stranger in the city where he was about to declaim, introduced his main discourse by a short speech designed to conciliate his auditors' goodwill.[1] This introductory speech might, of course, take any form, but it usually contained a few words in praise of the city and depreciatory of the speaker's ability.[2] Sometimes a short narrative was introduced and the moral drawn that the audience should receive the speaker with favor.[3]

The introductory speech finished, the sophist then proceeded to the matter in hand. This might be (1) a διάλεξις,[4] a more or less informal discourse, in the nature of a talk, on any subject of popular interest, such as the sophist's art,[5] or, possibly, on some more philosophical theme or a theme of ethical interest;[6] or it

[1] Called λαλιά, or, more distinctively, προλαλιά, or, from its character, διάλεξις (Förster, in *Rhein. Mus.*, 49, pp. 481 *ff.*); also πρόλογος (Choric., p. 200; see Förster), and προαγών (Eunap., pp. 82, 101). Examples are Lucian's *Dream, Herodotus, Zeuxis, Hercules*, etc. See Themis., 329 d. Libanius mentions a sophist who made a reputation on his prologues (i. 210, 5). People learned Libanius's prologues by heart, and perhaps sang them (*ib.*, i. 40, 12; 63, 9). Libanius's students used to applaud so much that they broke the connection of the discourse, and he urged them in a prologue to reform their ways (*ib.*, i. 179, 17).

[2] Philos., 535, 572; Lib., i. 276, 15.

[3] As in the προλαλιαί of Lucian. Sometimes the sophist was introduced (Aristeid., ii. p. 534). See, however, Rohde, *Gr. Rom.*, p. 336, n. 5. Libanius was introduced by his uncle on one occasion (Lib., i. 63, 4).

[4] The διάλεξις, though sometimes an introductory speech, was not always so (see Himer., *or.*, vi, xvii, xxij). It was prepared beforehand or given extempore (*ib.*, *or.*, vi). The discourses of the philosophers were διαλέξεις (Themis., 312 b). See, further, Rohde, *Gr. Rom.*, p. 346, n. 1.

[5] Philos., 528.        [6] Here would be included the θετικά.

might be (2) one of the epideictic, or encomiastic, speeches, to be described later;[1] or it might be (3) a speech of the sort called μελέται, dramatic, or semi-dramatic, representations or interpretations of character in given situations, or arguments for or against certain imagined lines of conduct.[2] It is with this third sort of speech that we have to do at present.

Sometimes the sophist prepared his speech beforehand, and then either recited it or read it, when the time for display came. This was the case with Aristeides, who was never able to summon his thoughts on the spur of the moment, and of whom it was a saying that he was not one of those who cast up their words undigested, but one who gave them careful treatment.[3] He required twenty-four hours for the preparation of his theme, and during that time labored at it phrase by phrase and thought by thought. "Such work," says Philostratus,[4] "is that of a person chewing, not eating, for extempore speech is the accomplishment of a fluent tongue." Apollonius of Naucratis,[5] Scopelian,[6] and Polemo[7] were accustomed to withdraw from the room for a short space after the theme had been propounded, in order to collect their thoughts in private, and Isæus required half a day to put his argument into shape.[8]

[1] P. 263.

[2] συμβουλευτικά (suasoriæ) and δικανικά (controversiæ).

[3] Philos., 583; Eunap., p. 82. Proclus was another who required that his theme be given him the day before (Philos., 604). See also Lib., i. 51, 3; ep., 407.

[4] 583.   [5] Philos., 600.   [6] Philos., 519.   [7] Philos., 537.

[8] Philos., 514; but see next note. Sometimes the sophist thought over his theme for a few moments in his seat (ib., 572: καιρὸν δ' ἐπισχὼν βραχύν). Isaeus put on his gown, in the presence of the audience, after he arose (Plin., ep., ii. 3).

More often, however, the sophist spoke extempore, and ready wit was sure of ready applause. Even Aristeides, scoffer as he was, admired this accomplishment and labored hard to acquire it.[1]

The theme for discussion was usually given by one of the audience, or, if some distinguished person was present, the choice was left to him.[2] Sometimes, out of several themes that were propounded, the speaker selected one or allowed the audience to select one.[3] If the display was given at the request of a magistrate, the magistrate generally set the theme, and, in case a contest among several sophists was on hand, either a single theme was set for all to discuss[4] or a different theme for each.[5] Occasionally a sophist practised deception upon his audience. By skilful depreciation of all the different themes propounded, he could, by a process of suggestion similar to that employed by the prestidigitator in forcing a card, compel his audience to select a particular theme,[6]

[1] Philostratus (620) tells of a sophist who could speak extempore with the readiness of one reading what was familiar to him. So Pliny says of Isæus, *dicit semper ex tempore, sed tamquam diu scripserit. . . . statim omnia ac pœne pariter ad manum, sensus reconditi occursant. . . . multa lectio in subitis, multa scriptio elucet* (*ep.*, ii. 3). *Cf.* Quint., *Inst. or.*, x. 7. Speed was a characteristic of the Greek speech as practised by the sophists (Sen., *Contr.*, iv. *praef.*, 7).

[2] Philos., 529, 572. Various expressions are used for 'propounding a theme,' as προβάλλειν τὸν ὅρον (Eunap., p. 83), προβάλλειν τὴν ὑπόθεσιν (Philos., 529), προβάλλειν τὸ πρόβλημα (Eunap., p. 81), προβάλλειν τὸ ζήτημα (*ib.*), ὑποβάλλειν ὑπόθεσιν καὶ ἀφορμὰς τῶν λόγων (Luc., *Rhet. præc.*, 18), πρόβαλλειν (Philos., 583), προβάλλεσθαι (*ib.*, 529), ὑπόθεσιν διδόναι (*ib.*), ὑπόθεσιν ὁρίζειν (*ib.*, 579).

[3] Luc., *Rhet. præc.*, 18; Plin., *ep.*, ii. 3, 2. Isæus even allowed the audience to select the part to be defended.

[4] Eunap., pp. 81, 86.     [5] Eunap., p. 81.

[6] Luc., *Rhet. præc.*, 18.

or he could instruct a friend stationed in the audience to see that the theme desired was propounded and accepted.[1] Herodes Atticus, on one occasion, hearing that the sophist Philager was accustomed to repeat his own speeches and pass them off as new, secured a copy of the sophist's most successful speech—one that had already been published—and then propounded this very theme for the sophist to discuss. After Philager had finished speaking, Herodes quietly read aloud from the copy which he held before him. Philager was laughed out of the room.[2]

The theme once fixed upon, to see it in all its aspects and in all its bearings, and to select that point of view and that method of treatment which promised to be the most effective, were for these extempore speakers the work of but a moment.[3] Their whole training was de-

---

[1] Luc., *Pseudolog.*, 5.     [2] Philos., 579.

[3] Hermocrates impressed his audience by his power to grasp a theme, ἐν στιγμῇ τοῦ καιροῦ (Philos., 612). Ptolemy was blamed by some for not being able to distinguish his themes or to see wherein the στάσις (*status*), the point of view, or the point on which the case is to be made to rest, lay (*ib.*, 595, 596). Thus, in the theme wherein the Thebans charged the Messenians with ingratitude for not receiving the Theban fugitives who had been driven from their homes by Alexander, it was said there was no στάσις; for, if the charge was made while Alexander was living, no one would be bold enough to vote in condemnation of the Messenians, while, if it was made after his death, no one would be so easy as to vote for their acquittal. Philostratus justifies the theme by saying that the defence is made on the ground of pardon (ξυγγνώμην) in view of the fear in which the Thebans stood of Alexander (see Volkmann, *Rhetorik*, p. 99). Compare the case of the sophists at Athens wrangling over the point of view, or chief point of contention (στάσις), in a theme propounded to them by the proconsul Anatolius (Eunap., p. 87). Each took a different στάσις; and if there had been more than a dozen sophists, said Anatolius, the result would have been the same.

signed to give them this facility, and constant practice kept it ever alive.[1] The sophist Marcus, we are told,[2] used to go through the streets with knit brows and abstracted air, pondering his themes even in his hours of leisure. Being on one occasion asked how he had succeeded in a declamation the day before, he replied, "Very well before myself, but before my students, poorly." "How is that?" asked the astonished hearer. "Even when I am silent, I am busy," returned the sophist, "and, though I interpret one theme in public, two or even three themes are running through my head." *Ready Speakers*, resembling perhaps our *Guides to After-Dinner Speaking*, were written, and doubtless often served to jog the tired sophist's wit.[3]

The themes which were propounded to the sophists were similar to those which were made use of by the sophists themselves in the class-room, and of which we have already had examples. They were deliberative or judicial in character, and, if the imaginary circumstances were attached to definite names, instead of being, as was often the case, given without definition of time and place, the matter was almost exclusively drawn from the ancient history and mythology. The Spartan, urging his brother Spartans not to receive those coming back from Sphacteria without their shields;[4] Demosthenes, defending himself against a charge of bribery

[1] The sophist studied by night (Philos., 518; Lib., i. 75, 15; Syn., *Dion*, 11; Themis., 312 b). Constant practice necessary for the sophist (Himer., *or.*, xvii. 6; xxiv. 4; Luc., *Dem.*, 36). *Cf.* Pliny, of Isæus (*ep.*, ii. 3, 4): *Ad tantam ἕξιν studio et exercitatione pervenit: nam diebus et noctibus nihil aliud agit, nihil audit, nihil loquitur.*

[2] Philos., 528, 529.   [3] Philos., 581; *cf.* 565.   [4] Philos., 528.

brought by Demades;[1] an unknown accusing Epicurus of impiety on the ground of his denial of Divine Providence;[2] the poor man accusing the rich man who had ruined the poor man's happiness;[3] an unknown urging that those who by reason of dwelling on the plain were in ill health should remove to the mountains[4] — these are but a sample of the situations which the sophist was required to expound. Some of the situations imagined were purely fictitious, but more often they were those either of actual or of probable occurrence.

In these deliberative and judicial themes the orator was required to imagine himself in the positions of the different characters, and to portray, in suitable words and action, their thoughts and feelings in the given situations; or he was required to speak, in the rôle of advocate, appropriate arguments for or against certain definite lines of conduct. In theory there was here involved more than the actor's trade, which is to interpret by action and manner words that have been written by another; the sophist's problem (at least in the impersonation themes) was to write, or, more often, to speak on the spur of the moment, the words appropriate to the character assumed, and by his own action to interpret these. It is evident that in such a representation there was much that was dramatic. "The most of the 'business' and the aim of dancing (or the pantomimic art)," says Lucian,[5] "is, as I have said, representation

---

[1] Philos., 538.     [2] Himer., *ec.*, iii.     [3] Himer., *ec.*, iv.
[4] Philos., 575.
[5] *De saltat.*, 65. In 35 he says that rhetoric and 'dancing' have this in common, that they both aim to express character and feeling ($ἦθος$ and $πάθος$). On imitation in dancing, see Libanius's

(ὑπόκρισις), the same kind of representation that is practised by the sophists, especially in their so-called declamations. For in these, too, representation gains most credit when it fits the parts that are taken, and when the words that are spoken are not out of harmony with the characters of the princes and the tyrant-slayers and the poor men and the farmers who are introduced, but express, in the case of each of these, that which is characteristic of it and belongs to it alone."

Recognition of the fact that there existed a close connection between the sophistic oratory and tragedy is expressed in many of the utterances of the sophists themselves. "It was the Ionians," says Himerius,[1] "who, finding oratory poor and meanly clad and dwelling about the courts, raised it to something more grand and tragic than tragedy itself;" and the sophist Nicagoras remarking on one occasion that tragedy was the mother of sophists, Hippodromus filled out his words by saying, "And Homer the father."[2] Tragedy formed a part of the course of study of the sophists, and some sophists, we are distinctly told, aimed at the tragic grandiloquence or at other characteristics of the tragic style.[3] Philostratus tells us[4] that Scopelian was particularly satisfactory in themes relating to the Persian kings, because

---

oration lxiii. (iii. 345–395). The writer of speeches is at a disadvantage when compared with the writer of plays, in that he cannot introduce costumed characters (Choric., p. 6). Stage-acting was a step beyond the sophistic representation. See p. 232, n. 2, and Quint., *Inst. or.*, xi. 3, 181, 182.

[1] *Or.*, xi. 2.

[2] Philos., 620. It was another of Hippodromus's sayings that Homer was the voice and Archilochus the breath of sophists.

[3] Philos., 518, 590.    [4] 519, 520.

he was very successful in *representing* the high spirit of those parts and at the same time the levity of the barbarian character; and of similar suggestiveness is the story that is told of Polemo. Polemo, while walking through the market-place, caught sight of a sophist laying in a store of sausages and sprats and other such cheap fare. "My friend," he said,[1] "you cannot hope to represent well the high spirit of Darius if you eat such stuff as that." Pointing in the same direction is the frequent use of theatrical terms — ὑποκρίνεσθαι, ἀγωνίζεσθαι, etc.— in connection with the sophist's trade.[2]

The action of the sophist in declaiming, we shall not be surprised to find, was much more violent than is that of the modern orator. Indeed, among both the Greeks and the Romans in ancient times, far greater freedom was allowed in this respect than is the case with us at the present day.[3] Thus, Cicero recognized that there were occasions when it was necessary for the orator to strike his forehead with his hand or to stamp on the ground,[4] though such gestures as these were in general forbidden by the more moderate Quintilian.[5] But even Cicero would probably have taken offence at the

[1] Philos., 541.

[2] ὑποκρίνεσθαι (Philos., 541); ἀγωνίζεσθαι (*ib.*, 514); διεξιέναι (*ib.*, 522). *Cf. ib.*, 537: τὴν δὲ σκηνὴν τοῦ ἀνδρὸς, ᾗ ἐς τὰς μελέτας ἐχρήσατο· *ib.*, 595; Himer., *or.*, xvii. 6. On ὑπόκρισις, see Volkmann, *Rhetorik*, p. 573. Aristocles, when he became a sophist, frequented the theatre and took on its ways (Philos., 567).

[3] See Volkmann, *Rhetorik*, p. 576.

[4] *Brut.*, 80, 278; *De or.*, iii. 59, 220; *cf.* Quint., *Inst. or.*, x. 7, 26; xi. 3, 123 and 128.

[5] See *Inst. or.*, i. 11, 1–3; ii. 12, 9 and 10; iv. 2, 39.

gestures of some of the later Greek sophists, for all that was in any way theatrical was excluded from his code.[1] We have seen in a previous chapter how Proæresius on one occasion pranced about the stage like one inspired, and Polemo, it is said, such was his superabundance of energy, used to spring from his seat with a bound when he came to the crucial point of his speech.[2] "He came forward to speak," says Philostratus, "with a calm and confident air;" and then, farther on, "Herodes says that . . . when he rounded off a period, he spoke the final clause with a smile, showing thereby that it caused him no trouble; also that in certain parts of his theme he struck the ground with his foot, like Homer's horse." Scopelian had a habit of striking his thigh with his hand occasionally, while speaking, to arouse the interest of his hearers and himself, and this seems to have been a not uncommon practice among the speakers of that day.[3] Scopelian, further, when engaged on his Medic or Persian themes, would sway from side to side like one in a frenzy.[4] Alexander gave effect to certain words in one

[1] *De or.*, iii. 59, 220.

[2] Philos., 537; *cf.* Seneca, *Contr.*, vii. *præf.*, 1. Hippodromus would sometimes jump from his seat before he began (Philos., 619). The practice seems to have differed about speaking from the seat. Proæresius on one occasion spoke the προαγών, or introductory remarks, from his seat, but rose when he came to the ἀγών, or main theme (Eunap., p. 82); so also Alexander (Philos., 572). Scopelian spoke, sometimes from his chair, sometimes standing (*ib.*, 519). Isæus rose before beginning to speak (Plin., *ep.*, ii. 3, 2). Probably the practice of most speakers was to speak the ἀγών, or the most impassioned part thereof, standing, and the προαγών sitting.

[3] Philos., 519; Luc., *Rhet. præc.*, 19; Quint., *Inst. or.*, ii. 12, 10; xi. 3, 123. Sometimes the orator walked about the stage in an insolent or affected manner (Luc., *Rhet. præc.*, 19).

[4] Philos., 520.

of his speeches by weeping as he spoke them,[1] and a speaker of an earlier age is said to have thrust his tongue from his mouth and smacked his lips, to illustrate more vividly the action of eating. When Libanius was lecturing at Constantinople, he drew large audiences; some of the people came to hear him speak, but the most, he says, to see his gestures.[2] The whole manner of the sophist on the stage was, as is evident from the expressions that are used with regard to it,[3] typically one of pompous aggressiveness. It was designed both to impress and to impose upon the audience. Nor was this manner always confined to the stage; even in private life the sophist was often by force of habit overbearing and arrogant.[4]

[1] Philos., 574. *Cf.* Seneca, *Contr.*, iv. *præf.*, 11; Quint., *Inst. or.*, vi. 2, 36. The hair of Timocrates's head and beard, it is said, stood on end when he spoke (Philos., 536).

[2] Lib., i. 54, 12. His audiences at Constantinople had, however, very little literary appreciation. *Cf. ib.*, i. 43, 1: ἐπεδεικνύμην κινούμενος τὰ εἰωθότα· iii. 199, 18: οὐδὲν φαιδρότερον ἐν θεάτρῳ σοφιστοῦ τὰ πρέποντα κινουμένου τε καὶ σχηματιζομένου. Libanius was once taunted with being an actor rather than an orator (*ib.*, *ep.*, 127; *cf.* Gell., i. 5).

[3] *E. g.*, Themis., 243 a: καθήμενον ἐπὶ θρόνου τινὸς ὑψηλοῦ μάλα σοφιστικῶς καὶ σοβαρῶς· Choric., p. 6: οὐ τὰς ὀφρῦς ἐπαιρούσης, οὐ βαδίσματι σοβαρῷ κεχρημένης, κἂν ἐκ φύσεως ἔχῃ τὰ τοιαῦτα 'Ρητορική· Syn., *Dion*, 11: ἐσθῆτι καὶ σχήματι σοβαροῖς, . . . καὶ προσγελᾷ τῷ θεάτρῳ καὶ χαίρει δῆθεν, ἡ δὲ ψυχὴ κατατείνεται. Smiling seems to have been a characteristic proceeding: Polemo smiled, as stated in the text, and so did Libanius (Lib., i. 63, 5).

[4] Greg. Naz., *ep.*, 233: τὸ χρῆμα εἶναι θαυμάσιον, οἷον σοβαρὸν φθέγγεσθαι, μέγα βλέπειν, βαδίζειν ὑψηλὸν καὶ μετέωρον. *Cf.* Lib., i. 37, 1; Procop., *ep.*, 69, 72, 85. See Schlosser, *Univ., Stud. u. Prof. d. Griech.* in *Archiv. für Gesch. u. Lit.*, pp. 258 *ff.*, for the Christians. Compare further on the sophist's manner, Luc., *Rhet. præc.*, 15; Aristeid., ii. p. 533 (the sophist brandishes his arms, draws his lips awry, loads his person with clothes, and prances back and forth); Themis., 341 b; Syn., *Dion*, 11.

The voice of the sophist was carefully attuned,[1] and resembled in its flexibility and melodiousness some delicate musical instrument. Often, we may believe, the utterance had much of the character of sing-song, and at its best it may have been a kind of modulated intonation.[2] "The voice of Polemo," says Philostratus,[3] "was clear and sustained, and his tongue gave forth a wonderful ring." Proæresius, we remember,[4] also closed his periods with a sonorous ring. "The Romans," says Philostratus again,[5] "listened to Adrian as if he were some sweet-voiced nightingale, wondering at his flow of words, and the quality and flexibility of his voice, and the rhythms, both prose and metrical;" and Favorinus charmed his hearers by the sound of his voice, the keen glance of his eye, and the rhythmic flow of his words.[6]

A musical and well-modulated voice and an harmonious flow of language may be considered as being supplementary to each other, and the Greek ear was delicately susceptible to both. Great stress was, of course, laid by the sophist on the perfection of his literary style, and the language tended to become in his hands more and more a thing of the hot-house, forced

---

[1] Syn., *Dion*, 1: εἴ τις ἀξιοῖ τὴν ἐπιμέλειαν τῆς φωνῆς σοφιστικὸν ἀγώνισμα οἴεσθαι· Lib., *ep.*, 172: ἥ τε φωνὴ χρόνῳ πρὸς τὸ κάλλιστον ἥξει. According to Synesius, the sophist ate tragacanth to make his voice flexible (*Dion*, 11). Sometimes he would turn around in the middle of his display, take a bowl from his slave's hand, and gargle before going on with his song. *Cf.* also Philos., 577: λαμπρᾷ τῇ φωνῇ καὶ ἠσκημένῃ. Libanius tried his voice and got the pitch before speaking (Lib., i. 51, 9). In general, the ancient utterance was much more musical than the modern, Anglo-Saxon, utterance.

[2] *Cf.* Quint., *Inst. or.*, xi. 3, 57 *ff.*; Cic., *Or.*, 8, 27; 18, 57.
[3] 537.  [4] P. 157. See also Philos., 327.  [5] 589.  [6] Philos., 491.

and artificial in character. The ordinary and well-felt, if not always well-understood, prose rhythms — such rhythms as characterized the artistic prose of the Greeks in an earlier age and belong in some measure to all prose that is harmonious in any language — were, in the prose of the sophists, often supplemented and sometimes displaced by the metrical rhythms — the rhythms of poetry. The sophist Varus, we are told,[1] made his language so rhythmic that one could almost dance to it, and Herodes once introduced into a speech rhythms more varied than those of the lyre or the flute.[2]

So characteristic and well-recognized a feature of the prose of this period had the poetic style — not poetic rhythms alone, but poetic words and expressions and forms of thought — become, that the word ᾄδειν, "to sing," is hardly to be distinguished in its use in the sophistic writings from the word λέγειν, "to say," while not infrequently the prose compositions of the sophists were called by the name ᾄσματα, "songs," or some similar name.[3] This usage is significant of a change in the world's attitude toward the two great departments of literature, prose and poetry. Prose, as an artistic production, had usurped in men's minds the place which poetry once held, and of real poetry there was at this time a singular dearth. Poets, it is true, are frequently mentioned in the writers of the fourth century, but generally in conjunction with sophists and public

[1] Philos., 620.   [2] Philos., 573.
[3] For ᾄδειν, see Radermacher, in *Jahrb. f. Phil.*, 1896, i. p. 116. For the connection of epideictic literature and poetry, see Burgess, *Epideictic Literature*, pp. 166 ff. ᾄσματα (Lib., i. 518, 22); ῥητορικὸς (ἀνατιθεὶς) ὕμνον ἄνευ μέτρου (ib., i. 225, 10).

speakers.¹ It is apparent that the functions of the three classes were considered to be similar. The poets, like the sophists, held displays, they dealt with 'epideictic' themes, and their compositions, like many of those of the sophists, were probably often directed at the auditor rather than at the reader of later time. The poets, indeed, received their training in the sophistical schools, and men were there moulded into poets, as they were into rhetors or sophists. For if ever it was true, it was so at this time, that *poeta fit, non nascitur*.² The extent to which the rhetorical literature had usurped the forms and the spirit of poetry is perhaps best seen in the compositions of Himerius, some of which are as near being on the line between prose and poetry as it is well possible to be.

Under these conditions we are not surprised to learn that some sophists, through their excess of emotion, burst forth into song in the midst of their recitations.³ Such prose style and such delivery charmed many ears, but the saner critics, even among the sophists themselves, recognized the perniciousness of the practice.⁴ Isæus once reproved a student for making his language and delivery over-musical, by saying, "My lad, I have not taught you to sing."⁵ "For all over-rhythmical writ-

---

¹*E. g.*, Lib., i. 34, 12; 652, 8; ii. 372, 20; Themis., 254 b.

²*Cf.* Himer., *or.*, xiv. 22: ῥήτωρ τε ἐπιστήμων καὶ ποιητὴς ἔνθεος γίνεται· Theon, 2, p. 168 (Speng., *Rh. Gr.*, ii. p. 70): εἴ τις ἢ ποιητῶν ἢ λογοποιῶν ἢ ἄλλων τινῶν λόγων δύναμιν ἐθέλει μεταχειρίζεσθαι.

³ Luc., *Pseudolog.*, 7.

⁴ *E. g.*, Philos., 601, 602, 607, 620; Luc., *Hist. conscr.*, 46. For the affected speech of the sophists, see Plut., *De rect. rat. aud.*, 7.  ⁵ Philos., 513.

ing," says the author of the περὶ ὕψους,[1] "is at once felt to be affected and finical and wholly lacking in passion owing to the monotony of its superficial polish. . . . Sometimes, indeed, the listeners knowing beforehand the due terminations stamp their feet in time with the speaker, and as in a dance give the right step in anticipation."

The charm which a musical voice and sweet language, even when unaccompanied by sense, had for the ancient ear, is well illustrated by the story that is told of the manner in which the Romans were affected by the eloquence of the Greek-speaking Adrian at the time of the latter's stay in Rome.

He so charmed the city [says Philostratus [2]] that he caused even those who were unfamiliar with the Greek language to wish to hear him. . . . When the Romans were engaged in celebrating their religious festivals, . . . it needed but the appearance at the stage door of the messenger announcing a recitation by Adrian, and all would jump up, the senators from their seats and the knights from theirs, and hasten to the Athenæum, chiding as they went those who were slow of foot; and it was not alone the Greek-educated people, but even those who had been taught only Latin at Rome, who were filled with this zeal.

[1] 41 (Mr. Roberts's trans.). Sometimes the lines were filled in with unmeaning or disconnected words (Luc., *Rhet. præc.*, 19; Cic., *Orat.*, 69, 230), or a sort of tag, or refrain, was given at the end of each clause, which the audience would anticipate (Aristeid., ii. p. 564). Sometimes the speaker ranted (Luc., *Rhet. præc.*, 19; Lib., iii. 362, 15). *Cf.* Quint., *Inst. or.*, ii. 12. For the singing of sophists, public speakers, and even philosophers, see Dio Chrys., xxxii. 686 R. See also Norden, *Die antike Kunstprosa*, i. pp. 55, 57, 294, 376.

[2] 589; *cf.* 488 (of Dion's speech). See also Norden, *Die antike Kunstprosa*, i. p. 5.

With this we may compare the following:

Such peace and such sweetness blossomed from his speech and were poured about the ears [says Eunapius, of Eustathius, in his flowery and not always logical style[1]] that those who listened to his voice and his words, yielding themselves, like men who had tasted of the lotus, to their influence, hung, charmed, from his voice and his words.

And, again, Eunapius's description of Chrysanthius's eloquence:[2]

Just as the sweetest and most beautiful melodies are attuned to every ear, and flow, gliding peacefully and soothingly, even into the souls of unreasoning beasts, as is said to have been the case with the measures of Orpheus, so the speech of Chrysanthius was fitted to every listener, and, though characters and dispositions are various, it was in harmonious accord with each.

It is clear from the frequent allusions to the voice and the language of the sophists that the study of the harmonious accord of these was cultivated to an extent which we of to-day perhaps hardly realize.[3]

But it was not alone in manner and in voice, in gesture and in tone, that the sophist had to portray character. He must also select and arrange words that were appropriate and that expressed by their meaning the

---

[1] P. 28.  [2] P. 112.

[3] Polemo's language is spoken of as being well-rounded and full, like the tone of the Olympian trumpet (Philos., 542). Polydeuces is said to have spoken a certain passage in a voice that was "honey-sweet" ($\mu\epsilon\lambda\iota\chi\rho\hat{a}\ \tau\hat{\eta}\ \phi\omega\nu\hat{\eta}$, ib., 593). It was noticed that Pausanias, who was a Cappadocian, spoke with a thick utterance, running together his consonants and making long vowels short and short vowels long (ib., 594).

thoughts and the emotions of the one he was impersonating. It is evident that in the manner of handling a theme a good deal of latitude was possible. The sophist might by his method of treatment give to a subject otherwise one of the commonest an individual character, while one and the same subject might in different hands put on entirely different aspects. The display was doubtless often regarded as an intellectual study, wherein the sophist introduced to his students and to the public new methods and new ways of treatment. Generally he would introduce his declamation by a few words of preface, in which he would take occasion to explain briefly the technical features of the theme he was about to discuss, mention any novelties in the way of treatment which he would introduce, and call upon the audience to observe with what success he put into practice the principles which he taught. Let us hear from Himerius and Choricius examples of this sort of introduction. The first example, from Himerius, is the introduction, not to a deliberative or judicial theme, but to a so-called Προπεμπτικός, or speech of farewell,[1] one of the many forms of speeches cultivated in the sophistic schools.

Themes which are common property [says Himerius] are given an individual character by the method of treatment. Thus, so-called farewell speeches, though they are a modern invention, may by artistic handling be made to smack of antiquity. Such handling I have here given a farewell speech. The present theme I have put into the form of a dialogue, but, in so doing, I have neither injured

[1] *Ec.*, x.

the subject-matter nor have I neglected the stately elegance which is peculiar to dialogues. I have, after the manner of Plato, though my subject is ethical, introduced physical and speculative matter, and have mingled this with the ethical. Plato, further, disguised the more divine parts of his argument by putting them into the form of myths, and you must observe whether I have successfully imitated him in this. The other characteristics of dialogues, the interruptions, the descriptions, and the digressions, as well as the various beauties of style and the general dramatic quality, all these my speech itself will best show whether I have attained. Dialogues begin with a plain style, in order that the simplicity of the style may enhance the simplicity of the matter, but, as the ideas swell and increase, the style also becomes fuller and rounder. Whether I have in this matter adhered to the rule, those of you whose ears have been trained by technical instruction to the judging of such matters may determine.

Of the speech of which this was the introduction we have only excerpts.

The second and third examples,[1] from Choricius, the fifth century sophist of Gaza, are the introductions respectively to the two speeches on opposite sides of a judicial theme. The theme is this: A certain wealthy and covetous old man has determined to marry his son to a well-to-do but ill-favored girl. The son falls in love with another girl, who is poor but handsome, and he asks his father for permission to marry her. This the father refuses to give. War occurs, and the son distinguishes himself on the field of battle. According to the law, the son is now at liberty to ask for any reward he may wish. He asks for the hand of his beloved.

[1] *Rhein. Mus.*, 49, pp. 484, 504.

The father objects. The orator, at this time a young man, takes the part, first of the son, then of the father, each of whom is represented as speaking in his own behalf. The introduction to the son's speech is as follows:

The laws of the art (*i. e.*, sophistry) admit also of sons contending with fathers. For all the kinds of suits that occur in real life are imitated in the fictitious cases. Now there are many reasons why this young man has the sympathy of the people: he has gained a victory on the battlefield, he has rescued his country from danger, he comes here with the law on his side, he asks for a reasonable reward — a girl brought up in modest circumstances. But although he has all these advantages weighing on his side, he is still not free from anxiety, and he is not confident that he will win his suit without a struggle. For son is opposed to father, and poverty to wealth — the latter a thing which all men like, but which is especially dear to him who is covetous. Therefore it is with reason that the son is at once boastful and flattering; the war has given him boldness and confidence, but before his father, notwithstanding his victory, he is humble and submissive. For he would not have any of his audience judge his whole life from the present controversy, and, inferring that he is by nature contentious and brazen toward his parents, be less favorably disposed toward him. Now, of course, it would have been best for the boy to overcome his love, but since he did not, the second best, as the saying is, is that he should appear not to have acted in an immoderate fashion; his contention is that this is the first time that he has been in love, that he did not carry the girl off by force, and in general that he did nothing that could lead to any disgrace, nothing of the sort that lovers usually do. He thus clears his own character and at the same time gives his beloved an added brightness by showing that her excellence has attracted the love of a modest young man. This is what he will do, and he will try, to the best of his ability, to make it clear that the object of his affection, rather than the well-to-do girl, should be chosen; and if he shall happen to seem to praise the former overmuch, he must be pardoned, since he is a lover. The father I hand over as a study to the old and covetous, who are of like habits with him; I have naturally assumed the part of the young man, for like takes to like, as the old proverb says.

The orator afterward decides to defend the part of the father, and he introduces the father's speech by the following explanation:

The old man, in the study, has also fallen in love — but not with a beautiful maiden, for old age has no dissipations of that sort, but with a large dowry, and if he shall seem to be urging his son to an orderly course of life and to be upbraiding him for his love of the girl, he directs all his words to one end, the end toward which he decided at the outset to direct his life. He considers the well-to-do girl as more preferable, not, it may be, because he finds her very comely, for his intelligence is blinded by his love of the dowry, and the beauty of the poor girl is dimmed in the eyes of the covetous judge. In fact, the judgment of both is at fault, that of the son owing to his love for the girl, that of the father through his desire for money. Now the latter's reason is interfered with by several emotions — desire and fear and pain; he loves money, he is suspicious of the alliance with a poor girl, he is grieved at losing a sweet hope which allowed him a glimpse of gold as the result of his son's prowess; for he expected his son to ask as his reward that which was the object of his own desire. But though tormented in all these ways, he does not yet show great rage toward his son, for fear that he shall irritate the people by attacking too bitterly the savior of the city, but he at one time gives vent to his anger, as at once a father and an old man — for age is naturally quick-tempered — and at another time he puts a check on his feelings and shows himself mild in consideration of his son's prowess. And the youth having given proof of his early modesty and having shown that he knows how to honor his parents, the father, naturally, falls in with this line of proof, in order that he may exhort his son to be true to himself and may show that he has laid himself open to greater blame. For when a man changes from a good course of life to the opposite, the disgrace is twofold. Thus I will assume the rôle of the covetous father, though I am not, I believe, naturally a great lover of money, nor am I a father of children; but I will take the imitation of both characteristics from my art.

It is worth while to have dwelt thus long on this aspect of our subject, for we gain from it an idea of what the tasks were which these men set themselves. Of course, the tasks set the students in the schools were similar in all respects to those undertaken by the sophists themselves. We see that the question was not simply one of harmoniously grouped words, well-modulated voice, and graceful manner; there was, besides, a real intellectual problem involved — often, as in the case here dealt with from Choricius, a careful study of character. It was this, we may believe, no less than the charm of voice and manner and the music of words, that in most cases pleased the audience and drew forth their applause.

It would be interesting to examine some of the display speeches of Himerius and others, in order to see how these sophists treated their themes and what it was that appealed so strongly to the intellect of the people of those days. We should find, perhaps, that in many cases the so-called originality of treatment was nothing more than a recurrence to old forms and methods. Often it was a clever saying, or a clever way of putting an old saying, a striking simile or metaphor, an antithesis either of word or of thought, that called forth the applause. For such examination, however, we have not at present the space, but we may glance at a few of the samples of style contained in the pages of Philostratus, and from these, perhaps, gain a suggestion of what these sophists' methods were like.

One of the favorite themes of Herodes Atticus was that wherein he impersonated the wounded Athenians in Sicily begging of their brother Athenians, who were preparing to depart for home, death at their hands.[1] With tears in his eyes, he uttered the words: ναὶ Νικία, ναὶ πάτερ, οὕτως Ἀθήνας ἴδοις, "In the name of Nicias, in the name of father, may you then see Athens." At these words the sophist Alexander, who was Herodes's auditor, is said to have exclaimed, "Ah, Herodes, we other sophists are all only fragments of you." Much of the effect of Herodes's words was doubtless produced by the manner and the tone of voice in which they were spoken, but we can well understand how this appeal of those who never expected to see Athens again to those who were on the point of departing for home was designed to touch the hearts of the listeners. The words of Herodes became famous and were hummed on the street.

One of Secundus's themes was this:[2] The man who begins a revolution is to be put to death, the man who

[1] Philos., 574.  [2] Philos., 545.

ends one is to be rewarded; the same man begins and ends a revolution, and then demands a reward. This theme Secundus summarized thus: Now which did you do first? Started the revolution. Which second? Ended it. Very well, pay the penalty for your wrong deed, and then take the reward for your good, if you can. This kind of ἀπορία, or mental puzzle, was a favorite exercise with the sophists, and the interest of the audience was engaged to see how the orator would dispose of the perplexity in a striking and effective way.

Sometimes our author passes judgment on the extracts that he gives. Thus, the following, from the pen of the great Lollianus, is described as being a brilliant lightning-flash of wit:[1] Lollianus is inveighing against the law of Leptines, which has closed the Hellespont to Athenian vessels, and he says: "The mouth of the Pontus has been closed by law, and a few syllables shut off the supplies of the Athenians. Lysander waging war with ships, and Leptines waging war with law, are equally powerful" (κέκλεισται τὸ στόμα τοῦ Πόντου νόμῳ καὶ τὰς Ἀθηναίων τροφὰς ὀλίγαι κωλύουσι συλλαβαί, καὶ ταὐτὸν δύναται Λύσανδρος ναυμαχῶν καὶ Λεπτίνης νομομαχῶν). It is impossible for us, without the sound of the orator's voice, and with our imperfect appreciation of rhythm in prose, fully to imagine what the passage, when spoken, would be, but we can see that the bold use of the word *syllables*, and the parallel mention of Lysander with his ships and Leptines with the law bring into vivid relief the point which Lollianus is impressing.

[1] Philos., 527.

The following is characterized by Philostratus as dignified and pleasing (σεμνῶς τε καὶ ξὺν ἡδονῇ διελέγετο):[1] Μαρσύας ἦρα Ὀλύμπου καὶ Ὄλυμπος τοῦ αὐλεῖν, "Marsyas loved Olympus, and Olympus loved to flute."

Aristeides was thought by some to be at times too violent in his form of expression. Thus he was blamed on this score, when he said, in his plea against walling in Lacedæmon, "Let us not crouch in fear within a wall, clothing ourselves in quails' nature" (μὴ γὰρ δὴ ἐν τείχει ἐπιπτήξαιμεν ὀρτύγων ἀναψάμενοι φύσιν).[2]

A student once expressing in the presence of Isæus admiration for the inflated speech of Nicetes in the Xerxes theme, "To the royal galley let us fasten the isle Ægina" (ἐκ τῆς βασιλείου νεὼς Αἴγιναν ἀναδησώμεθα), Isæus, with a loud laugh, said, "How, you fool, will you set sail then?"[3]

Many features of style that are commonplace enough to us to-day, metaphors that we hardly longer recognize as metaphors, and the like, were then being discovered by the Greeks for the first time, and they bore all the charm of novelty; especially in a language whose directness in general precluded the over-free use of such figures.

The literary style of the different sophists varied, and it is therefore difficult to fix upon any well-defined idiosyncrasy or mannerism and to say that that was probably characteristic of the style of all. Certain general tendencies, however, it may be presumed, were present to each man, coloring, to a greater or less degree, his language and his manner of thought.

[1] 574.   [2] Philos., 583.   [3] Philos., 513.

Two of these may be mentioned. First, there was the tendency to clothe a single thought in manifold expression. We know that this was a tendency, because, as we shall soon see, the ability to do this thing was greatly applauded by the audiences of those days and admired by the critics.[1] The ability testifies once more to the wonderful command which these men had over words, shuffling and arranging them as the juggler shuffles and arranges his cards. It has also left its mark on the sophistic writings, in the form of a certain inability to leave a good point when once made, a tendency to play around it and to view it from several different sides, and often to an undue dwelling on unessential or trivial matter.[2] Secondly, there was the tendency to disguise one's thoughts, to put them in an indirect way, or, perhaps, figuratively. This tendency was fostered in the schools; in its nature it was not so far removed from the other tendency just mentioned, and it often led to obscurity and ambiguity, if these were not sometimes even aimed at.[3]

In order to gain an idea of the personality of some of these men and of their appearance on the stage, let us

---

[1] There were some, however, who opposed the principle, saying that there was one best way of saying a thing, which, when found, should not be changed: Theon, i. p. 152 (Speng., *Rh. Gr.*, ii. p. 62). Theon argues strongly against this view. Cf. Cic., *Pro Arch. poeta*, viii. 18: *Quotiens revocatum eandem rem dicere, commutatis verbis atque sententiis;* and Seneca, *Contr.*, iv. *præf.*, 7.

[2] See, for examples, Lib., i. 277, 286.

[3] Philos., 519: ἄριστος μὲν οὖν καὶ σχηματίσαι λόγον καὶ ἐπαμφοτέρως εἰπεῖν. For the general ornateness and artificiality of the sophistic style, see Brandstätter, *Hermes*, 15, pp. 131-274. See also Norden, *Die antike Kunstprosa.*

## PUBLIC DISPLAYS

turn to the description of Scopelian's manner, given by Philostratus, and to the picture drawn by Eunapius of the great Proæresius.

He came before his auditors [says Philostratus of Scopelian[1]], not in a scornful or swaggering way, nor as if scared, but as one should come who is about to enter a contest in which his reputation is at stake and in which he is confident of making no slip. When he spoke from his seat, he spoke with elegance and grace, but when he spoke standing, his words were full of strength and energy. His theme he examined, not in his own house, nor in the presence of the audience, but in a side room, where it took him but a moment to look it over in all its parts. His voice was clear and loud, and pleasing in quality, and he often struck his thigh, while speaking, to arouse his audience and himself.

And of Proæresius, Eunapius says:[2]

The writer of these lines crossed from Asia to Europe and Athens at the age of sixteen. Proæresius had then reached his eighty-seventh year, according to his own statement. Notwithstanding his great age, his hair was still curly and remarkably thick, and, being very gray, it resembled the sea when covered with foam, and it had also a silvery tinge. He was then at the height of his powers as a speaker, and the youthfulness of his spirit gave to his aged body strength and vigor, so that the present writer looked upon him as one who was immortal and destined never to grow old, and attached himself to him as to some god who had come, self-bidden and without labor, among men. . . . His[3] physical beauty was such that one could well doubt if any person in youth had ever been so beautiful as he was in old age. . . . His size was

---

[1] 519.  [2] P. 73.  [3] P. 77.

beyond all credence and hardly conjecturable, for he seemed to be almost nine feet high, and he looked, when seen by the side of the tallest men of his time, like a veritable colossus.

Scopelian and Proæresius were two of the greatest of the sophists, and they were free, as were doubtless all the really great sophists, from many of the more offensive mannerisms of the class. A strong personality, as we see from the words of Philostratus and Eunapius, was at the back of their popularity.[1]

Much, in the displays of which we have been speaking, depended on the inspiration and enthusiasm of the

---

[1] We may notice, in passing, the advanced age to which many of these men attained. Proæresius lived to be ninety-one, Priscus was over ninety when he died, Chrysanthius was eighty, Libanius was about eighty, Himerius was over seventy, and Themistius was about seventy-five or eighty. These were of the fourth century. Of the forty-one sophists of the two preceding centuries whose lives are contained in the pages of Philostratus, one died at the age of ninety, two others at the age of eighty or over, seven others at the age of seventy or over, five others at the age of sixty or over, and five others at the age of fifty or over. Eight others are called "old" or "very old" at the time of their death, and two "middle-aged;" one is called "not old." In the case of eight the age is left uncertain. Two died young, one of them at the age of twenty-five or twenty-eight. Of the eight about whose age nothing is said in Philostratus, Herodes died at the age of about seventy-five, and Isæus lived to be over sixty (Plin., *ep.*, ii. 3). Hermogenes was an Infant Phenomenon. At fifteen he attracted the attention of the emperor Marcus by his power as a sophist, but when he reached man's age, this power suddenly and unaccountably forsook him, and he died in obscurity. The author of the *Macrobii* (18) accounts for the longevity of teachers on the ground that they take better care of their health than other men. "Fifty-six," says Philostratus (543), "the end of youth in the other arts, and the beginning of old age, is for the sophist still youth; for this art, as it grows old, gathers wisdom." *Cf.* Lib., i. 208 *ff.*

moment, and the orator was often as if in a frenzy during his performance.[1] "The moment the light of the god flows about the speaker," says Aristeides,[2] ". . . and, like a draught from the spring of Apollo, enters into his soul, then does the soul straightway become tense, and it is filled with heat and a kind of tranquillity; he lifts his eyes upward and his hairs stand apart; he looks at nothing . . . but at his words and the springs from which they flow." The audience also did not remain impassive, but met the orator half-way and encouraged him with hand-clapping and words of praise. These were things that he could not do without.[3] Wildly frenzied speakers, working, by their words and actions, on the feelings of emotional audiences, are not unknown to-day: preachers have at times been heard to break forth, in the midst of their sermons, into song, and to clap their hands and stamp the ground. One great point of difference, how-

---

[1] The display is sometimes spoken of as if it involved great physical or mental strain; e. g., Philos., 541: ἰδὼν δὲ μονόμαχον ἱδρῶτι ῥεόμενον καὶ δεδιότα τὸν ὑπὲρ τῆς ψυχῆς ἀγῶνα, οὕτως, εἶπεν, ἀγωνιᾷς, ὡς μελετᾶν μέλλων. The sophist often advanced to speak with fear and trembling (Lib., i. 335, 16; ii. 288, 6; Syn., *Dion*, 11). For the inspiration of the sophist, see Aristeid., ii. pp. 525, 528, 533. The custom of speaking as if inspired is said to have begun with Æschines (Philos., 509: τὸ γὰρ θείως λέγειν οὔπω μὲν ἐπεχωρίασε σοφιστῶν σπουδαῖς, ἀπ' Αἰσχίνου δ' ἤρξατο θεοφορήτῳ ὁρμῇ ἀποσχεδιάζοντος, ὥσπερ οἱ τοὺς χρησμοὺς ἀναπνέοντες.

[2] ii. p. 528.

[3] Philos., 614. *Cf.* Lib., ii. 80, 14; 81, 2; Themis., 246 a. Aristeides, when about to speak before Marcus, asked to have his students present and allowed to shout and clap (Philos., 583). The audience must meet the orator half-way (Aristeid., ii. p. 529). *Cf.*, further, Rohde, *Gr. Rom.*, p. 335, n. 2. See p. 252, n. 2.

ever, there is between such religious addresses of the present day and the ancient displays. In the former the appeal is almost wholly to the emotions, and the congregation is, as a whole, uncritical; in the latter the basis of the enthusiasm was intellectual. "Then," says Aristeides,[1] "every auditor grows dizzy and knows not whether he is standing on his head or his heels; surrounding the speaker, like a host marshalled for battle, they shout their approval, and one praises his correctness of language, another his subtlety of thought, a third the beauty and grace of his style, each selecting that feature to which his natural bent or his training inclines him." We should have difficulty in imagining any modern audience, religious or not, displaying equal enthusiasm for elegance of style or mental acuteness. Probably admiration for the great singer is the nearest modern approach to the enthusiasm aroused by the ancient sophist.

Such, then, were the displays, and such the men, that young and old in those days flocked in crowds to see and hear — even staying at times, as Libanius tells us,[2] overnight in the lecture-hall, in order to be on hand

[1] ii. p. 530. At Antioch the people used to flock to the courts to hear the speakers (Lib., i. 317, 10). For the æsthetic sense of the people of Antioch, see Lib., i. 335, 5: νόημα νοσοῦν, καὶ σχῆμα ἡμαρτημένον, καὶ ῥῆμα διεφθαρμένον εὐθὺς ἥλω. A weak idea, a wrong figure, or an inappropriate word was at once detected.

[2] i. 63, 4. Men of all ages flocked to Libanius's displays at Constantinople (Lib., i. 57, 3; cf. ii. 219, 12), and men and women of all conditions at Antioch (see below in text); women at Constantinople also (Themis., 304 b). The οἱ πολλοί, as well as the better class of people, attended Aristeides's displays at Smyrna (Aristeid., ii. 562). Again, the sophist's audience is spoken of as

in the morning — much as men do nowadays when a favorite actor or singer comes to town. In some places, the moment a professor's gown appeared, the people ran, and, as Themistius says,[1] clung to it as iron clings to a magnet. "I have met a number of people from Antioch," writes the Christian orator Basil to the pagan sophist Libanius,[2] "who have spoken most admiringly of your eloquence. They said that you held a display under the most brilliant auspices; and the performance, they said, attracted so much attention that everybody flocked to it, so that the city seemed as if divided into two camps: Libanius, who was contending, and everybody else, who was listening. Nobody wished to be left out, from the nabob, high in dignity and station, and the military commander, distinguished for his rank, to the common workman. Even the women came in crowds. Now, what was this performance? What was the discourse that could thus bring the whole city together? They told me that you represented the character of a fretful man. Send me without delay this speech which is so much admired, that I, too, may be one of your admirers." Sometimes a distinguished sophist would be followed from place to place by his students, who would settle wherever the sophist settled.[3] The presence of Proæresius at Athens was sufficient to

being made up of all sorts of people (Themis., 201 a, 313 d). See also Lib., i. 335, 11; ii. 80, 18. An audience of one thousand is mentioned in Epictet., iii. 23, 19.

[1] 299 a; *cf.* 289 a, 293 d. In Athens a certain class of people made it their business to tag after the sophists (Philos., 578, 587).

[2] *Ep.*, 351, Migne (Lib., *ep.*, 1596).

[3] Luc., *Dem.*, 31; Lib., i. 54, 15; 70, 14.

attract to the city the educated men from all parts of Greece.¹ The enthusiasm in the lecture-hall was, as we have already seen, often great; hand-clapping and shouting were the approved methods of expressing admiration, and old men and men that were sick were at times known to jump from their seats and wildly gesticulate.² Libanius used sometimes to chuckle in secret over the thought that he had one student who shouted like fifty ordinary students.³ Being thus forced

[1] Eunap., p. 90.

[2] Lib., i. 63, 10. For clapping and shouting, see Lib., iii. 378, 19; Themis., 243 b, 282 d; Eunap., p. 69; Luc., *Nigr.*, 10; and p. 249, n. 3. At a funeral oration on one occasion the audience shouted at every word (Procop., *ep.*, 49), but Plutarch advised against such practices (*De rect. rat. aud.*, 13). *Cf.* Lib., i. 87, 3. See also Norden, *Die antike Kunstprosa*, i. pp. 274, 275, 295, 296. Sometimes unruly students tried to prevent those who were well disposed from shouting (*ib.*, i. 200, 12). Men occasionally shouted themselves hoarse (*ib.*, ii. 375, 10), and people on the street were disturbed by the hooting in a sophist's hall (Plut., *De rect. rat. aud.*, 15). See, further, Lib., ii. 80 *f*. For jumping from the seat, see Themis., 311 c, 315 c, 343 b, 366 c; Luc., *Rhet. præc.*, 21; Lib., *ep.*, 348, 613, 1593. At times the audience became so excited that they all but turned somersaults (Lib., ii. 375, 10; *cf.* p. 262 of the text). Gesticulating with the hands was also common, as well as waving the cloak (Luc., *Rh . præc.*, 21; Eunap., p. 73). τοὺς ἐν ταῖς ἐπιδείξεσι πάντα ποιοῦντας, says Libanius, i. 211, 3. The audience tried to find extravagant words of praise, such as θείως, θεοφορήτως, 'divine,' 'inspired,' ἀπροσίτως, 'inimitable' (Plut., *De rect. rat. aud.*, 15; *cf.* Lib., i. 179, 9); ὑπερφυῶς, 'marvellous' (Epictet., iii. 23, 11); θαυμαστῶς, 'wonderful,' Οὐᾶ, 'Rah' (Epictet., iii. 23, 24). The usual words were καλῶς, σοφῶς, ἀληθῶς. Antipater, who taught the children of the emperor, was called θεῶν διδάσκαλος (Philos., 607). See also Luc., *Rhet. præc.*, 21. It was considered a sign of distinction to enter late at a display (*ib.*, 22). See, further, on this subject, Sievers, *Leben des Lib.*, p. 27; Rohde, *Gr. Rom.*, pp. 335, 336. Hissing was a sign of disapproval (Luc., *Nigr.*, 10); also howling (Plut., *De rect. rat. aud.*, 4).

[3] Like Stentor, *Il.*, v. 786 (Lib., *ep.*, 280).

to pause in his speech, Libanius would smile upon the student, and even step down from the platform and run up to him.[1] Proæresius, as we saw in a previous chapter,[2] was hailed as a god on one occasion by his ecstatic audience, and escorted from the hall by the proconsul in person and his body-guard. Sometimes, when the rivalry between different sophists was great, the audience was packed, and the applause given at a pre-arranged signal, and in concert, under the leadership of one of the band.[3] When a sophist was famous and his speeches 'took,' snatches of them were hummed on the street,[4] or the students, congregating after lecture, would try to patch together the parts they had brought away in their memory.[5] Adrian's students escorted their master home after lecture.[6]

[1] *Cf.* Themis., 314 a.    [2] P. 157.  *Cf.* Luc., *Rhet. præc.*, 21.
[3] Themis., 283 a; Eunap., p. 81; Aristeid., ii. 542; Luc., *Rhet. præc.*, 21. A band of partisans or claqueurs was called φάλαγξ (Lib., i. 33, 1), μερίς (*ib.*, i. 51, 1).
[4] Philos., 574.    [5] Lib., i. 201, 6.
[6] Philos., 587. Compare the conduct of the people of Greece toward the aged philosopher Demonax, described by Lucian (*Dem.*, 63, 64): "He so endeared himself to the Athenians themselves and to all Greece that, when he appeared in an assembly, the officials arose and every voice was hushed. Finally in extreme old age, whenever, even though unbidden, he entered a house, he was always invited to dine and to spend the night, the occupants looking upon his presence there as a manifestation of god, and believing that a good spirit had entered among them. When he passed on the street, the bread-women rivalled one another in suing for his attention, each urging him to take of her bread; and the one from whom he took rejoiced as at a piece of good fortune. Even the children offered him fruit, and called him 'father.' Once dissension having taken place in the Athenian assembly, Demonax entered, and his simple presence caused all to become silent. Then, seeing that the members had come to their senses, he departed without, on his part, saying a word."

Haughtiness and vanity, we have already seen,[1] were characteristic of the sophist. Not infrequently he presumed upon his reputation, and many are the anecdotes that are told of his overbearing manner and self-confident ways. Polemo, according to Philostratus,[2] acted toward cities as their superior, toward provinces as anything but their inferior, and toward divinities as their equal. On the occasion of his first visit to Athens, he did not, as sophists generally did, begin his address by referring to the glory of the city and the insignificance of his own fame, but said, "They say, Athenians, that you are intelligent listeners: I shall see." When Adrian, a Phœnician, took the chair of sophistry at Athens, he began his inaugural address thus: "Once again come letters from Phœnicia."[3] Himerius was frank enough to intimate to his audience on more than one occasion that he regretted that all men were not wise enough to send their sons to him to be educated.[4] Occasionally there is a note of extravagance in the sophist's words. Polemo is said to have given instructions, just before he died, that he should be buried before the breath had left his body, and, when the door of his tomb was about to be closed, to have cried, "Hurry! hurry! I would not be seen above ground with my mouth shut."[5]

Haughtiness and vanity, however, were not incompatible with much genuine human feeling. It was a part of the sophist's trade to assume an air of superiority, and if the sophist sometimes carried his arrogance and

---

[1] P. 232. See also Themis., 251 b.
[2] 535.
[3] Philos., 587.
[4] *Or.*, xxxiii. 2 *ff.*; xxxiv. 1, 2.
[5] Philos., 543, 544.

haughtiness into private life, it was no more than most people did at a time when the feeling of rank permeated nearly all society, as was the case in the fourth and following centuries. Indeed, the sophists probably made a better showing in this respect than most others. We feel, as we read their biographies and their works, that the humanity of their profession was not wholly without influence on their character.

One of the most pleasing features of the academic life of the second and third centuries is the professional honesty that existed among certain great sophists — the ready willingness to recognize ability even in a rival. This is in distinct contrast to the spirit of the fourth century, which was one of enmity and petty jealousy,[1] and it is to be feared that even in the earlier period only the greatest of the sophists could rise to this height of magnanimity. Sometimes sophists travelled long distances to see and hear their brother sophists who were famous, and gave them generous praise. Herodes, who was a great admirer of extempore speaking, went on one occasion to Smyrna to hear the sophist Polemo, whom he had never seen. After embracing Polemo and kissing him on the lips, he said, "Well, father, when shall I hear you speak?" He thought that Polemo would shrink from speaking before one so famous as himself, and would make excuses, but Polemo said, "To-day; come and you shall hear me now," and when he spoke, Herodes wondered at his readiness of tongue and mind. "This," says Philostratus, referring to the action of Polemo,[2] "shows the man's spirit and his

[1] See pp. 152 *ff.*  [2] 537.

great wisdom, but the following shows his modesty and good breeding: for when Herodes entered to hear him speak, he received the man with every mark of respect and in a manner befitting the latter's words and deeds."

At another time the aged sophist Dionysius, arriving one evening at Sardis and learning that the great Polemo, who was then at the height of his fame, was in town and about to speak the following day on a law case, said to his entertainer, Dorion, "What a piece of good fortune, if I am to hear Polemo, whom I have never yet seen!" "You seem," said Dorion, "much affected by this young man, who has already acquired such a name." "I am," replied Dionysius. "By Athene! I can hardly sleep; my heart jumps and my head is in a whirl, when I think how many there are who speak in his praise; some say he has twelve springs to his tongue, while others measure his speech by the yard, as they do the risings of the Nile." Dionysius, be it said, was somewhat alarmed for his own reputation, but on the next day he heard Polemo speak, and regained his courage. "Polemo has strength," was his comment, "but not well-trained strength." Polemo, hearing of this remark, went to the sophist's door and challenged the man to a friendly contest. Dionysius went, but came off second best.[1]

The custom of engaging in friendly contest has been remarked upon above.[2] Marcus of Byzantium was rough and unkempt, and resembled much more a countryman than a man of wit and learning. Coming once to Smyrna, where Polemo was holding forth, he

[1] Philos., 524, 525.   [2] P. 218.

dropped into the latter's lecture-hall, when all the audience was seated and ready to listen to the speaker's words. Somebody, who happened to have been at Byzantium, recognizing the newcomer, passed the word to his neighbor, and so the news went through the whole audience that Marcus, the sophist, was present. When Polemo asked the audience for a theme, all turned to Marcus, but Polemo, not knowing the man, and thinking him some rustic who had come to town, said, "Why do you look at that countryman? *He can't give a theme.*" But Marcus, as was his way, throwing back his head and raising his voice, said, "I can give a theme, and I can discuss one, too." Then Polemo recognized Marcus's Doric tongue, and, stepping down, he conversed long and pleasantly with his visitor; and afterward they both declaimed, and each wondered at the other's power.[1]

The sophistical displays, which have formed the subject of the present chapter, will be more fully understood if we give from the original a few descriptions of what actually took place on these occasions. There are here given translations of three passages, two from the pages of Philostratus, illustrative of academic life as it was at Athens in the second century, and one from Libanius, describing an event which took place at Antioch in the fourth century.

Hippodromus [says Philostratus[2]], though rather countrified in appearance, gave indication in his eyes, which were bright and keen, of wonderful spirit. This fact Megistias of Smyrna says he noticed, and Megistias had

[1] Philos., 529.      [2] 618, 619.

a wide reputation as a physiognomist. The story he tells is this: Hippodromus, some time after the death of Heracleides, paid a visit to Smyrna. He had never been there before, and, after leaving the vessel, he walked up to the centre of the town, to see if he could fall in with any one who was educated in the native style of oratory. Seeing a temple, and some pedagogues and foot-boys sitting outside with bundles of books slung from their shoulders in bags, he inferred that some distinguished man was teaching inside, and so walked in. Giving a word of greeting to Megistias, he sat down without asking any questions. Megistias thought that he had come to have a conversation about the class, and that he was perhaps the father or the guardian of one of the boys, and so he asked him which boy he wished to talk about. "You shall hear," said Hippodromus, "as soon as we are alone." Accordingly, after Marcus had finished quizzing his students, he said, "Now tell me what you have to say." "Let's exchange cloaks," said Hippodromus—Hippodromus had on a travelling cloak, and Megistias the speaker's gown. "What for?" asked Marcus. "I wish to give you a sample of my oratory," replied Hippodromus. When he heard this, Megistias thought the man must be beside himself and really mad, but, seeing the sharp gleam of his eyes, and observing that he acted sensibly and as if in his right mind, he exchanged cloaks, and then, being requested so to do, set a theme. The theme was: The mage maintaining that he should die because he could not slay the mage who was a rake. When Hippodromus seated himself in the sophist's chair, and then, after a few moments, jumped to his feet, Megistias was confirmed in his first impression that the man was deranged; and this that was art on Hippodromus's part, he thought madness. But when Hippodromus began his theme and spoke the words, "But, in my case, I am able . . ." (ἀλλ' ἐμαυτόν γε δύναμαι . . .), Megistias could not contain himself for admiration, but, running up to him, begged to know who he was. "I am," said the other, "Hippodromus of Thessaly, and I have come to practise in your presence, because I wish, through one man of your learning, to receive instruction in the Ionic style of speaking. But now hear me to the end." When he was near the end of his speech, all the people of education in Smyrna flocked to the door of Megistias's school, for the report quickly spread everywhere that Hippodromus was in town. Hippodromus, taking up again the theme he had just discussed, repeated in different form the ideas he had before expressed, and, when he appeared in the public assembly, the people wondered at him and thought him worthy to be placed among the ancients.

The second passage from Philostratus refers to the sophist Alexander and his visit to Athens.[1]

Hearing that Herodes was staying at Marathon and that all the young men had followed him thither, he sent a letter, asking for the Greeks, and Herodes replied, "I will come myself and bring the Greeks." The audience had now assembled in the theatre called the Agrippeium, which is in the Ceramicus, and, as the day wore on and Herodes did not appear, the Athenians began to get uneasy, thinking that they were to be cheated out of the show, and they complained that it was a trick. Alexander was, therefore, obliged to come forward and begin his talk before Herodes came. His talk was an encomium upon the city and a defence of himself for not having come to Athens before. It was of fitting length, resembling the epitome of a Panathenaic speech. Alexander made so good an impression on the Athenians that, even before he began to speak, a murmur ran through the crowd, showing that they were pleased with his appearance. The theme that was chosen

[1] 571–573.

for him to discuss was: The urging of the Scythians to a return to their former nomad life, since to live in cities made them sick. After a moment's hesitation, the sophist leaped from his seat with a beaming face, as if bringing to his auditors an earnest of what he could say. While he was speaking, Herodes came in, wearing, as was his custom at Athens in summer, his Arcadian cap, to shield his face from the sun, and at the same time perhaps to show that he had just arrived from a journey. Alexander, taking advantage of the occasion, spoke in dignified and clear-ringing terms of the presence of Herodes, and then left it to him to decide whether he would listen to the theme that had already been started or would himself set another. Herodes looking at the audience and saying that he would do whatever seemed best to them, all agreed that Alexander should go on with the Scythian theme; and, indeed, he was treating the theme most brilliantly, as is evident from the speech itself. In another way also Alexander displayed wonderful power: for, although, before Herodes came, he treated his theme most brilliantly, he expressed the same ideas, after Herodes's arrival, in different words and different rhythms so successfully, that his hearers, who heard him twice, did not feel that he was saying the same thing over. The most famous passage in the first speech, "From standing, even water contracts disease" (ἑστὸς καὶ τὸ ὕδωρ νοσεῖ), he afterward changed thus, "Even of waters, those that are in motion are the sweeter" (καὶ ὑδάτων ἡδίω τὰ πλανώμενα). The following, too, is from Alexander's *Scythians:* "When Ister froze, I rode to the south; when Ister opened, I went to the north, entire of body, and not, as now, on a bed of pain. For what harm can come to man if he follow the seasons?" (καὶ πηγνυμένου μὲν Ἴστρου πρὸς μεσημβρίαν ἤλαυνον, λυομένου δὲ ἐχώρουν πρὸς ἄρκτον ἀκέραιος τὸ σῶμα καὶ οὐχ ὥσπερ νυνὶ κείμενος. τί γὰρ ἂν πάθοι δεινὸν ἄνθρωπος ταῖς ὥραις ἑπόμενος;). At the end of the speech, when inveighing against the city as a stifling habitation, he closed thus: "Spread wide the gates, I wish to take breath" (ἀλλ' ἀναπέτασον τὰς πύλας, ἀναπνεῦσαι θέλω). Then, running up to Herodes and embracing him, he said, "Now you entertain me," and Herodes replied, "Indeed I will, seeing that you have entertained me so brilliantly."

The ability to express the same thought in several different ways was, we see, a thing highly prized, and its effect on the sophistic writings has been remarked upon before.[1]

The third passage describes the return of Libanius to his home, Antioch, after long absence and in the height of his fame, and the welcome accorded him by his countrymen.[2]

Fortune favored me . . . when I found that I had to prove my mettle in a contest. For, first, there was no need that men should go about from house to house to raise an audience by flattery — the news had but to be spread abroad that I was going to speak. Secondly, the people did not wait for daybreak before they filled the council-chamber in every part; on that occasion for the first time the room seemed not large enough to hold the crowd that wished to enter. When I asked my foot-boy if anybody had come, he told me that there were some who had slept there overnight. My uncle, with fear and trembling, led me in; I followed, smiling — for Fortune filled my heart with confidence — and, looking upon the throng, as Achilles looked upon the armor, I was glad. Thus, at the very outset, before a word was spoken, I filled the audience with wonder. How can I fittingly describe the tears that followed my introductory speech? Not a few learned

[1] P. 246.   [2] Lib., i. 62, 12.

that speech by heart before they left the room. How can I describe the frenzy with which my second speech was greeted? There was not a man who, in the matter of leaping and showing in every way his delight, was anything but young, not a man who was anything but quick and active, not a man who was anything but full of strength. Even such as had the gout and could not comfortably stand, still stood; and when I told them to sit down, they said they could not, for the speech. Many times they interrupted me while I was speaking and begged the emperor to restore me to my home and countrymen. Having kept this up till they grew tired, they turned once more to the speech, and blessed both themselves and me. . . . No more glad was that day to Agamemnon whereon he captured Troy, than was this day to me, when I met with such success. Even when I passed on my way to the bath, the people followed at my heels, eager to touch my person.

We have, however, not yet exhausted the fields of the sophist's activity. For it must be remembered that the sophist was not only a teacher of youth, who at times came forth from the school-room to give in public an exhibition of his art; he was the orator—the Court orator of the times. If a temple was to be dedicated, if an officer of the government—a provincial magistrate or the ruler of a diocese—was to be welcomed to his district, if a petition was to be preferred to the emperor or the emperor's representative, the sophist was the one man to whom all turned to perform that duty; and on numberless other occasions his services were called into requisition. At public festivals he was always in prominence, and, when travelling from place to place, he frequently addressed in more or less formal discourse the people of the towns through which he passed. The speeches that were delivered on all these occasions were of the kind called *epideictic*, and were generally eulogistic in character. The rhetorician Menander has left us a curious treatise dealing with this class of speeches, and in it he has given us detailed instructions as to how we are to handle this or that person or thing. We are told,[1] for instance, how to praise a country, how to praise a city, how to praise an acropolis, how to praise a harbor, how to praise a gulf, and so on. If the object that you wish to praise has both good and bad qualities, it is always better to dwell on the good and omit to mention the bad, or, making little of the bad, show how the good predominate. If it is a city that you wish to eulogize, you may do so from the point of view of its situation or from that of its inhabitants. If you take the point of view of its situation, you may speak of its climate, of its position with regard to the sea and the land, of its streams, etc. If the city lies on a plain, with mountains about it, you should speak of the defence that these mountains offer against a foreign foe; if it is built on hilly ground, with a plain before it, you should compare it to a lighthouse, serving as a welcoming beacon to approaching friends.

Not all the epideictic speeches, however, were so ostensibly encomiastic as these, though all that were not actually in the line of censure were of an encomiastic nature. Wedding speeches, birthday speeches, speeches of welcome and of farewell, these and many others

[1] Speng., *Rh. Gr.*, iii. pp. 344 *ff*.

came within the province of the orator in those days, and each had its own peculiar form and style, being cast in a mould of its own and constructed according to fixed rules.¹

[1] It is not the intention in this book to speak at length of the literary, as distinguished from the oratorical, activity of the sophists, but one curious tendency may here receive casual notice. This is the tendency which produced such encomiastic enormities as Lucian's *Encomium on a Fly* and Synesius's *In Praise of Baldness*. Other authors went even further in this line, as when they wrote in praise of vomiting, or of fever, or in commendation of a porridge-pot (Plut., *De rect. rat. aud.*, 13). It is, of course, not always easy to say what was spoken and what was not; nearly all compositions were written as if to be spoken. The sophist Heracleides wrote a piece called πόνου ἐγκώμιον. Another sophist, seeing him engaged on the work, waggishly erased the π of πόνου, and handed him back the book (Philos., 614, 615). For the literary activity of the sophists, see Rohde, *Gr. Rom.*, pp. 343 *ff*. For the epideictic literature, see Burgess, *Epideictic Literature*.

## CHAPTER XII

### SCHOOL-HOUSES, HOLIDAYS, ETC.; THE SCHOOL OF ANTIOCH

THERE remain to be considered, in the present chapter, a few matters relative to the more or less external features of the class and class-room instruction, together with the question of the arrangement of the school system as a whole in Antioch in the fourth century.

At the beginning of the academic year the sophist commonly opened his course with an introductory lecture, or address, to his students.[1] Old students were welcomed back, and new were taken into the fold. Himerius on these occasions usually had a graceful and appropriate word for each of the different nationalities represented in his class — some myth, it might be, or a flattering allusion to the students' country or countrymen. Sometimes he recommended to the care of the older students those who had just come, and at other times he explained to his class what they were expected to do and what not to do. "Come, then," he says in his

[1] Lib., *ep.*, 407 (probably a public address or one open to all students, for at its close seventeen new students joined the class; it was accompanied by a ἅμιλλα πρός τι τῶν Δημοσθένους); Himer., *or.*, xii. (inscribed εἰς ἀρχὰς σπουδῶν). Apparently such addresses as Himer., *or.*, x, xi, xv, xxviii, xxix.; *ec.*, xv, xviii, xix, xxii. were of this order.

flowery style,[1] "before I initiate you into the rites of my school, let me tell you what you are allowed to do and what you are not allowed to do. Let every one give ear, whether he now comes for the first time to be initiated or has already reached the last stage of initiation. You must throw aside the ball, and put your attention on the pencil. Close the playground, and open the Muses' workshop. Run no more about the lanes and alleys of the town; stay at home and write instead. Avoid the public theatre; give ear to a better theatre. Luxury and daintiness do not fit well with study; show yourselves, while with me, severe in your lives and superior to luxury. This is my proclamation, this my law—much in little. Those of you who listen and obey, shall sing *Iacchus, Iacchus* many times, for those of you who heed not my words and disobey, I hide my light and close the temple of my wisdom. This proclamation is for you all, but especially for you, young men, who are newcomers and have just joined my class." At the end of the term the sophist took leave of his students in a farewell speech.[2]

The sophist met his class, sometimes in a public building, as a temple, a city hall, or the like, sometimes in hired quarters, and sometimes in his own house, where he often had a private theatre, or lecture-hall, fitted up after the pattern of the public halls. In the fifth century, at Constantinople, as we have elsewhere seen, sophists who held state appointments had rooms assigned to them in the Capitol. At Antioch, Athens,

---

[1] *Or.*, xxii. 7. In *or.*, xv. 3, the younger students are recommended to the care of the older. [2] *Cf.* Himer., *ec.*, xi.

and probably other places, school buildings were erected at the public expense. At Rome the Athenæum was the centre of university life. Libanius, during the most of the time he was at Antioch, held his school in the city hall — the βουλευτήριον.[1] When he settled at Antioch,

[1] In a temple: ἱερόν (Philos., 618), τὸ τῆς τύχης ἱερόν (Lib., *ep.*, 86), ἐπί τι τῶν ἱερῶν (*ib.*, i. 71, 6). The βουλευτήριον of Lib, i. 238, 4 was a temple (τὸ ἱερόν, 236, 4; τὸν νεών, 240, 9). It would seem, from the words which the old man addresses to Libanius in Lib., i. 71, 5, that certain temples were open to the occupancy of anybody. The suggestion from Lib., ii. 377, 4, and 378, 14, is that a room in the βουλευτήριον, once occupied, was for the private and sole use of the occupant. It is possible that Libanius, after his appointment as sophist at Antioch, was given such an apartment. In that case, however, he received his appointment as early as 354 (see below). Notwithstanding the reasonable doubt that may be raised whether he was receiving a salary at Antioch at the same time that he was receiving one at Constantinople (see pp. 176, 177), there are not lacking other slight indications that he was holding an official appointment at Antioch as early as 354 or 355. Zenobius, who was at the head of a school of rhetors at Antioch (Lib., ii. 204–223; 312, 17 *ff.*; p. 192, above), died in 354 (see below), and Libanius succeeded to his position. The salary which Zenobius had enjoyed, however, instead of being given to Libanius, was assigned to the four rhetors. We may conjecture, as the reason for this transference, the fact that Libanius was now given an imperial salary; the salary of Zenobius, which was a municipal donation, was thus left available for the under-teachers. (The Twenty-ninth Oration of Libanius [the Thirty-first in Förster], in which Libanius appears as the sophist of Antioch, Förster, ed. Lib., iii. p. 119, assigns to 355 or thereabouts; it certainly belongs to the period 355–361, but a few passages [204, 1; 205, 15 *ff.*; 210, 15 R] suggest a date nearer 361). Again, Libanius seems, in *ep.*, 1247, to refer to a salary held by himself in Antioch in 355. Libanius constantly speaks of the βουλευτήριον as the scene of his labors — as display-room and as school-room (*e. g.*, i. 73, 4; 77, 8; 134, 12; 238, 4; ii. 375, 11; 378, 14; 430, 15; 471, 14; iii. 176; *ep.*, 367, 1083). *Ep.*, 1083 dates, according to Seeck (*Briefe d. Lib.*, p. 322), from 355. In fact, we find Libanius in the βουλευτήριον shortly after his occupancy of the room near the market-place and before Zeno-

he was in great distress because his students were so few. "I had, meeting at my house," he says,[1] "a class of fifteen, the most of whom I had brought with me from Constantinople, but I did not yet hold a public appointment. My friends were discouraged, and I was thoroughly disheartened. Oppressed, like Peleus's son, by inactivity, I called myself 'a weight upon the earth,' and even had recourse to drugs to save my mind. I had found things at Antioch not what I had expected, and to Constantinople I could not return without encountering ridicule. At this time there came to me an old man, who told me that it was no wonder that I did

bius's death, which was in 354 (Lib., i. 73, 4). After his removal to Antioch in the spring of 354, therefore, Libanius taught first in his own house (*ib.*, i. 70, 13), then in the hired apartment by the market-place (*ib.*, i. 71, 8), and, thirdly, probably after his appointment as official sophist and still in the year 354, in the βουλευτήριον. The question then arises, When did he teach in the temple of Fortune (*ib.*, *ep.*, 86), and when, if at all, in the Museum (*ib.*, i. 71, 10)? The letter in which the temple of Fortune is mentioned as being the former scene of his labors was written in 359. His occupancy of this temple, therefore, must have been in 354, after he moved out of the hired quarters and before he entered the βουλευτήριον, or it must have been a temporary occupancy between 354 and 359. As regards the Museum, the single passage in which this building seems to be mentioned under this name (*ib.*, i. 71, 10) does not make it clear that Libanius ever had quarters therein, while from other passages it would seem that, though Libanius was stationed in the βουλευτήριον, the other sophists, or, at least, all others except his own χορός (*ib.*, ii. 210, 218), had quarters elsewhere (*ib.*, ii. 375, 11; 430, 15). The Museum may at this time have been the centre of the university life at Antioch, as the Athenæum was of that at Rome, and, later, the Capitol of that at Constantinople. Libanius was occupying the βουλευτήριον as late as 393 (*ib.*, *ep.*, 986, 995). There were public recitation buildings at Antioch (*ib.*, i. 334, 14), and at Athens (Eunap., p. 69: τῶν δημοσίων θεάτρων.) At Nico-

[1] i. 70, 13.

not succeed when I lay at my ease in my own house, for, of course, those who sat in public had the advantage. 'If you wish,' he said, 'to see how many there are who thirst for knowledge, go to some temple.' This advice of the old man I did not precisely follow, but, inducing a shopkeeper down town to move, I installed myself in his quarters, and thus set up my chair close to the market-place. The situation did something, for the number of my students — fifteen, as I have just said — was increased more than threefold. The Museum, however, which was a great help to those that held it, was in the hands of my rivals."

media Libanius at one time held his classes in the public baths (Lib., i. 40, 9), but this was unusual. Displays were given at Athens in the Agrippeium and in τὸ τῶν τεχνιτῶν βουλευτήριον (Philos., 571, 580), perhaps also in the Lyceum (Schemmel, *Neue Jahrb.* 22, p. 499). Public theatres for sophistical displays were erected at Smyrna (Aristeid., i. 376). A building for school purposes at Trèves was the Mæniana (Eumen., *Pro rest. scol.*, 2). For the Athenæum at Rome, see p. 85, Dio Cass., lxxiii. 17; Jul. Capit., *Pert.*, 11; Lamprid., *Alex. Sev.*, 35; Script. Hist. Aug., *Gord. sen.*, 3; Hulsebos, *De educ. et instit. apud Rom.*, p. 207. Of course, private teachers often taught at the pupils' houses (*Cod. Th.*, xiv. 9, 3 [*Cod. Jus.*, xi. 19]). Hime ius gave some of his speeches ἔνδον, 'at home' (*e. g., or.*, xv. xvii.; *cf.* Lib., i. 367, 9). Sosipatra taught in her own house (Eunap., p. 38). Private theatres (*ib.*, p. 69: ἐν τοῖς ἰδιωτικοῖς θεάτροις). See also the description of Julian's theatre (*ib.*). The theatre is also spoken of as a place for displays at Antioch (Lib., *ep.*, 767, 782). The common words for 'recitation building' are διδασκαλεῖον (Lib., ii. 207, 9), μουσεῖον or μουσεῖα (*ib.*, i. 213, 8; *ep.*, 1215), παιδαγωγεῖον (Themis., 258 b); but other words were sometimes used, as σχολή (Plut., *Pericl.*, 35), παιδευτήριον (Diod. Sic., xiii. 27), διατριβή (Himer., *ec.*, xvii. title); less prosaically, ἐργαστήριον σοφιστῶν (Lib., ii. 79, 11), ἐργαστήριον Μουσῶν (Himer., *or.*, xxii. 7), ἐργαστήριον λόγων (Lib., i. 103, 15), τῶν Μουσῶν σηκός (*ib., ep.*, 1594). A 'lecture-room' is θέατρον (Eunap., p.69), διατριβή (Philos., 529), ἀκροατήριον (Himer., *or.*, 22, title), φροντιστήριον (Procop., *ep.*, 114, 138).

Of the school system of no ancient Greek city of this period have we so much information as of that of Antioch. And yet the details even of this system are often hard to make out: Libanius, our principal informant, leaves us all too often to conjecture and inference. The matter is most important, however, for, aside from its intrinsic interest, its determination may cast light on the school systems of other Greek cities of the second, third, and fourth centuries A. D.

In the speech [1] which Libanius addressed to the municipal council of Antioch when, some time between 355 and 361, he came before that body to plead for a special dispensation in favor of the four rhetors to whom had been assigned the single salary of the sophist Zenobius, he tells the relation in which he stood to these four rhetors. They were, he says, his associates and his fellow-workers in the same ranks, they 'sang' (*i. e.*, taught and declaimed) in company with him and were members of the same 'chorus' (χορός), or circle;[2] they lived with him;[3] they were under his direction;[4] he was thoroughly acquainted with their condition;[5] he was the 'coryphæus,' or leader, of the 'chorus';[6] for all these reasons he appeared as their spokesman. These expressions seem sufficiently clear, and yet we are immediately confronted by several questions. The

---

[1] *Or.*, xxix. R (ii. 204 *ff.*).

[2] ii. 218, 5: τῶν συνόντων, τῶν συντεταγμένων, τῶν συμπονούντων, τῶν συνᾳδόντων, τῶν τὸν αὐτὸν πληρούντων χορόν.

[3] ii. 217, 19.

[4] ii. 207, 10: εἰσὶ δὲ οὗτοί μοι τέτταρες ἡγούμενοι τοῖς νέοις ἐπὶ τὴν γνῶσιν τῶν ἀρχαίων.

[5] ii. 208, 25; 218, 5.          [6] ii. 210, 13.

first question relates to the constitution of the school itself, if school we may call it. Were these five — the four 'rhetors'[1] and Libanius — the sole members of the school or were there others? No mention of others is made in this speech, but it is not improbable that the school, if not at this time, at least later, had in its corps of teachers one or more 'grammarians,' as well as a teacher of Latin eloquence. One 'grammarian' Libanius cer-

[1] They are consistently called 'rhetors,' and not 'sophists,' in this oration, but apparently the name here is simply a less distinguished one than 'sophists,' and refers to teachers of eloquence who were sub-masters; perhaps they taught the more elementary and technical parts of the subject, or, possibly, they dealt with the more practical, as distinguished from the 'sophistical,' or literary, aspects of it. *Cf.* p. 220, n. 4. They are referred to in ii. 221, 9 as οἱ χώραν μὲν ἔχουσιν ἣν ἴστε καὶ προσηγορίᾳ τῇ νῦν κρατούσῃ στέργουσιν, ἦσαν δ' ἄν, εἴπερ ἐβούλοντο, τοῦ παντὸς ἡγεμόνες, ὡς ἥ γε δύναμις πάρεστιν, the meaning of which seems to be that they are satisfied with being simply 'rhetors,' or sub-masters, though they could, if they wished, set up schools of their own and be known as 'sophists.' The reference in the similar passage, iii. 446, 18: ὃς ἀγαπᾷ μὲν τῇ δευτέρᾳ χώρᾳ, is to the position of 'grammarian.' *Cf.* also i. 203, 15: εἰς ἄλλους θρόνους καὶ προσηγορίας (professors of other branches). The same distinction between 'rhetor' and 'sophist' is probably made in Jul., *ep.*, 42, 422 D. The word 'rhetor' is often used of a public speaker (Lib., i. 617, 18; *cf.* Brandstätter, *Leipz. Stud.*, 15, p. 239); frequently it is used as identical with 'sophist' (compare *Dig.*, xxxviii. 5, 27 and *C. I. G.*, xii. 1, No. 83; see also *Dig.*, xxvii. 1, 6, where σοφισταὶ ῥήτορες is also used). *Orator* is similarly used of a sophist (*Cod. Th.*, xiv. 9, 3). ἐπαγγέλλεσθαι διδάσκειν, *profiteri*, is found (Jul., *ep.*, 42, 422 C), but it is doubtful if the absolute use of ἐπαγγέλλεσθαι recorded by Hatch (*Hibbert Lectures*, 1888, p. 44, n. 1) was propagated. ἐπαγγελία and ἐπάγγελμα with defining word are found (Epictet., iv. 8, 14; 8, 9). In the Latin, we have *magister* (*Cod. Th.*, xiv. 9), *professor* (*ib.*, vi. 21, 1), *doctor* (*ib.*, xiii. 3, 5), *præceptor* (*ib.*, xiii. 3, 16), *antistes* (*Cod. Jus.*, x. 47, 1), and (of the law) *antecessor* (*Dig.*, *præf. omnem*, title), some of these with defining word. For δύναμις, *facultas*, branch of knowledge, see Epictet., i. 20, 1. See p. 277, n. 3; p. 296, n. 1.

tainly had assisting him in the year 361,[1] and in several letters of the years 356 and 357 Libanius urges a certain Olympius to return from Rome and take charge of the Latin department of his school, under appointment from the city.[2] Frequent reference is also made to under-teachers who were assisting Libanius in his work, but whether these teachers were all rhetors or not is uncertain.[3] The assistants in Libanius's school were in receipt of an official salary,[4] and it was their duty to conduct such lessons as the sophist imposed upon them.[5]

[1] Calliopius (Lib., *ep.*, 540; *cf. ep.*, 591; iii. 446, 18, if this is the same man: see Seeck, *Briefe d. Lib.*, p. 102).

[2] *Ep.*, 448, 453, 481.

[3] Gaudentius in 356–7 (Lib., *ep.*, 457); Uranius in 358 (*ib., ep.*, 360); Eusebius in 388 (*ib., ep.*, 822, 823, 824, 825, 826, 827); Calliopius (*ib., ep.*, 971, 983); Thalassius, Libanius's secretary, who also assisted in the management of the boys and as a teacher (*ib., ep.*, 842, 844, 847, 856; ii. 393, 14; 404, 14; *cf. ep.*, 850; ii. 390, 10; 401, 15; 409, 12). The members of the school are again referred to in *ep.*, 813. Libanius had an assistant in Constantinople (*ib., ep.*, 215). See Sievers, *Leben des Lib.*, p. 42. There seems to be a reference to under-teachers in Greg. Naz., *or.*, xliii. 24, where the departure of Basil from Athens is described (see p. 332): "The members of our college corps, and with them many even of the teachers, standing in a ring about us" (περιστάντες ἡμᾶς ὁ τῶν ἑταίρων καὶ ἡλίκων χορός, ἔστι δὲ ὧν καὶ διδασκάλων). Also in Eunapius's account of Libanius; Libanius, says Eunapius (p. 96; see p. 298, below), did not join the school of the sophist Epiphanius, nor that of the far-famed Proæresius, "fearing that he should be swamped in the crowd of students and the great reputation of the teachers" (ὡς ἐν τῷ πλήθει τῶν ὁμιλητῶν καὶ τῷ μεγέθει τῆς δόξης τῶν διδασκάλων καλυφθησόμενος). Possibly, however, in the latter passage the plural refers to the two teachers, Epiphanius and Proæresius, especially as the singular is used farther down on the page (ταῖς μὲν ὁμιλίαις καὶ συνουσίαις . . . ἐλάχιστα παρεγίνετο, καὶ τῷ διδασκάλῳ τις ὀχληρὸς οὐκ ἦν).

[4] See *or.*, xxix. R, and *ep.*, 825.

[5] On one occasion a pupil of Libanius, before he could advance to τὰ τελεώτερα γράφειν, had to go through a certain book (Lib., ii.

## THE SCHOOL OF ANTIOCH, ETC. 273

In case the sophist was sick or for any other reason was unable to meet his classes, one of the assistants took his place. The sophist seems to have had a certain amount of authority over the assistants even in matters not connected with the class-room.[1] Whether Libanius was the Head of the school simply by virtue of his distinction as a teacher and orator, or by special appointment, either from the council or the emperor, is not perfectly clear, but apparently his position was official and carried with it an official salary.[2]

Other questions which arise are: Did these five sophists constitute the entire sophistical outfit of the city at this time, or were there other teachers of eloquence at Antioch, either teaching individually or forming a school or schools similar to this school, and, if there were other schools, did the members of these also, as did the members of Libanius's school, have official appointment and salary? Notwithstanding that from one passage in this speech we should be inclined to infer that these were the only sophists teaching at Antioch at this time,[3] we can hardly believe that such was the case. The city was a famous seat of sophistry, and the mention of other teachers of the subject work-

273, 1 ff.). Libanius did not wish to make a class for the subject smaller than nine or ten, and, this number not being forthcoming, he handed the boy over to another teacher, presumably an assistant. In the meantime he himself continued with the advanced work. Lecturing on the interpretation of history and speeches was done among the Greeks, according to Quintilian (*Inst. or.*, ii. 5, 3), by assistant teachers.

[1] Lib., ii. 224, 13 ff.  [2] See p. 176 f.
[3] ii. 218, 13: τοῖς μέν γε ῥήτορσιν ἡ Ζηνοβίου συναγωνίζεται γῆ. πρὸ δὲ τῶν ἄλλων κ. τ. λ. It is possible that they formed the only *official* school.

ing there at various times is not infrequent.¹ It is even probable that in some cases these were members of schools. Thus, Eudæmon, a 'grammarian,' and Harpocration, a sophist, were working together in some sort of educational partnership at Antioch in the year 358.² Further, the mention in the passage above referred to and elsewhere of a 'chorus of sophists' seems to impart to the term a certain definiteness as a unit that suggests the possible presence in a city of as many as two or three schools at once.³ Such schools, if schools there were, may have been private schools, in the sense

¹ Thus, Harpocration in 358 (Lib., *ep.*, 367); Acacius up to 361, when he finally withdrew to Phœnicia (*ib.*, *ep.*, 277, 292, 407, 469, 666, 1254); another previous to 360 (*ib.*, ii. 220, 20), believed by Sievers (*Leben des Lib.*, p. 199), and by Seeck (*Briefe d. Lib.*, p. 245), to be Priscio; it can hardly be Acacius, as Förster believes (ed. Lib., iii. p. 144), unless *or.*, xxix. R was delivered in 361 (see p. 267, n. 1), for Acacius did not finally leave Antioch until that year; Latin sophists about 387 (Lib., i. 153, 7; ii. 345, 1; iii. 261, 5); an Egyptian and a Phœnician in 384 (*ib.*, ii. 372, 9); after the death of Julian (*ib.*, iii. 451, 23); *cf.* ii. 276, 5 (not long after 387); 311, 17 (in 386); 115, 10 (in 385); 353, 11; 354, 9; 359, 17 (before 384); see also *or.*, xliii. (ii. 420–432). For the dating of Libanius's orations, see Förster's ed.

² Lib., *ep.*, 367; *cf.* 258, 371.

³ Lib., i. 305, 16: τὸ δὲ μεῖζον ἢ (κατὰ) πολλὰ στόματα καὶ σοφιστῶν χορὸν ὡς οἷόν τε μέγιστον· 317, 7: ὥστε φαίης ἂν αὐτὴν χορόν τινα εἶναι σοφιστῶν. In Lib., ii. 256, 18: τῶν ῥητόρων τὸν χορόν, and i. 335, 11: τρεῖς χοροὶ ῥητόρων, the reference is to public speakers (also in *ib.*, *ep.*, 248) —'companies' or 'firms,' possibly; though may they not also, perhaps, have been members of schools? χορός was sometimes used of a 'ring,' a 'gang' (*e. g.*, Lib., i. 437, 9; 459, 17); sometimes of the audience of a sophist (Luc., *Rhet. præc.*, 21). Lib., iii. 86, 12: ᾔει δέ ποτε καὶ ὁ τῶν φιλοσόφων ἐξ Ἀπαμείας χορός, ὧν ὁ κορυφαῖος θεοῖς ἐῴκει, καὶ μικρὰ συγγενόμενος ἀνέστρεφεν, however, seems to suggest but a single χορός (of philosophers) to a city, or at least to Apamea. For χορός, of a student-corps, see p. 296.

that the members had no official appointment and salary, though doubtless subject to official supervision and direction.

Sophists and rhetors, however, were not the only teachers who were established at Antioch: there were also philosophers, 'grammarians,' lawyers, and various others of lower grade.[1] All these, together with the sophists and rhetors, constituted the School of Antioch, and of this School — not simply of his own corps of rhetors — Libanius was Head. He had general oversight and supervision of matters pertaining to the teachers and schools of the city, subject, of course, to the implied direction of the municipal council and the emperor,[2] and he acted as the mouthpiece of council and teachers in their dealings with each other. It even seems to have lain within his prerogative to make the selection of a new teacher, and his power was great enough to compel at times a teacher's acceptance of a call or to increase a teacher's salary. When it was determined to establish a chair of law at Antioch, and the council had passed an order putting the determination into effect, Libanius set about to secure a man to fill the place. He fixed upon Domnio, or Domninus, who was then teaching at Berytus. In the letter which Libanius wrote to Domnio offering him the chair and urging him to come to Antioch, he spoke as one who

[1] The mention of schools and teachers at Antioch is frequent (*e. g.*, Lib., ii. 600, 14; 601, 13; iii. 261, 4).

[2] Lib., ii. 207, 8 *ff.* Doubtless, as a sophist himself, he had more intimate relations with the sophists than with the other teachers of the School (*ib.*, ii. 218, 5), and he, of course, had closer relations with the members of his own χορός than with other sophists.

was in charge of affairs and whose privilege it was to select the teachers and, if he so desired, to compel their attendance.¹ On another occasion Libanius was instrumental in increasing a sophist's salary.² Sometimes parents brought their boys to Libanius for guidance and advice in the matter of studies, and Libanius placed the boys among the different sophists.³ Again, the sophists themselves would come to Libanius after school hours and make such complaints with regard to their condition as occurred to them.⁴ By no means were the different sophists of the town always harmonious, however; we see them receiving one another's renegade students and vilifying one another's good name, and Libanius found it necessary once, in the general interest of all, to recommend common action putting an end to this state of affairs.⁵ The importance of the position which Libanius held as Head of the School of Antioch is shown by the fact that, as he says of himself when at the height of his career, he had no rival. The under-sophists, being none of them superior to another, were obliged to compete for the favor of the students, but

---

¹ *Ep.*, 209 (360 A. D.; Seeck, *Briefe d. Lib.*, p. 372). *Cf. ib.*, *ep.*, 1240 and 1277 a (which Seeck, pp. 322, 327, assigns to the years 355 and 356 respectively, but which seem to belong to about the same time as *ep.*, 209). See also Libanius's letters to Olympius, urging him to accept a position at Antioch (p. 272, n. 2), and his letter to Acacius, in which he says that he could compel Acacius to return to Antioch if he desired (*ep.*, 277). So Themistius called sophists from various places to build up the University of Constantinople (Lib., *ep.*, 367, 371).

² Lib., i. 76, 7.   ³ Lib., ii. 420, 16.

⁴ Lib., ii. 430, 15. It appears from this that while Libanius (and, probably, his staff) taught in the senate-house, the other sophists had other quarters (see p. 267, n. 1).

⁵ Lib., *or.*, xliii. (ii. 420–432). See p. 326.

not so he, who was overseer of them all.[1] It was in virtue of this position as Head of the School that he was called by John Chrysostom "the Sophist of Antioch."[2]

In a passage in one of his orations Libanius takes occasion to describe the etiquette that was observed in the conduct of the members of the School toward their Head.[3] There had been two Heads preceding himself. The first of these had been a native of Ascalon, in Palestine — a man tyrannical in temper and strict in his requirement of the observance of form. Whenever he appeared in the school-room,[4] all the teachers had been expected to rise and attend him as long as he remained or until he gave them permission to sit. No one was to raise his eyes or look his master in the face, but all were to acknowledge his supremacy. He had even been known to threaten or to strike a teacher on occasion. Imposing a certain tax (the nature of which is unknown)

---

[1] Lib., ii. 421, 1.

[2] *Or. de S. Babyl. contra Jul. et gent.*, 18 (Migne, i. p. 560: ὁ τῆς πόλεως σοφιστής); Suidas, s. v. Λιβάνιος.

[3] ii. 312, 4–314, 12. The reference here seems to be to the whole School, and not to the 'circle' of sophists simply. τούτων, in 312, 6, which Reiske supposes to refer to the students, evidently refers to the teachers, while in 313, 4–6 the teachers are, as the context shows, again meant; though it is true that συνεῖναι is a common word referring to the intercourse of teachers and students. If the 'circle' of sophists is meant, it is hard to see how the Head could fail to know all their names, their number being small, but this might well be the case if all the teachers of all grades are referred to. It is to be noticed that Libanius here speaks of 'the teachers' (τοὺς διδασκάλους, 312, 5), whereas the sophists are called 'the teachers of eloquence' (τοὺς διδασκάλους τῶν λόγων, 206, 21; τοὺς διδασκάλους, 204, 3, is again the teachers in general). *Cf.* καθηγητής (Greg. Nys., *De castigat.*, 312) and λόγων καθηγητής (Agath., ii. 29, p. 68 c).

[4] Several taught in the same room, therefore.

on the students, he had made the teachers responsible for the payment of this. The second Head, also a native of Palestine, had been of an entirely different disposition from the first. He had not aimed at the same personal ascendancy, nor had he even been acquainted with all the teachers by name. Libanius, as he himself affirms, was different from either. Affable and genial, he mingled freely and on equal terms with the teachers, allowing them to jest in his presence and oftentimes himself taking part in the sport.

It is probable that the school system of Antioch found its counterpart, though generally on a smaller scale, in most cities of the Greek world at this time. There was apparently a school at Gaza similar to that of Harpocration and Eudæmon mentioned above,[1] and another at Apamea resembling Libanius's,[2] while Themistius, doubtless, held much the same position in the School of Constantinople that Libanius held in that of Antioch. Those who filled the chair of sophistry at Athens in the second and third centuries seem to have been at the same time Heads of the School of Athens, and the position for which there was such competition after the death of the sophist Julian in the fourth century was doubtless the same as that held by these men in the preceding centuries.

At Antioch teaching was usually confined to the forenoon, the hours after the mid-day meal being left free of lessons,[3] but this rule was probably often broken;

---

[1] Lib., iii. 189, 8 ff.     [2] Lib., iii. 86, 12.
[3] Lib., ii. 430, 16; 600, 1; iii. 256, 5; *ep.*, 473; *cf. ep.* 923; ii. 316, 2.

Libanius at one time had so many students that he could not get to the end of them till evening,[1] while Acacius sometimes taught till night.[2] At other places the custom in this regard may have been different. Philostratus says that the most of the sophist's day was devoted to teaching.[3] Lucian intimates that children went to school both in the morning and in the afternoon.[4] Probably a difference was made between the elementary and secondary schools and the university. Sometimes a man taught rhetoric in the forenoon and 'grammar' in the afternoon,[5] and Eunapius, while engaged in teaching rhetoric in the morning, himself took lessons in philosophy under Chrysanthius in the afternoon.[6]

The long vacation extended from the early part of the summer until well into the autumn.[7] Often, however, sophists gave displays during the summer months, and these were sometimes attended by the students who were in town.[8] Occasionally a sophist broke

---

[1] Lib., i. 73, 4; 74, 7; *ep.*, 407. Sometimes the time was shortened (*ib.*, *ep.*, 119).   [2] Lib., *ep.*, 277.
[3] 614.   [4] *De parasit.*, 61; *cf. Amores*, 45.
[5] Strabo, xiv. p. 650. See also Lib., *ep.*, 1383.
[6] Eunap., p. 114. See, further, Grasberger, *Erzieh. u. Unterr. im klass. Alterth.*, iii. 429, and Sievers, *Leben des Lib.*, p. 23.
[7] Generally winter is spoken of as the time when the schools were in session at Antioch, and summer as the time of vacation (*e.g.*, Lib., *ep.*, 319, 382, 394 a, 1036 a; i. 64, 10, 17; 199, 10; *cf. ep.*, 57, 1150). Once the middle of summer is mentioned as being the time when the schools closed (*ib.*, i. 76, 1 and 3). At Athens (Himer., *or.*, xiv. 3; xxii. 6). Libanius arrived at Athens, when he went to study there, in the autumn (Lib., i. 13, 5), and Eunapius at the time of the autumn equinox (Eunap., p. 74). At Constantinople (Lib., i. 55, 5 and 9; 62, 1).
[8] Lib., i. 64, 11 *ff.*; *ep.*, 394 a.

through the custom here referred to, and, as a mark of special consideration, took a student even in the summer.[1] Holidays regularly occurred on the days of the pagan festivals.[2] Custom, however, prescribed that on certain other occasions as well the regular exercises of the day should be omitted. Thus, at Antioch, it was usual, when some distinguished man or the relative or friend either of the teacher or of one of the students died, for the teacher, perhaps accompanied by his class in a body, to honor the funeral with his presence. If this was not done, he spent the day in eulogizing with his students the dead man's virtues.[3] Again, when any one of the sophists held a public display, it was customary for all the students of all the sophists in the city to be released from further work on that day, and, in Libanius's school at least, the display of one of the students was the occasion for a similar holiday.[4] Irregular 'cuts,' due to unforeseen circumstances, doubtless often occurred. Libanius lost every year a number of days by reason of his health,[5] and at the time of the great riot at Antioch the schools were closed for thirty-

[1] Lib., *ep.*, 87.
[2] At the New Year's (Lib., i. 258, 16). At one time, at the festival of Artemis at Antioch (*ib.*, i. 236, 15 *ff.*). Libanius took few holidays when he was at Athens (*ib.*, i. 19, 8). At Antioch, when the public officials attended the theatre or the hippodrome, it would have been quite in order, says Libanius (ii. 427, 16-428, 5), for the sophists to observe holidays, but, instead of that, they preferred to keep school.
[3] Lib., ii. 277, 5-279, 10.    [4] Lib., ii. 279, 11-281, 9; 268, 3.
[5] Lib., ii. 276, 1; 277, 2; iii. 145, 4. Sometimes the philosopher caroused too freely and was then obliged to omit his lessons on the following day (Luc., *Hermot.*, 11). He then posted a notice on a board in front of his door, to the effect that there would be no school on that day.

four days.[1] Otherwise the occasions when students who lived out of the city interrupted their studies to go home seem to have been few; the death or urgent need of some member of the family was generally required.[2]

[1] Lib., ii. 269, 1. Sometimes students complained of the loss of time (*ib.*, ii. 268, 11 and 18).

[2] Lib., iii. 194, 9; 195, 10; *ep.*, 291, 1336. Outbreak of a pestilence (*ib.*, i. 142, 14). In *ep.*, 57, Libanius mentions a boy who was called home to console his father, because all the other children had gone away from home and the father was left alone; also in some way to assist his father by his eloquence. Libanius rather reluctantly allows the boy to go, but reminds the father that it has been stipulated that the boy shall return before the end of the summer. Titianus went home to attend his sister's wedding (*ib.*, *ep.*, 374, 376). Calycius interrupted his studies to be married (*ib.*, *ep.*, 374, 376, 382, 383). See, in general, Lib., *or.*, lvi. (iii. pp. 185–205), and Sievers, *Leben des Lib.*, p. 23

## CHAPTER XIII

### THE BOYHOOD OF A SOPHIST

WE have in the preceding chapters traced the course of collegiate instruction in Grecian lands from the time when that instruction began, in the centuries before Christ, to the time when it was brought to a close, in the year 529 A. D., have taken a glance at the professor's standing in the community, the manner of his appointment, his salary, his privileges and immunities, have dropped into the Muses' workshop, as Himerius calls it,[1] and observed the professor and his students at their daily task, and have also seen the professor in those grand moments of triumph when he came before the public in the character of interpreter of his own art. We are now to look at Greek university life from still another point of view — the point of view of the student. Did the ancient student, we should like to know, have the same aspirations as his brother in modern times; did he, if he happened to be born in a distant province, turn with the same longing eyes and wondering thoughts to the great university afar off of which he had heard so much; did he engage in the same, or similar, college practices, and have the same, or similar, college customs; and did he, finally, in his old age look

[1] τὸ τῶν Μουσῶν ἐργαστήριον (*or.*, xxii. 7).

back with the same fondness and regret to the years spent in study and to the friendships then formed? We should think it strange, indeed, if, when there is so much in our knowledge of ancient life and thought that is only fragmentary, we could answer all these questions fully. But we can say something — not, by any means, so much as we could wish, but still something that is really definite — on every one of them. The most of our information bearing on the student life is of the fourth century, and here we are fortunate in having, first of all, that rich mine of information on many subjects, Libanius, who is perhaps the greatest of the fourth-century sophists, if not of the sophists of all time.[1] So much of the material contained in the pages of Libanius is autobiographical in character that we shall find it at once profitable and interesting in this account to group as many of the facts as we can about his early life; and, so far as may be, we will let him tell the story in his own words.

Libanius's life was nearly coincident with the rise and fall of fourth-century sophistry: sophistry, after its decline under the ruinous conditions which prevailed in the latter half of the third century, once more came into prominence under Constantine, at the beginning of the fourth century, but again declined toward the end of that century; Libanius was born in 314, and he died in 394 or 395. He was born at Antioch, that city

[1] Second in point of importance, perhaps, is Eunapius, whose *Lives of Philosophers and Sophists* contains much that is interesting and curious. Other authors from whom we obtain valuable information are Himerius, Themistius, Gregory Nazianzene, and so on.

where the followers of the new faith were first called Christians, a city famed for its beauty and size — it was reckoned by the ancients themselves the third city of the world and the first of the Roman Empire in the East [1] — but also notorious for the free and easy life of its inhabitants. In its streets, as in those of Alexandria, the East and the West jostled each other, and, while the architecture and the culture were Greek, the general tone of the life was Eastern. Here the pursuit of pleasure was the chief business of life, and, side by side with the Greek sophist, the actor, the singer, the ballet-dancer, and the circus clown clamored for the popular favor.

Built by Seleucus not long after 300 B. C., and subsequently enlarged by other members of the Seleucid line, Antioch was a typical example of the foundations established by the followers of Alexander in many parts of the East. It stood in a narrow plain, between the Orontes River on the north — at a point about thirteen miles inland, where that river, coming from the south, turns abruptly to the west, and then flows down to the sea — and Mount Casius on the south, and had, at the time of Libanius, one broad thoroughfare about four miles long, running east and west through the centre of the town and flanked on either side by colonnades and public buildings, and, crossing this at right angles at its middle point, another similar thoroughfare running north and south. Narrower streets ran at right angles

[1] Lib., i. 471, 16; 673. 7; ii. 254, 15; Jos., *Bell. Jud.*, iii. 2, 4; Procop., *Bell. Pers.*, i. 17, p. 87, 12. It was pre-eminent for its size, wealth, beauty, and prosperity. Rome and Alexandria alone surpassed it.

from each of these thoroughfares, and along the river and in the neighborhood of the mountain were many handsome residences and beautiful gardens.

Libanius, who is fond of dwelling on the charms of his native town, thus speaks of the hillside, or southern, section of the city:[1] "Some of these (*i. e.*, the narrower streets just mentioned) stretch toward the south to the foot of the mountain, gradually carrying forward the inhabited part as far as is possible, while at the same time preserving the symmetry of the city as a whole and not raising this section so far above the rest as to make it stand apart. . . . The mountain stretches along like a shield raised on high for the protection of the city, and those who live farthest up on the side have nothing to fear such as one might expect from the neighborhood of a mountain, but, instead, inducements to perfect cheerfulness — streams of running water, trees and plants, gardens, breezes, flowers, the songs of birds, and the enjoyment, earlier than those below, of the delights of spring."

This was the form of the old city so-called; the new city was built on an island in the river, and was connected with the old city by five strong bridges; here were other thoroughfares and other colonnades, and here was the palace, the residence of the rulers of the East. "The palace itself," says Libanius,[2] "occupies as much of the island as would constitute a fourth part thereof. For it touches the centre . . . and extends to the outer branch of the river; so that the wall, instead of being battlemented, is surmounted by pillars, and, with

[1] i. 338, 4.      [2] i. 340, 12.

the river flowing beneath and the suburbs on all sides rejoicing the sight, makes a picture fit for a king."

It would be interesting to follow Libanius through his description of the beautiful grove, Daphne, which lay among the hills, about four and a half miles to the south-west of Antioch, and was filled with every sort of delight, and then, accompanying him farther, to hear him discourse on the hundreds of fountains, both public and private, that were found in every part of the city, and on the crowds that thronged the streets at all hours of the day and night — "To one stopping and gazing at the spectacle for the first time," he says,[1] "it would seem as though there were, outside the city, before each gate, a festival, and as though the populace, dividing itself by its preferences, were pouring out in accordance with some custom to visit these"— and on the many kinds of goods that were displayed before all the shops, and the illumination by night, which rivalled that of the sun by day; but for all this our space is at present too limited. We may remark simply, as supplementary to what has already been said, that the population of Antioch, at the time of which we are speaking, was, according to ancient statements, between 150,000 and 200,000, not including the women, children, and slaves, or those dwelling in the various suburbs, and that about one-half of the inhabitants are said to have been Christians.[2]

---

[1] i. 329, 2.

[2] For the last statement, John Chrysostom is our authority (see Benzinger in Pauly's *Real-Encyc.*). Libanius (*ep.*, 1137) gives the population as 150,000; John Chrysostom, at the beginning of the fifth century, as 200,000. The most important an-

The family to which Libanius belonged was one of the old respected families of Antioch, the members of which had for generations been noted for their culture and public spirit. The little account that was in those days made of Latin in the eastern part of the Empire is hinted at in the fact that one of Libanius's great-grandfathers was thought by many to have come from Italy, because he wrote a speech in the Latin tongue;[1] this was a feat that was then quite beyond the power of most men in that part of the world. The family had at one time possessed considerable wealth, but, as a result of political disturbances in the reign of Diocletian, this had been confiscated, and Libanius's parents had at first been in straitened circumstances; a meagre part of the family fortune had, however, been recovered before the father's death. Libanius was the second of three sons; when Libanius was eleven years of age, the father died, leaving the three children to the care of the mother and her two brothers. We now obtain in Libanius's account some pleasing pictures of the family life of that time. "My mother," says Libanius,[2] "standing in dread of the wickedness of guardians, and, such was her natural modesty, shrinking from the possibilities of litigation, undertook to bring us children up herself.

---

cient description of Antioch is given by Libanius in the oration called *Antiochicos* (i. 275-365). Additional information is contained in the Byzantine historian Malalas, who also was a native of the city. The most important modern authorities are K. O. Müller, *Antiquitates Antiochenæ* (1839), and R. Förster, in the *Jahrbuch d. kaiserl. deutsch. arch. Inst.*, xii. pp. 103 *ff.* (1897); see also H. C. Butler, in *Publ. of the Amer. Arch. Ex. to Syria in 1899-1900*, pt. ii.

[1] Lib., i. 3, 9. [2] i. 5, 6.

In the main she held to her task with great success, though it cost her much labor. But in the matter of our education, though she paid out many a sum for teachers, she could not bring herself to be severe if one of us fell asleep over his books, for she considered it the part of a fond mother never to oppose her son in anything. So that, as a result, we spent the most of the year running about the fields instead of at our studies."

This sort of thing lasted four years, till Libanius reached his fifteenth birthday. Then, suddenly, he was seized with a passionate desire for learning, which carried him as far in the other direction. He sold his tame pigeons, stayed away from horse-races and public shows, and gave up running about the fields. One of the teachers whom he had had in the earlier time was "a man," as he says,[1] "from whose lips poured forth eloquence in streams." In those days Libanius had paid slight attention to this man's instruction, and now that he was himself interested in study, the man was dead. "So," says Libanius,[2] "I continued to yearn for him who was no longer there, and, like those who eat barley-bread for want of something better, made use, as a last resort, of such teachers as were at hand — mere shadows of sophists; but making no progress and finding myself in danger of falling into a pit of ignorance by following these blind guides, I finally said good-by to them, and refrained thenceforth from exercising my brain with composing, my tongue with

---

[1] i. 8, 6. This cannot have been Zenobius, as Förster in his edition of Libanius (pp. 84, 289) intimates, for Zenobius did not die till many years later.    [2] i. 8, 10.

speaking, or my hand with writing. One thing only did I do, and that was to memorize passages from the ancients. I had as a teacher in this line a man with an excellent memory — one quite capable of introducing boys to the beauties contained in those old authors. I clung to him so closely that not even after school hours did I leave his side, but, book in hand, followed him through the market-place, and made him recite to me whether he would or not. It was evident that he did not fancy this sort of thing at the time, though he praised me afterward." We here see illustrated in brief the respective duties of the sophist and the 'grammarian,' or teacher of lower grade: the duty of the sophist was to teach the brain to compose, the tongue to speak, and the hand to write; that of the 'grammarian' was to interpret the ancient authors.

Once Libanius met with an accident, the effects of which he never ceased to feel to the end of his life. "I was one day," he says,[1] "engaged on Aristophanes's *Acharnians;* my teacher was seated and I was standing by his side. Suddenly the sun became obscured by heavy clouds and it seemed as though day were turned to night. There came a loud clap of thunder and at the same instant a flash of lightning. My eyes were blinded by the flash, and my head was stunned by the noise. I did not suppose that I had received any permanent injury, but thought that the confusion in my head would pass away soon. After I had gone home, however, and while I was at breakfast, I seemed again to hear the thunder crash and to see the bolt fly past the

[1] i. 9, 13.

house. Fright started the sweat out on me, and, jumping up from the table, I fled to my bed. I thought I must say nothing, but must keep the matter secret, for fear that, if I should tell the doctors, I might have to take some medicine or undergo some treatment that would cause me the inconvenience of interrupting my studies. By this very course the trouble became firmly fixed upon me, whereas, if it had been taken in the beginning, it might, I am told, easily have been cured."

Five years Libanius continued in this path, till he was twenty. Then came the first impulse toward the sophist's life. "I had thus stored my mind," he says,[1] "with the writings of the best authors, when I received my first impulse toward the sophist's life. One of my companions was a Cappadocian named Jasion — a backward scholar, but a lover of hard work if there ever was one. Day in and day out, one may say, he rehearsed to me the stories he had heard from his elders about Athens and the doings there; strange accounts he gave me of one Callinicus and Tlepolemus and other mighty sophists not a few, and of the contests and the victories and the defeats. All this inspired me with a longing for the place, but not until later, I thought to myself, would I make known my intention of sailing thither." We see the young man, in his far-away home, his thoughts filled with glowing pictures of the life at Athens, forming in his mind the determination some day to visit this spot and taste the spring of learning at its source. For it was always Athens, "golden Athens," that exercised the charm over men's minds, and no

[1] i. 10, 14.

matter where else one had studied, one's thoughts fondly turned at last to the real home of letters, Athens. The Christian orator Basil, after studying at Cæsarea and Constantinople, "was sent," says Gregory,[1] "by God and his own noble and unquenchable thirst for knowledge to the real home and seat of learning, Athens." That the history and associations of the city exercised a powerful influence over the imaginations of men at that time, as, indeed, they exercised through all antiquity, is evident from many passages in the authors.[2]

At length, after many months, Libanius broached the subject that was in his mind, for he could contain himself no longer. "I think," he says,[3] "that, like Odysseus, I should have spurned even a marriage of the gods for one glimpse of the smoke of Athens." His mother, as may be supposed, could not bear to think of his leaving home. "Now my mother shed tears and could not endure even to hear the subject mentioned. Of my two uncles, the elder, thinking that he must uphold my mother, bade me desist from striving for the impossible; no matter how much I wished to go, he said, he

---

[1] *Or.*, xliii. 14.

[2] "Nymphidianus," says Eunapius (p. 101), "*although* he had never shared in the learning and education that are to be had at Athens, was *still* worthy of the name of sophist." Themistius devotes a whole speech to the consideration of the question, why it is that young men, in selecting a university, look to the antiquity and associations of the city rather than to the ability of the teachers (331 d–341 a). The reference is, of course, to Athens (*cf.* 336 d). "Athens, the most ancient, the wisest, the most divinely favored of cities, the common love of men and gods," says Libanius (i. 410, 10) One Ecdicius complimented Libanius by saying that in sending his sons to him he was sending them to Athens (*ib.*, *ep.*, 1529). See pp. 337 *ff*. [3] i. 11, 23.

would not allow it. But then came the Olympic games instituted by my younger uncle, and after that, when I was at last becoming reconciled to the inevitable, Fortune sent to the city, or rather to the whole land, the affliction of Panolbius's death. (Panolbius was the name of my elder uncle.) My mother's tears no longer availed to the same purpose with Phasganius, for he was not a man to yield to idle grief. So he persuaded her to bear the pain, which, he said, would not be for long and promised great reward, and then opened wide the door for my departure." [1]

Libanius was at this time twenty-two years of age.[2] This was above the average age of university students, although there were, without doubt, many students at Athens as old as that, or even older. From fifteen to twenty may have been the usual age; the Emperor Julian, however, when a student at Athens, was twenty-four, Basil was twenty-five, and Gregory Nazianzene was, when he left the city, nearly thirty. Probably, as at the present day in a large university centre, all periods of youth and early manhood were well represented in the crowds of students that flocked to Athens in the fourth century of our era. At Rome students were forbidden by an edict of 370 to stay in the city for pur-

---

[1] i. 11, 24.
[2] At least two years elapsed between the time when he first conceived the idea of going to Athens and the time when he finally set out, for the Olympic games just mentioned (*cf.* iii. 110) took place in the year 336. He was at Athens during his twenty-fifth year (i. 20, 3), and it is probable that the four years of his university study extended from his twenty-second to his twenty-sixth year, that is, from 336 or 337 to 340 or 341 (see Sievers, *Leben des Lib.*, p. 43, n. 2).

poses of study after the age of twenty, and at Berytus the limit was fixed for law students at twenty-five. In other places all ages were again probably represented. Libanius apparently studied under a sophist at Antioch before he was fifteen, and he refers to a student of his own who, when he began to study, was over twenty.[1]

Libanius had at first evidently had it in mind to go to

---

[1] See Sievers, *Leben des Lib.*, p. 20. The sophist Adrian was eighteen when he went to study at Athens (Philos., 585). Eunapius was sixteen (Eunap., p. 74). For Rome, see *Dig.*, xxvii. 2, 3, 5; *Cod. Th.*, xiv. 9, 1. For Berytus, *Cod. Jus.*, x. 50, 1 and 2. The reason for the setting of a limit to the period of study was to prevent students from evading their public duties. For Libanius, see p. 288 (*cf. ib.*, i. 526, 9, of Julian). For Libanius's pupil, *ib.*, *ep.*, 605. Lucian speaks of a boy of eighteen who had made good progress in his philosophy (*Philops.*, 14). For the age of fifteen or under, see Orelli, *Inscr.*, No. 2432: *studioso eloquentiæ, vixit annis xv;* Kaibel, *Ep. Gr.*, 229: ἔτη δ' ἐπὶ πέντε λόγοισιν εἰν Ἐφέσωι σχολάσας εἰκοσέτης ἔθανον· and compare Philos., 594: Ἀριστοκλέους μὲν γὰρ ἤκουσε παῖς ἔτι, and *ib.*, 598: ἀκροατὴς δὲ Ἡρώδου μὲν ἐν παισίν, Ἀριστοκλέους δὲ ἐν μειρακίοις γενόμενος (*cf. ib.*, 568). Libanius had a pupil of fifteen (Lib., ii. 267, 9). Hippodromus had one of twenty-two (Philos., 617). Libanius urges a former pupil, who has gone home to be married, to return to his studies and bring his wife with him (Lib., *ep.*, 374, 376, 382, 383). Another of his pupils was a married man (*ib.*, *ep.*, 1535, 1536, 1537; *cf.* Luc., *Symp.*, 32), and still another was a member of the council at Antioch (*ib.*, *ep.*, ii. 222, 16). Even advocates sometimes attended his course (*ib.*, *ep.*, 203). Libanius, when teaching at Constantinople, attended the lectures of Didymus (*ib.*, *ep.*, 321), and Eunapius studied under Chrysanthius while he was himself teaching rhetoric (Eunap., p. 114). One of Libanius's fellow-students at Athens was of the same age as Libanius (Lib., i. 21, 12). A member of the Senate at Constantinople studied under Themistius (*ib.*, *ep.*, 84, 1510 a). In general, Themistius's students probably averaged somewhat older than those of the sophists (Themis., 288 c). Soranus, in the second century, says (*Ars obs.*, 92) that from fourteen to twenty-one the boy studied mathematics and philosophy. See, further, Rohde, in *Rhein. Mus.*, 40, pp. 73, 74.

Athens by sea, but when he departed he went overland to Constantinople. Perhaps the lateness of the season determined him to take this course. He departed with mingled joy and regret. "So I drove forth, and only then did I realize how bitter a thing it is to leave behind those who are dear to us. Thus, it was with tears and lamentations that I was carried on my way, and often did I turn my eyes back, longing to catch a glimpse of the city walls. As far as Tyana, tears; from there onward, a fever, but ever tears. Two longings fought within me, but shame, casting in its weight, turned the scale, and I went on, perforce, sick as I was. My sickness increasing with the journeying, I was little better than dead when I at length crossed the Bosporus; and my mules were in much the same condition."[1] It took about a week in those days, travel as fast as one could, to go from Antioch to Constantinople by land;[2] in Libanius's case the time must have been very much longer.

Libanius had counted on being forwarded from Constantinople to Athens by Imperial Post, but the man — a friend of the family, apparently — through whose influence he had hoped to secure this privilege, had fallen from favor, and so Libanius was obliged to turn to the

[1] i. 12, 13

[2] When Cæsarius drove from Antioch to Constantinople after the uprising at Antioch, and allowed himself no time for food or sleep, it took him until noon of the sixth day to reach his destination (Lib., i. 684, 14 ff.). The road passed through Tarsus, Ancyra, Nicæa, and Nicomedia, and the distance was seven hundred and ninety-two English miles. Libanius travelled in a wagon drawn by mules. See Palestine Pilgrims' Texts, 5, *Itinerary from Bordeaux to Jerusalem.*

THE BOYHOOD OF A SOPHIST 295

sea to find a means of reaching his destination. Few captains were venturing out at that time of the year, but Libanius finally found one who for a consideration was willing to undertake the voyage. "So," he says,[1] "I embarked, and, being favored by the powers of the deep, was carried on my way in high spirits. Perinthus and Rhœteum and Sigeum, as we sailed along, and the city of King Priam of many woes, I looked upon from the deck; then across the Ægean we scudded under as fair a breeze as favored Nestor. So that, as it proved, my friend's inability to provide conveyance by Post was a gain to me." Thus did Libanius approach the land of enchantment.

[1] i. 13, 7.

## CHAPTER XIV

### STUDENT DAYS

At the time when Libanius landed at the port of Athens, the rivalry among the different sophists was intense, and the spirit which animated the sophists themselves was reflected in the conduct of their students. Attached to each sophist was a sort of corps, or incorporated student body, composed of those students who, having sworn allegiance to the sophist's cause, attended his lectures as his regularly enrolled pupils. Each of these corps (called commonly a χορός)[1] had its own student leader (κορυφαῖος, προστάτης, χορηγός,

---

[1] *E. g.*, Lib., i. 16, 1. Also called φρατρία (Greg. Naz., *Poem. de se ipso*, ii. 1, 215); συμμορία (Lib., *ep.*, 139). Other terms for a sophist's corps, or class, were διατριβή (Eunap., p. 75); ἀγέλη (Lib., i. 258, 16); ποίμνη (Choric., p. 4); ποίμνιον (Lib., i. 119, 15). The sophist was the 'shepherd' of his flock (ποιμήν, *ib.*, i. 19, 14); also the 'leader' (ἡγεμών, *ib.*, i. 16, 5), and the 'ruler' (ἄρχων, *ib.*, i. 15, 1); see, further, *ib.*, ii. 429, 3; *ep.*, 454. The students were called μαθηταί, 'learners,' 'disciples' (*ib.*, iii. 255, 17); ὁμιληταί, 'associates' (Philos., 523); ἀκροαταί, 'auditors' (*ib.*, 494); γνώριμοι, 'acquaintances' (*ib.*, 522); στασιῶται, 'partisans' (*ib.*, 536); φοιτηταί, φοιτῶντες, 'frequenters' (Lib., *ep.*, 187; i. 178, 13); πῶλοι, 'colts' (*ib.*, *ep.*, 154); θαυμαζόμενοι, 'admirers' (Syn., *Dion*, 13); ἐπιτήδειοι, 'friends' (Themis., 291 a); πλησιάζοντες, 'associates' (Jul., *ep.*, 42); ἑταῖροι, 'companions' (Lib., *ep.*, 160); χορευταί, 'corpsmen' (*ib.*, *ep.*, 285); θιασῶται, 'classmen' (Procop., *ep.*, 108); θρέμματα, 'children' (Lib., *ep.*, 343); συνουσιασταί, 'associates' (*ib.*, *ep.*, 521); νέοι, 'young men' (*ib.*, i. 11, 18). Newcomers were νεήλυδες (Himer., *or.*, xv. title).

Ἀκρωμίτης),[1] and expected of its members mutual co-operation in upholding and promoting the interest of its teacher. When a young man went for the first time to Athens to begin his studies at the university there, he probably, in most cases, if allowed to enter the city unmolested, betook himself to a sophist of his own nationality or to one of prominence and enrolled himself forthwith as a pupil under his instruction.[2] Thus, Eunapius men-

[1] Lib., *ep.*, 755, 804, 1058; i. 16, 15; Phot., *Bibl.*, cod. 80, p. 60; Themis., 294 a. For the meaning of Ἀκρωμίτης, see Sievers, *Leben des Lib.*, p. 32, n. 153. τὸ κεφάλαιον τῶν χορευτῶν (Lib., *ep.*, 1518). See the description of a χορός, Themis., 293 c–294 a. For κορυφαῖος τοῦ χοροῦ in another sense, see p. 270.

[2] Other reasons at times influenced the student: a boy joined Libanius's class because he knew that his uncle was a friend of Libanius (Lib., *ep.*, 22). Sometimes the young student was brought to the sophist by his father (*ib.*, ii. 342, 10; iii. 200, 15; *ep.*, 940), or his mother (*ib.*, *ep.*, 288), or some other relative (*ib.*, *ep.*, 87, 640), or he came recommended by letter (*ib.*, *ep.*, 940), and on occasion the sophist seems to have given the boy an examination before admitting him to the class (*ib.*, *ep.*, 358, 460, 1048; *cf.* 187, 1203). In view, however, of the competition that existed among the sophists, it is likely that the examination was often waived. Schlosser (*Univ., Stud. u. Prof. d. Griech.*, p. 232) says that students were won for this or that sophist before leaving home, and that they even sometimes engaged as early as that to become leaders of a corps. There is no authority for the last statement, and the fact is extremely unlikely. It is doubtful if they were, except possibly in rare cases, even sworn to any particular sophist before leaving home. Libanius had apparently selected his teacher before arriving at Athens, but purely in a voluntary way. Eunapius and his companions were taken to Proæresius, because the skipper of the ship in which they were brought to Athens was a friend of Proæresius. At the time of the great contest for the chief chair of rhetoric at Athens, the different nations sent their students, according to the respective nationalities of the teachers, to Epiphanius, Diophantus, and Proæresius; but it does not appear that any canvassing or press-gang work was done in the provinces. The reader who has some acquaintance with the customs pre-

tions it [1] as a fact worthy of notice that Libanius, when he reached Athens, did not join the school of the sophist Epiphanius, who was a Syrian and had a wide reputation, nor that of the far-famed Proæresius, "fearing that he should be swamped in the crowd of students and the great reputation of the teachers"; but that, instead, he attached himself to a third sophist—one Diophantus of Arabia. Again, as we may remember, at the time when these three distinguished sophists, Epiphanius of Syria, Diophantus of Arabia, and Proæresius of Armenia, were all competing for the official chair of sophistry at Athens, the Roman world in the East was divided in its sympathies among these three; the Orient held to Epiphanius, Arabia supported Diophantus, while nearly the whole of Asia Minor, as well as Egypt

vailing among the students at the German universities at the present day will be reminded, in reading of the Greek χοροί, of the German *Corps*. It is probable that at first the Greek χοροί were, as were the German *Corps*, based on nationality. This is suggested by the use of such terms as 'the Greeks' (οἱ Ἕλληνες, Philos., 571), 'the Greek crowd' (τὸ Ἑλληνικόν, ib., 587), 'the Armenians' (οἱ Ἀρμένιοι, Greg. Naz., or., xliii. 17), 'the Laconians' (Eunap., p. 73). For long the majority of the students of any one sophist may have been of the sophist's own nationality, but other students were from the first doubtless welcomed, and even sought. In the second half of the fourth century nationality was probably, in ordinary times, a lesser bond of union. The captain of Julian's Spartan band was an Athenian (Eunap., p. 70). Himerius at Athens had students from a variety of countries, as did Libanius at Antioch. It would seem to have been the case at one time in Antioch that teachers did not have the liberty of rejecting students who were brought to them (Lib., i. 213, 9: οὐκ οὔσης τοῖς διδασκάλοις ἐξουσίας, οἷς βούλοιντο, κλείειν τὰς θύρας), though perhaps we must not press this statement too far. Reference may also be made, in connection with the χοροί, to the *Nations* which formerly existed at European universities.

[1] P. 96.

and the regions toward Libya, sent their pupils to Proæresius. Not always, however, or perhaps in the majority of cases, was the young man allowed to reach his journey's end without interference. The various student corps, performing the part of press-gangs in the service of their respective teachers, not only paraded the streets of Athens, but beset every avenue of approach, for the purpose of obtaining recruits for their ranks. Interesting descriptions of this press-gang service and of the initiatory rites practised upon the would-be Freshman in ancient times are given by the fourth-century Gregory Nazianzene in his *Life of Basil* and by Photius in a summary from the work of the historian Olympiodorus of the early part of the fifth century. Though of different periods, the two accounts supplement each other.

The most of the young men at Athens [says Gregory [1]] — the more foolish among them — are sophist-mad; being not only the base-born and the insignificant, but even such as are of good family and prominent station; for they are a mixed crowd, and young, and not easily restrainable in their impulses. They do just such things as we see done at horse-races by lovers of horses and public shows. These jump and shout, throw dust into the air, play the charioteer from their seats, lash the air for a horse with the finger as a whip, and make believe to shift their horses from one chariot to another, though really they can do none of those things which they pretend to do. With the greatest ease they exchange drivers, horses, stalls, and managers. And who are they that act thus? The poor often and the needy, who perhaps have not enough for their own sup-

[1] *Or.*, xliii. 15.

port for a single day. Exactly similar are the actions of the young men with reference to their teachers and the rival sophists, in their endeavors to increase their own numbers and to bring by their efforts added prosperity to their professors. The whole proceeding is, indeed, quite astonishing and absurd. Towns, roads, harbors, mountain-tops, plains, and frontier lines — in fact, every inch of Attic, and, indeed, of Grecian, soil is preoccupied, and even the inhabitants are, for the most part, taken possession of, for they, too, are divided in their sympathies.

When, now, a young man arrives and becomes a captive (for this always happens, either with or without his consent, such being the Attic custom, a form of sport not unmingled with seriousness), he is first entertained at the house of one of his captors, or of one of his friends or relatives or fellow-countrymen, or, it may be, of one of those who, adepts in the sophistic practices and clever at securing gain for their teachers, are for that reason greatly honored by the latter (for it is as good as money to these to have enthusiastic supporters); then he is made the object of jest and banter by all who wish to take part in the sport. The purpose of the last-mentioned proceeding is, I think, to humble the conceit of the new student and to bring him at once under the authority of the corps. The bantering is either rough and insulting, or it is moderate in tone, according as the object thereof is himself boorish or refined. To the inexperienced the proceeding looks most frightful and cruel, but, when one knows beforehand what is to occur, it is very pleasant and humane; for the demonstration made by these threateners is greater than the performance. After the bantering, the victim is marched in procession through the market-place to the public bath. The procession is made up as follows: Those who form the escort arrange themselves in a double line, two by two, with a space after each couple, and so conduct the youth to the bath. When they come near,

## STUDENT DAYS 301

they begin to jump, and to shout at the top of their voices, as if possessed, those in front calling to those behind not to advance, but to halt, as the bath cannot be entered; and at the same time they batter the door and terrify the young man with the noise. At length they allow him to enter and give him his freedom, putting him, now that the ordeal of the bath is over, on an equal footing with themselves and receiving him as one of their number. This, indeed, is the most pleasant feature of the initiation, that the deliverance from the ordeal is speedy and the dispersal immediate.

In the summary of Olympiodorus we come upon a new feature — the student's gown. We are familiar with the coarse gown worn, more or less regularly, by philosophers from the time of Socrates, as a badge of humility and studiousness; this was of a dark color, but the sophist's gown, we are told, was red or purple.[1] We recollect that, when Hippodromus dropped into

[1] Schol. in Greg. Naz., Migne, p. 906: τρίβωνες δὲ περιβλήματά τινα, τῶν ῥητόρων μὲν ἐρυθροί τε καὶ φοινικοί, φαιοὶ δὲ τῶν φιλοσόφων. παράσημον δὲ τοῦτο ἦν αὐτοῖς καθ᾽ ἑκάστην φορούμενον. *Cf.* Themis., 246 d, and *Cod. Th.*, xiii. 3, 7, and see Diels, *Doxographi Græci*, p. 254; also Agathias, ii. 29, p. 68 c, and Rohde, *Gr. Rom.*, p. 331. Philosophers are included under the 'men in white' in the Synesius passage, *ep.*, 153 (καὶ γὰρ τῶν ἐν λευκοῖς ἔνιοι τρίβωσι, καὶ τῶν ἐν φαιοῖς, ἔφασάν με παρανομεῖν εἰς φιλοσοφίαν), while the 'men in black' are the monks and clergy. (*Cf.* Themis., *or.*, xxi, xxiii, xxvi, from which it is evident that Themistius was also criticised by philosophers, as well as by sophists, for holding displays of his eloquence.) To be sure, it is surprising to learn that philosophers were clad in white, but perhaps by this time the philosophers had begun to imitate the style of dress of the sophists. The sophists also are ridiculed for their white flowery dress (Luc., *Rhet. præc.*, 15). See Epictet., iii. 23, 35: κομψῷ στολίῳ ἢ τριβωναρίῳ, of a philosopher's dress. Philosophers were sometimes called σοφισταί by way of reproach (see Luc., *Jup. trag.*, 14, 19, 30; also Schmid, *Gr. Renais.*, p. 37, n. 11).

Megistias the sophist's school-room during school-hours,[1] Megistias had on the speaker's gown, and that Hippodromus thought it necessary to don this before he could speak. The gown is elsewhere mentioned as the distinctive garb of those engaged in academic study or teaching,[2] but in this passage we shall find that at Athens, in the early part of the fifth century, its use, in the case of students, was subject to certain fixed regulations.

Olympiodorus [says Photius [3]] further says that he repaired to Athens, and that through his efforts and attention Leontius was elevated to the chair of sophistry, though he in no way desired that honor. He also speaks of the student's gown, saying that at Athens no one, above all no stranger, was allowed to assume this unless he had been granted permission by vote of the sophists and had had his worth confirmed by the rites performed in accordance with the scholastic regulations. These rites were as follows: First, the newcomers, both large and small, were conducted to the public bath, and, included among these, were also those who, having arrived at the proper age, were ready to assume the gown, and whom the conducting students had thrust into the middle of the line. Then some ran before and tried to prevent the advance, while others resisted from behind and pushed in the opposite direction; and all those who tried to prevent the advance shouted "Stop! Stop! No bathing here!" Finally those who were pushing to get the student in were considered to have prevailed, and, after much contention over the aforesaid cus-

---

[1] See p. 258. See also Synesius, *Dion*, 11, of the sophist on the day of declamation: he appears ἐσθῆτι καὶ σχήματι σοβαροῖς.

[2] See Greg. Naz., *or.*, xxxvi. 12; Lib., i. 411, 9; ii. 432, 5; iii. 438, 23; *ep.*, 389, 471, 713, 937. The student was said λαμβάνειν τὸν τρίβωνα (Greg. Naz., *or.*, xliii. 17). Both professors and students wore the gown.    [3] *Bibl.*, cod. 80, p. 60.

tomary words, he was at length brought into the warm apartment and there given a bath. Then, after he had dressed, he received the privilege of the gown, and immediately departed clad therein and escorted by an honorable and distinguished procession; having previously laid out a considerable sum in honor of the leaders of the corps, the so-called Acromites.[1]

How did Libanius fare when he landed in the midst of this life? "So," he says,[2] "touching at Geræstus, we passed on and came to anchor at last in one of the harbors of Athens, where I lay over night. On the

[1] Not all students, it is evident from this account, were allowed, immediately after their arrival at Athens and initiation at the hands of the older students whose captives they became, to wear the gown. While, according to Olympiodorus, every new arrival, young or old, was put through the initiatory rites, only such students as were of a suitable age and had further received the approval of the sophists themselves, were granted this privilege. (So, in Lib., *ep.*, 763, 937, the gown is spoken of as the prospective reward of a proficient student.) What was the fate of the unsuccessful candidates — whether they were later admitted to the ranks of the gownsmen, and whether, if so, they were required to undergo a second initiation, as also in what relation they stood to their more fortunate fellow-students — is not clear. If the interpretation is correct which makes the second of the qualifications mentioned above (ᾧ μὴ τῶν σοφιστῶν ἡ γνώμη ἐπέτρεπε) imply united action on the part of the sophists, the fact is noteworthy, and serves to supplement what we know of united action among the professors at Antioch in the time of Libanius (see pp. 270 *ff.*, 326). A further suggestion of combined action— this time on the part of the different student-corps — may be contained in the final words of Olympiodorus given above (εἰς τοὺς τῶν διατριβῶν προστάτας τοὺς λεγομένους 'Ακρωμίτας). Bernhardy (*Gr. Lit.*, p. 710) sees a reference in Phot., *Bibl.*, cod. 242, p. 352 a, 16: λόγους . . . ἐπεδεικνύμην πρότερον, τὸν ἐπὶ ῥητορικῇ τρίβωνα περιθέμενος, ὥστε ἦν καὶ τρίβων ῥητορικός, ὡς καὶ φιλόσοφος, to a sort of Doctorate. Sometimes the hazing seems to have consisted of an intellectual browbeating, as when the band of Armenians attempted to argue Basil down (Greg. Naz., *or.*, xliii. 17). [2] i. 13, 13.

next evening I was in the city and in hands I little liked; and on the following night, in still other hands, as little to my liking as the former. But of him whom I had come to see and hear, not a glimpse was to be had, for I was confined in a cell not much larger than a wine-jar; such were the tricks they played on the new arrivals as they came. We shouted, my sophist and I, he from one room and I from another, deprived of each other's presence; but my gaolers paid no attention to our cries. Like another Aristodemus, I was guarded, Syrian though I was, until I took the oath; but after I had sworn allegiance to the party whose captive I was, the door of my cell was opened, and from that time forth I attended the lectures of all three sophists: those of the one, without delay and as a regularly enrolled pupil, those of the other two, according to the regulation in force governing attendance at lectures." [1]

[1] i. 14, 4: ἠκροώμην τοῦ μὲν εὐθὺς ἐν τάξει μαθητοῦ, τοῖν δυοῖν δὲ κατὰ νόμον δὴ τὸν τῶν ἐπιδείξεων. The regulation here referred to may have been similar to that in force at Antioch, whereby, when any one of the sophists held a display, the students of all the other sophists in the city were released from work on that day and allowed to attend the lecture (see p. 280). Cf. Philos., 578, where a student of one sophist seems to have had the opportunity of attending the ἀκροάσεις of another (see also ib., 617). At Antioch students seem at times to have been attached to two sophists at once (Lib., ep., 474, 498; iii. 262, 2 ff.). Of course, it was not unusual for a student to attend the lectures of two or more sophists at different periods of his course. With ἐν τάξει μαθητοῦ, cf. Lib., i. 527, 3: ἦ μὴν ἐμὸν μήτε γενέσθαι μήτε κληθῆναι φοιτητὴν μήτ' εἰς τὸν κατάλογον ἐγγραφῆναι τῶν ἐμῶν ὁμιλητῶν, and, for the oath, see ib., ep., 407. The sophist by whom Libanius was impressed was Diophantus (Eunap., p. 96; Suidas, s. v. Λιβάνιος). The sophist whom he went to hear is supposed to have been Epiphanius, and the third sophist referred to, Proæresius. The reference to the last two, however, is rather in-

It would seem, from this account, that Libanius escaped the usual initiatory rites as described by Gregory and Olympiodorus; but such was not the case: in one of his letters [1] he refers, in a reminiscent vein, as to a part of his own experience, to the bath which followed his arrival, and — a new feature, not mentioned by either Gregory or Olympiodorus — to the 'spread' which came after, and the conversation that there took place. Probably a 'spread,' provided at the expense of the initiate, was the last act in the drama of initiation, and for this the money which, according to Olympiodorus, was laid out in honor of the Acromites may have served.[2]

It did sometimes happen, but only rarely, that the rigor of the process here described was, as a mark of special recognition, relaxed in favor of a new pupil. Thus, Basil of Cæsarea, the great Christian orator, was, thanks to the efforts of his friend Gregory, already well known when he arrived at Athens at the age of twenty-five or thereabouts, and in his case the initiatory rites were omitted, out of respect for his reputation and dignity.[3] Eunapius was sick when he arrived, and by

definite, and if it were not for the difficulty of making τοῖν δυοῖν δὲ include τοῦ μὲν in the passage given above, we should be inclined to believe that two sophists only are referred to here; especially as two only are mentioned in the further account of Libanius (i. 15-19). Libanius seems to have heard also the lectures of the philosophers Priscus (Lib., *ep.*, 866) and Maximus (*ib.*, *ep.*, 685) while at Athens. Gellius speaks of attending several teachers at one time (xviii. 2, 2).   [1] 1071.

[2] See Sievers, *Leben des Lib.*, p. 32, n. 153.

[3] Greg. Naz., *or.*, xliii. 16. Libanius once wrote to the proconsul of Greece requesting him to protect from hazing a student who was about to go to Athens (*ep.*, 1347).

special request of Proæresius, the sophist to whom he attached himself, the rites were in his case also only in part carried out. Eunapius's own account of this event is worth perusal, both for its own sake and because it well supplements what has already been said:[1]

He (*i. e.*, Eunapius, the author) arrived at the Peiræus about the first watch, suffering from a violent fever, wherewith he had been attacked on the voyage; a number of others, his relatives, accompanied him, and the skipper, notwithstanding the hour, set out immediately for Athens, before any of the usual proceedings had taken place — for the vessel hailed from Athens, and crowds of students, fanatically bent on promoting the interests of their respective schools, were always lying in wait near the landing-places. The others walked, but the writer, being unable to walk, was carried to the city in the arms of his companions, who relieved one another at supporting him. It was now midnight, at the time of the year when the sun, verging toward the south, makes the nights longer; in fact, it had already entered Libra, and the autumn equinox was at hand. The skipper had an ancient bond of friendship and hospitality with Proæresius, and so, knocking at his door, he introduced us all into his house; — so many were we that, when later several battles took place over a youth or two, we who came that night made by ourselves a complete sophist's school. Some of these had physical strength, some had great wealth, while there were others who had neither strength nor wealth; the writer was in a sorry plight, for his sole possession was a fairly complete knowledge of the works of the ancients, which he had at his tongue's end. At once there was rejoicing throughout the house, and a running about of men and women, and some laughed, and some threw jokes

[1] P. 74.

at us. Notwithstanding the hour, Proæresius sent for some of his kinsmen and bade them take the newcomers under their charge. . . . These, taking possession of the newcomers, conducted them into the neighboring streets and about the baths, making a general display of them, while the boys treated them to ridicule and laughter. And so the others, when they had received the bath, were once and for all freed from their troubles, but the writer, the force of his sickness increasing, lay near to death. Neither Proæresius nor Athens did he see, and the things that he had desired he seemed but to have dreamt. . . . [After his life had been almost despaired of, Eunapius was at length taken in hand by one Æschines, a physician whose reputation was not of the best, and was by him unexpectedly and quickly restored to health.] The most divine Proæresius, who, though he had never seen the writer, had yet, when he heard of his sickness, grieved for him, did now, when he learned of his unexpected and joyful recovery, call to his side the strongest and most valiant-hearted of his students — those whose feats of strength were most loudly applauded — and say to them: "I have sorrowed for this youth whose life has now been saved, though I have never seen him; still I sorrowed for him when he lay at the point of death. If you wish, therefore, to do me a favor, you will give this young man his purification at the public bath, but you will spare him all ridicule and jesting, and deal easily with him as though he were my own son." And this was what took place.

Eunapius was at that time sixteen years of age, and Proæresius eighty-seven.

We notice with pleasure in this passage the tender consideration which Proæresius showed for the sick Eunapius. The attitude of the sophist toward the student was in general a parental one, and indeed he is often called the father of his students.[1] He not unfrequently kept a careful watch over their daily life, accompanied them on their walks, visited them when they were sick, and in other ways showed his interest in their welfare.[2] The term 'father,' however, as used in this connection, referred quite as much to an intellectual relationship as to any actual parental care exercised by the sophist toward the student. The sophist was the intellectual parent of the student; it was through him that the student came into a new life. This relationship formed a bond between the two that was hardly less sacred than that existing between the real father and the son,[3] and we find that the feeling of the sophist toward the student was as a rule reciprocated.

We observed in a previous chapter the admiration and respect with which Eunapius wrote of the personality of the aged Proæresius — that patriarchal figure which he recalled out of the days of his boyhood. The same admiration and respect breathes through his description of the sophist Julian's house, which he saw

[1] *E. g.*, Themis., 20 b; Choric., p. 21; Lib., *ep.*, 1452. Libanius calls one of his former pupils his son, and says that he stood to the boy as a father (*ep.*, 137). The students are called the children of the sophist (*ib.*, iii. 444, 5; Eunap., p. 70). *Cf.* Quint., *Inst. or.*, ii. 2, 4; ii. 9.

[2] Eunap., p. 113; Lib., ii. 311, 12. Libanius sometimes defended his students from the attacks of the police (*ib.*). He writes on one occasion to the uncle of one of his pupils, telling him that he does not allow his nephew enough money; if the uncle were poor, says Libanius, and could not afford the money, he (Libanius) should himself consider it his duty to see that the boy did not want (*ep.*, 22).

[3] *Cf.* Philos., 536: πατέρα καλῶν αὐτὸν τῆς ἑαυτοῦ γλώττης· *ib.*, 617: τοῖς ἐμαυτοῦ σπλάγχνοις (of a pupil).

when at Athens. This house was evidently sacred in his eyes. "When at Athens," he says,[1] "the writer saw Julian's house. It was small and simply furnished, but breathed the air of Hermes and the Muses; in no respect did it differ from a holy shrine. Julian had bequeathed it to Proæresius. There were busts in it of some of Julian's friends — those whom the sophist most admired — and a theatre of polished marble, built in imitation of the public theatres, but smaller and such as befitted a private house." Philostratus says[2] that the sophist Adrian engaged with his students in all their pastimes quite like one of them, so that he was looked upon as an agreeable and kind-hearted father. "Some of them I have seen," continues Philostratus, "when anything has recalled the man to their mind, shed tears, and fondly imitate his voice, his walk, and the graceful manner he had of wearing his cloak." On one occasion, when Adrian was made the object of a bitter attack by a certain pettifogging rhetorician, but himself paid no attention to the abuse that was heaped upon him, his students, taking up their professor's cause, ordered their servants to waylay the rhetorician and give him a sound thrashing. This they did, and about a month later the man died, though the cause of his death was not evident. Adrian, however, was arraigned, and then his students appeared in court, and with tears and words of explanation sued for his release.[3] So, when Heracleides was adjudged guilty of cutting down some cedar-trees, the wood of which was sacred, and was mulcted by the court of a sum nearly equal to the

[1] P. 68. [2] P. 587. [3] Philos., 588.

whole of his fortune, his students accompanied him from the court-house, consoling and supporting him, and one said, "Well, Heracleides, no one can take away your eloquence or the glory that has brought you."[1]

Libanius was now duly matriculated at the University of Athens and ready to begin his studies there. How did he improve his time? The opinion which he formed of his lecturers was not an exalted one. "Now the applause," he says,[2] "was great, being designed to mislead those who were tasting this spring of learning for the first time, but I gradually began to realize that it was nothing very wonderful that I had come to hear, for the charge of these boys had been seized by men who did not themselves differ much from boys. It was held an unpardonable offence on my part toward Athens that I did not express admiration for the professors, and it was with difficulty that I appeased the indignation of the students by telling them that I admired in silence and that I was prevented from shouting

---

[1] Philos., 614. Libanius says that he is sure that his students would attack and pommel his enemies, without waiting for a case at law, if they knew who his enemies were (ii. 308, 8). This was their duty (cf. ib., ii. 266, 1 ff.). Compare the love of Severus, Libanius's former pupil, for his master in after years (ib., iii. 231, 1 ff.), and the regard of Libanius for the memory of his teacher Zenobius (ib., ep., 100, 101, 118, 119). See also ib., i. 203, 4. Sometimes a student gave financial aid to his teacher (ib., ep., 232), and one of Libanius's former pupils sent to the professor a χιτών made by his wife (ib., ep., 829). Nicknames were common in antiquity, and doubtless the ancient student often made use of them in connection with his teacher. One particularly trenchant Peripatetic (Luc., Symp., 6) was called by his students 'Brand' (ξίφος) and 'Cleaver' (κοπίς). The sophist Secundus was called 'Peggy' (ἐπίουρος), because his father was a carpenter (Philos., 544). [2] i. 14, 6.

by my ill health." And yet Diophantus, the sophist to whom Libanius attached himself, was one of the most famous sophists in the city; it was both in Libanius's own nature, however, and in the spirit of the times to carp at rival eminence.[1] As it was, Libanius devoted himself to the study of the ancients, and paid not much attention to his lectures. In after times he professed to have benefited by this proceeding. "In the very matter of my style," he says, addressing an Antioch audience,[2] "I should have become the imitator of the sophist under whom I was studying — my love for the man would have brought that about — and I should then have followed in the footsteps of men whom you yourselves know only too well and whom it is better that I should not mention. Imagine, if, instead of the masters of style whose forms you now recognize in my speeches, my sentences were to suggest to you some poor starveling rhetorician." We may compare with this account Eunapius's description of Libanius's method of study :[3] "Having been impressed by Diophantus's pupils, he attached himself to Diophantus; and, as those who became well acquainted with the man said, he, understanding the purport of what had been done, very rarely presented himself at the lectures and the meetings of the class, and afforded no trouble to the teacher, but confined himself to the practice of declamations, and forced himself into conformity with the ancient type, moulding his mind and his speech.

[1] It is not impossible, however, that the real virtues of Athens fell behind her reputation (see pp. 337 *ff.*). Even as a boy Libanius had failed to find any good in the sophists of Antioch (Lib., i. 8, 11 *ff.*).   [2] i. 18, 12.   [3] P. 96.

As, in the case of those who shoot again and again and sometimes hit the mark, continued practice begets, as a rule, through use of the instruments, not an understanding of the art of sharp-shooting, but a knowledge of the way how to shoot straight, so Libanius, attaching himself, and keeping close, to the best guides, the ancients namely, and following the correct masters, did, by dint of emulation, and imitation after comparison, enter upon the right path and enjoy to the full the fruits of his course."

In the matter of corps-service also Libanius was not a loyal supporter of his professor. The waylaying of new arrivals at the ports of entry was not the only form of service which the various corps undertook in the interests of their masters: rival corps often came to blows in the streets of Athens,[1] and students and even professors were attacked and roughly handled. Even in a previous century, when the rivalry was less bitter than it was in the fourth century, Heracleides had been driven from his chair at Athens by the party of Apollonius and had retired to Smyrna to teach,[2] and in the fourth century, as we have already seen, Proæresius was in a like manner compelled to leave the city for a time. The populace sometimes took sides and perhaps even assisted in the frays,[3] while the professors themselves were generally only too ready to abet their pupils

---

[1] Also at Antioch in the second half of the century (Lib., ii. 345, 6; iii. 254, 20), and doubtless elsewhere. In the time of Libanius's boyhood student battles were probably unknown at Antioch (see p. 314). [2] Philos., 613.

[3] Eunap., p. 69. They are even accused of being the prime offenders (Lib., iii. 254, 8). *Cf.* Eunap., p. 76.

in this form of warfare. On one occasion, as we read,[1] Athens was as if in a state of siege, and the streets were so dangerous by reason of the terrorization practised by the student-corps that no professor dared go downtown to the public school-rooms, but each held his class in his private auditorium, which was built in his own house. We read in Libanius [2] how a certain Arabian professor, while going to his breakfast, or mid-day meal, from the bath, was attacked by two hired agents of a rival band of students and had his face plastered with mud, and how another, from Egypt, was hounded from the city and his profession. In the latter case the poor sophist was actually dragged from his bed and carried to a well, where he escaped a ducking only by promising to leave the city. Himerius [3] was on one occasion so

[1] Eunap., p. 69.
[2] i. 60, 12. The professor was probably Diophantus.
[3] *Or.*, xxii. The Emperor Justinian put an end to all such proceedings on the part of students at Constantinople and Berytus (*Dig.*, *præf. omnem*, 9). With the liberty which prevailed at Athens it is interesting to compare the strictness of the regulations governing the movement of students at Rome (*Cod. Th.*, xiv. 9, 1): "Whoever comes to Rome for the purpose of study must first present to the head of the board of censors a letter from the judges of his province (from whom he in the first instance received permission to come), containing the name of his city, and a statement of his age and qualifications. As soon as he arrives, he must signify to what studies he intends to devote himself. The board of censors must be kept informed of his residence, in order that they may see that he follows the course which he has laid out for himself. The censors must likewise see that, when the students come together, they conduct themselves as persons who have a proper regard for their reputation, and who consider that those societies which we hold to be next to criminal are to be avoided; also that they do not attend public shows too often, or banquets that last far into the night. Furthermore, if any student acts in a manner unbecoming his condition as one pursuing a course of liberal study, he shall, under authority by us

severely handled by the students of a rival sophist that he was obliged for a considerable time to intermit his lectures. From all such escapades Libanius held himself aloof. "I had heard . . . ," he says,[1] "ever since I was a boy, of the battles between the student-corps waged in the very streets of Athens; of the clubs and swords and stones and wounds; of the indictments that resulted from all this, and the defences that were made, and the sentences that were pronounced; of all the wild and daring deeds undertaken by the students to win for their teachers gain and glory. I held these fellows brave for the dangers that they ran, and their cause a just one; not less so than that of those who take up arms in their country's defence. And I prayed to the gods that it might fall to my lot, too, to win such laurels; to run down to the Peiræus and to Sunium and the other ports and waylay the new arrivals as they disembarked from the trading-vessels; and then to go to Corinth [2] and

given, be publicly flogged, and then straightway put on board ship, taken from the city, and transported back to his home. Those who devote themselves assiduously to their studies may remain in the city till their twentieth year; after that time, whoever neglects to return to his home of his own accord shall be made to do so by the city-prefect under disgrace. That these regulations may be carefully observed, it shall be the duty of Your Sincerity to advise the board of censors that they each month make a list of those who are studying in the city, stating whence they come, and how many, by reason of their age, are ready to return to Africa and the other provinces; an exception being made in the case of those who are burdened with the duties of corporations. Similar lists are to be transmitted yearly to the office of Our Clemency, in order that, learning the qualifications and proficiency of each, we may judge whether, and at what time, he is necessary to Our service."     [1] i. 15, 16.

[2] Corinth was at this time the seat of government for the province of Achaia, and it was there that the proconsul had his residence and administered justice.

stand trial for my conduct; and to string dinner on dinner in endless succession, and, after quickly going through my money, to cast about for somebody from whom to borrow more. But the goddess, Fortune, well aware that I was headed straight for what would have been my ruin — that snare so fair in appearance and with so fair-sounding a name, a corps-captaincy — very wisely, as it is her wont to do, withdrew me from that sophist in whose defence I considered it obligatory upon me to undertake such service, and, hurrying me apart, put me under another, with whom I was to know only the labors done for study's sake. This result came about in the following way: Owing to the indignity which had been put upon me in the matter of the oath, I would not myself undertake any of the services I have mentioned, and, inasmuch as my condition of bondage was not a voluntary one, no one would order me to do what I would not do willingly. Furthermore, the students were not without fear that I might become annoyed at the burden of such duties, and, assigning as my excuse the compulsion under which I lay, take it into my head to revolt against my oath. I was therefore relieved from the necessity of taking part in their expeditions and campaigns and battles and reviews, and even in the Great Battle, in which everybody, not excepting those who were exempted by reason of their years, engaged, I sat apart by myself and received from others the account of what befell." [1]

[1] It would seem from the last sentence that the older students were exempted from service of the sort. In later life, when Libanius came to speak to his own students, he expressed himself on occasion quite differently with relation to the customs which he as a youth condemned (i. 202, 20).

The Great Battle here referred to was a contest memorable of its kind; it was fought in the Lyceum, east of the city proper.[1] Another memorable contest took place many years before Libanius came to Athens. The case that grew out of this contest was celebrated in the annals of sophistry. The description of this event is preserved to us by Eunapius,[2] who based his account on the narrative of an eye-witness; the case well illustrates the customs prevailing at Athens at this time.

It had happened, in the course of this civil warfare, that the boldest of Apsines's pupils got the better, in a hand-to-hand contest, of the pupils of Julian; and having, in truly Laconic fashion, roughly handled them, they then, as though they were themselves the injured party, made a public accusation against those whom they had thus severely treated and brought to within an inch of their lives. The case was carried to the proconsul, and he, showing himself a stern and formidable officer, gave orders that both the teacher and all those against whom the accusation had been lodged should be arrested and imprisoned, like common cutthroats. The man seemed, however — naturally, being a Roman — to be well educated, and not to have been reared in a rough and unpolished school. Julian came at the appointed time — for he had been summoned to appear — and Apsines also was present — though he had not been summoned, but came to speak in behalf of those who made the charge.

When the time set for the examination was at hand, the plaintiffs were allowed to enter. The leader of this unruly Spartan band was Themistocles, an Athenian, who was also the originator of the trouble; being over-violent and arrogant, he was a disgrace to his name. The proconsul,

[1] Lib., *ep.*, 627.   [2] P. 69.

straightway eying Apsines fiercely, said, "Who ordered *you* to come here?" "I have come," answered Apsines, "to plead for my children." The governor concealed his thoughts by saying nothing, and the prisoners, who were the injured party, were allowed to enter in their turn, and with them came their teacher. Their hair was unkempt, and their bodies were battered and bruised; so that pity might have been awakened even in the heart of the judge.

The plaintiffs were given the floor, but Apsines had hardly begun to speak when the proconsul, interrupting him, said, "Stop! this is not the Roman way of conducting a case. Let the one who first made the accusation now come forward and conduct the trial." They were quite unprepared to undergo the ordeal of a trial then, and Themistocles, who had made the original accusation, finding himself compelled to take the floor, first changed color and bit his lips in his embarrassment, and then, looking stealthily at his companions, asked under his breath what was to be done. They had come into court simply to shout and applaud their teacher's speech, and consequently the silence and embarrassment were great. . . . First Julian remarked plaintively, "Let me speak." Then said the proconsul, raising his voice, "Let there be no applause, either on the part of you who are practised speakers or on the part of the students. You shall soon know what Roman justice is. Let Themistocles carry through the accusation, and be the defence made by whomever you, Julian, select as best." No one rose to accuse, Themistocles proving a disgrace to his name, but, when the proconsul ordered whoever could, to make answer to the original charge, then said the sophist Julian, "By your strict observance of justice, Proconsul, you have made of Apsines a veritable Pythagoras, for he has learned, though late, a needed lesson, the way to hold his tongue. Long ago — and of this you yourself have experience — he taught his pupils the Pythagorean art of silence. If, now, you bid us defend ourselves, release from bondage one of my pupils, Proæresius by name, and you shall yourself judge whether he has been taught the art of Pythagoras or that of the Attic people." . . .

At once quite calmly . . . Proæresius, one of those under accusation, came forward unfettered, and, his teacher crying to him loudly and in a high tone of voice — like those who incite and urge on the runners at the games — and sharply withal, the words, "Speak, Proæresius, now is the time to speak," he pronounced the opening of a speech. . . . He broke forth into a lament over the indignities he and his companions had suffered, and here and there in the introduction were words in praise of his teacher; there was also, scattered through it, reproof, conveyed in the turn of a phrase, of the precipitancy of the proconsul, who had made them undergo and endure things which they ought not to have undergone even if they had been convicted. The proconsul sat with bowed head, deeply impressed by what Proæresius had said, and by the dignity, the ease, and the well-rounded sonorousness with which he spoke; and then, while the whole audience, eager to applaud, but awed as before an omen sent from Zeus, sat wrapped in a mysterious silence, Proæresius, putting his words into the form of a second introduction, began again thus . . .: "If," he said, "one is permitted to do every wrong, to accuse his neighbor and have his words believed even before the defence is made, well and good, let the whole city go with Themistocles." Then the proconsul, stern and inflexible man, jumping to his feet and waving his purple-bordered robe . . . applauded Proæresius like a boy. Apsines also applauded — not that he wished to do so, but necessity knows no master; and Julian, the teacher, only wept. The proconsul ordered the defendants to be dismissed, and then taking aside, first the teacher from among the plaintiffs, and afterward Themistocles and the Laconians, reminded them of the festival called the *Scourging* at Sparta and also of the process called by that name at Athens.

Libanius has intimated that running into debt and giving 'spreads' were two of the favorite forms of amusement of students at Athens. There were others, however. "Never," he says,[1] "while I was at Athens, did I engage in a game of ball; and I was far from joining in a carousal or participating in the night raids made on the houses of the poorer people." Himerius, we remember, warned his students at the beginning of the term against playing ball, practising athletics, running about town, and going to the theatre. Drinking-bouts were frequent, and often at these bouts, as well as at the 'spreads,' intellectual entertainment and contests of wit were joined to good cheer. Favorite occasions for 'club' or 'class' dinners were the Saturnalia and other holidays.[2]

Student life at Athens and student life at Antioch probably differed very little. The rivalry between the various sophists was more intense at Athens than it was at Antioch, and the warfare between the student-bands was carried on with greater bitterness and fierceness; there may also have been at Athens certain traditional customs which had failed to take root at Antioch; but the main characteristics of the student life of the two places must have been essentially the same. We shall not be far wrong, therefore, if, in order to gain a clearer idea of the conditions that prevailed at Athens at the time of Libanius's stay there, we glance at the picture which

---

[1] i. 18, 2.
[2] Philos., 585, 586, 587; Gell., xv. 2; xviii. 2 and 13. Sometimes the students went a-hunting (Philos., 587). For further evidence that athletics sometimes interfered with studies, see Lib., *ep.*, 1119.

Libanius draws of his own experience as a teacher at Antioch.

Swearing at goldsmiths, insulting cobblers, drubbing carpenters, kicking weavers, hauling hucksters, threatening oil-dealers, were among the pastimes of Libanius's own students.[1] Libanius on one occasion delivered a lecture [2] wherein he dissuaded his students from taking part in any such unseemly pranks, as also from engaging in street-fights with the students of rival corps; he urged them rather to stand as an example to the townsmen of the advantages of an education.

It is evident that Libanius often had hard times with his students. "Perhaps some think," he says, when giving his reason for having intermitted for a time his usual displays,[3] "that I shall give as the reason the injustice that exists in connection with the fees." After describing how the student, having received money from his father to give to the sophist, squanders this on wine and dice, he continues:

And then, after behaving thus shamelessly toward his teacher, he bounds into the school-room, bawling at the top of his voice and threatening and using his fists; holding everybody in contempt and looking upon his simple presence there as sufficient pay for the sophist. Now the student of scanty means we can forgive, at the same time that we censure him; for he gives not because he has not; but when he arrays himself in line with the others and joins them in their insolence, how can anybody tolerate such

---

[1] Lib., iii. 254, 13.
[2] Or., lix (iii. 252). A student was once sent to Libanius, recommended by the promise he gave of turning out a good fighter (Lib., ep., 58).
[3] i. 197, 16.

conduct? Sometimes those who are poor go to even greater lengths than those who are rich, as though they hoped, by so doing, to conceal the fact that they have not paid their fees. Then, cringing at the feet of the rich, they spend their time in such flattery as this (flattery so creditable to them!), and, when they leave the school, they either ignore the sophist altogether or do their best to work him all manner of harm.

[Another man, then, might make this his excuse for not speaking in public, but not so Libanius; he had long been accustomed to charge nothing for his instruction, and the matter of fees could, therefore, have no influence with him.]

What is the reason, then, if this is not? Why, I fail to see that my students as a body care in the least for my declamations, or have the slightest appreciation of my worth. And of this the students themselves have given clear proof, both in spring and in winter, whenever I have spoken at either time of the year. For see: I send my servant out to invite them to a lecture; he hurries off and executes my order. They, instead of, as they ought, outstripping the servant, are absolutely unmoved by his example. Some linger over their songs, which they all know, others loiter away the time in idle foolery or in laughter. Then, after arousing by their deliberateness the ire of all beholders, they, if they ever do decide to come, walk, both outside and inside the room, as gingerly as young girls, or, rather, as men balancing on a tight rope. It is indeed enough to make those who are seated indignant, to have to wait for such dawdlers as these to enter the room. All this takes place before the speaking begins; after the sophist has entered upon his declamation and begun to speak, then the students keep up a constant signalling back and forth about drivers and mimes and horses and dancers, and about this or that battle that has taken place or is to take place. Further, some stand like statues, with one arm thrown over the other, while others delve in their noses with both hands at once; still others sit without moving a muscle, notwithstanding all the brilliant points that I make, or forcibly detain in their seats those who have been moved by my words. Some count those who come in after them, while others find it sufficient to gaze at the leaves, or are better pleased to chatter over chance subjects than to listen to the speaker. Surpassing all this in audacity is the act of those who interrupt genuine applause with spurious, choke the voice of enthusiasm at its source, and parade through the whole theatre, withdrawing from the lecture all whom they can influence, either by false messages or by invitations to come and bathe before breakfast — this also being an extravagance on which some spend their money. . . .

Now no one can accuse me of dealing in slander and of uttering false charges, on the ground that, if that was done which I say was done, I should have flown into a passion at once and have spoken then and there words of anger against the wrong-doers. You know well enough that that is the very thing I often did, and that I, on not a few occasions, raising my voice, bade my man seize the loafer by the neck and throw him out of doors. If this was not done, it was by reason of the prayers which were uttered in his behalf. . . .

Evidence that the students, when they attended a declamation, did not pay the attention they should have paid, is furnished by the fact that on no occasion did they carry away in their minds a word of what was said. Exactly the opposite was the case with those who preceded you in these halls. They departed from the lecture, each with some different scrap of what was said stored in his memory. Then, when they were outside, they tried to fit together what they remembered and so restore my speech; and if anything, however little, was forgotten, they felt grieved at the loss. And for three or four days after that they did nothing at home but recite my words to their parents, and here at school they kept this up for a much longer period. *You* go back to your songs, which you remember with the greatest facility. . . . If any one asks you whether I have spoken and on what subject, to the first question he will doubtless receive an answer, but, as for what I said, nobody can tell that.[1]

The principal reason given by Libanius for not expelling students is noteworthy:[2]

The greatest consideration of all is my regard for these students' parents and native cities. I greatly fear that, if they should hear of their sons' expulsion, they would treat those that were thus disgraced as if they were dead, at the very least; looking upon dishonor as worse than death and knowing that such dishonor as this is greater than that inflicted by the courts. For from the latter men may be freed, but the former remains with them forever, accompanying them, at every age, from boyhood to death, and depriving them of all sense of freedom. "Shameless, dog-eyed one, wert thou not banished from the holy rites of learning, because thou didst pollute the altar of the Muses?" It was, then, because I wished to spare their mothers and fathers, their cities, and their future children — for even to them this disgrace would have to descend —

---

[1] Ingratitude and rudeness were not uncommon on the part of students toward their teachers (Lib., i. 146, 1; ii. 311, 4; 422, 16; iii. 443, 5; Themis., 289 a; Himer., *or.*, xx; *ec.*, xvii). For talking 'horse,' etc., in school, see Tac., *Dial. de or.*, 29; *cf.* Cic., *De orat.*, ii. 5, 21. Compare the proceedings of students at Carthage (Augustin., *Confess.*, v. 8). Sometimes, according to Epictetus (ii. 21, 12 and 13; *cf.* iii. 24, 22 and 24), during the lectures, students from afar would let their thoughts wander homeward, and, recalling how their parents had sent them forth with great hopes, would wonder why no letter came from home and allow themselves to get discouraged at the arduousness of their task; then the lecturer's words fell on deaf ears.

[2] i. 207, 6.

that I did not expel from my class these unruly students, but, instead, decided to speak no more, and, as I believe, decided wisely.

The strap [1] and the rod [2] were the common instruments of chastisement, but Libanius, in his later years, abandoned the use of these; "for I have given up," he says,[3] "trying to bring my students into a path of rectitude by means of blows and stripes, finding that these often produce the opposite effect to that desired. Being of the belief that counsel and exhortation are more beneficial and can better effect a cure, I have recourse to them." Early in life, however, he was not averse to the use of the strap on lazy boys. Occasionally he received remonstrating letters from the boys' fathers, which he found it necessary to answer.

[1] σκῦτος (Lib., i. 479, 17); ἱμάς (ib., ii. 425, 12); ῥυτήρ (Themis., 261 c); μάστιξ (Lib., iii. 253, 5).
[2] ῥάβδος (Lib., ii. 425, 12).
[3] iii. 253, 5. Cf. ib., ii. 311, 6; iii. 270, 18. His students, he says, did everything for him willingly, without the fear of blows (i. 178, 15). In school, boys were laid on their stomachs and flogged on their backs and posteriors (ib., i. 646, 6), but possibly university students received more dignified treatment. Sometimes they were lashed about the legs (ib., ep., 1119). Gregory of Nyssa (De castigat., 312) recommends, first to whip the boy, then to keep him after school and deprive him of his breakfast. Libanius sometimes caused unruly students to be evicted from his displays (i. 200, 23). Himerius was also opposed on principle to corporal punishment (or., xv. 2). Philager, noted for his quick temper, is said on one occasion to have boxed the ears of a pupil whom he caught napping in the class-room (Philos., 578). Proclus, in order that his pupils might not hiss and jeer at one another, practices which, says Philostratus (604), were common in the class-room, had them enter in a body, and seated them, the older boys singly, and the younger boys and the pedagogues filling in the spaces between these (cf. Quint., Inst. or., ii. 2, 14).

The person who sent you word about the strap and the whipping [he writes on one occasion[1]] ought to have added the reason for the whipping. For then you would not have felt hurt, as is now the case. For your sorrow seems to be due, not to the fact that your son has received a whipping, but to the thought that, if he had not committed some great wrong, a whipping would not have been considered necessary. Now hear my attitude in regard to these matters. If one of my students commits a wrong which it is disgraceful even to mention, I expel him, and allow him not to taint my class with his infection. But if a student is lazy and neglects his studies, I use the lash. In the first case, I fear him as I should fear a festering sore, and drive him from my presence; in the second case, I arouse with the strap one who is sleeping. Now the latter was the error and the punishment of your son. He abandoned his books and became a sprinter, but he also made amends on his legs, and now practises his tongue instead. Now don't inflict on him a second chastisement, in the shape of your displeasure, or consider the boy bad, for he looks on his brother as an example, respects you, and will some day perhaps make his performances equal yours.

That teachers were often deterred from punishing their pupils by the fear of losing their patronage is clear enough.[2] Libanius says that the defection of students from one sophist to another was in the time of his youth a thing almost unheard of; a few had been known to transfer their allegiance, but the action had been considered dishonorable, and the students who engaged in it had been shunned by nearly all their friends. In his later life, however, hardly a day passed without its example of such defection, and sometimes a student

[1] *Ep.*, 1119.   [2] See Lib., ii. 425, 12 *ff.*

went the rounds of all the sophists, swearing allegiance to each in turn. To remedy this evil, Libanius once called the sophists of Antioch together and proposed that they should enter into an agreement whereby no sophist was to accept a student who came to him in that way. Any father who was dissatisfied with the sophist under whom he had placed his son was to have the privilege of examining his son or of having him examined by competent persons, in order to determine if the sophist was neglecting his duty. If there was apparent evidence that the sophist was neglecting his duty, then the father might enter a formal complaint against him and have the case tried before a board of his own selection, composed of teachers and non-teachers. In case this board adjudged the sophist guilty, the boy might be transferred to another sophist; otherwise no change could be made.[1] Such a contract, we learn, was actually made and put in force.[2]

On one occasion the students of Libanius's school

[1] *Or.*, xliii (ii. 420). The act of transferring one's allegiance from one sophist to another was called *apostasis* (ἀπόστασις; in Eunap., p. 80, μετανάστασις). Students often resorted thereto to avoid paying their dues, and they improved the occasion to insult their former teacher (Lib., ii. 422, 16; *cf.* Augustin., *Confess.*, v. 12). Owing to the custom of *apostasis*, the sophist was made the slave of the pedagogue, who, if things did not go to his liking, could induce his ward to transfer his allegiance (*ib.*, ii. 283, 7; 425, 7; iii. 445, 24). *Apostasis*, in the second half of the century, was common at Athens and elsewhere (Himer., *or.*, xxxiv; Synes., *Dion*, 13). Sometimes a student went from one university town to another (Lib., iii. 457, 1).

[2] Lib., ii. 314, 8. Some measure to forbid transference of allegiance Libanius seems to have recommended to the council, and even to have carried through, shortly after his settlement in Antioch (*ep.*, 407).

went to the length of tossing in a blanket a certain pedagogue who had incurred their displeasure. The process is thus described:[1]

They stretch a carpet on the ground and then take hold of it on all four sides — sometimes more, sometimes fewer, according to the size of the carpet. Then, placing the unhappy victim in the centre, they toss him as high as they can (and that is not a short distance), accompanying their action with laughter. Great is the amusement also of the standers-by, as they behold the pedagogue spinning in the air and hear him cry out as he goes up and again as he comes down. Sometimes he falls in the carpet, which is held high above the ground, and he is then saved; at other times, missing the carpet, he strikes the ground, and leaves the field, with some of his limbs maimed or bruised — danger being thus added to insult. And, worst of all, even such an event arouses the mirth of the students.

This attack on the pedagogue, however, was a unique case, for generally the pedagogue was held in high esteem and was much respected by both students and sophists.[2]

---

[1] iii. 259, 14.

[2] The pedagogue, in the Greek sense of the word, was a slave who was a sort of personal attendant of the boy and kept watch and ward over him. "He is the protector of his fresh young age," says Libanius (iii. 255, 13), "his guardian and his defence. . . . He beats off all attacks, as a barking dog beats off wolves. . . . The pedagogue has, as his sole care, the boy and the boy's welfare." He awoke the boy in the morning and made him learn his lessons. "What the boy has received from his teacher, it is the duty of the pedagogue to preserve for him; for the means of preservation belong to him: he urges the boy, he shouts at him, he produces the rod, he brandishes the strap, he endeavors, by laboring at his task, . . . to drive into his memory the lesson he has heard." When the boy went to school, he was accompanied by the pedagogue and by a foot-boy, the latter of whom

Such is the picture drawn by Libanius of the student life at Antioch in the second half of the fourth century, and similar, as has been said, must have been the student life at Athens when Libanius was himself a student there. During these years that he was a student there, he studied hard and faithfully. "Not a day," he says,[1] "was without its labors, except — which was not often the case, I think — when some holiday intervened to give me rest." He travelled about the country with an eager interest in its antiquities and its local customs. "I visited Corinth,[2] neither as a defendant nor as a prosecutor, but at one time when hurrying to attend a Spartan festival, the *Scourging*, at another time while on my way to Argos, there to be initiated in the local mysteries." He must have distinguished himself among the students at Athens, for, when a proconsul, who was determined to have peace in the town, deposed three of the most contentious of the sophists, he selected Libanius, who was then only

---

carried his books (Lib., ii. 80, 19; iii. 145, 2; 260, 13; *cf.* Luc., *Amor.*, 44, and the Philostratus passages referred to below). Girard (*L'Éd. athén.*, p. 116) and Becker (*Characles*, trans., p. 226) say that the pedagogue carried the books, but there seems to be no evidence for this (if we except the passage in Lucian, *Amor.*, 44, which is not decisive). The pedagogue was superior to such service. Sometimes the pedagogue and the foot-boy waited outside the school-room until the boy had finished his lessons (Philos., 618), sometimes they accompanied him inside (*ib.*, 604; Lib., iii. 200, 15). Many students, especially the older ones, were unaccompanied by a pedagogue. At times the pedagogue abetted the student in his resistance to the professor (p. 187, n. 1; Lib., iii. 445, 24; *cf. ep.*, 1173, 1508).

[1] i. 19, 8

[2] i. 18, 9. So Gellius visited Delphi and Ægina (Gell., xii. 5; ii. 21).

twenty-five years of age, to fill one of the vacant chairs. The anger of the proconsul becoming in time appeased, the three sophists were reinstated; "but the honor was mine," says Libanius,[1] "in that I had been deemed worthy of the place."

Many friends also Libanius made at Athens — friends who were a consolation to him in later years.[2] Lifelong friendships were formed at college in those days as they are in these. Two celebrated instances are those of Gregory and Basil, and of Proæresius and Hephæstion. "Thence he was sent," writes Gregory, referring to Basil,[3] "by God and his own noble and unquenchable thirst for knowledge to the real home and seat of learning, Athens; 'golden Athens,' it was indeed to me, if ever to anyone in this world, and the introducer to all things beautiful. For there my acquaintance with this man was cemented into firm friendship, and, seeking knowledge, I gained happiness; in another way having the experience of Saul, who, while seeking his father's asses, found a kingdom." Proæresius and Hephæstion were students together at Athens in the school of Julian. It was hard at that time to say which showed the greater ability or which was the more indigent, but they were firm friends. They had, we are told,[4] but one coarse cloak and one outer mantle between them, and three or four faded and threadbare

---

[1] i. 20, 6.

[2] E. g., Ecdicius (Lib., ep., 147); Flavianus (ib., ep., 556); Severus (ib., ep., 1145); Eugnomonius, to whom Libanius recalls old times (ib., ep., 473). Mygdonius, he says, was like a father to him at Athens (ib., ep., 471). See also ib., ep., 1135.

[3] Or., xliii. 13. [4] Eunap., p. 78.

blankets. One day Proæresius would go to lectures and Hephæstion would lie abed and study, and on the next day Hephæstion would appear in public and Proæresius would stay at home. We remember that, at a later time, when both Proæresius and Hephæstion had been nominated for the chair of sophistry at Athens, and party feeling ran high, Hephæstion withdrew from the city, so as not to interfere with his friend's success.

We should be glad to learn where Libanius lived while at college, but on this point he has left us little information. We know that his 'chum' was one Chromatius, with whom he had a room and with whom he took his meals.[1] So far as we are aware, there were no dormitories for students in those days, but the professor sometimes took the student into his own family.[2] Otherwise, the student took private lodgings, or, possibly, he sometimes found quarters at an inn.[3]

Libanius had been four years at Athens when the time came for his departure. He had intended to stay four years more. "I had the intention," he says,[4] "of adding, before leaving Athens, another four years to the four I had already passed in the city, my mind, as it seemed to me, requiring a more thorough training than it had yet received. For, however perfect I seemed to others, I by no means felt myself to be so, but I was disturbed by the fear that, no matter where I went, sophists would swarm about me and try by ten thousand

[1] Lib., *ep.*, 393.
[2] *Ep.*, 285, 290, 378, 379, 381. Libanius at one time allowed two of his students to room at Daphne (*ep.*, 1235).
[3] Lib., ii. 359, 21; Philos., 553; Themis., 293 d; Eunap., p. 75.
[4] i. 20, 15.

tests to pull me down. It seemed to me necessary, therefore, ever to seek and gain more knowledge."

Whether four years was the usual length of the college course, we are not informed. Libanius speaks[1] of one of his own students who was obliged to leave in the second year of his instruction, when he had hardly acquired even the rudiments of his art. Some students, we know, spent more than four years at college: Eunapius, for instance, five,[2] and Gregory Nazianzene from ten to twelve.[3] Of course, the expense was often a determining factor in the matter of the length of stay. Lodging, board, tuition, and, especially, books were among the chief sources of outlay,[4] and sometimes a father found it necessary to take up a contribution among his friends, in order to defray the cost of his son's education.[5]

[1] iii. 229, 1; *cf.* 202, 13 *ff*.  [2] Eunap., p. 92.
[3] See Sievers, *Leben des Lib.*, p. 31, n. 144. The law course at Berytus was four years, until Justinian made it five (*Dig.*, *præf. omnem*). In an earlier age, Isocrates's course was from three to four years (Isoc., *De antid.*, 87). Crispinus, mentioned in the text below, studied at Athens the same length of time as Libanius (Lib., i. 21, 10). Rohde (*Rhein. Mus.*, 40, p. 75) considers the usual length of time to have been five years. The fact that Libanius's school at Antioch contained four rhetors suggests a course of four years. See Luc., *Rhet. præc.*, 9. A letter of Hadrian suggests as a possibility a residence of at least ten years in a city for the purpose of study (*Cod. Jus.*, x. 40, 2).
[4] Lib., ii. 289, 9; *ep.*, 1192.
[5] Lib., *ep.*, 1192; *cf. ib.*, *ep.*, 322; Luc., *Somn.*, 1; John Chrys., *De sacerdot.*, i. 5. Travelling expenses were another item. Sometimes the sophist gave assistance (Lib., *ep.*, 22, 1452, and pp. 182, 183, 308, n. 2). Letoius, a senator of Antioch, once assisted needy students out of his own pocket (*ib.*, *ep.*, 464, 467). The Prætorian Prefect, Anatolius, sent to a poor student who was studying under Libanius one hundred staters, which, according to Libanius, would not go a great way toward defraying the

The reason which induced Libanius to change his mind and to leave Athens was one of the heart rather than of the head. One of his most intimate friends, Crispinus, had been summoned home to Heraclea in Asia Minor, and he strongly urged Libanius to accompany him. After much hesitation, Libanius determined to go, but, before leaving Athens, he made a vow to return at some future time.[1]

Regretfully in those days did the student look forward to the hour when he must say good-by to his college and his college friends. The scene that was enacted on the occasion of Basil's departure was not unusual.

And now the day of departure was at hand [writes Gregory [2]] and was marked by all the usual features of such an occasion — farewell speeches, good wishes, calls for us to return, laments, embraces, and tears. For nothing is ever so hard as for those who have lived together at Athens to tear themselves from the city and from one another. The scene that was then enacted was indeed mournful and worthy of long remembrance. Friends and fellow-students, the members of our college corps, and with them many even of the teachers, standing in a ring about us, refused, whatever should happen, to let us go, entreating us, holding us back by force, and using words of persuasion. What did they not say, and what did they not do, that beings in great sorrow would be likely to say

---

cost of the boy's education (*ib.*, *ep.*, 78). For other cases of assistance given to students, see *ib.*, *ep.*, 1237, 1308. Sometimes students worked their way through college (*ib.*, i. 162, 7). The student sometimes deposited his funds with his teacher (Luc., *Symp.*, 32; Lib., *ep.*, 78).

[1] i. 21, 9; 25, 11.

[2] *Or.*, xliii. 24. Julian, the emperor, wept at leaving Athens (Jul., *Ep. ad Ath.*, 275 a), and one of Libanius's students at leaving Libanius (Lib., *ep.*, 631). *Cf.* also Isoc., *De antid.*, 88.

and do? Here I do indeed blame myself, as well as that divine and incomprehensible soul, presumptuous though it be in me to say so. He, giving the reasons which induced him to depart, showed himself superior to those who tried to detain him, and secured, though not without the exercise of physical force, consent to his departure, but I was left behind at Athens; partly (for I will tell the truth) because I was too weak to persevere in my resolution, and partly because I was betrayed by my friend, who was induced to let me go from his side, though I relaxed not my hold on him, and to yield me to the mercy of those who pulled me back.

Libanius and his friend went, not by sea, but overland, to Constantinople; on their way through northern Greece and Macedonia they entertained many of the cities through which they passed with samples of their eloquence, and were greeted with great applause. From Constantinople to Heraclea the distance was short, and in the latter place they were entertained by one of Crispinus's relatives. Here Libanius took leave of his friend, and set out to return to Constantinople.[1]

[1] Lib., i. 23, 2.

## CHAPTER XV

### AFTER COLLEGE

WHEN Libanius left his friend, Crispinus, at Heraclea, and returned to Constantinople, he was intent upon carrying out the vow which he had made to revisit Athens. Arriving at Constantinople, he went down to the Great Harbor and proceeded to look about him for a shipmaster bound for Greece. "While I was thus engaged," he says,[1] "I felt a tug at my cloak, and one of the teachers of the place — you know him, Nicocles, the Lacedæmonian — whirling me around and bringing me face to face, said: 'This is not the tack for you; you should take a different course.' 'What different course,' said I, 'when I am bound for Athens?' 'Why, bless you,' said he, 'stay with us and take charge of the young men here; there are many rich fathers in Constantinople. Give up your voyage and listen to me. Would you injure the prospects of both of us and run away from all the great good fortune in store for you? When you can stay here and be professor, why go farther to put yourself under the instruction of another? I will engage to make you within twenty-four hours 'boss' of the town and lord over forty young men, the cream of the place. Once lay the foundation and you will find riches pour in upon you in floods.'"

[1] i. 24, 5.

Libanius, however, was deaf to all entreaties, and took ship to Athens. He appears not to have stayed long at Athens this time, but, mounting a two-wheeler, he was off again at the beginning of winter. On arriving at Constantinople, he at first met with discouragement. "When I entered the market-place at Constantinople," he says,[1] "I was just in time to see a Cappadocian professor taking his chair — one, it chanced, who had been appointed by the emperor in compliance with a request of the local council. He was an excellent speaker, and had received the call, I believe, as the result of a single contest. There he stood in all his glory. I made inquiries of an old man as to the name of the sophist, his country, the manner of his coming and the terms, and was struck to the heart by the answer I received. Going to Nicocles, who had offered to introduce me to the city, I referred to our previous conversation. 'You are simple,' he said, 'very simple, if you do not know the value of striking while the iron is hot, and this after you have been at Delphi. It is useless for you to think of the promises I then made or to remind me of them; you destroyed all that when you sailed away to Athens.'" Setting up a school of his own, however, Libanius soon drew large crowds of students. "Each man urged his neighbor, and it was not many days before my corps numbered more than eighty. Some poured in to me from without the town; others, deserting their former masters, flocked to me from within; those who had been all agog for the races and the theatre changed their interests and became devotees of letters."[2]

[1] i. 27, 1.  [2] i. 29, 6.

But the intrigues of rival sophists soon drove him from the city, and he retired, first to Nicæa, then to Nicomedia. In the latter place he spent five prosperous and happy years, at the expiration of which time he was obliged, much against his will, to return to Constantinople. During the period of his second residence at Constantinople, he received an invitation to go to Athens to teach, which he recognized as a great honor, but, remembering the bitter spirit that prevailed among the sophists there, he declined to accept the call.[1] One summer he visited Antioch. Sixteen years or more had passed since he left it, to go to the University at Athens. "I saw once more," he says,[2] "the roads and gates I loved so well, I saw the temples and the colonnades, I saw the house where I had lived as a boy, now old and gray, I saw the whitened hairs of my mother, I saw my uncle, still happy in the name of father, and my own elder brother, now called grandfather, I saw my many school companions, some of whom were in office, while others were acting as advocates, I saw the old family friends, though few, alas! their number, I saw the city, prosperous and happy in its wealth of learned men."

While at Antioch, he spoke before the people, and won such applause that he was moved to sue the emperor for permission to remove from Constantinople to his home. He was successful in his application, but just as he was about to start for Antioch, he received a bitter message. "My cousin," he writes,[3] "was dead, and my uncle lay stricken with grief. Fortune spoiled her gift, for I no longer had any care to return to the

[1] i. 58, 4   [2] i. 62, 2.   [3] i. 67, 5.

city of my birth, where I should see but the tomb of her who was to have been my wife." His uncle, however, was urgent that he should come. "Accordingly I went, but not with the same heart as before." [1] At Antioch, as at Constantinople, he at first met with disappointment, but in the end prospered, and before long received an official appointment.

We have now carried Libanius through his college days and seen him established as a professor of eloquence in his native town. At this point we should properly leave him. Let us, however, before we do so, see how in his mature years he looked back on the days spent at Athens and on the life there.

Notwithstanding his love for the city, he probably never lost his repugnance to the barbarous customs which prevailed there. "No wonder," he says in a letter to a friend,[2] "if one falls in love with the Attic land, for it is a land that naturally awakens love, whether one has seen it or not. Fathers believe that their sons will bring back from Athens either learning or, at least, the reputation for learning. Now, in that I respect Acacius, I approve of his having sent his son thither; but as I love the man, I should prefer that he had kept the boy at home. Of the teachers there, some are old fogies, fit only to eat and sleep at their ease, while others seem in need of teachers themselves, who shall teach them this first of all: that cases are decided, not by arms, but by arguments. As it is, they produce for us soldiers rather

---

[1] i. 67, 13.
[2] *Ep.*, 627. *Cf. ep.*, 330 (of Athens): μέγα γὰρ εἰς τὸν λοιπὸν βίον, τὸ μὴ τὴν πόλιν ἀγνοεῖν.

than orators.[1] Many a one have I seen bearing the scars of the wounds which he received in the Lyceum fight." But for the city itself and its associations he never had anything but the fondest remembrances. "Happy is he," he says in another letter,[2] "who can run through many places in a few days, and then say: I have seen the Areopagus, I have seen the Acropolis, I have seen the shrine of those who after great anger were reconciled, when he who had supported his father was freed from guilt, I have seen her who acquired the city as the result of a contest, the nurse of Erechtheus. Such a man I count happy for what he has seen, and you I count happy in that you can enjoy all these things and many more every day." "Berytus," he says again,[3] "I confess, I love for many things, but Athens for all." Occasionally some circumstance would unexpectedly recall the old days to his mind. "When I saw Clematius," he writes,[4] "I was reminded of the old happiness of the days when I first greeted Athens — the Athens of Theseus. I recalled the first evening, the bath, the 'spread,' and the conversation that there took place." Still, those days seemed much like a dream to him. "You will see again," he once more writes,[5] "our old friend, the gentle Severus, who has enjoyed

---

[1] Elsewhere the teachers at Athens are spoken of as being inferior to their reputation. *Cf.* Themis., *or.*, xxvii; and Eunap., p. 87, of Anatolius. But Anatolius was chronically disaffected to sophists (Lib., *ep.*, 78). See also Cicero, for a much earlier time (*De orat.*, iii. 11, 43). *Cf.* p. 311.

[2] *Ep.*, 881.    [3] *Ep.*, 10.

[4] *Ep.*, 1071. Then, as is the case now, those who had been to college used fondly to talk over their student days (*ib.*, iii. 268, 1).

[5] *Ep.*, 1511. See also *ep.*, 866, 1080, 1389; and p. 291.

Athens to the full. As for me, I seem to have passed quickly through there as in a dream, and to have gone on my way, but he, knowing how much this spot surpasses all other spots, prolonged his happiness there. Hence he has reaped from the land more profit than others have. The profit which one reaps from Athens is not learning only, but friends, in whom, indeed, Severus considers no land inferior to his own."

## CHAPTER XVI

### CONCLUSION

As we review in our minds the education that has here been described, we cannot fail to be impressed by the great part which personality played in it. Even in the fifth and fourth centuries B. C., as we have elsewhere seen,[1] the personality of the wandering teacher of ethics or of science was one of the chief forces which drew young men in the direction of a life of study. The same, or similar, was the case in the later period. The young man, brought up in his distant home at Antioch, is, to be sure, attracted to Athens by his own unquenchable thirst for knowledge and the halo that hangs about the city, but faint rumors of the men there and of their personality reach even his ears. When he arrives at Athens, he does not select this or that study to pursue, but he chooses a certain *man*. Indeed, the choice could not well lie among subjects, for if the boy did not, as comparatively few did in the fourth century, wish to devote himself to philosophy, he was sure to turn to the subject of sophistry. Now the subject of sophistry was the same for all teachers and for all students, and only by the personality of the man who taught it was it made to differ in the hands of one from what it was in the hands of another. In some cases, the establishment of

[1] P. 16.

a distinguished sophist in this or that city was sufficient to divert the stream of studying youth from all other centres,[1] and a man of the personality and force of Themistius could for a time draw students even away from the study of sophistry and toward that of philosophy. Not unfrequently it happened that, as in the case of Julian, who afterward became emperor, a student went from one university town to another, drawn each time by the name of some distinguished man whom he wished to hear. The place, if we except Athens alone, was not so important as were the men.

Owing to the important part which personality played in the popularity of the teacher, there grew up between the teacher and the student that strong personal relation which was characteristic of the Greek university life. The teacher, as we have seen, was the intellectual parent of the pupil, and he acted as the pupil's guide and protector; the pupil was under moral obligation to take an interest in his teacher's welfare and to support his teacher in all ways in which this was possible.[2]

Though the custom which prevailed, whereby a stu-

[1] When Libanius was teaching at Nicomedia, students flocked thither, instead of, as before, to Athens (Lib., i. 39, 10). So Heracleides, when teaching at Smyrna, drew young men, not only from Asia, but from Europe and Africa as well (Philos., 613). Julian drew young men to Athens from all quarters of the earth by the excellence of his oratory and his nobility of character (μεγέθει φύσεως, Eunap., p. 68; nobility of character distinguished Proæresius also, ib., p. 78). These are but a few out of many cases.

[2] The students were, of course, expected to fight in their teacher's behalf (Lib., i. 16, 4 ff.). See especially the two striking orations, Lib., xxxii (ii. 266) and xxxv (ii. 307), where a plea is made to the boys for support on the ground of moral obligation.

dent was required to attach himself to a single teacher, had its pleasant feature in this close personal relation between the teacher and the student, it apparently had in another way its unfortunate side. In some cases it probably led to servile imitation of the teacher and his literary style by the student, when the student could better have put his attention upon the old masters of style.¹ If it had been the custom for the student to attach himself to more than one teacher, he would, doubtless, by a broader acquaintance with men and with methods, have been able to avoid this evil. Perhaps, however, the evil was not so great as has sometimes been supposed,² for there seems to have been a regulation at Athens, as well as at Antioch, whereby a student was allowed to attend at least the displays, and possibly the instruction, of a second teacher, not the one to whom he was regularly bound,³ and the custom of changing from one teacher to another became more common as the fourth century wore on. The cases also are not infrequent in which we are told that this or that man attended at different periods of his course the lectures of more than one sophist.⁴

¹ Lib., i. 18, 12. The Emperor Julian is said to have imitated Libanius's style (*ib.*, i. 527, 10), and he succeeded so well in this that he was held to have been a pupil of Libanius (*ib.*, i. 452, 24). Favorinus was said to have been a pupil of Dio, but his style differed as much from Dio's as did that of those who had never heard the latter (Philos., 491). *Cf. ib.*, 522, 527, 535, 576; Himer., *ec.*, x. 13. Imitation of the ancient authors also, of course, played a prominent part in the sophistical education. *Cf.* Quint., *Inst. or.*, x. 2.

² *E. g.*, by Herzberg, *Gesch. Griech.*, iii. p. 350.

³ Lib., i. 14, 4; ii. 279, 280. See p. 304.

⁴ *E. g.*, Philos., 576, 594, 605.

## CONCLUSION 343

Another important feature of the ancient Greek university life was the great weight that was put, in the instruction of the day, on the spoken word. The spoken word, indeed, as we have already elsewhere seen,[1] was a matter of racial instinct, and the whole sophistical education was based on the communication of ideas by speech. The student did not so much learn from books as he did from the teacher's mouth, or at least the lessons that he obtained from books were expounded and enforced by oral instruction. This fact is emphasized by the word that was used to express the relation of student to teacher: 'to be the pupil of' was regularly ἀκροᾶσθαι, 'to hear.' The ancient student did not 'read' sophistry under such and such a teacher, nor did he 'take a course under' this or that professor, but he 'heard' such and such a sophist. It was the influence of the living voice and the contact of mind with mind on which stress was laid. This is seen most notably in the grand displays of the sophists themselves. In these much of the effect produced was doubtless due to the circumstances of the moment and arose from the personality and manner of the sophist, reinforced by the sympathetic encouragement of the audience, rather than to any more enduring qualities of thought and style.[2]

Still, it may be doubted whether the living voice was considered quite so potent a force in instruction in the centuries after Christ as it had been in the time of Socrates. As we have seen, memory played an im-

[1] Pp. 5, 25.
[2] It was recognized by the ancients themselves that extempore speech did not conduce to thorough work (Syn., *Dion*, 12; Philos., 583, 607; Luc., *Rhet. præc.*, 20).

portant part in the sophistical training, and the cultivation of the memory resulted in, if it was not necessitated by, the accumulation of stores of facts in the minds of the students. Facts, as well as a thorough knowledge of the ancient authors, the student was obliged to have. Thus it happened that *polymathia* (πολυμαθία), much-learning, was considered at this time a valuable part of a man's education, and the πολυμαθής, the man of many facts, was looked up to and admired.[1] This attitude toward education was quite opposed to that of an earlier time. In the fifth century B. C. an harmonious development of the parts of man — moral, mental, and physical — and a rational adjustment of these toward the outer world were considered of more importance than much knowledge.

The custom of the present day is rather to decry the ancient sophistical training. Its weaknesses are so apparent, and its insufficiency, as judged by modern standards, is felt to be so great, that it is easy to denounce the whole system as artificial and barren. And yet, perhaps, the better way is to see what there really was in this education and what it professed to do in the world as it was at that time. Artificial and barren, in a certain sense, the education was. By laying too great stress on the form in which a thing was said, we may

[1] Longinus is called by Eunapius (p. 7) "a living library and a walking museum" (βιβλιοθήκη τις ἦν ἔμψυχος καὶ περιπατοῦν μουσεῖον). *Cf.* Philostratus (618), of Hippodromus: πλεῖστα μὲν ἐξέμαθεν Ἑλλήνων τῶν γε μετὰ τὸν Καππαδόκην Ἀλέξανδρον μνήμην εὐτυχησάντων, πλεῖστα δὲ ἀνέγνω μετά γε Ἀμμώνιον τὸν ἀπὸ τοῦ Περιπάτου, ἐκείνου γὰρ πολυγραμματώτερον ἄνδρα οὔπω ἔγνων. Also of Polemo (541). πολυμαθής and πολυμαθία are common expressions in this period (*e. g., ib.*, 627; Porphyr., *Vit. Plotin.*, 20).

admit, it led to all manner of excesses and extravagances in the matter of style; and this, too, we cannot deny: it did not contain within itself the possibilities of great speculative or scientific truths. If we look, however, to the grand displays of the sophists themselves, we can say — as has been said by others [1]—that we no longer have the means of judging of these aright. Many things in them are lost to us to-day, and of others we have but an imperfect understanding and appreciation. The play of accent and rhythm, the delicate adjustment of sound and sense in the selection and arrangement of words, the harmony of form, we try to understand, but do so only imperfectly. The orator, his personality, the rise and fall of his voice, the variety and appropriateness of his gestures — these we can only imagine. Even the bare words which were spoken are in most cases unknown to us.

But — and this is a thing that is more often lost sight of — however the case may be with these displays, it does not seem that it is from these alone, or from these primarily, that the sophistical education is to be judged. They were admittedly the sublimation of the sophist's art. The great university of to-day is judged, not so much by the comparatively small number of specialists whom it fits to be teachers, as by the great body of students whom it sends out into the world. Greek sophistry did not profess to teach men scientific knowledge or abstract theories — the performance of that task was left to the specialists and to the various schools of philosophy, as long as these existed — but it did profess to

[1] *E. g.*, by Rohde, *Gr. Rom.*, p. 334.

prepare men for the active duties of citizenship — the citizenship of those days — and to provide them with a broad and liberal culture, and this task it performed on the whole satisfactorily and effectively for several hundred years. The fact should be emphasized that rhetoric meant in those days more than what we understand by the term. It was the common heritage of the Greek-speaking peoples and that which distinguished them from barbarians.[1] In this sense it meant education, culture, humanism, civilization even. It provided a literary training on classic lines, and at the same time developed the mental and moral parts of the boy. The sciences in their elements, it should be remembered, the boy had, if he had been properly brought up, studied before he entered the sophist's school, and, if he studied them further than that and to the neglect of sophistry, he was in danger of receiving a purely technical education. Of the product of the schools it is unjust to judge by the school exercises that we possess. With more reason do we turn to the orations of the few sophists of whom we have literary remains, and here, if we have Himerius with his mincing, dainty style and meagre thought, we have also Libanius, direct, forceful, sincere, and often truly eloquent.

[1] See p. 4. *Cf.* Isoc., *Paneg.*, 50: (ἡ πόλις ἡμῶν) τὸ τῶν Ἑλλήνων ὄνομα πεποίηκε μηκέτι τοῦ γένους ἀλλὰ τῆς διανοίας δοκεῖν εἶναι, καὶ μᾶλλον Ἕλληνας καλεῖσθαι τοὺς τῆς παιδεύσεως τῆς ἡμετέρας ἢ τοὺς τῆς κοινῆς φύσεως μετέχοντας· Lib., *ep.*, 372: τούτους (*i. e.*, λόγους) ἂν σβέσῃ τις, εἰς ἴσον ἐρχόμεθα τοῖς βαρβάροις. λόγοι (rhetoric) and παιδεία or παίδευσις are often identified; *e. g.*, Lib., i. 365, 9: Ἑλληνικῇ παιδείᾳ καὶ λόγοις· *ib.*, i. 452, 20: ἄνδρες ἐν παιδεύσει καὶ λόγοις τεθραμμένοι. *Cf. ib.*, i. 502, 8: παίδευσιν καλεῖτε τὰ ἔπη, and the eulogy of letters, *ib.*, ii. 303. It was rhetoric that made Lucian a Greek (Luc., *Bis accus.*, 30).

## CONCLUSION

It has been made matter of reproach to the ancient education of the early Christian period that it dealt so extensively with mythology and the life of a past age. Such a reproach has justification. And, yet, it should be remembered that this mythology and this life of a past age were of the nature of a *corpus vile;* they formed a traditional body of material, of which the sophist made use in his class-room instruction, and which the sophist and the student moulded and kneaded into various forms to suit their purposes. The principles which were involved in these processes were later applied to the conditions of daily life. As Choricius says,[1] "all kinds of suits that occur in real life are imitated in the fictitious cases." What matter, one may say, whether the principles were illustrated by Demosthenes and Demades or by John Doe and Richard Roe? Notwithstanding that even in ancient times there were some who asserted that the student, on emerging from the sophist's school, was ill-prepared for the problems of real life — a complaint that was doubtless in many cases justified — it is apparent that on the whole, the sophistical education did provide a satisfactory preparation for the professional and the official life of those times. No system of education is likely to go unquestioned in any age, and complaints similar to that mentioned above are common even to-day.

We may enumerate, then, the means by which sophistry in ancient times sought to accomplish its aim of preparing men for the duties and successes of life and of giving them a broad and liberal culture.

[1] See p. 240, above.

First, by giving the student a thorough grounding in the literature of the Greek people, the only literature which, in that part of the world and at that time, was thought to have any value. The student who went through his course in 'grammar' and sophistry with faithful adherence to duty should have been familiar with the best Greek authors, in a way to be able to quote them and to feel them a part of himself. They permeated his life and thought. His knowledge of them was a more or less critical knowledge, for he had been required in the schools to judge and discuss them from many points of view.

Secondly, by giving the student a mass of incidental information on many subjects. He acquired, in the course of his 'grammatical' and rhetorical studies, a good knowledge of Greek antiquities — of the laws, the customs, the institutions, of former times — and he became steeped in the spirit of the Greek religion and mythology. The history of the Greek people from the time of Solon to that of Alexander he learned thoroughly in the sophist's school, while Greek literary history he obtained from the 'grammarian.'

Thirdly, by training the student to write and to speak the Greek language correctly and effectively, and to arrange his material in the best way for the purpose in hand. Much practice and study of the best models were the means employed to this end.

Fourthly, by teaching the student to think, and to exercise his judgment and imagination. The practice of arguing cases and of taking sides for and against was helpful in the training of his reason and judgment, while the other practice of impersonation could not but tend to develop his imagination.

Fifthly, by cultivating readiness of thought and speech.

And, sixthly, by training the ethical side of man. We remember that under Socrates rhetoric was regarded as having a moral force; and Aristeides, the second-century sophist, says: "There being four parts of moral excellence"— prudence, temperance, justice, and fortitude (φρόνησις, σωφροσύνη, δικαιοσύνη, ἀνδρεία[1]) — "all these have been produced by rhetoric, and what gymnastic and the physician's art are in the case of the body, that rhetoric is shown to be in the case of the soul and matters of state." This view that there was an ethical value in the study of letters is expressed in one form or another in many authors.[2] The man of literary train-

[1] ii. p. 72. The cardinal virtues. *Cf.* Menander, Speng., *Rh. Gr.*, iii. p. 361; also Syn., *Dion*, 8, and Themis., 146 d.

[2] *E. g.*, Lib., *ep.*, 1143: τὰ γὰρ ἐκ πεπαιδευμένης ψυχῆς οὐκ ἔνι μὴ κάλλους μετέχειν· Theon, *Progym.*, 1, p. 148 (Speng., *Rh. Gr.*, ii. 60): ἡ διὰ τῆς χρείας γυμνασία οὐ μόνον τινὰ δύναμιν λόγων ἐργάζεται, ἀλλὰ καὶ χρηστόν τι ἦθος. According to Aristeides, rhetoric is connected with all the virtues: it is begotten of prudence, upholds justice, is supported by temperance and fortitude (ii. p. 72; *cf.* pp. 58, 64–66, 128, 132). It holds together and is the ornament of communities (p. 136). It aims at what is best, and is the instructor of the people (pp. 56, 58). The orator will himself be a good man. In so far as he does or advises wrong, he is an imperfect orator (pp. 76, 77, 80, 81, 154). His goodness, however, is apparently primarily a matter of policy (p. 83). Whether Aristeides understands that there is a sort of reflex action produced by rhetoric, such that the orator, simply by practising his profession, is himself benefited morally, is less clear. The view of Aristeides is that of Quintilian, who defines the orator as *a good man skilled in speaking* (*Inst. or.*, xii. 1; *cf. præfat.*, 9, and ii. 15, 1). This was also Marcus Cato's definition (see, further, Seneca, *Contr.*, i. *præfat.*, 9; Cic., *De orat.*, ii. 20, 85; and *ib.*, De

ing could by his wise guidance preserve the state, and he possessed within himself the means for his own salvation.

The ideal of the education of these centuries is stated in the words of Julian, the emperor, and has already

*invent.*, i. 3, 4). Goodness, with Quintilian, is a part of the intent of the word *orator*. In so far as the orator is not a good man, he is no orator. The orator gets his morality through study (xii. 2, 1). The view of Aristeides and Quintilian is, of course, far in advance of the prevailing view of the fifth century B. C., when oratory was commonly held to be fully as often on the side of wrong as on the side of right (for Plato's view, however, see the *Gorgias* and the *Phædrus*, and Quint., *Inst. or.*, ii. 15, 28 *ff.*), and, apparently, somewhat in advance of the view of Isocrates. Isocrates enumerates the benefits which oratory has conferred on mankind: it has civilized men and enabled them to live in communities, it has established laws about the good and the bad, the just and the unjust, etc. (*De antid.*, 253-257). But this is all the part of the (morally) good oratory; there might also, apparently, be a (morally) bad oratory. Isocrates seems not to have arrived at the point of declaring that the bad orator is no orator, though this seems almost to be implied by his point of view. Thus, he says that "*true* and *right* and *just* speech is the reflection of a good and faithful soul" (255), but it is only the true and right and just speech that has any worth for him. Isocrates's orator is a good man chiefly as a matter of policy, for it is seen that words supported by character carry more weight than words alone (285); but still the civilizing effects of the study and practice of oratory on the orator's character are recognized (254). Aristotle's view is about that of Isocrates, except that Aristotle affirms that there may be bad orators as well as good orators. With him, the orator is considered with reference to his art, not with reference to his moral principle (*Rhet.*, i. 1, 14). Rhetoric is a good which may be misused (i. 1, 13). Its ends, however, are the expedient, justice, and honor (i. 3, 5). In Theon the ethical effect is more definitely stated: "it produces not only command over words, but a kind of good moral disposition" (see above). This disposition may be supposed to be produced in two ways: by the general humanizing effect of the study of literature, and by the habit engendered in the orator by constant dealing with noble and honorable themes and with matters involving questions of justice, tem-

## CONCLUSION

been given above.¹ "Right education I consider to be, not the gracefulness that resides in words and on the tongue, but a healthy disposition of an intelligent mind, and true opinions about the good and the bad, the noble and the base." This ideal, however, received its embodiment in the man who had been trained, morally, intellectually, and æsthetically, to use his powers in the interest of the state. Such a man was the orator. The orator was not the man of fluent tongue and graceful speech solely; nor was he the man of scientific attainments or technical knowledge; he was the man of broad learning and general culture, trained to see the distinctions of right and wrong, and to act with reference to them in the service of his πόλις, or native city. The teaching of the best educators of the day, men like Libanius and Themistius, was in full accord with the profession of Julian, just quoted.

These, then, are some of the things that sophistry in ancient times professed to do. Not always did it carry out its professions, and it led to excesses and abuses which were recognized, even in those days, by such men

---

perance, and the like. With Himerius, λόγος is the handmaid of ἀρετή and carries out her behests (ec., xvi. 2). Libanius constantly recognizes the beneficial effect of education on character (e. g., ep., 192, 1048), and the sophists in general realized that they were the guardians and educators of the morals, no less than of the intellect, of their students; Herodes Atticus was reproved by another sophist for neglecting (as was charged) the conduct of his pupils (Philos., 579), while Julian says (ep., 42) that the teaching of morals was a part of the sophist's profession. From the beginning of the Attic education to the close of this Hellenistic education the moral development of the student always played a leading part.

¹ P. 125, n. 2. See Jul., ep., 42, 422 A.

as Lucian and Themistius. Both Lucian and Themistius, however, were sophist-bred, and to both was opened up the rich inheritance of the race — the storehouse of ancient thought — in the 'grammarian's' and the sophist's school.

# INDEX

Acacius, sophist, his salary, 175 n.; held an imperial chair, 177; trick played on him by Libanius, 186 n.; left Antioch in 361, 274 n.; sometimes taught till night, 279.

Academic school, foundation of, 27; in first three centuries A. D., 101, 102; after Diocletian, 105, 107, 171, 199.

ᾄδειν, 234.

Adrian of Tyre, sophist, receives appointment, 91; as he went to and returned from his lectures, 134; took part in sports of his students, 187; his eloquence, 236; eighteen when he went to study at Athens, 293 n.; affection of his students for, 309.

Ærarium, 172.

Æschines, transplants the study of rhetoric to Rhodes, 35; on educational legislation, 59, 60.

Agathias, trans. from, on emigration of Neo-Platonic philosophers, 127, 128.

ἀγών, 231 n.

ἀκοντιτσής, 36.

ἀκροᾶσθαι, 220 n., 343.

ἀκρόασις, 220 n.

'Ακρωμίτης, 297, 305.

Alaric, 121.

Albinus, Lucius Postumius, 52.

ἀλειτουργησία, 164 n.

Alexander, sophist, 259-261.

Alexander of Aphrodisias, 102 n., 138.

Alexander the Great, events following his death, 41, 42; one result of his death, 44; his regard for Athens, 45, 46.

Alexander Severus, 99.

Alexandria, foundation of, 48; museum and libraries at, 49; seat of scientific learning and philosophy in the second century A. D., 95; attitude of Caracalla toward the Peripatetic philosophers at, 99; in the fourth century A. D., 115, 116, 124; in the third century A. D., 124; in the fifth century A. D., 124; Neo-Platonism at, 125.

Alexandrian period. See Macedonian period.

ἅμιλλα, 211 n., 265 n.

Ammonius Saccas, 125.

ἀμοιβαί, 179 n.

ἀνασκευή, 209.

Anatolius, 142 n., 226 n., 331 n.

Ancyra, 116 n., 124.

Annona, 178.

Antigonids, 42.

Antioch, foundation of, 50, 284; library and museum at, 50; in the second and third centuries A. D., 95; in the fourth century A. D., 115, 116; in the fifth century A. D., 124; teachers at, by whom appointed, 140; number of teachers at, 144-146; salaries of professors at, by whom paid, 172, 173, 176,

## INDEX

177; condition of the sophists at, in the fourth century A. D., 191-194; displays at, no fee charged for, 220; Libanius's first display at, 261, 262; school buildings at, 267; the School of, 270-278; teaching at, generally confined to the morning, 278; an important city of the East, 283, 284; situation of, 284; description of, 284-286; number of its inhabitants, 286; student life at, 319-327; Libanius settles at, 337.

Antiochus IV, 46, 47.
Antiochus the Great, 45, 50.
Antiochus Grypos, 47.
Antiochus XIII, 50.
Antoninus Pius, gives honors and salaries to philosophers and rhetoricians, 86-91.
Apamea, 140 n., 278.
Aphthonius, 209.
Apollonius of Rhodes, 49.
*Apostasis*, 326 n.
Applause, methods of, 252.
Appointment to professorial chairs, methods of, 134-142.
Areopagus, Court of the, 63, 66.
Aristarchus, 49.
Aristeides, sophist, compared to Demosthenes, 95; writings of, 95; not an extempore speaker, 220 n., 224; his audiences, 220 n., 250 n.; trans. from, on the inspiration of the sophists and the enthusiasm of the audiences at displays, 249, 250; on the relation of rhetoric and moral excellence, 349.
Aristippus, 29.
Aristophanes, the *Clouds* cited, 17.
Aristophanes of Byzantium, 49.
Aristotle, on the subjects of education, 22; on good and bad oratory, 349 n.

Arithmetic, 24, 25, 197.
Arnim, H. v., his account of the course of the struggle between the rhetorical and the philosophical education, 79 n.
Asia Minor, condition of, in first century A. D., 69, 77, 78.
Asiatic oratory, 73 n., 76 n.
Assistant teachers, 272.
Astronomy, 25, 96.
*Ateleia*, 164.
Athenæum, established by Hadrian, 85; the name, how used, 152 n.; the centre of university life at Rome, 267.
Athens, education at, in the fifth and fourth centuries B. C., 10-40; raised to a place apart in the imaginations of men, 44, 48; attitude of Macedonian princes and others toward, in Macedonian period, 44-48; in the third century B. C., 51; in the second century B. C., 53; in the first century B. C., 53-57; attitude of the state toward education in, in pre-Christian times, 58-63, 66; in the time of Domitian, 82; connection of Hadrian with, 83-86; connection of Herodes Atticus with, 86; University of, established by Antoninus Pius and Marcus Aurelius, 86-94; University of, from Marcus Aurelius to Constantine, 97-108; in the fourth and fifth centuries A. D., 122-124; in the second century A. D., 130-134; University of, relation of the proconsul of Greece to, 139, 140; number of teachers at, 142, 143; contest for the headship of the school at, 153-158; visit of Hermogenes to, 195; dis-

## INDEX 355

plays at, uncertain whether fees were charged for, 220; pictures of academic life at, in the second century A. D., 257–261; student life at, 296–319, 328–330; perhaps fell behind its reputation, 311, 337, 338; regrets of students at leaving, 331–333; Libanius's feeling for, 337–339.
Athletics, 266, 319.
Audiences at displays, character of, 249–253.
*Auditorium, auditorium Capitoli,* 152 *n.*
Augustus, his attitude toward teachers, 79 *n.*
Aurelian, emperor, 106, 124.
Aurelius, Marcus, establishes the University of Athens, 91–94.
Autun, University of, 141 *n.,* 172.
*Axiochus,* trans. from, 19 *n.*

*Bacchæ,* the, of Euripides, 47.
Bactria, 47.
Ball-playing, 266, 319.
Banquets, 28, 133.
Basil the Great, held that there was no antagonism between pagan learning and Christianity, 110, 111; Gregory's account of his education, 196, 197, 291; trans. of a letter to Libanius, 251; age as a student, 292; escaped hazing, 305; and Gregory, friendship of, 329; departure from Athens, 332, 333.
Baths, public, classes held in, 267 *n.*
Battles of student corps, 312–318, 320.
Berytus, celebrated for its law school, 95, 115, 116, 124; age of students at, 293; course at, length of, 331 *n.*
Board of electors, 135–138.
βουλευτήριον at Antioch, 267.

Cæsar, Julius, his attitude toward teachers, 79 *n.*
Cæsarea in Cappadocia, 124.
Cæsarea in Palestine, 124, 140 *n.,* 146, 173.
Callimachus, 49.
Capitol, the, at Constantinople, 149, 150, 266, 267 *n.*
*Capitolium,* the word, 152 *n.*
Caracalla, 99, 168.
Cassander, 46.
Catana, 63, 64.
Cato, his ideal of the orator, 349 *n.*
Centumalus, Gnæus Fulvius, 52.
Chairs, of eloquence, endowed at Rome, 81; of rhetoric, 'grammar,' and philosophy, established at Athens and elsewhere, 87, 88, 91, 92; the political chair at Athens, 87 *n.,* 94 *n.;* the sophists' chair at Athens, 94 *n.,* 142 *n.,* 153; the educational chair at Athens, 94 *n.,* 142 *n.,* 220 *n.;* the chair at Rome, 94 *n.;* other references to, 142 *n.;* methods of appointment to, in the second and third centuries, 134–138; methods of appointment to, after Diocletian, 138–142.
Chalcis in Syria, 116 *n.,* 172.
Charondas, 63, 64.
χορηγός, 296.
Choricius, professor at Gaza, 124; trans. from, on Procopius, 210, 211; trans. from, introductions to themes, 239–242.
χορός, 270, 274, 296.
Christianity, ethical teaching of philosophical schools taken up by, 102; conflict of, with the ancient religion and education, 109–129.
Chrysanthius, philosopher, 237, 248 *n.*

## INDEX

Cicero, trans. from, on Athens, 55; on gesticulation, 230, 231.
Claqueurs, 253.
Class, words for, 296 n.
Class dinners, 319.
Classes, size of, 185–187, 272 n.; where they were held, 266–269.
Class-room methods, 211 n.
Claudius, emperor, 80.
Claudius Gothicus, emperor, 106.
Comedy, studied in the schools in second century B. C., 22.
Commodus, 98, 165.
Constantine the Great, 106, 108.
Constantinople, founded by Constantine, 108; celebrated for its schools of law and philosophy, 115, 116, 126; University of, put on a new basis by Theodosius II, 124, 148–151; number of teachers at, 143–146; the Capitol the University building at, 149, 150, 152 n., 266, 267 n.; Libanius's experiences at, 160 n., 333, 334; Libanius's salary at, 173–177; Themistius professor at, 178; uncertain whether fees could be taken by professors at, 179; Themistius the head of the School of, 278.
Constantius, emperor, his attitude toward the ancient education, 112, 113, 116 n.
Constantius Chlorus, 172.
'Construction,' 204, 209, 210.
Contests of sophists, 218, 256, 257.
*Controversiæ*, 224 n.
Corinth, destruction of, 53; seat of the proconsul of Achaia, 139, 314.
Corps, student, 296–304, 312–318.
Cos, 50.

Councils, connection of rhetoric and, 78 n., 119; their power of appointing and assigning salaries to professors, 134 n., 139–141, 172–177. *See* Municipalities.
Cratippus, 63.
Crete, constitution of, 63.
Cynicism, 26 n.. 100 n.
Cyzicus, 116 n., 140 n.

Damianus, sophist, 181, 182.
Dancing, 228, 229.
Daphne, grove near Antioch, 286.
Daphne-Apollo legend, briefs of, 209, 210.
Defection of students, 325, 326.
Deliberative oratory, 75, 76.
Delivery of the sophists, 233–237.
Delphi, inscription at, about Attalus, 65; oracle sent to Julian from, 115.
Demetrius of Phalerum, 45, 49.
Demetrius Poliorcetes, 45, 46.
Demonax, philosopher, 253 n.
δημόσιον, 173 n.
Denarius, the, 172 n., 184, 185.
'Description,' the, 7, 204, 208.
Dexippus, schoolman and historian, 105.
διάδοχοι of the philosophical schools, 102.
διάλεξις, 220 n., 223.
δικανικά, 220 n., 224 n.
Dio Cassius, trans. from, on the establishment of the University of Athens, 93.
Dio Chrysostom, 82, 83, 95.
Diocletian, his accession, 106; and Maximian, edicts, 166, 167; his maximum scale of prices, 184, 185.
Diodorus Siculus, trans. from, 6 n.
Diogeneion, the, 38, 133.
Dionysius, sophist, 215, 256.
Dionysius of Halicarnassus, trans. from, 21 n.

# INDEX

Diophantus, sophist, competes for chair of rhetoric, 154, 298; Libanius attaches himself to, 298, 304 n., 311; hounded from Athens, 313 n.
Displays, held by sophists of the first century A. D., 72 n.; of judicial and deliberative themes, introduced into the sophistical schools, 74, 75, 220 n.; given by students, 211 n.; time of year when given, 218; generally public, 219; generally free, 220; an integral part of the sophist's course, 221, 222; introduced by short speech, 223; the main speech, of various kinds, 223, 224; speech prepared or given extempore, 224, 225; theme, how selected, 225, 226; power of sophists to grasp the nature of a theme, 226, 227; samples of themes, 227, 228; dramatic character of, 228–230; action of the sophist in, 230–232; voice, language, and delivery of the sophist in, 233–237, 245, 246; samples of introductions, and passages from themes, 238–245; descriptions of the manner of certain sophists in, 246–248; enthusiasm at, 248–253; involved strain, 249 n.; people flocked to hear, 250, 251; examples of, 255–262; in what buildings held, 267 n.; we cannot judge of, aright, 345.
*Dispositio*, 211.
Doctorate, 303 n.
Domitian, 82.
Domnio, lawyer, 275.
Dramatic character of displays, 228–230.
Drawing, 22.
Drinking-bouts, 319.
δύναμις, 271 n.

Educated man, Isocrates's ideal of, 33 n.
Education, Greek, was continuous, 9; at Athens in the fifth and fourth centuries B. C., 10–40; and the state, 58–67; cost of, 183, 331; the sophistical, 195–217; the ideal of the sophistical, 350, 351.
ἐγκύκλια παιδεύματα, μαθήματα, 79 n., 198 n.
ἐγκύκλιος παιδεία, 198 n.
Elementary instruction at Athens, 10–13, 18–23.
*Elocutio*, 211.
Elusa, 172.
Encomia, 264 n.
Encyclopædias, 7.
Enthusiasm at displays, 248–253.
ἐπ' ἄλλῳ, 211 n.
ἐπαγγελία, ἐπάγγελμα, 271 n.
ἐπαγγέλλεσθαι, 271 n.
ἐπαναγνῶναι, 211 n.
Ephebi, College of the, 26, 35–40.
Ephesus, 77 n., 95.
Epicurean school, foundation of, 29; and Hadrian, 84, 85.
Epicurus, founds the Epicurean school, 29; apparently the first man to use the word *sophist* in a purely technical sense, 75 n.
Epideictic, oratory, taught by Isocrates, 32, 71; oratory, given a wider significance by the introduction of judicial and deliberative themes, 74, 75, 220 n.; speeches, character of, 263, 264.
ἐπιδείξεις. See Displays.
ἔφηβος, 35.
Epiphanius, sophist, 154, 298, 304 n.
Epistle, the imaginary, 7.
Epistle-writing, 211 n.
Epitaph, trans. of, 56.
Eratosthenes, 49.

Eudæmon, 172, 274.
Eumenius, appointed professor at Autun by the emperor, 141 n.; offers salary for restoration of university building, 163 n.; his salary, 172.
Eunapius, biographer, 107; discussion of passage in, 142 n.; trans. from, on contest for chair at Athens, 153–158; of himself, at sixteen, 214; on Libanius's declamations, 203; on characteristics of Libanius, 205, 206; trans. from, on Eustathius and Chrysanthius, 237; trans. from, on Proæresius, 247; taught in the morning, took lessons in the afternoon, 279, 293 n.; important source of information, 283 n.; trans. from, on Nymphidianus, 291 n.; age at which he went to Athens to study, 293 n.; escaped full initiatory rites, 305, 306; trans. from, account of his arrival at Athens, 306, 307; his description of the sophist Julian's house, 308, 309; his description of Libanius's method of study, 311, 312; trans. from, the case of Apsines and Julian, 316–318; remained five years at college, 331.
Euphorion of Chalcis, 50.
Eusebius, sophist, 170.
Eustathius, 237.
Examinations, for the Ephebic College, 38; for philosophical and sophistical chairs, 135, 147 n., 153; for a sophist's class, 297 n.
Excusatio, 164 n.
Expenses of students, 331.
Extempore speaking, 224–227, 343.

'Fable,' method of treatment of, 207–210.

Farewell speeches, 238, 263, 266.
Fees, taken in the philosophical schools, 29; of Isocrates, 32; of the sophists, 179–184, 187–189.
Fielding, Henry, *Tom Jones* quoted, 171 n.
Fiscus, the, 172.
Flamininus, Titus Quinctius, 45, 52.
Friendships made at college, 329, 330.

Gaza, 112 n., 124, 278.
Gellius, Aulus, on student life at Athens, 132, 133.
Geography, 25, 96, 197.
Geometry, 24, 197.
Gesticulation of the sophists, 230–232.
Gorgias, 6 n.
Goths, the, 104, 121.
Gown, academic, 301–303.
Grades in education, 18, 19, 64.
Graduate professional schools, 120 n.
Grammar, meaning of the word, as used by the Alexandrians, 20; the study of, promoted by the fifth-century sophists, 20, 21; method of learning, in the time of Dionysius of Halicarnassus, 21 n.; Greek, foundations of syntax laid, 96.
'Grammar,' chairs of, 88, 143–145; character of the course in, 23, 24, 201, 202.
'Grammarians,' their course of study, 23, 24, 201, 202; immunities of, 81, 87–90, 165–170; officially appointed, 88, 134 n., 143–145; honored with title, 150; salaries of, 172, 178; in Libanius's school, 271; at Antioch, 275.
γραμματιστής, 11, 18, 21, 23, 24, 25.

INDEX 359

Greece, ancient, extent of, 1, 2; claimed as an appanage by Macedonian kings, 42; raised to a place apart in the imaginations of men, 44, 48; attitude of Macedonian princes and others toward, in Macedonian period, 44-48; in the third century B.C., 51, 52; in the second century B.C., 53; in the first century B.C., 53-57; attitude of the state toward education in, in pre-Christian times, 58-67; condition of, in the first century B.C., 68-70; attitude of the emperors toward, 80-94, 97-99; plundered by the Heruli, 105; overrun by the Goths, 121; decrease of the political and commercial importance of, 130.

Greek language, bond of union between diverse races, 3, 4.

Greek literature, study of, in Alexandrian times, 48; of the first century A.D., 68 n.

Greeks, a people of speakers, 5, 343; sense of proportion highly developed in, 5; intolerant at times, but intellectually curious, 17.

Gregory Nazianzene, held that there was no real antagonism between pagan learning and Christian belief, 110, 111; his account of Basil's education, 196, 197, 291; age as a student, 292; trans. from, on the hazing of students, 299-301; and Basil, friendship of, 329; remained from ten to twelve years at college, 331; trans. from, description of Basil's departure from Athens, 332, 333.

Gymnastic, 10.

Hadrian, his Hellenism, 83; his relation to Greece, 83, 84; and the Epicurean school, 84, 85; establishes the Athenæum at Rome, 85.

Hand-books, 213, 227.

Harpocration, sophist, 274.

Hazing, 296-307.

Hellenism, meaning of, 2; in what it consisted, 43, 44.

Hephæstion and Proæresius, friendship of, 154, 329, 330.

Heracleides, sophist, 309, 310, 312, 341 n.

Hermogenes, proconsul of Achaia, 195, 196.

Hermogenes of Tarsus, rhetorician, 95, 248 n.

Herodes Atticus, his attitude toward Athens, 86; put at the head of the philosophical department at Athens, 93, 134; entertains students, 133; death of, 135; said to have held a chair at Athens, 142 n.; and Scopelian, 180, 181; and Philager, 226; his theme of the Athenians in Sicily, 243; age at death, 248 n.; and Polemo, 255; and Alexander, 259-261.

Heruli, the, overrun Greece, 104.

'Higher learning,' 14.

Himerius, important sophist at Athens in the fourth century, 107; on the life and education of Hermogenes, 195, 196; trans. from, introduction to a theme, 238, 239; age at death, 248 n.; his frankness to his audiences, 254; his introductory addresses, 265, 266; severely handled by his students, 313, 314; opposed to corporal punishment, 324 n.; his view of the relation of oratory and virtue, 349 n.

## 360  INDEX

Hippodromus, sophist, 257–259.
Holidays, 218 n., 279–281.
Horace, quoted, 69, 131.
Hypatia, 125.

Iamblichus, 125.
Ideal of education, Isocrates's, 33 n., 349 n.; sophistical, 350, 351.
Imitation, 342.
*Immunitas*, 164 n.
Immunities, granted by Vespasian, 81, 164, 165; granted by Antoninus Pius, 86–91; further grants of, 98, 165; fell into abeyance in second half of the third century, 105; restored in the fourth century, 106, 107; of philosophers, 166, 167; basis on which they were granted, 167–169; attempts to deprive teachers of, 169, 170.
Impersonation, 217, 224, 228, 229.
Impressing of students, 299, 300.
Initiation of students, 296–307.
Inspiration of the sophists, 248, 249.
*Inventio*, 211.
Isaeus, sophist, 225 n., 248 n.
Isocrates, his view of music, grammar, etc., 22 n., 33; and his school, 31–35, 40; length of his course, 32, 331 n.; his fees, 32, 183 n.; his ideal of the educated man, 33 n., 349 n.; said to have held a chair at Athens, 142 n.
Isthmian games, 52, 53.

John Chrysostom, 121, 198, 277.
Jovian, emperor, 116 n.
Judicial oratory, 75, 76.
Julia Domna, 98, 168.
Julian, emperor, trans. from, letter on the pagan teaching, 110 n.; accession of, 114; death of, 114; oracle sent to, from Delphi, 115; his education, 198, 199; and Libanius, 219 n.; his age as a student, 292.
Julian, sophist, 107; contest for chair at his death, 153; drew men from all quarters, 163 n., 341 n.; Eunapius's description of his house, 308, 309; the case with Apsines, 316–318.
Justinian, emperor, rescript of, suppressing schools of philosophy, 126; put an end to hazing at Constantinople and Berytus, 313 n.

κατασκευή, 209.
Κλεψύδριον, the, 211 n.
κορυφαῖος, 270, 296.
κοσμητής, 37.
κριτικός, 23.

Lagidæ, the, 42.
λαλιά, 223 n.
Language of the sophists, 233–237.
Latin, increase of, at the expense of Greek, 120, 121, 191; chairs of, 143, 145, 146, 149; teachers of, at Antioch, 272.
Law, teachers of, their privileges, 90 n.; schools of, at Constantinople and Berytus, 116, 124, 126, 149; usurped the place of Greek, 119–121, 191; students of, took preliminary course in sophistry, 120 n.; chairs of, in various cities, 145, 146; teacher of, honored with title, 150.
Lecture-rooms, 267 n.
Libanius, distinguished sophist, 107; trans. from, on Constantinople, 108; his attitude toward the Christian religion, 112–118; trans.

from, on Constantius, 112, 113; feelings of, at the accession and the death of Julian, 114, 115; trans. from, on the monks and clergy, 117, 118; trans. from, on the decline of sophistry, 119–121; his remark that he would wish to bequeath his school to John Chrysostom, 121; receives an appointment at Athens, 139 *n.*, 142 *n.*; called to Athens, 140 *n.*; to Egypt, 140 *n.*; to Nicomedia, 140 *n.*; how he was transferred from Constantinople to Antioch, 141, 142; trans. from, on acts of disgruntled sophists, 158, 159; his account of what happened after his return to teaching after a sickness, 159, 160; his experiences at Constantinople, 160 *n.*; his experience in the matter of his salary when he removed to Antioch, 175–177; when he first received a salary at Antioch, 176, 177, 267 *n.*; his fees, 183 *n.*, 187, 188; size of his classes, 185, 186; trans. from, on poor condition of teachers at Antioch, 191, 192; trans. from, on the condition of the four rhetors, 192–194; showed ignorance of technical details in his declamations, 203; Eunapius's description of characteristics of, 205, 206; trans. from, introduction to a theme, 217; age at death, 248 *n.*; trans. from, his first display at Antioch, 261, 262; buildings in which he taught at Antioch, 267–269, 276 *n.*; his school, 270–273; head of the School of Antioch, 275–278; sometimes taught the whole day, 279; his works rich in information on many subjects, 283; birthplace, date of birth, and date of death, 283; his description of Antioch, 285, 286; boyhood of, at Antioch, 287–292; on Athens, 291 *n.*, 337–339; departs for Athens, 292–295; his age as a student, 292; arrival at Athens, 303, 304; undergoes the initiatory rites, 305; his opinion of his teachers, 310; devotes himself to the study of the ancients, 311; Eunapius's description of his method of study, 311, 312; takes no part in the student battles, 314, 315; trans. from, on the indignities he suffers from his students, 320–323; trans. from, his reason for not expelling his students, 323, 324; his use of the strap and the rod, 324; induces the teachers to make a contract to prevent *apostasis*, 326; his students toss a pedagogue in a blanket, 327; his life in Greece as a student, 328; makes friends at Athens, 329; his 'chum,' 330; his departure from Athens, 330–333; returns to Athens, 334, 335; returns to Constantinople and sets up a school there, 335; settles at Antioch, 336, 337; his feeling for Athens in later years, 337–339; when at Nicomedia, drew men from all quarters, 341 *n.*

Libraries, at Alexandria, 49, 50, 124; at Antioch, 50.

Literature, Greek, study of, in Alexandrian times, 48; of the first century A. D., 68 *n.*

Lodge, H. C., quoted, 4 *n.*

Lollianus, sophist, 87, 183, 244.

Longinus, trans. from, 101; "a living library and a walking museum," 344 n.
Lowell, J. R., quoted, 187 n.
Lucian, sophist, 96; trans. from, on Athens, 131, 132; his description of a contest for appointment to a philosophical chair, 135, 136; trans. from, on representation, 228, 229; trans. from, on Demonax, 253 n.
Lycon, 28, 30.

Macedonian period, the, 41–57.
Macedonian princes, their attitude toward Greece, 44–47.
Mæniana, the, at Trèves, 267 n.
Malalas, historian, 286 n.
Marcus of Byzantium, sophist, 256, 257.
Marseilles, 70.
Mathematics, 96, 197. See Geometry, Arithmetic.
Medicine, in the first three centuries A. D., 96; in the fourth century A. D., 116; students in, took preliminary course in sophistry, 120 n.
Megistias, sophist, 257–259.
μελέτη, meaning, 220 n., 224.
Memory, the training of, in the sophist's course, 214, 215.
Menander, rhetorician, 220 n., 263.
μετ' ἄλλον, 211 n.
μετανάστασις, 326 n.
μισθός, 179 n.
Monroe, Paul, quoted, 12 n.
Morality, result of the sophistical training, 349–351.
Municipal chairs. See Political chair, Chairs.
Municipalities, of Asia, in the first and second centuries A. D., 77, 78; salaries paid by, 87; allowed to grant immunities to teachers, 89, 90; sometimes tried to withdraw privileges, 169, 170; extent to which they paid salaries of teachers in the fourth century, 172–177.
Museum, at Alexandria, 49, 86, 152 n.; at Antioch, 50, 152 n., 267 n.
Music, in fifth century Athenian education, 10–12; change in point of view toward, 23.
μῦθος, 207–210.

Neo-Platonic philosophy, 125–129.
Neo-Platonic school at Athens, 126, 139 n.
Nero, 80, 81.
Nerva, 82.
Nicæa, 50, 146.
Nicetes, sophist, 77, 163 n.
Nicknames, 310 n.
Nicomedia, foundation of, 50; seat of sophistry, 115, 116, 124, 146; Libanius at, 140 n., 160 n., 267 n., 341 n.
Nicostratus, 134 n.
Nigrinus, 131.
Note-taking, 211 n.
Novel, the, 7.

Olympiodorus, a summary from, trans. of, 301–303.
Olympius, sophist, 272, 276 n.
ὁμιλία, 220 n.
ὁπλομάχος, 36.
Orator, the word, 271 n.
Orator, the embodiment of the ideal of education, 351.
Oratory, as taught by Isocrates, 32; course of, from the fifth century B. C. to the first century A. D., 71–79. See Sophistry, Rhetoric.

παιδευτικὸς θρόνος, 142 n., 220 n.
παιδοτρίβης, 36.
Pan-Hellenia, the, 83.
Parthia, 47.
Paulus, Lucius Æmilius, 52.
Pay. See Salaries, Fees.

# INDEX 363

Pedagogues, sold their wards to the highest bidder, 187 n.; induced their wards to transfer their allegiance, 326 n.; tossed in a blanket, 327; held in esteem, 327 n.

Pella, 50.

Pergamum, 42, 50, 65.

Peripatetic school, foundation of, 28; long maintained itself, 101; after Diocletian, 199.

Περὶ ὕψους, trans. from, 235, 236.

Personality, 16, 248, 341, 342.

Pertinax, 98 n.

Philager, sophist, 226, 324 n.

Philip V of Macedon, 51-53.

Philiscus of Eordæa, sophist, 98, 99, 168, 169.

Philodemus, 72 n.

Philosophers, granted immunities by Vespasian, 81; granted honors and salaries by Antoninus Pius, 86-91; method of appointment to chairs of, 93, 134-136; qualifications required of, 136-138; number of, at Constantinople, 144, 149; immunities of, 165-167; salaries of, 171; have recourse to the law to collect their debts, 188, 189; feeling that they should be indifferent to pay, 189-191; at Antioch, 275; their gown, 301; sometimes called sophists, 301 n.

Philosophical schools, foundation of, 26-29, 40; internal management of, 30; compared with Isocrates's school, 32, 33; at Rhodes, 50; in the third century B.C., 52; in the first century B.C., 54; attitude of Hadrian toward, 84, 85; endowed by Marcus Aurelius, 92-94; in the first three centuries A.D., 100-102; after Diocletian, 107, 138, 199. *See* Academic school, etc.

Philosophy, legislation affecting, in pre-Christian times, 62; decrease in importance of, in the second and following centuries A.D., 100-102, 107; the Neo-Platonic, 125-129; as taught in the first centuries of the Christian era, 197-200; in what part of the course studied, 201.

Philostratus, biographer, 95, 96; his *Life of Apollonius of Tyana*, 98; trans. from, on a family in thriving circumstances, 163; on the memory, 215; on Polemo's manner, 231; on Adrian, 236, 309; on Scopelian, 247; on the age of sophists, 248 n.; scenes at displays, 257-261.

Photius, his trans. of a summary from Olympiodorus, 301-303.

Physicians, granted immunities by Vespasian, 81; granted immunities by Antoninus Pius, 87-90; early, treated as benefactors, 87; given salaries by Septimius Severus, 99; under Constantine, 106, 107; granted immunities by Commodus, 165; basis on which they were granted immunity, 167.

Plato, trans. from the *Protagoras*, 12 n.; the *Protagoras* cited, 15-17; the *Theages* cited, 16; founds the Academic school, 27; trans. from, on educational laws, 59, 61.

Plotinus, 125.

Plutarch, trans. from, on capture of Athens by Sulla, 54; Ninth Symposiac, 133.

Plutarch, Neo-Platonist, 125.

Poets, 81, 234, 235.

Polemo, sophist, a speech of, preserved, 95; his distinc-

tion at Smyrna, 163; and Herodes, 181, 255; anecdotes of, 215, 219 n., 254; sprang from his seat while speaking, 231; his voice, 233; and Dionysius, 256; and Marcus, 256, 257.
Political chair, 87 n., 94 n.
Polybius, trans. from, on state of Greece, 51; trans. from, on the Rhodian education, 65; on the Roman education, 66.
Polymathia, 344.
Polysperchon, 45.
Porphyry, 125.
Primary instruction at Athens, 10-13, 18-23.
Priscus, philosopher, 122, 248 n.
Privat-Docenten, 147.
Private teachers, 146-148.
Proæresius, sophist, 107; said to have been a Christian, 111; competes for the chair at Athens, 153; his personal appearance, 247; his age at death, 248 n.; and Hephæstion, friendship of, 329, 330.
προαγών, 223 n., 231 n.
Proclus, philosopher, 125.
Proclus, sophist, 132, 182, 324 n.
Procopius, 124, 210, 211.
Professional schools, graduate, 120 n.
Professor, those who were entitled to the name, 148; words used for, 271 n., 277 n., 296 n.
Professors, honored with title, 150. See Sophists, etc.
προλαλιά, 223 n.
πρόλογος, 223 n.
Pronuntiatio, 211 n.
Προπεμπτικός, 238.
προστάτης, 296.
Ptolemaion, the, 38.
Ptolemies, the, 42.
Ptolemy Philadelphus, 49.

Ptolemy Soter, 49.
Punishment of students, 323-325.

Quintilian, appointed to chair at Rome, 81; his ideal of the orator, 349 n.

Reading, 25.
Recitation buildings, 267 n.
'Refutation,' 204, 209, 210.
Representation, 228-230.
Rhetoric, Isocrates's school of, 31-35, 40; schools of, at Rhodes, 50; legislation affecting, in pre-Christian times, 62; taught at Athens from the time of Isocrates down, 74; connection of local councils and, 78 n., 119; chairs of, at Rome, 81; chairs of, at Athens, 87, 91; the study of, cultivated in the first two centuries A. D., 96; and philosophy, the two great departments of instruction, 197, 198. See Sophistry, Oratory.
Rhetoricians. See Sophists, Rhetors.
Rhetors, mentioned by Strabo, 73; granted immunities by Vespasian, 81; granted honors and salaries by Antoninus Pius, 86-91; granted salaries by Septimius Severus, 99; the four, in Libanius's school, 192-194, 267 n., 270, 271; the word, how used, 271 n.
Rhodes, Æschines transplants the study of oratory to, 35; schools of rhetoric and philosophy at, 50; a resort of the Romans, 55, 56; public education at, 65.
Romans, their diplomatic relations with Greece, 45, 52, 53; resort to Greece, 55, 56, 70; their attitude toward mu-

nicipalities, 77, 78; their appreciation of eloquence, 236.
Rome, University of, 81, 85, 94 n., 267; age of students at, 292; regulations with regard to students at, 313 n.

Salaries, of teachers, at Teos, 64; at Delphi, 65; at Rhodes, 65; granted by Vespasian, 81; granted by Antoninus Pius, 86-89; granted by Marcus Aurelius, 91, 92; granted by Septimius Severus, 99; fell into abeyance in second half of the third century, 105; restored by Constantine, 106; size, 171, 172; by whom paid in the fourth century, 172-177; paid in kind, 178, 179; words for, 178 n.; often difficult to collect, 191, 192.
Scholarch, 27, 30.
School of Antioch, 270-278.
School buildings, 266-269.
Schools, philosophical. *See* Philosophical schools, Academic school, etc.
Scopelian, sophist, and Herodes Atticus, 180; his fees, 182; his manner when speaking, 231, 247.
Secondary instruction, 18, 19, 23-25.
Secundus, sophist, 243, 244.
Seleucids, the, 42.
Seleucus, 50.
Septimius Severus, 98.
Severi, the, 97-99.
Short-hand-writing, 121, 191.
Socrates, his influence on education, 15, 18.
Soli, 50.
*Sophist*, the name, 75.
Sophistical chair, the, 94 n., 142 n., 153.
Sophistry, a protest against barbarism, 4 n., 346; the word, 5; its rise and spread, and its influence, 5; its essence, 6; its influence on Greek letters, 6-9; Isocrates's statement of what it does for a man, 33 n.; training in, a preparation for life, 73, 75, 78 n., 345-352; rise of, in the first and second centuries A. D., 70-79; chairs of, established in the second century A. D., 86-94; the fourth century, second flourishing period of, 107; decline of, 115-122; in the fifth century, 124; and philosophy, the two great departments of instruction, 197, 198; the overrating of, 200, 201; how in general the teaching of it differed from the teaching of 'grammar,' 202; what it was and how it was taught, 202-217; the training in the schools of, modern judgments of it, 344, 347; what it did and what it did not profess to do, 345-347; the means by which it sought to accomplish its purpose, 347-352.
Sophists, of the fifth and fourth centuries B. C., 13-18, 31; connection of the earlier and the later, 71-79; of the first century B. C., as pictured by Philodemus, 72 n.; their number, 142-146; jealousy among, 152-161; their position in society, 162-164; their immunity from burdens, 164-170; their fees, 179-184, 187, 188; their profession profitable, 184; their fees as affected by Diocletian's scale of prices, 184, 185; size of their classes, 185-187; sometimes resorted to the law to recover their debts, 188, 189; deterioration of their condi-

tion toward the close of the fourth century, 191; sometimes difficult for them to collect their salaries, 191, 192; their teaching, 195–217; the displays of, 218–262; their haughtiness and vanity, 232, 254; the advanced age to which many of them lived, 248 n.; professional honesty of, 255–257; their contests, 256, 257; Court orators, 262; varieties of their epideictic speeches, 263, 264; began course with introductory address, and ended it with farewell speech, 265, 266; where they held their classes, 266–269; 'chorus' of, 270, 274; their gown, 301–303; stood as fathers to their students, 307, 308, 341.
Sophocles, son of Amphicleides, 62.
σωφρονισταί, 37.
Soterus, 134 n.
Sparta, constitution of, 63.
Spencer, Herbert, quoted, 22 n.
Speusippus, 27, 29.
Spoken word, the, 5, 25, 343.
σπουδή, 220 n.
Spreads, 305, 319.
στάσις, 226 n.
State, education and the, 58–67.
Stoic school, foundation of, 28.
Strabo, on Marseilles and Tarsus, 70; rhetors mentioned by, 73.
στρατηγοί, 37.
στρατηγὸς ἐπὶ τὰ ὅπλα, ἐπὶ τῶν ὅπλων, 66, 76 n.
Straton, 28.
Students, gave displays, 211 n.; took notes of lectures, 211 n.; questioned teachers, 211 n.; age of, 292, 293; their corps, 296–304; words for, 296 n.; the impressing and hazing of, 296–307; their gown, 301–303; stood as sons to their teachers, 307, 308, 341; battles of their rival corps, 312–318, 320; their amusements, 319, 320; their conduct at the lectures, 320–324; punishment of, 324, 325; defection of, 325, 326; toss a pedagogue in a blanket, 327; friendships among, 329, 330; expenses of, 331; regrets of, at leaving Athens, 332, 333.
Style, the study of, for its own sake, 6; the study of, in the sophist's school, 208, 209; literary, of the sophists, 245, 246.
Suasoriæ, 224 n.
Successors, the, of Alexander, 42, 43, 45–47; of the philosophical schools, 102.
Sulla, 53, 54.
συμβουλευτικά, 220 n., 224 n.
συνουσία, 220 n.
Synesius, trans. from, on Athens, 122–124; on envy among teachers, 152 n.
Syrianus, 125.

Tarsus, 50, 70, 95, 116 n.
Tatian, on salaries of philosophers, 87 n.
Taurus, philosopher, 133, 211 n.
Taxes, immunity from, 86, 164–167.
τέχναι, text-books, 72 n.
τέχνη, 59 n.
Teles, trans. from, 19 n.
Teos, 61, 64.
Theagenes, 181 n.
Theatres for displays, 267 n.
Themes, set in the schools, 205, 215–217; the propounding of, 225, 226; the power of the sophists to grasp the essential point of, 226, 227; samples of those

propounded at the displays, 227, 228; representation in, 228–230; manner of the sophists in dealing with, 230–238, 246–250; samples of introductions to and passages from, 238–246; descriptions of sophists discussing, 255–262.

Themistius, philosopher, 107; trans. from, on envy among teachers, 152 *n.*; helped needy students, 163 *n.*; honors of, at Constantinople, 164 *n.*; the salary to which he was entitled, 178; did not take fees or salary, 179 *n.*, 183; accused of buying students, 187; his philosophy, 199; age at death, 248 *n.*; head of the School of Constantinople, 278; on the question, why students look to the city rather than to the teachers, 291 *n.*

Theodosian Code, trans. from, 148–150, 313 *n.*

Theodosius the Great, 122.

Theodosius II, 124.

Theodotus, sophist, 91.

Theon, philosopher, 125.

Theon, rhetorician, trans. from, on the study of rhetoric, 200, 201; his account of the sophistical course, 203 *n.*; trans. from, on individual aptitudes, 205; trans. from, on methods of teaching, 206.

Theophrastus, 28.

Thessalonica, 116 *n.*

θετικά, 72 *n.*, 223 *n.*

θρόνοι. See Chairs.

Tigranes, 47.

Titles, given to teachers, 150, 164 *n.*

τοξότης, 36.

Trajan, 82, 83.

Trèves, 178, 267 *n.*

Troezen, 65 *n.*

Tuition, cost of, 183, 331.

Tutors, private, 146–148.

Tyre, 116 *n.*, 124.

Ulpian, 189.

Under-teachers, 272.

University, wherein the ancient differed from the modern, 150–152; the name for, 152 *n.* See Athens, etc.

ὑπόκρισις, 229, 230.

*Vacatio*, 164 *n.*

Vacations, 279–281.

Vespasian, 81.

Voice of the sophists, 233–237.

Xenocrates, 27.

Zenobius, 192, 267 *n.*, 288 *n.*

Zenodotus, 49.

For Product Safety Concerns and Information please contact our EU representative GPSR@taylorandfrancis.com
Taylor & Francis Verlag GmbH, Kaufingerstraße 24, 80331 München, Germany

www.ingramcontent.com/pod-product-compliance
Lightning Source LLC
Chambersburg PA
CBHW071145300426
44113CB00009B/1090